women and globalization

women and globalization

edited by Delia D. Aguilar
and Anne E. Lacsamana

Humanity Books

an imprint of Prometheus Books
59 John Glenn Drive, Amherst, New York 14228-2197

Published 2004 by Humanity Books, an imprint of Prometheus Books

Inquiries should be addressed to
Humanity Books
59 John Glenn Drive
Amherst, New York 14228–2197
VOICE: 716–691–0133, ext. 207
FAX: 716–564–2711
WWW.PROMETHEUSBOOKS.COM

08 07 06 05 04   5 4 3 2 1

Library of Congress Cataloging-in-Publication Data

Women and globalization / edited by Delia D. Aguilar and Anne E. Lacsamana.
p. cm.
Includes bibliographical references and index.
ISBN 1–59102–162–6 (pbk. : alk. paper)
1. Women in development. 2. Women—Social conditions. 3. Women—Economic conditions. 4. Globalization—Social aspects. I. Aguilar, Delia D. II. Lacsamana, Anne E.

HQ1240.W652 2004
305.42—dc22   2004003626

Printed in the United States of America on acid-free paper

Contents

Introduction   **11**
  Delia D. Aguilar

**1. Globalization and Its Impact on
   Women Workers in Malaysia**   **25**
  Rohana Ariffin
    Introduction   25
    Female Employment   27
    Health and Safety of Women Workers at the Workplace   32
    Retrenchment   39
    Unions and Workers' Rights   41
    Standards of Life, Urban Living, and Poverty   43
    Gender Relations   45
    Conclusion   48

**2. The Context of Gender and Globalization
   in the Philippines**   **52**
  Elizabeth Uy Eviota

**3. The Restructuring and Privatization of
   Women's Industries in Nicaragua**   **68**
  Nancy Wiegersma

5

Methodology   70
Background   71
The Restructuring Rationale   75
Restructuring of the Garment-Textile Industry
    and Gender Discrimination   76
Impact of Privatization on Working Women   80
Labor Union Gender Bias in Restructuring   83
Conclusion   84

4. **Six Years of NAFTA: A View from Inside
   the Maquiladoras**   **90**
   Border Committee of Women Workers,
   with a foreword by Rachael Kamel
   Introduction   94
   The End of the Mirage: Six Years
       of NAFTA in the Maquiladoras   100
   Workers and the CFO Respond   114

5. **Maquiladoras, Migration, and Daily Life: Women and
   Work in the Contemporary Mexican Political Economy 120**
   Nancy Churchill
   Introduction   121
   NAFTA, the Mexican Political Economy,
       and Women's Labor   124
   Maquiladora Assembly Plants   128
   Migration   135
   The Growth in the "Informal Sector"   139
   Changing Social Relations in "Everyday Life":
       Prospects for Liberation   142

6. **Haitian Women in the New World Order**   **154**
   April Ane Knutson
   Introduction   155
   History   156
   Economic Domination and Superexploitation
       of Women Workers   159
   The Informal Economic Sector   161
   International Monetary Fund Policies   162

Alternative Development Models   164
Language and Revolutionary Change   166
Women's Role in the Revolutionary Struggle   168
Haitian Literature: Portraits of Strong Women and Victims   170
The Haitian Diaspora: Intellectual Expatriates
    and Economic Refugees   176
Current Political and Economic Situation   177
Conclusion   178

7. **Internationalization of Capital and the Trade in**
   Asian Women: The Case of "Foreign Brides" in Taiwan 181
   Hsiao-Chuan Hsia
   The Phenomenon   182
   The Problematique   184
   Research Methods   187
   Internationalization of Capital
       and "Marriage Immigration"   190
   Formation of Dependent Relations
       between Taiwan and Southeast Asia   194
   Distorted Development and the Formation
       of "Marriage Immigration"   198
   Contribution of Transnational Marriages
       to Capital Internationalization   219
   The Personalization and Engendering
       of International Division of Labor   222
   Conclusion   225

8. **Globalization in Living Color: Women of Color Living**
   under and over the "New World Order"   **230**
   Grace Chang
   Testimonies on Living under Globalization   233
   "Filipinos for the World"   242
   Women Turning the "New World Order" Upside Down   252

9. **Who Needs Yehudi Menuhin?**
   Costs and Impact of Migration   **262**
   Bridget Anderson

The Troubling Relationship
    of Domestic Labor to Capitalism   264
Commodification and Domestic Labor—
    a "Win-Win" Situation?   266
Kalayaan: A Case Study in Organizing
    Migrant Domestic Workers   269
Conclusions   275

10. South African Women:
    Narratives of Struggle and Exile   278
Thelma Ravell-Pinto
    Introduction   279
    Historical Overview   283
    Women's Writings   296
    Conclusion   308

11. The Cultural Debate over Female Circumcision:
    The Sudanese Are Arguing This One
    Out for Themselves   313
Ellen Gruenbaum
    Is Female Circumcision a Maladaptive Cultural Pattern?   317
    Forces for Continuity and Change   322
    Forces for Change: Cultural Debates in Sudan   326
    Toward a Political Ecology of Health   339

12. Gender, Race, Militarization, and
    Economic Restructuring in the Former Yugoslavia
    and at the U.S.-Mexico Border   347
Anna M. Agathangelou
    Globalization and Militarization:
        Two Sides of the Same Coin?   349
    The Political Economy of Militarization in Yugoslavia   355
    Militarization, Gender, and Race   360
    The Militarization of the U.S.-Mexico Border   367
    Feminist Perspectives on Militarization in the
        Former Yugoslavia and at the U.S.-Mexico Border   372
    Feminist Resistance and Revisioning   375

13. **Sex Worker or Prostituted Woman? An Examination of the Sex Work Debates in Western Feminist Theory** 387
   Anne E. Lacsamana

14. **Questionable Claims: Colonialism Redux, Feminist Style** **404**
   Delia D. Aguilar
   Woman as Empowered Agent   406
   From Academe to the "New World Order"   407
   Making Sense of "Resistance" Feminism   411
   Escape from Class and Political Economy   413
   An Alternative to "Essentialism"   416
   Toward a Reinstatement of Class   417

Contributors   **423**

Introduction

Delia D. Aguilar

The USA dominates the United Nations (UN), the World Bank, the IMF, GATT, and SAPs, etcetera. Through these international agreements and institutions the North is strengthening its grip on the world economy. The USA and powerful European countries in the North have become a de facto board of management for the world economy, protecting their interests and imposing their will on the South.

—Nawal El Saadawi,
The Nawal El Saadawi Reader (1998)

[W]e insist on asserting that the construction of Empire is a step forward in order to do away with any nostalgia for the power structures that preceded it and refuse any political strategy that involves returning to that old arrangement, such as trying to resurrect the nation-state to protect against global capital. We claim that Empire is better in the same way that Marx insists that capitalism is better than the forms of society and modes of produc-tion that came before it.

—Michael Hardt and Antonio Negri, *Empire* (2000)

One wonders whether, with the events of September 11, 2001, and the declaration of a "war on terror" by U.S. president George W. Bush, a paradigm shift would be forced on the academic mind from Hardt and Negri's view of a benign "Empire" to that of El Saadawi, who sees the United States as the world's ruling power that is neither kind nor gentle either at home or overseas. Moreover, while for the moment overshadowed by these events and their aftermath, there is no doubt that the efforts of activists against economic globalization that were launched with the 1999 "battle of Seattle" have had their repercussions in the popular consciousness as well as on the international bodies whose regulations they protested. Whatever else might be said about these activists, they have successfully put poverty on the agenda for the International Monetary Fund and World Bank to address, however superficially (Rodrik 2002).

Interestingly enough, in his State of the Union address in 1999 —a time, it should be remarked, when the U.S. stock market was near peak performance—President Bill Clinton made a call "to put a human face on the global economy." Recognizing that "the world economy is becoming more and more integrated," he urged that "we have got to do in the world what we spent the better part of this century doing at home." Now, the president was not exactly agreeing with Egyptian militant feminist physician Nawal El Saadawi's open charge that the United States is an imperial power managing the international economy in its own interest. But his remarks certainly indicate more cognizance of global ills than is evinced by many a U.S. academic today. He may not have been aware that the integration of all the nations of the planet into one world order has resulted in a "disorganized capitalism" (Lash and Urry 1987), or that this presumed disorganization has been optimistically viewed and lauded as a "borderless world" of transnationalism (Miyoshi 1993) that now radically decenters or displaces Western culture. Nor would he have been informed that such a resulting "transculture" is

seen to usher in global cultural flows or "scapes" in which deterrito-
rialized individuals can negotiate their identities within newly
opened interstitial spaces (Appadurai 1999). Finally, he couldn't
possibly have understood that the nation-state is in imminent
demise, if not already dead, even though he would probably have
been in total concurrence with Hardt and Negri that it would be
futile for nation-states to go against global capital.

Instead, President Clinton's remark brought to the surface a
contrary concern that even in a period of thriving commerce, things
may not be quite right with the world. It is more than likely, then,
that despite the burgeoning of the U.S. economy during the years of
his administration, he shared the knowledge that those in governing
circles must all possess. In a meeting at the posh Fairmont Hotel in
San Francisco in 1995, for example, the world's business and conservative intellectual elites discussed the state of future global
society in a pair of numbers: 20:80 (Martin and Schumann 1997).
These numbers indicate that in any given country in the world, only
one-fifth of the population would have access to production and
consumption; that is all the labor power required to produce all the
goods and services that global society can buy. For the 80 percent
without employment, the choice, if any exists, would be "to have
lunch or be lunch" (p. 4).

Indeed, inequality within and between countries today has
reached a new magnitude. Within the United States, the average
income of the top 20 percent of families rose to 13 times the income
earned by the bottom 20 percent by the late 1990s. In the late
1970s, it was only 10½ times greater (Phillips 2002). This polarity
of wealth is greater than at any time since the 1930s; in this it is currently matched only by Russia among industrialized countries
(Hassan 2000). In 1995 the net wealth of Bill Gates alone was
greater than the combined net worth of the poorest 40 percent of
Americans, numbering 106 million people. The World Bank reports
that about half of the world's population (2.8 billion people) sur-
vives on less than two dollars a day, and 1.2 billion on less than one

dollar a day (Yates 2003, p. 55). According to the UN Development Program (1996), "Between 1960 and 1991 the share of the richest 20 percent rose from 70 percent of global income to 85 percent—while that of the poorest declined from 2.3 percent to 1.4 percent." In 1991, "more than 85 percent of the world's population received only 15 percent of its income." Lastly, a total of 358 people own the combined wealth of 2.5 billion put together, almost half of the world's population! Clearly, globalization is paying off rather well for those on top while wreaking untold misery on those on the bottom, a state of affairs that the former U.S. president wished to mask with a "human face."

For the majority of the world's population, contrary to the opinions of academics cited early on, globalization has brought on a predicament that is far from being cheered or exalted. In the public mind in developing countries it is associated with the debt burden and structural adjustment programs, both of which are linked to "conditionalities" imposed by the International Monetary Fund and the World Bank. Former chief economist and senior vice president of the World Bank Joseph E. Stiglitz has now provided insider information on the bank that makes it less easy for skeptics or a misinformed populace to dismiss antiglobalization activists' charges that the policies of these international bodies primarily benefit the already affluent. And the irony cannot be missed that it is elite white men like Stiglitz and financier George Soros (2002) who would now write about how year after year the flow of money has been from the poor nations to the wealthy, rather than the other way around, as assumed by common wisdom and fostered by the major media.

Today the international debt exceeds two trillion dollars, placing the poor majority of the world in virtual debt bondage. To ensure debt payment, the IMF/WB injunction has been the production of goods for export. In this export-oriented scheme, the employment of women and children as cheap labor has been the key ingredient, as has the deployment of women as migrant workers overseas. From yet another reading of Clinton's exhortation, admittedly with a twist, it is the human faces of women and children that are reflected back to us if we subject economic globalization processes to thoughtful perusal. The subjugation of women and children to the demands of capital notwithstanding, analyses of these processes have remained a purview of male intellectuals (Brah et al. 2002). In Hardt and Negri's much touted and widely reviewed *Empire*, to cite an example, the labor of women in sweatshops or as migrants is given no mention.

While we recognize the existence of theoretical differences among those who have sought to explain the phenomenon of globalization, it is in these economic realities that we wish to contextualize this collection of essays on women. We take the following broad features of the globalized order as the backdrop and framing device for comprehending the lives of women: iniquitous North-South relations of power, in which transnational corporations, their instruments of regulating trade (WTO, NAFTA, APEC, MAI), and international lending agencies (IMF and WB) play a major role; the increasing polarization between rich and poor, within and among nations; a redefinition of the role of the nation-state vis-à-vis the power of transnational corporations; the hypercommodification of culture and the accelerated rate of cultural transmission; and time-space compression.

The most pronounced change in the world's workforce today is probably in its composition and numbers: it has become radically feminized and sports a literally different complexion (Harvey 2000, Hassan 2000, Sassen 1998). It doubled in size between 1966 and 1995, according to the World Bank (1995). "Globalization in its modern form is . . . based less on the proliferation of computers than on the proliferation of proletarians," states David Coates, and "the change in the center of gravity" defines globalization as much as the extraordinary mobility of capital (quoted in Tabb 2000, p. 37). Moreover, this much larger labor force is also more heterogeneous and migratory. The United States, for instance, has the greatest proportion of foreign-born residents since the 1920s. Not less important, geographical and social differentials in wages and social provisions within the global proletariat are greater than they have ever been (Harvey 2000).

Examining changes in the employment trends in the United States—in her words, "not simply a quantitative transformation . . . [but] a new economic regime"—Saskia Sassen (1998) explains how economic globalization has resulted in the increasing inequality of different types of workers and their heightened insecurity due to the "casualization of employment relation." The deindustrialization of the 1970s was accompanied by the rise of service-sector jobs and the recruitment of women. The service sector today is sharply polarized: at one end are labor-intensive retail trade, health, and business services, mostly low-paid and not requiring a high-school education. At the other end are finance and specialized services calling for a college degree. Sassen notes that the "valorization" of the finance industry, because of the superprofits it commands, has been achieved in direct contraposition to the "devalorization" of women, people of color, and immigrants in global cities like Los Angeles and New York. In both cases, informalization by firms of all or some of their operations has bred an insecurity in workers heretofore not experienced by professional and skilled employees.

To speak of globalization without center-staging women of color would be a grave mistake. In the era of globalized economics where a race to the bottom is critical for superprofits, it is primarily the labor power of "Third World" women—and unfortunately, of children, 70 percent of whom work as unpaid family members in rural areas (Tabb 2000)—that is the cheapest of all. From the maquiladoras in Mexico even prior to NAFTA, to assembly plants and export processing zones in Central America, the Caribbean, and the Pacific Rim, to subcontractors and garment sweatshops in global cities and in nations of the periphery, it is women's labor that allows and guarantees maximum profitability for the corporate elite, a tiny minority of the world's inhabitants. Qualities presumed to be inherently female—docility, nimble fingers, patience—spring to the lips of many a manager, no matter his race, when asked why the preference for women workers (*Global Assembly Line* 1986).

In peripheral nations, the development model shaped by "conditionalities" of structural adjustment programs has made them particularly vulnerable to the onerous practices of global capital. Deregulation, liberalization, privatization, casualization of labor, and export production are some key words that "globalization" immediately rings up in developing countries. Regular workers have been replaced by casuals who have paradoxically become permanently so, and who might now constitute a larger proportion of the workforce than regular, unionizable employees. Production of garments and cash crops has displaced the production of staples that people require for their basic daily consumption, prices of which they can no longer afford. While women have always been an important source of labor power, their active recruitment in low-paid labor, mainly in the service industry, is a new feature of globalization. But perhaps the most distinguishing mark of globalization is the unprecedented diaspora of migrant women workers from poor exploited nations to more affluent countries of the North. In many cases, their remittances keep their otherwise IMF/WB debt-ridden countries in relative economic viability.

The kernel of this book is labor, even though not all the essays in the collection directly deal with it, because we believe that labor and class relations lie at the heart of global economic processes. Ironically, most academic accounts of globalization have merely glossed over these processes, directing attention, instead, to its presumably potentially liberating cultural features. In line with this, a prevailing emphasis on culture and discourse in the academy has also caused many feminist studies on women and globalization to train the spotlight solely on women's subjectivities, to the diminution of the significance of the global order itself. Against the main trend, a number of scholars are calling for the urgent need, in the face of intensifying economic globalization, to come to intellectual grips with the production relations that serve as its foundation

(Wood 1999, Ebert 1996, Harvey 2000). We view this project as heeding that call. We wish to recuperate the use of the academically repudiated metanarrative, in this case the global political economy, and to underscore its impact on women's lives both in the productive and reproductive spheres. We also delineate the importance, not the decline or demise, of the nation-state.

Several of the articles in the book, then, deal with women as workers. Globalization has created an international division of labor, producing a female proletariat consigned to the lowest-paid and least secure jobs with the worst working conditions. This is the case in Malaysia where, as Rohana Ariffin's study shows, an export-oriented industrialization policy beginning in the seventies drew women out of the farms into the urban areas to occupy the lower rungs of the labor market. In these places of employment an authoritarian government has seen to it that profit-making is unhampered by unionization, effectively shutting off any venues women might use to alleviate their exploitation. In the Philippines the same export-led design, according to Elizabeth Uy Eviota, has forced women to choose between sweatshop employment in the home country or service-oriented occupations like domestic work overseas. Nancy Wiegersma's essay on Nicaraguan women suggests, however, that factors beyond export-oriented production and the establishment of free trade zones intercede to influence the position that women are made to occupy. Under the Sandinistas, women already comprised a significant portion of the labor force; but with the move to the National Opposition Union (UNO) they were edged out of the formal labor force into the informal sector. Wiegersma explains this to be the consequence of Nicaragua's departure from a society with socialist features to one modeled on capitalist development.

Undertaking the task of defining their most pressing health problem, the Comite Fronterizo de Obreras (Mexican Border Committee of Women Workers) draws up a report in which "stress" winds up as the unanticipated culprit, instead of toxic exposure and industrial accidents. Noteworthy because it is maquilas who speak for themselves, the report supplies an insider's view of the impact on women of altered conditions of work—speed-ups, longer work days, lowered standard of living, etc.—that are couched by management in euphemisms like "labor flexibility" and the "new culture of labor." Nancy Churchill also writes about Mexican women, examining the rapid expansion of maquiladora factories and the changing patterns of labor migration. She explores the effects of these changes on women's activities at work and at home, noting that women's participation in production has considerably increased their reproductive labor. Given this situation, she contends that any program for the liberation of women must therefore reckon with women's embeddedness in the realm of reproduction along with their involvement in the realm of production.

April Ane Knutson's essay on Haitian women exemplifies a historicized perspective that covers broad territory: the economy with emphasis on the informal sector, IMF policies and the operations of U.S. corporations, and the Lavalas movement and its vision of an alternative system. In her explication of the Lavalas movement Knutson maneuvers a cultural turn, using novels to demonstrate how women cope under conditions of occupation and economic devastation. Hsiao-Chuan Hsia investigates the mail-order-bride industry in Taiwan and contends that it is capitalist development and its resulting relations of dependency that have attracted "foreign brides" from poorer countries like Indonesia, Vietnam, and the Philippines to marry Taiwanese grooms and to take up residence in a foreign land. The product of empirical research initiated in 1994, the study includes interviews with brides and grooms in these "transnational commodified marriages" that reveal that their unions were contracted as a means of meeting societal and familial demands.

Grace Chang indicts structural adjustment programs as the cause of the suffering of women of color in the United States and in the "Third World." She argues that one of the most egregious by-products of globalization is the displacement of women from the South, which disrupts their families, and their forced migration to the North, where they become caregivers or servants in the households of strangers. Indeed, any query about the international migration of women today inevitably leads to the issue of domestic work. Bridget Anderson trains her sharp eye on this subject and probes its myriad ingredients in order to conceptualize it within the rubric of social reproduction. She argues that domestic work, the particular features of which are always historically and socially contingent, is socially necessary labor and that it entails much more than the mere reproduction of people. More crucially, migrant domestic work reproduces patterns of consumptions, lifestyles, and status. Recognizing the complexity of her thesis, she summons her practice, her long-standing membership in a migrant workers' organization, to vouch for the empirical soundness of her arguments.

Writing about South African women, Thelma Ravell-Pinto addresses the gender gap in mainstream historical accounts by giving a historical overview of the pass system and the ways in which women fought against its institution. Like Knutson, she deploys the use of literature—in this case women's narratives—to supplement and change the way that history has transcribed South African women. Ellen Gruenbaum takes issue with analyses that have tended to view female circumcision as a "maladaptive cultural pattern." She also differs from feminists who have identified tradition as the main reason for the evolution and persistence of the practice. Instead, she uses historical and ethnographic data to trace the ongoing debates surrounding female circumcision in the Sudan, in the process delineating women's agency.

Anna M. Agathangelou draws attention to the links between globalization and militarization and asks: Is globalization constituted through militarization? What part do gender and race play in the militarization process? To resolve these questions, she examines militarization in the "ethnic conflict" in Yugoslavia as well as at the U.S.-Mexican border. She closes by proposing transnational feminism as a site where militarization and the inevitability of globalization could be challenged collectively.

Finally, given an international division of labor that indubitably favors the North, it is not surprising that feminist formulations are prone to replicate such an asymmetrical relationship. Anne Lacsamana plunges head-on into the prostitution versus sex work debate and rejects outright the proposition that prostitution is work just like any other. She refutes sex work advocates' contention that practitioners exert agency or that prostitution is a form of emotional labor that they can manage or control. She turns to the Philippine case where prostitution has proliferated with increasing poverty, and maintains that a sex work perspective actually functions to buttress an exploitative world order. Delia D. Aguilar likewise argues that contemporary feminist theoretical production dominated by the metropolis, though posing notions of "empowerment" and "resistance" as mechanisms to redress previous marginalization of the "other," in truth accomplishes nothing of the sort. For her it is through the recuperation of class analysis and the concrete positioning of women within global economic arrangements that feminist theory can give substance to and make real its emancipatory claims.

In sum, this book hopes to show that it is only with an unequivocal articulation of the global order that women can be adequately grasped in their complexity as laboring and desiring subjects. Lastly, although the evidence presented in the following chapters indicates that economic globalization weighs most heavily upon women and extracts from them the greatest suffering, they have been rendered neither immobile nor quiescent. Nor have they quietly resorted to individualized, largely ineffectual expressions of resistance. Grassroots women's organizations such as the Mexican Border Committee of Women Workers, Kalayaan, Vancouver Committee for Domestic Workers' and Caregivers' Rights, Workers' Voices Coalition, and Philippine Women's Centre demonstrably testify that women around the world have never ceased to work together and to collectively envision a system more humane than the one that currently exists.

The world is not quite the same now as it was before September 11, 2001. It is a very different world largely because of flagrant unilateralist moves by the United States that, an increasing number of commentators agree, denote a stark and compelling transmogrification from republic to empire (Henderson 2002). This transmogrification, needless to say, has angered and dismayed the world's peoples who have never been as uninformed or apathetic about the U.S. imperium as those within the country, to begin with. A year after the events of September 11, feminist activist Charlotte Bunch (2002) raised an urgent call for U.S. women to protest the Bush administration's actions, bringing to notice the puzzlement of women elsewhere over U.S. feminists' utter lack of influence on their country's foreign policy. In light of these changes, academic and feminist analyses will have to undergo substantive revision if the academy is to maintain a veneer of relevance. This book is intended as a contribution in that direction.

REFERENCES

Appadurai, Arjun. 1999. Disjuncture and difference in the global cultural economy. In *The cultural studies reader*, ed. S. During, pp. 220–30. New York: Routledge.

Brah, Avtar, H. Crowley, L. Thomas, and M. Storr. 2002. Globalization. *Feminist Review* 70 (May): 1–2.

Bunch, Charlotte. 2002. Whose security? *Nation* 275 (9) (September): 36–40.

Ebert, Teresa. 1996. *Ludic feminism and after*. Ann Arbor: University of Michigan Press.

The global assembly line. 1986. VHS. Produced by L. Gray et al. New York: New Day Films.

Hardt, Michael, and Antonio Negri. 2000. *Empire*. Cambridge, MA: Harvard University Press.

Harvey, David. 2000. *Spaces of hope*. Berkeley and Los Angeles: University of California Press.

Hassan, Khalil. 2000. The future of the labor left. *Monthly Review* 52 (3) (July–August): 60–83.

Henderson, David. 2002. The course of empire. *Harper's Magazine* 305 (1831) (December): 15–19.

Lash, Stephen, and J. Urry. 1987. *The end of organized capitalism.* Madison: University of Wisconsin Press.

Martin, Hans-Peter, and H. Schumann. 1997. *The global trap: Globalization and the assault on democracy and prosperity.* London and New York: Zed Books.

Miyoshi, Masao. 1993. A borderless world? From colonialism to transnationalism and the decline of the nation-state. *Critical Inquiry* 19 (4) (summer): 726–51.

Phillips, Kevin. 2002. *Wealth and democracy: A political history of the American rich.* New York: Broadway Books.

Rodrik, Dani. 2002. Globalization for whom? *Harvard Magazine* 104 (6) (July–August): 29–31.

Sassen, Saskia. 1998. *Globalization and its discontents: Essays in the mobility of people and money.* New York: New Press.

Soros, George. 2002. *On globalization.* New York: Public Affairs, 2002.

Stiglitz, Joseph E. 2002. *Globalization and its discontents.* New York: W. W. Norton.

Tabb, William. 2000. Turtles, teamsters, and capital's designs. *Monthly Review* 52 (3) (July–August): 28–45.

United Nations Development Program. 1996. *Human development report.* New York: United Nations.

Wood, Ellen Meiksins. 1999. *Democracy against capitalism: Renewing historical materialism.* Cambridge and New York: Cambridge University Press.

World Bank. 1995. *World development report: Workers in an integrating world.* New York: World Bank.

Yates, Michael. 2003. *Naming the system: Inequality and work in the global economy.* New York: Monthly Review Press.

1. Globalization and Its Impact on Women Workers in Malaysia

Rohana Ariffin

According to Ariffin, the development of an export-oriented economy in the 1970s has exerted an enormous impact on women workers in Malaysia. In a detailed study, Ariffin's essay explores women working in both the industrial and service sectors of the economy as well as their migration from rural to urban centers. Over the past several years, women working in Malaysia have felt the brunt of global economic expansion: attempts to unionize have been thwarted by authoritarian regimes intent on protecting profits rather than people. By tracing the employment patterns of women from the 1970s to the present, Ariffin carefully notes how global capitalist expansion has led to an increasingly feminized and flexible workforce.

INTRODUCTION

"Globalization represents changes in the operation of global capitalism.... It has expanded its potential for producing inequalities.... Those with the least power, whether defined in state, class, 'race,' or gender terms, are being forced to compete on an increasingly intense basis with one another" (Koffman and Young 1996, p. 4). This process allows for greater intratrade, foreign direct investment, and an intensified division of labor between developed and developing nations. It brings about a supraterritorial world-wide set of social relations; old relations of the past are transformed into new relations, while others are further entrenched.

In terms of labor standards, globalization has brought about a disparity between the North and South. Labor standards include level of wages, conditions of employment, working hours, health and safety measures at the workplace, and security of work (Manning 1998, p. 2). Women workers in Asia have been increasingly drawn into the new international division of labor since the early seventies and seem to be the most exploited class of workers due to their lower level of skill training and lack of organized representation. The state, in its attempt to attract direct foreign investments, has curbed unions as well as workers' rights and discouraged unionization. Because women were the most recent recruits into the industrial sector and subsequently into the service sector, they were discouraged by the state and their employers from forming unions. The new "human resource management" concept that was encouraged in the United States in the eighties in their multinationals throughout the world both undermine the practice of industrial relations and the presence of unions in many companies and workplaces in Malaysia.

This paper attempts to evaluate the position of Malaysian women workers in the sixties and seventies, comparing this with that of the nineties in order to gauge the effects of the process of globalization. *Women workers* in this paper denotes women workers in the industrial and service sectors, including sex workers. In any discussion of women workers, job security and unionization are very important. When focusing on women workers, it is also necessary to contextualize them within the new urban environment and to look at class and gender relations in the country. Migrant women have to be mentioned as well, since they make up a substantial proportion of women workers, especially in manufacturing and services, domestic work in particular. Out of an estimated 8 million workers in the labor market, almost 2 million are foreign workers. They make up about 13 percent to 20 percent of the labor force (National Economic Action Council [NEAC] 1998, Tenaganita 1998b). Local women make up over 38 percent of the existing labor market. About half of the students in the schools and in postsecondary education are female.

FEMALE EMPLOYMENT

Globalization encouraged industrialization in many Third World countries. Malaysia's period of export-oriented industrialization caused a large internal migration of youth, especially women from the rural to the more urban areas of the Free Trade Zone (FTZ). Thousands of women leave their villages to become part of the working class. The vast majority have very little skills and basic education (seven to eleven years), and as a result, the jobs most frequently available to them are either as machine operators or as operators in the expanding textile, food, electrical, and electronic industries. The growing number of working women began to fill the lower positions of the job hierarchy both in the industrial (see Lim 1978, Fatimah 1985, J. Ariffin 1994a) and public (R. Ariffin 1997) sectors. Women mainly filled jobs located in the primary labor market that are low-skilled, semi-skilled, repetitive, and with a slow chance of advancement in their career (see Tables 1.1 and 1.2).

Comprising 10 percent of the labor force in the fifties, women moved up to about 25 percent in the seventies (see various Ministry of Human Resources Reports from the 1950s to the 1970s) and 38 percent in the nineties.

In the sixties women were mainly found in agriculture, in the eighties in manufacturing, and in the nineties, in the service sector.

Table 1.1. Female composition of the labor force

Industry	Distribution (%)							
	1970		1980		1985		1990	
	M	F	M	F	M	F	M	F
Agriculture and fishing	49.6	67.9	37.5	49.3	28.6	33.7	28.9	28.2
Mining and quarrying	2.3	0.7	1.4	0.3	1.1	0.2	0.7	0.2
Manufacturing	9.3	8.1	11.8	16.3	13.0	18.9	15.2	24.3
Construction	3.1	0.5	6.4	1.0	10.7	1.2	8.7	0.7
Electricity, gas, water	1.0	0.1	0.2	0.1	0.8	0.5	0.9	0.1
Wholesale, transportation, storage, and communication	5.0	0.5	6.9	2.3	9.7	5.2	9.9	5.4
Services	18.1	16.4	22.7	19.5	19.3	21.2	18.8	21.4
Total	100	100	100	100	100	100	100	100

Source: Sixth Malaysia Plan (Kuala Lumpur: Government Printers, 1991).
Note: M = male; F = female.

In the nineties, 19.0 percent were found in agriculture, 30.3 percent in manufacturing and 47.7 percent in services (*Hawa Fact Sheet 1994* 1996).

Legislation relating to women was changed twice with the EOI process and the coming of transnational corporations (TNCs) into the country. Before the seventies women were not allowed to work after 10:00 PM, except in essential services such as nursing and bus conducting for the municipalities. Then the law was amended in 1968 to allow women to work an hour later, until 11:00. The law was changed again in 1970 to allow women workers to work three shifts in the TNCs with the qualification that the prime minister deemed it would not cause inconvenience to these women workers (R. Ariffin 1997, pp. 3–4).

The fact that women were employed in large numbers caused a considerable transformation in the composition of the labor force and the urban population, for the labor market before the seventies

Table 1.2. Employment distribution by industry and sex, 1990 and 1995

Industry	Male		Female	
	1990	1995	1990	1995
Agriculture, forestry, livestock and fishing	65.5	71.6	34.4	28.4
Mining and quarrying	87.1	88.1	12.9	11.9
Manufacturing	53.6	56.6	46.4	43.4
Construction	93.1	87.6	6.9	12.4
Electricity, gas, and water	95.7	92.2	4.3	7.8
Transportation, storage, and communication	61.4	88.8	38.6	11.2
Wholesale and retail trade, hotel and restaurants	88.9	62.4	11.1	37.6
Finance, insurance, real estate, and business services	65.8	59.7	34.2	40.3
Other services	62.1	60.8	37.9	39.2
Social and related community services	47.2	44.9	52.8	55.1
Personal and household services	47.0	49.4	53.0	50.6
Public administration	81.5	78.4	18.5	21.6
Total	68.6	66.3	31.4	33.7

Source: Ministry of Human Resources, 1996

was mainly male dominated, with ethnic Chinese comprising the largest number of workers. After the seventies women made deep inroads into the labor market, and Malay workers have increased substantially. This led to tension and stress for women who then had to adapt to their new work and social environment. Not only did they have to adapt to the strict regime of work in general, but also to shift work, the paternalistic or management style of the workplace, and the handling of machines as well as of over seven hundred chemicals (Malayan Trade Union Congress [MTUC] 1990).

Globalization in the nineties has further increased women's labor force participation. Due to structural adjustment, women shifted from agriculture and the informal sectors into manufacturing and services in the formal sector. Women then made up about

Table 1.3. Women (age 15–64) labor force participation

Year	1957	1970	1980	1990	1995	1996	1997	1998
%	30.8	36.3	39.3	46.8	44.3	45.8	47.4	44.2

Source: Ministry of Human Resources, 1996.

38 percent of the labor market (see Table 1.3). Of the total population of women, about 44.2 percent were gainfully employed, as compared to 83.4 percent of men in 1996 (*Economic Report 1999/2000* 2001).

There has been some variation in the second half of the nineties, with over 44 percent of women working. However, in comparison to men's labor force participation, which was still 83.3 percent in 1998 (*Economic Report 1999/2000* 2001), women lagged behind men, and growth has been very slow over the last decade. The other factor that might explain the low figures is the fact that some of women's work in the informal sector (e.g., unpaid family work) is still not accounted for as waged work in the national economy.

Women are increasingly found in the service sector as this sector expands in a more developed economy. For example, the service sector's contribution to the GNP was 36 percent in 1970 and 44 percent in 1993. In addition, it provided for over 42.2 percent of all jobs in 1993 (*Hawa Fact Sheet 1994* 1996), whereas manufacturing provided 23 percent and agriculture, 21.1 percent. While men are mainly found in the subsectors of transportation, finance, and utilities (water, gas, electricity, etc.) within the service industry, women are mainly found within several other subsectors. By 1989, over 50 percent of women were found in jobs characterized by low pay and poor conditions such as domestic work and waitressing. However, in the nineties, there had been some improvement in social services and self-employment, where women numbered 554,100 in 1992 and 589,700 in 1993; in wholesale, retail, restaurant, and hotels, where they numbered 488,000 in 1992 and

495,000 in 1993; and in finance, insurance, real estate, and business, where they accounted for 112,200 in 1992 and 121,900 in 1993. In the subsectors where men dominate, the nature of work requires technical skills that women frequently do not possess.

Even as students in colleges and universities, women tend to study the arts and social sciences, while more technical courses of study such as engineering are largely male dominated. In contrast, there has been much improvement in the number of female students taking business, science (with education), and medicine since the mid-eighties (J. Ariffin 1994b, pp. 86–87).

At the managerial level, in 1988 women made up 0.7 percent of total managers. In 1995, this increased to 1.8 percent, and in 1997, it was 2.2 percent (*Labour Force Survey 1997*). The following year, in decision-making occupations, women made up 0.7 percent (63,400), as compared to 3.1 percent of men (266,100) (*Labour Force Survey 1998* 2000).

Overall, we can conclude that although the increase in the number of women in technical-related jobs and decision-making is slow and the overall number remains very low, there has been a gradual improvement in the last decade or so. Because education, skills, and technical training are the road to upward mobility in the job hierarchy, the government and private sectors must take remedial measures to hasten the vocational and technical training of more women and to prepare women to participate more in decision-making and managerial positions. It is important to note that although quantitatively the proportion of female labor has improved, qualitatively much is left to be desired; that is, women should be able to earn enough for a decent living and to work in a safe and clean environment, which in the long term would not jeopardize their safety and their health.

Another area in the service sector is sex work, or prostitution. With the opening of international boundaries and the existence of poverty, many women have turned to prostitution to survive. The earnings of the majority of prostitutes are located at the lower end of the pay scale, as demand and affordability are found here (see *New Straits Times* [Malaysia], January 20, 1999). This would include girls in karaoke lounges and pubs. Demand for upper-class call girls and mistresses has recently been quite badly affected, as many businessmen have either lost their business or gone bankrupt. As Malaysia's official religion is Islam, many people feel that prostitution is well contained; yet many hundreds of girls reported missing have gone into this trade. Furthermore, Malaysia has not escaped from the global trafficking of women. Studies by Tenaganita (1998a) and some nongovernmental organizations (NGOs) have revealed that Malaysian women have been exported to Japan, Taiwan, Hong Kong, Europe, and Australia for this purpose.

HEALTH AND SAFETY OF WOMEN WORKERS AT THE WORKPLACE

As available work moved from agriculture to industry, after 1987, the main health and safety challenges came from the use of machinery and chemicals. The constant upgrading of machinery and the introduction of a variety of new chemicals has resulted in health risks of various types: biological, brought on by dust, liquid, gas, or radiation; ergonomics, caused by vibration of machinery or the inappropriate design of furniture and machinery; and socio-psychological, caused by stress, the repetitive nature of work, boredom, and isolation.

All data have pointed to an increase of accidents since the eighties, because at that time more machinery began to be used in all sectors except among professional, administrative, and clerical workers. But because the nature of their work is different from those handling machines and chemicals, clerical workers are affected by different workplace health issues such as ergonomic problems and stress-related work, which are categorized not as accidents but as health issues.

So far government data has concentrated mainly on the safety issue and very little on health aspects of the workplace. This is partly due to the difficulty in assessing such effects, as health problems related to such risks only surface after many years of working in a specific situation with the handling of machines and chemicals. Another problem is the dire shortage of doctors qualified in health and safety, which has resulted in a failure to record cases arising from and related to workplace situations. Substantially fewer studies have been conducted in this area of concern in Malaysia than in other countries. Because it is relatively difficult to prove the correlation of a certain health problem to a job, most research tends to discuss only the probability of health problems arising from the nature of some jobs and industries (Lim 1978, MTUC 1990, Nicholas and Wangel 1991, Ng and Kua 1994).

Since the nineties, changes in conditions of production have taken place in most factories; so has the socioeconomic demographic profile of the workers. Whereas before, the majority of workers were below thirty years of age, many workers are now over thirty-five and have worked for more than ten years. Newer machines have replaced older ones; for example, visual display unit (VDU) screens have replaced the microscope. Instead of looking through one microscope for many hours, workers now have to monitor six VDU screens. They are constantly looking at several screens at once and have to continually turn their heads for many hours. Many workers have complained of neck problems, eyestrain, and other musculoskeletal problems. Since workers now have to handle several screens, they have no time to interact with other workers. Although many microscopes have been abandoned, there still are a few remaining, to be used in times of computer breakdown so as not to disrupt production schedules.

In some Japanese factories, workers are made to stand for eight long hours while performing their work; according to employers, this facilitates efficiency. Such assembly-line work includes, among other tasks, inserting screws and fastening casing covers. In several audio (electrical) factories, workers have to be in constant motion to finish a product. One union organizer reported that a worker making a combo unit has to move fifty-three times to finish a unit. With the target set at twelve hundred units per day, one can just imagine the thousands of movements per day that a woman worker has to make to achieve this (interview with unionist, December 20, 2000). Eventually, this will cause many musculo-skeletal problems for these workers.

In many high-tech factories, robotic machines are used. For instance, in a factory producing hard disks, the robots are supported by tester machines. The "technical" workers that operate these testers have to stand for many hours to ensure the smooth operation of these machines. When the tester breaks down, which is quite often, the worker has to bend down to repair it, and most workers have complained of backaches as a result of this (interview with worker, December 21, 2000).

In the service sector before the nineties, women were concentrated in more marginal jobs characterized by low pay and poor employment practices; over 50 percent were found to be maids, housekeepers, laundresses, cooks, and waitresses. After the nineties more women were found in the "newer" services of retail trade, sales, hotels, and banking (R. Ariffin 1997). Thousands or more are found in the civil service as clerks, operators, typists, and lower-level office jobs. Although in general the service industry has a lower accident rate, over fourteen hundred cases were reported in 1998 by the Social Security Organization (SOCSO).

The service industry is increasing its use of computers, and as a result, less labor power is required in many work organizations. Although there is greater efficiency with the use of computers, it has often resulted in greater intensification of work. For most public-sector offices now, a clerk who used to handle a single job before computerization is now expected to handle several jobs and be multiskilled.

Many workers are now required to work with computers for

many hours to key in information. In a study by Cecilia Ng and Jamilah Ariffin in 1991 on a statutory body, it was found that workers suffered from musculoskeletal problems such as backache, pain in the wrists and forearms, headaches, and eyestrain. In a later study of four workplaces (PUBS, a public agency; TELMAl, a telecommunications organization; MANAS, an airline agency; and BANKAM, a bank), it was found that most of the managerial positions are occupied by men but with variation in these organizations, a higher percentage of women in banking are sliding down to MANAS (Ng and Kua 1994, p. 33).

With higher productivity expected from the new working system, women workers feel more pressure, leading to greater stress and tension at the workplace. Women workers are also dissatisfied with the lack of opportunity for promotion despite undergoing sufficient training. In their 1994 study, Ng and Kua pointed out that with computerization, there is a clear gender divide; more men are found in the highly skilled jobs such as computer programmers, whereas women are found in lower-level jobs such as data processing.

Unions have complained that they do not play a major role in the health and safety of workers in many factories, mainly because most employers do not inform unions of accident cases. Only when unions were present on health and safety committees were they consulted and informed of these incidences (R. Ariffin 1997). Generally, most unions are very financially weak, which limits their ability to provide health and safety education to their workers.

With the new health and safety law in the United States (OSHA 1994), more workers are covered in various industries, but a code of practice needs to be developed for effective implementation of the law. The setting up of the National Institute for Occupational Safety and Health (NIOSH) and the earlier Society for Health and Safety has gone a long way toward creating more health and safety awareness among workers and the general public, which is important as the costs, both direct and indirect, are heavy if health and safety matters are not reduced (MTUC 1990, pp. 10–11). Direct cost includes compensation to the victim, while indirect cost includes inability to work, emotional pressures on the victim and the family, and the loss of future earnings.

Up to 1994, SOCSO has paid a compensation of over 142.1 million Malaysian ringgits (RM), which is over US$37 million, not to mention the fact that there was a great loss of "person" power, which is generally an important asset to a country.

More studies are needed to look into the long-term effects of specific work on the health of workers. As technology changes in the form of new machinery and as work relations are reorganized, women in the manufacturing sector are faced with more complex health and safety problems. And as more and more women work in the service sector, greater attention should be paid to musculoskeletal health problems as well as emotional-psychological problems that could affect the mental health of women workers.

Immigrant Women Workers

With the recovery that took place after the 1985 recession, foreign labor was gradually imported into the country to take up jobs in the construction, plantation, and service industries (especially as domestic helpers). These are known as the "3-D jobs"—Dirty, Dangerous, and Demeaning. It was estimated that this group makes up over 2 million workers, or of about 13 percent of the labor market (see Table 1.4). They do not enjoy protection under the employment regulations, cannot join unions, and are subjected to much hardship in their daily living with improper housing, sanitation, etc.

In general, all workers in Malaysia including migrant workers are supposedly covered by the Malaysian Employment Act (1955), which provides for increased working hours, holidays, and workers' rights to other benefits such as medical insurance, social security, and maternity leave. But this law does not cover all migrant workers, especially in the case of domestic helpers, and it is often left to the goodwill of the employers to determine the terms

Table 1.4. Immigrant workers in Malaysia according to
country and economic sectors, July 1992–January 1997

Sector/ Country	Domestic	Plantation	Construction	Services	Manu-facturing	Other	Total	%
Indonesia	79,167	108,778	94,561	3,062	30,568	1,347	317,483	62.7
Thailand	3,879	11,120	6,540	1,492	298	848	24,177	4.8
Philippines	28,587	49	1,160	828	1,401	668	32,643	6.4
Bangladesh	56	17,366	27,578	5,803	72,538	416	123,757	24.4
Pakistan	53	183	1,356	427	1,682	3	3,704	0.7
India	54	306	1,347	444	194	27	2,372	0.5
Sri Lanka	5	4	43	39	28	—	119	0.0
Myanmar	17	125	675	282	123	16	1,238	0.2
Nepal	—	25	17	97	262	—	401	0.1
Nigeria	—	—	—	—	—	5	5	<0.1
Other	7	—	137	11	54	526	735	0.2
Total	111,775	137,956	1,333,414	12,485	107,148	3,856	506,634	100.0

Source: Malaysian Immigration Department, Kuala Lumpur.

of employment. Migrant workers in the factories and on plantations are not covered under the social security scheme, which covers Malaysian workers earning RM2,500 (about US$658) or less. Employers are required to buy insurance policies for their workers as stipulated under the workers' compensation law, and foreign workers are protected should any mishaps occur in the workplace.

As the terms of domestic employment are dictated by employers, migrant workers are subjected to long hours of work, are given no leave, and have no right to negotiate their terms of employment, based on observations and opinions of friends, relatives, and the public, as well as and my personal observations. In addition, they are barred by law from joining unions and have practically no channels through which to air their grievances.

A National Family Planning Board study (1996) listed the

nationalities of maids working in Malaysia. Of the households included in the study, 67.0 percent were Indonesian, 23.0 percent native Malaysian, 5.4 percent Filipino, and 3.3 percent other. It seems rather indicative of the actual situation in Malaysia.

Immigrant Women Workers' Experience

Many legal workers are spared the agony of landing by boat at the various coastal areas of the country. The boats are often over-crowded and will land at various points in Johore, Selangor, Negri Sembilan, and Malacca. Many illegal immigrants are brought in under the dark cover of night and have to jump into the sea as the boats near the shore, making a run for the mangrove swamps. At this point the land Taikong transport them by taxi or bus. If they are caught by the police, they have to bribe their way through. Some workers are asked for sexual favors by the police and immigration officers if caught. For those who make it through, they are then taken to an agent, after which they are sent to various workplaces.

Migrant domestic workers have various experiences with their employers. Generally the pay ranges from RM400 to RM800 (US$10 to $20), with Filipino maids earning at the higher end and Indonesian maids at the lower. Several factors contribute to this: primary among them is that Filipino maids have a better supportive system back home as well as within the recipient country (e.g., agencies, NGOs, and the state). Filipino maids are given rest days off, mainly Sundays for religious and recreational activities. Many Filipinos can be seen congregating at churches or supermarkets. They have some NGOs in Malaysia to air their grievances.

This is quite absent for Indonesian maids, who are not given any days off. They have no place to gather for religious or social interactions. Their embassies until lately have been lackadaisical and less forthcoming in helping their maids in distress. There have been many cases of maid abuse in all forms, and it is only now that the embassies are showing some interest.

Many horror stories, reported in the media, have exposed some of the terrible treatment suffered by domestic helpers at the hands of their employers. As the Asian Migrant Centre (1997) puts it, "They are usually treated as faceless labourer-economic tools—and not as human beings. Because they are foreigners, they are subjected to dehumanising conditions and various forms of discrimination" (p. 17).

RETRENCHMENT

With the increasing mobility of TNCs from country to country due to globalization, cyclical demands for semiconductors and other products, upgrading of technology for competitive edge, many workers are adversely affected and lose their jobs. From 1980 to 1982, 10,000 workers lost their jobs; in 1983, over 1,600 more were affected. When the country underwent a recession in 1985, over 7,000 women from the industrial sector lost their jobs. Men working in this sector were also affected, as well as those from the tin mines and plantations.

Recently, for example, from January to December 1998, at least 83,865 workers were retrenched. Women bore much of the brunt: over 43.5 percent, or 36,284, were female. The manufacturing sector once again topped the number of layoffs (53.8 percent, or 45,000), followed by wholesale, business, restaurants, hotels, and sundry sectors, counting as one group (12.4 percent, or 10,343). The third group was the construction sector, with 11.4 percent, or 9,334 workers (Ministry of Human Resources, 2000; *Sun* [Malaysia], September 20, 1998). Unemployment rose to 5.5 percent in 1998. Employment growth was about 1.1 percent by 2002.

Of the total retrenched workers, over 89 percent were local workers, and the rest migrant workers. According to an official report, about 80 percent of those retrenched have been re-employed. Over one hundred thousand migrant workers have been repatriated, and the government has threatened to send back more (about a million), except for those workers who are willing to work in the plantation and selected industries. Other anti-migrant measures include nonrenewal of working permits, imposing higher levies to discourage hiring of new migrants, and deportation of undocumented migrants (Battistella et al. 1998, p. 112). Some NGOs and trade unions were of the opinion that it was grossly unfair to dispense of these workers when they have contributed to the economic growth of the country (Tenaganita 1998a).

Efforts have been made by the Malaysian Ministry of Human Resources to provide retraining of skills for retrenched workers. Under its Human Resource Development Act (1992), retrenched workers can apply to the Human Resource Development Council through their former employer to receive training in a chosen area. Such courses include hotel catering, information technology, office administration, and human resource management. RM2.2 million (about US$580,000) was allocated for this purpose (*Star* [Malaysia], June 28, 1998). Initial feedback showed that retrenched workers were not taking advantage of this training, due most likely to lack of awareness of the program. In the existing skill training centers, male students formed the majority of trainees. Attachment schemes were initiated by the Free Trade Zone Penang Companies Association whereby temporary placement would be made for retrenched workers before they could find another job (*New Straits Times*, July 20, 1998). However, this mainly applied to "technical" staff, consisting mostly of male workers. Many retrenched women have turned to petty trading and small enterprises such as making and selling of foodstuffs (e.g., making of tofu and noodles). A substantial number of women are still engaged in agricultural work such as vegetable production (*New Straits Times*, October 14, 1998).

The trade unions and consumer associations have suggested to the government to set up a Retrenchment Fund (*New Straits Times*, May 24, 1998). The discourse between these groups and that of employers indicated different interests and perspectives. The latter viewed this as unnecessary because if a safety net is provided for workers, it will "create a corporate culture where workers feel they do not need to contribute so much to the well-being of the company" (ibid.). The unions and the consumer groups felt that this fund would be able to support the retrenched workers for a few months before they found another job. The resultant decision was that the fund was not set up by the government.

But in months where the government has felt threatened by political opposition and religious extremism, which have made efforts to win over NGOs, unions, and workers, it has gravitated toward a favorable response to form the fund, provided the employers agree to this.

UNIONS AND WORKERS' RIGHTS

The need for direct foreign investments made most governments in Asia impose tighter control on unions. This provides a conducive environment for industrial harmony so as to attract TNCs. Trade unions in Malaysia came under heavy control by the state through its Trade Union Law of 1948 and its Industrial Relations Law of 1967, both of which have been amended many times after that. With the prime minister emulating the Japanese (and to a lesser extent, the Koreans) in his Look East policy in the mid-seventies, workers were encouraged to form an enterprise (or in-house) union if they wished but were correspondingly discouraged from affiliating or forming state or national unions. Thus from 1985 until the present, most new unions have been in-house unions, accounting in 1998 for over 55 percent of all existing unions (R. Ariffin 1998). The fragmentation of the union movement by the formation of these smaller unions was achieved through the process of the Japanization of unions (Wad 1988). In general, union functions were curbed and strikes were made difficult, while management's prerogatives were widened to include hiring and firing, as well as

promotion and demotion of workers. The minister of human resources has a major say in matters related to industrial relations and
conflicts between workers/unions and management.

Since thousands of women joined the electronic industries in
the seventies, unions have been disallowed for these workers. Since
1974, the Electrical Industry Workers' Union (EIWU) and MTUC
have made great efforts to encourage women in the electronics
industry to form a national union or to join the EIWU; however, the
Registrar of Trade Unions (RTU) thwarted all these efforts. For
fourteen years women workers struggled, with the cooperation of
the MTUC, against the reluctance of the government to form a
national union. The case was taken to the High Court but was ruled
out by the judge, who decided that the MTUC was not the directly
aggrieved party. However, the government did relent somewhat in
1988 and allowed for only enterprise in-house unions for electronic
workers (R. Ariffin 1997, p. 82). If the national union for electronics workers had materialized, it would have been one of the
biggest, if not the biggest, union in the country.

Some women workers in the electrical and textile industries
have joined the existing unions, but in general, most women
workers in the industrial sector are non-unionized or unorganized,
and even if they are, it is mainly in enterprise unions. Of course,
there are a few big enterprise unions, but in general, enterprise
unions are fairly small, easily manipulated, and controlled by the
company management.

The suppression of unions is not only on a material level but
also in the ideological realm. The government-controlled media
have in the past painted the unions as subversive trouble makers
and disrupters of productivity. Unions are made to be seen as irrelevant and nonfunctional by the "propaganda programs" of the
employers.

Women workers' consciousness has been structured in many
factories by the management along human resource management
lines, such that any work problems and workers' rights issues are

perceived to be resolved directly (or indirectly) through the human resources department. In such situations, unions are perceived as irrelevant to the workplace. The concept of a plurality of interests, where the stakes and interests of workers, employers, and shareholders widely differ, is completely submerged in the workplace environment. Women workers are taught to identify closely with employers through various symbols and programs such as songs, games, motivational talks, and in-service training. In the bigger TNCs, where pay and other fringe benefits are better than in smaller and local companies, this perception is strongly entrenched. Thus the functions of unions, as a channel for grievance and as a manifestation of worker solidarity, are no longer needed. Over the last three decades, union membership in the country has been low, consisting of about 8 to 10 percent of the working population, with women members at the lower end of this range.

STANDARDS OF LIFE, URBAN LIVING, AND POVERTY

As a result of the increase in population in urban areas due to the influx of workers as well as growth in the birth rate, the demand for housing and other basic amenities has increased in these areas as well. Several factors have caused property and land to become more expensive in the urban areas, and the profit orientation of developers has caused a mushrooming of high-rise, high-density buildings in most towns. Many of the apartments within are very small, with one or two rooms, a small kitchen, and no drying areas. Rules for the provision for a green space or park for children, youth, and elderly are not implemented. The skyscrapers in Malaysian cities are beginning to resemble those in the west, such as those in Chicago, New York, and London. With them come the problems of high-density living and urban slums. Social problems tied to the process of industrialization have arisen that are also connected to urbanization and the system of work. Drug addiction has become a major problem, followed by juvenile delinquency, missing and runaway children, and unwanted pregnancies; many of these problems have involved factory women. The number of single mothers has increased to about eight hundred thousand or about 18 percent of the population, due either to the death of a spouse, divorce, or abandonment. Single mothers are generally poorer than a "couple family" with joint income. In the seventies, most factory women were young and single, but in the nineties, the majority are married with children. As most factory women are required to work two to three shifts and the majority have children in school, work often clashes with their domestic and child-rearing activities. This gives ammunition to many segments of society who accuse working mothers of neglecting their children. This is relevant especially when the mother is a single parent who has to bring in the income and work twice as hard in many cases. Most working-class families including factory workers are housed in high-density, low-cost apartments, which creates even more problems for their children.

Regarding poverty, the Ministry of Finance (2001) reported that the poverty rate was 5.5 percent in 2000, down from 6.1 percent in 1997. The number of hardcore poor households had decreased from the 1997 figure of 294,400 to 276,000 by 2000. National income per capita has remained the same. For most people, therefore, their real income has dropped, as inflation has increased over 5 to 6 percent. Many basic food staples such as fish, flour, vegetables, milk, and cooking oil have become more expensive. Since between 40 and 50 percent of the budget of the lower/working-class families is spent on food items, this has caused considerable hardship for them. Some mothers have resorted to buying cheaper alternative food; for example, instead of giving milk to their infant in between meals, they now give syrup water (*New Straits Times*, March 7, 1999). The cost of transportation and school uniforms has also increased, which further adds to the burden. For the middle class, other adjustments were made, such as cutting down on luxury items, vacationing locally rather than abroad, buying fewer brand goods, and entertaining less frequently.

Poverty among single mothers is also rampant in the rural areas, as their husbands have abandoned them, and they usually have many children but little education and few skills. For those in the urban areas, the high cost of living adds more burdens to their modest income. As a result, a study in Penang revealed, it is common for single mothers to work more than nine hours per day in order to earn extra income (Nawesi 1999). Thus they are often tired when they get home. They then have to perform household chores such as cooking and washing clothes, which leaves them too tired to spend "quality time" with their children.

The recession had its effects on crime rates: police reports revealed a 13 percent increase in crimes by juveniles (such as vehicle thefts and breaking and entering) between 1997 and 1998, along with a 19.6 percent increase in the adult crime rate. Crime against women such as domestic violence has also increased. From about 400 cases in 1996 and 600 in 1997, it jumped to about 5,000 in 1998 (R. Ariffin 1998; *New Straits Times*, April 5, 1999). However, there is no study yet to show the positive correlation between the recession and the violence. A previous study (R. Ariffin and Samuel, 1997; *New Straits Times*, April 5, 1999) has shown that a strong contributing factor was financial difficulties. In a recession, financial difficulties are felt by many families in addition to the normal stress of modern living. A definite factor leading to the sudden increase in the crime rate, however, is the increased awareness of women regarding domestic violence following the implementation of the Domestic Violence Act in 1996.

GENDER RELATIONS

How do we evaluate gender relations and the position of women in Malaysia? Perhaps the words of an organizer of a women's conference in resisting globalization best illustrates this when she says, "The people's resistance movements within certain countries experiencing political crisis and current economic downturn are being led by fundamentalist groups . . . as the backlash will result in more suffering for women—which is already being experienced in this region" (Pesticide Action Newtork 1998).

Many segments of society are critical of Western capitalism and, more so, of Western culture, brought about primarily by the electronic media. As a result, they are beginning to turn back to religious teachings, which reconstruct gender relations. So how do we evaluate women's position and gender relations? There are variables such as class position, rural versus urban residence, economic sector, and ethnicity. Over the years, women's representation in the political arena has increased from 1 percent in the fifties to about 8.7 percent in the nineties (R. Ariffin 1998). Over the last twenty years, civil laws for non-Muslim women have given more rights and greater equality to women, for example the outlawing of polygamy as well as the establishment of rights of divorce and custody. Educational opportunities for female students have almost equalled those for male students at all levels of education, including the universities. Although all women are subject to the patriarchal nature of this society, gender relations vary quite widely.

Highly educated women in the service sector have some autonomy, income, and access to worldwide information through television and the Internet. They most probably have a foreign maid to run the household and take care of the children. Middle-class women enjoy a similar life, except that they may have the dual burden of being wage workers as well as housewives, since they cannot afford a servant. Non-Muslim women administrators and executives wear "power"-fashioned three-piece suits and such for creating the right image of the modern woman, whereas Muslim working women wear headgear of various brands and tones with the more modest Malay dress as a compromise between the requirements of modernism and their cultural norms (Stevens 1998, pp. 91–95).

Things got worse for lower-class women, with their dual burden, when thousands became involved in the three-shift system in the industrial sector. Their access to information regarding their rights is limited by their busy schedule and lesser degree of education. Women in the rural areas tend to be similarly burdened; many of them are living in hardship and poverty. According to many NGOs (see Isis International 1998) there has been a revival of strong, chauvinistic, antiglobal fundamentalist movements, which have intensified social conflicts: "Women asserting their economic and political rights are under attack by fundamentalists" (ibid.). This has been going on in Malaysia since the seventies; Muslim ideology discourages women from waged work in the public sector. In fact, in March 1999, a leading Muslim leader called upon Muslim women to give up their waged work to spend time at home looking after their husbands and children, the assumption being that social problems among youth are attributable to working mothers. Islamic laws have been tightened over the years with stiffer penalties, such as imposing heavier fines and even whipping. Whipping had not been the practice over the last few decades but has been reintroduced recently to deter "social ills" such as sexual promiscuity, prostitution, incest, and sodomy. Although, as stated earlier, the secular/civil laws seem to work toward equality for non-Muslim women in the country, Islamic laws tend to remain the same or even go in reverse. For example, women's groups recently have advocated for amendments to the Guardianship Act, where the father is considered to have the sole parental rights over the child; they wanted both parents to have the rights. Muslim women are not included here, though they have requested to be included (*Star*, November 11, 1998; *New Straits Times*, November 19, 1998).

Studies have shown that many Malay families, especially those in rural areas, are reluctant to practice modern contraception (*New Straits Times*, March 1999). Many of the men assume that such methods are contrary to Islamic teachings, as children are seen as gifts from God. Thus Malays have the largest average number of children among the three principal ethnicities in Malaysia. Women's sexual rights are therefore not their own.

Overall, however, within this last decade, with more women working in the waged sector, there has been a general improvement in their financial independence, personal autonomy, and economic and political status.

CONCLUSION

The Bank Negara Annual Report of 1998 predicted a GDP growth of 1 percent. It also stated that inflation has moderated and that the CPI has remained subdued. The employment rate will increase again with more investments coming from abroad. The World Bank has lauded Malaysia for its efforts in improving the lives of the poor. It has given Malaysia a $1.5 billion loan over 3 years for investing in social work and related sectors (*New Straits Times*, April 1, 1999). The minister of special function, Daim Zainuddin, was optimistic when he said that measures such as capital control and a stable exchange rate will improve the economy in the near future (Daim 1998).

Civil society seems to have expanded since the economic recession and the sacking of the deputy prime minister. Unions can play a more positive role by concentrating not only on economic issues but on a broader spectrum of social and political issues. The broader struggle would mean closer cooperation with NGOs and interest groups. Women in general, especially women politicians, are asking for changes to male-biased gender laws. They are also clamoring for 30 percent representation in the hierarchy of all spheres. Muslim women want female judges in the religious departments. In November 1989, over one hundred women NGOs gathered in Malaysia to discuss and resist the negative repercussions of globalization on women and children (Asia-Pacific People Assembly [APPA] 1988). They reasserted, "We say No to Globalization! We say Yes to resistance and common actions." Furthermore, they stressed that "Asian women have become the cheapest source of labor, as they work longer hours, are paid the lowest of wages, and are subjected to miserable working conditions" (APPA 1999, p. 45). They have come out with a plan of strategies for further action by women NGOs. Thus women everywhere are beginning to unite in order to stake their claim in the world and their lives.

REFERENCES

Ariffin, Jamilah. 1994a. *From Kampung to urban factories: Findings from the Hawa study*. Kuala Lumpur: University of Malaya Press.
————. 1994b. *Reviewing women's status*. Kuala Lumpur: Population Studies Unit.
Ariffin, Rohana. 1997. *Women and trade unions in peninsular Malaysia*. Kuala Lumpur: University of Malaya Press.
————. 1998. Violence against women. In *Gender, culture, and society*, edited by Rokiah Talib and S. Thambiah. Kuala Lumpur: University of Malaya Press.
————. 2001. Domestic work and servitude. Working paper, Hawke Institute, Adelaide, Australia.
Ariffin, Rohana, and Maria Chin. 2000. Religion, politics, and violence against women in Malaysia. In *Resurgent patriarchy*, edited by ARENA. Hong Kong.
Ariffin, Rohana, and R. Samuel. 1997. Domestic violence in Penang. Report for HAWA, Kuala Lumpur.
Asian Migrant Centre. 1997. *Asian migrant yearbook*. Hong Kong: AMC and APEC.
Battistella, G., M. Asis, and Scalabrini Migration Center. 1998. The impact of the crisis on migration in Asia. In *Economic crisis . . . and our rice pots are empty*, edited by Consumers International. Penang, Malaysia: Consumers International.
Cheng, Lucie. 1999. Globalization and women's paid labour in Asia. *International Social Science Journal* 51 (June).
Daud, Fatimah. 1985. *Minah Karen*. Kuala Lumpur: Pelanduk.
Economic report 1999/2000. 2001. Kuala Lumpur: Department of Statistics.

International Labour Institute. 1998. *Globalization with equity*. Bangkok: International Labour Institute.

Isis International. 1998. *Women envision* (November–December). Philippines: Isis International.

Jones, Sydney. 2000. *Making money off migrants*. Hong Kong: Asia 2000.

Hawa fact sheet 1994. 1996. Kuala Lumpur: Department of Women's Affairs.

Koffman, E., and G. Young. 1996. *Globalization: Theory and practice*. London: Pinter.

Labour force survey 1998. 2000. Kuala Lumpur: Ministry of Human Resources.

Lim, Linda. 1978. *Women workers in multinational corporations: The case of the electronics industry in Malaysia and Singapore*. Ann Arbor: Women's Studies Program, University of Michigan.

Malayan Trade Union Congress. 1990. *Occupational health and safety issues in Malaysia*. Kuala Lumpur: Malayan Trade Union Congress.

Malaysian Industrial Development Authority. 1990. *Annual report*. Kuala Lumpur: Malaysian Industrial Development Authority.

———. 1991. *Annual report*. Kuala Lumpur: Malaysian Industrial Development Authority.

———. 1993. *Annual report*. Kuala Lumpur: Malaysian Industrial Development Authority.

Malaysian Society for Occupational Safety and Health. n.d. *Sharing OSH Experiences with APOSHO experts*. Kuala Lumpur: n.p.

Manning, Chris. 1998. Does globalization undermine labour standards? Lessons from East Asia. *Journal of International Affairs* 52 (July).

Ministry of Finance. 2001. *Midyear report of Seventh Malaysia Plan*. Kuala Lumpur: Ministry of Finance.

Ministry of Human Resources. 2000. Report of employment (May). http://www.jarring.my/ksm.

National Economic Action Council. 1998. *National plan for economic recovery*. Kuala Lumpur: Government Printers.

Nawesi, Peter. 1999. Single mothers in Penang. Masters Thesis, University of Sains, Malaysia.

Ng, Cecilia, and Muaro Kua. 1994. *Keying into the future*. Kuala Lumpur: WDC.

Nicholas, C., and A. Wangel. 1991. *Safety at work in Malaysia*. Kuala Lumpur: University of Malaya.

Pesticide Action Network, Asia and Pacific. 1998. *Pesticide Monitor* (Penang) 7, nos. 3–4 (December).

———, and Tenaganita. 1999. *Women resist globalisation! Assert women's rights*. Proceedings from APPA Conference, Kuala Lumpur.

Stevens, Maila. 1998. Sex, gender, and the making of the Malay middle class. In *Gender, power in affluent Asia*, edited by K. Sen and M. Stivens. London and New York: Routledge.

Tenaganita. 1998a. Implications of the economic crisis on migrant workers. Paper presented at the seminar "Implications of the economic crisis on migrant workers," Kuala Lumpur.

———. 1998b. Trafficking in women: A growing phenomenon in Malaysia. Paper presented at the seminar "Trafficking in women: A growing phenomenon in Malaysia," Kuala Lumpur.

Wad, Peter. 1988. The Japanisation of the Malaysian trade unions movement. In *Trade unions in the new industrialisation of the third world*, edited by R. Southall. London: Zed Press.

Zainuddin, Daim. 1998. The national economic recovery plan—why and how. In National Economic Action Council 1998.

2. The Context of Gender and Globalization in the Philippines

Elizabeth Uy Eviota

Arguing against the notion that globalizing processes (economic liberalization, privatization of state enterprises and deregulation) will eventually improve the welfare of the world's countries, Eviota explores the impact of global economic restructuring on the Philippines in general and Filipino women in particular. Far from making the Philippines a more competitive country in the world market, rapid capitalist expansion has only translated into increasing poverty for the majority of the population.

As a result of structural adjustment programs mandated by the IMF and World Bank, the Philippine economy has been completely transformed into export-oriented production. Accompanying this shift in production has been the arrival of foreign-owned transnational corporations (TNCs), which have recruited a more feminized and flexible workforce. These profound economic changes have had the greatest impact on Filipino women, who are either forced to labor in sweatshop conditions or find work abroad as overseas contract workers (OCWs) in low-skilled, low-paying, service-oriented jobs such as domestic work. Like so many other countries in the South, the impoverishment of the Philippines, as a

result of globalization, has been especially acute for Fil-
ipino women, who bear the brunt of both productive and
reproductive labor.
  Aside from examining the economic effects of global-
ization on the Philippines, Eviota highlights the cultural
changes as well. The predominance of Western TNCs has
resulted in the creation of a Western monoculture. Essen-
tially, this has meant that the actual needs and wants of
the Filipino people are dictated by foreign, specifically,
Western interests. Eviota's article illustrates the way in
which globalization has produced a power divide
between the "First World" and the "Third World."

In spite of a much-heralded regime of economic growth in the early nineties, Philippine society remains profoundly unequal. While the population in absolute poverty has decreased from 49 percent in 1985 to 40 percent in 1994 as a result of rising average incomes and increasing productivity (United Nations Development Programme [UNDP] 1997), income distribution has not improved much. In 1995 the poorest 40 percent still received only 13.7 percent of total incomes, a proportion that was actually smaller than the 14.3 percent it received in 1985. By contrast, the richest 20 percent took in 52 percent of all incomes—a distribution almost unchanged for several decades (ibid.). In the 1950s, the poorest 40 percent received roughly 10 percent; the richest 20 percent, more than 55 percent of all incomes (International Labour Office 1974).

The context of inequality this past decade is the project of economic restructuring to make the country more globally competitive. Structural adjustment, initiated by the IMF in the eighties, has paved the way for the liberalization of trade, the deregulation of markets and prices, and the privatization of state enterprises—

This paper is a slightly revised version of the afterword to the Japanese translation (Akashi Shoten 2000) of my book *Political Economy of Gender: Women and the Sexual Division of Labour in the Philippines* (London: Zed Books, 1992).

processes encapsulated in the term *globalization*. These processes are meant to promote greater global production efficiency and improve global welfare. But this latest phase of capitalist expansion, which is proceeding with unprecedented speed and range, is being achieved at great cost to many sectors of the population. Because globalization favors the powerful and the strongest—it has beggared vulnerable groups by marginalizing basic human needs,[1] enfeebled laboring classes by rendering their livelihood and entitlements insecure, and despoiled the environment by engaging in indulgent commercialism. In so doing, globalization has sharpened inequalities of class, state, ethnicity, and gender. Transnational corporations (TNCs) are the major players in global restructuring, aggressively safeguarding profits by reorganizing productive and marketing activities and making labor more "flexible." Together with international institutions such as the IMF and the World Bank, TNCs have undermined the ability of national states to intervene in the economy.

The key features of economic liberalization, such as export development, reduction of trade barriers, and the opening up of the economy to international competition have rapidly transformed the Philippine physical and social landscape. Agricultural lands are increasingly being converted into either plantation estates for export cash crops or industrial zones for export firms. Tens of thousands of farm families are deprived of sources of livelihood (Puod 1998). Since 1988 an average of fourteen thousand hectares per year have been lost to these industrial and commercial activities (ibid.).[2] Basic staple agriculture in these areas has been replaced by cut flowers, castor beans, rubber, and raspberries (Calderon 1996).

The government has adopted a program of food security based on food imports instead of fully implementing land reform that would have enhanced productivity and boosted demand for local products. Cheap imports now flood the markets, driving down prices of local produce and cutting into household incomes.[3]

The lands of cultural minorities have been taken over by "ecotourism ventures" (such as golf courses and resorts), "forestry management agreements," and extractive (open-pit) mining, creating beggars of many men, women, and children or driving them deeper into the interiors (Malig 1997; Perante 1998; Malanes 1998a, 1998b; Due 1998).[4] These commercial activities initiate a process of social differentiation in cultural communities while degrading the environment. Soil erosion resulting from deforestation has endangered many lives during the rainy season.

The country's coasts are crowded with large commercial trawlers, as the laws have allowed them to enter municipal waters, leaving thousands of small fishers with much diminished harvests. Seaside villages are forced to give way to construction of international trading ports. In the meantime, island towns in the south are being weaned away from fishing and agriculture to pearl farming ("Fisheries code . . ." 1998). Numerous coastal areas have been converted to shrimp cultivation to stimulate local economies, but this has provided little employment and has led to the pollution of the seas.

All these economic activities lower the living standards of affected rural families and leave their women worse off. Women in these sectors bear the major burden of raising and caring for their families and producing food for them. They now must intensify their workload and lengthen their working hours, look for employment to make up for income losses, or forage for food. Wives of small fishers are left to scavenge along the shorelines. Women and children of cultural minorities are forced to eat roots from the wild in order to survive (Tacio 1997; Cadelina-Manar 1998). Many rural women have had to migrate to towns and cities in search of paid work or economic opportunities in an already crowded informal sector. If men migrate, women are forced to tend the farms by themselves. In many households, young children, especially daughters, are taken out of school and pushed into often oppressive work (UNDP 1997). The cost of economic restructuring is measured in terms of growing hunger, diminished children's and women's health, expanding poverty, and social dislocation.

Export manufacturing and agribusiness offer employment for a growing number of women and regular paid work enables some women to gain some autonomy. But the very nature of the work makes them more expendable for capital and thus tends to sharpen gender inequalities. These jobs often re-create disadvantages generally associated with the informal sector: workers' right to organize and take collective action is suppressed, employment is insecure, the minimum wage is frequently waived, productivity quotas replicate the intensity of piece work, and especially in the case of electronics work, labor is casualized through apprenticeship status (see my discussion of this topic in Eviota 1992, pp. 102–26). Recent international processes of labor "flexibilization" (Standing 1989) have led to even more unprotected employment for women and a weakened bargaining position for the working class and trade unions. Such schemes as "labor-only contracting," contracting out or subcontracting, casual hiring, rotations, and contractualization— old forms of labor appropriation reoriented to meet market requirements—have become more widespread (Arboleda 1997, 1998a; Rebong 1998; de la Cruz 1996).[5] By 1992, 73 percent of factories were directly implementing various forms of flexible work arrangements, most in "economic growth centers" and export processing zones (Arboleda 1997). Firms have also resorted to more intensified use of labor, with fuller application of shifts and longer working hours (ibid.). While most common in manufacturing employment, these arrangements are also found in plantations and agribusiness, where some form of contractual production for export (e.g., horticulture and food processing) recruit women for intermittent wage employment. In all of these schemes, workers are hired and fired at will, deprived of their traditional entitlements of job security and benefits. Typically, these labor arrangements mean that labor standards are nonexistent, there is little monitoring of health hazards, and in the absence of institutional procedures, women have no redress against sexual harassment or physical abuse.

Filipino women have thus been at the forefront of labor flexibilization. They are the preferred labor force in export-oriented production and services because of their auxiliary position in the labor market and their reduced pay, which arises from social relations of subordination to men. Thus the very characteristics that make women more prominent in export-led development render them, with economic liberalization, more flexible.

Transnational corporations and their local agents adopt these schemes in order to cut costs and make them more responsive to changes in consumer tastes of niche markets in more affluent societies. Transnational corporations are accountable to no one; in their search for low-cost and flexible labor, they play labor-surplus countries against each other (e.g., the Philippines against Vietnam or Bangladesh) and even regions within one country (Hale [1996a?]).[6]

Technology improvements that fuel globalization may also offer more work for women, but technology has always had mixed effects on them. No doubt new technologies have eased the work of women, such as the use of computers by secretaries and clerks. In addition, they have opened up new economic opportunities for women in the internationally traded industrial services sector, although these are still along lines of labor-intensive or low-skilled, and therefore relatively low-paid, work in an analogy of export-manufacturing employment. For example, as TNCs decentralize their work processes through offshore subsidiaries in countries such as the Philippines, the expanded use of new technology for information processing gives rise to a need for women to do low-skill data entry work.[7] In contrast, higher-skilled software and programming work go to men, suggesting the persistence of a gender hierarchy of activities (Pearson and Mitter 1993). While most export manufacturing continues to use labor-intensive processes, as is the practice in subcontracted work in garments, others are beginning to adopt computer-aided technology to make labor-intensive work less significant and so replace women workers. Women's assembly work in electronics, for example, is changing qualitatively from a manual assembly line to machine-feeding, machine-minding, quality control, and maintenance work using less labor. In cases where work is carried out by improved technologies requiring higher skills, women do not progress to the higher category; men are hired instead (Elson 1994; O'Connor 1987). Practices of labor recruitment among TNCs thus tend to widen the disparities between skilled and unskilled work, and as skill and technology are gendered, the disparities between women and men widen as well.

What these trends show is that the gains to women's employment with the expansion of export-oriented industries is fleeting. This type of work has no long-term benefits for women relative to their position in the labor market and to their improved access to better future employment; thus it does not provide for a steady and equitable integration of women into the workforce. Nor is there evidence that the export sector diminishes the wage gap by gender (Standing 1989). All these points suggest that as the country progresses along the spectrum within this development path, so does the inequality between women and men with respect to access to jobs and wages.

Women continue to carry the larger burden of export orientation, including exporting themselves. The export of labor power remains a development tool of the state. In fact, the economic growth reported by policy-makers has been based largely on the remittances of overseas workers (roughly $5.2 billion in 1998 [Arboleda 1998b]). In 1995 approximately 4.5 million Filipinos, representing 17 percent of the total employable labor force, were working overseas (Son 1995; based on a report by the International Organization for Migration). Most are women, with one estimate as high as a ratio of twelve to one (Hale [1996b?]). Many are teachers, nurses, and other better-educated or skilled groups of women working mainly as domestic workers in the Middle East, Europe, and East Asia, and as entertainers (many of them prostitutes) in Japan (UNDP 1997; Arboleda 1998b). The social cost to women of overseas work includes physical, emotional, and sexual abuse as well as racial discrimination. In the meantime the skill drain goes unabated, as adequate-paying jobs are not made available. In 1996, out of the one million jobs the economy is said to have "generated," 62 percent were actually overseas placements (Arboleda 1998b). Throughout the decade, as the GDP and the GNP grew, so did the number of unemployed; and as industrial output rose, so also did the number of industrial workers made redundant—in both cases, with greater proportions of women (UNDP 1997; Oviedo 1998). The economic growth of the nineties has been a case of "jobless" growth (UNDP 1997; "Growth did not spell . . ." 1997).

As a result, women have to create their own jobs in the informal sector or intensify their work in it; at the same time, those who already work in it have a precarious existence. Women are slowly being squeezed out of their physical spaces in the sector: the privatization of public markets has increased user fees for stalls, leading to diminished earnings for women or driving them out of business altogether (Judy Taguiwalo, Center for Women's Studies, University of the Philippines, personal communication). The informal sector is expanding as it absorbs the many women government workers laid off by the privatization of several government agencies and corporations (Baylosis 1998). Thus an expanding informal sector is far from an indication of increased commercial activity; rather, it is an indication of deteriorating economic conditions.

As conditions worsen, sex work becomes a viable economic option for many women. The numbers of prostitutes and women engaged in other forms of sexual servicing are consistently high. In one instance, women's sex work waxes and wanes with the trajectory of Philippine-U.S. geopolitics. When the U.S. bases closed down in 1991 after their lease was not renewed, the demand for sex work in the areas surrounding them was drastically cut. The prostitutes then relocated their activities to "boom" cities, such as Metro Manila, Cebu, Davao and Angeles, as well as tourist destinations where whole areas are now engaged in "community servicing" (Taguiwalo, pers. comm.). But the demand in Subic is likely to grow again when U.S. military presence is reintroduced into the country with the signing of the Visiting Forces Agreement. This connection between foreigners or foreign military and sexual servicing by Filipino women has figured prominently in the country's economic and political autonomy—from the women who serviced the conquering Spanish and American forces of the colonial period to the sexual slaves or "comfort women" of the Japanese military during World War II to the prostitutes of the visiting U.S. military and overseas men today.[8] The bodies of Filipino women are a constitutive element of the country's traded services.

The Philippine experience of the 1997 Asian economic crisis exposes the disastrous consequences of the country's program of indiscriminate liberalization and unqualified endorsement of globalization. The crisis has weakened the Philippine currency considerably and comes at a time when the economy is still heavily burdened by a huge foreign debt. It has also unmasked the country's fundamentally unsound economic policies. In the first three months of 1998 alone, hundreds of manufacturing and business establishments shut down, and tens of thousands of workers were laid off or placed on a rotational basis, the majority of them from manufacturing firms (Baylosis 1998; de la Cruz 1998a, 1998b; Navarro 1998; Arboleda 1998c).

An economic crisis affects women differently from men. Because of women's multiple roles as producers of goods and services, reproducers of people, and maintainers of their family's well-being, women are especially vulnerable during these times. As the economy slows down, women are the first to be let go, often in the interest of protecting jobs for men, who are seen as the traditional breadwinners. Fewer jobs are made available to women, and the jobs that are offered are unrewarding or insecure. At the same time, the state cuts back on expenditures on health and services, especially those directed to the poor. Women thus make up for what they are unable to purchase or receive from the state—with added inputs of their own energy and their own time, both in the workplace and in the home. These types of self-help responses of women also tend to exclude them from more remunerative activities. Furthermore, when women seek to take charge of their own subsistence, they are largely unable to because high interest rates combined with a tight monetary policy make money unavailable in informal credit markets, the primary source of credit for many poor urban and rural women.

Studies have already shown how economic restructuring and cutbacks in government expenditures on health and services have undermined previous gains in women's well-being (UNDP 1997). Indeed, measures of gender disparity derived from human and gender development indices this past decade show that in many areas of the country, any worsening in socioeconomic conditions has been disproportionately borne by women; and in the few cases of improvements, women obtained a disproportionately smaller share (ibid.).

Downward pressures on real incomes and high unemployment rates for both women and men, combined with growing demands on household expenditures, have often led to situations where men are unwilling or unable to meet their traditional breadwinner responsibilities. Often, to compensate for this loss, men violently assert their dominance over women and children by physical or psychological abuse or abandonment (Eviota 1995a, 1995b).

On a larger scale, global restructuring disempowers workers as their lives are increasingly shaped by TNCs and international institutions rather than by local employers or the state. The practical result is that it is becoming more difficult for workers and other groups to develop a strong bargaining position locally; flexibilization has eroded the trade union movement's constituency (Arboleda 1997). Nonetheless, some space exists for public articulation, dissent, and debate; interest groups have become more vocal, more organized, and more sophisticated through lobbying, advocacy efforts, and the use of global networks in behalf of economic and social justice. Women's groups, for example, have used creative means to engage government and the market to fight against policies and programs inimical to their interests.[9] The responses of these various groups to globalization have ranged from disengagement to a selective integration into the global economy accompanied by, among other things, democratization of national economic policy-making, accelerated land reform, orientation toward the domestic market, and a trade policy with a judicious mix of protection and liberalization (see Ocampo 1996; Bello 1997).

But globalization is more than an economic phenomenon. Globalization of media, communications, and transportation technology likewise creates a globalization of culture—a Western economic monoculture. Western-based TNCs and global forces tell us what to buy, when to buy it, and how much to pay for it. They have begun to shape our needs and wants. To do so, many exploit the connection between sensuality and profit. Thus sex has come to figure more prominently in the profit equation—from advertising to film and various media presentations to the selling of sex itself. Newer and varying forms of communications networks such as the Internet are co-opted into a global objectification of women's bodies and the commodification of female sexuality. New technology has erased the boundaries of culture; it has popularized the manifold forms of sex as industry, including access to exploitative sex. This goes hand in hand with a growing incidence of sex tourism by men from predominantly affluent countries visiting the Philippines and other disadvantaged Asian countries for sexual services such as pornography and prostitution (Dimaano 1998). The exploited population is also getting younger largely because of increasing impoverishment on the one hand and the fear of AIDS on the other; already an estimated 60,000–100,000 Filipino children (some as young as nine years old and most of them girls) engage in sex work (Ocampo 1997).[10]

On the other extreme of culture is the rise in religious fundamentalism, whose spread is fueled by globalization through the popularization of televangelism and the easy entry of assorted religious groups into the country. Religious fundamentalism advocates a relationship between genders that valorizes "places"—of women in the home and men outside of it. Gendered places are insisted upon in the face of the pressing need for women to leave their homes in order to earn income.

The path to NIChood—to become a Newly Industrializing Country—is proving to be a long, drawn-out, and contradictory process for the Philippines. The integration of the Philippines into the global economy lays bare the vulnerability of a weak actor on a decidedly unequal stage. Premised on producing higher living standards and a more just society, globalization instead has produced the opposite. The fetish for profit has deepened the abyss between rich and poor, between women and men, and between North and South.

The challenge to globalization is for vulnerable groups—workers, women, the poor, especially the ethnic minorities among them—from countries of the South (and those from countries of the North, as well) to band together to fight for a better system of global economic regulation and governance—one that is characterized by transparency, democracy, and accountability, and one sensitive to the issues of basic human needs, gender, and environmental sustainability.

NOTES

1. See World Bank (1997a, 1997b); Talosig (1997), which is based on a UN report, "Economic and social survey of Asia and the Pacific for 1997"; and Reyes (1995), based on a study by Robert Manuel, "The debacle of inflation: Its impact on the 30% bottom population" (1994).

2. My figure of 14,000 is the midpoint of the figures reported by the Department of Agrarian Reform (roughly 8,000 a year from 1988 to 1996) and the Philippine Peasant Institute (200,000 in the past ten years).

3. "Philippine corn farmers . . ." (1996), which is based on a study by K. Watkins, "Prosects of the Philippine yellow corn sector under the GATT-UR; "GATT has failed . . ." (1997).

4. Other examples of "ecotourism ventures" are cable cars and shopping malls. Hundreds of Aeta (aborigine) families in Pampanga are threatened with ejection to make way for these ventures.

5. Subcontracting is defined as an arrangement under which the sub-contractor provides the principal with products that are used and marketed by the principal under the principal's sole responsibility. (This may include processing, transformation, or finishing of materials or parts.) "Labor-only" contracting occurs when the person supplying workers to an employer does not have substantial capital or investment (e.g., equipment or work premises) and the workers placed by such persons perform activities directly related to the business of such an employer. The intermediary is considered an agent of the employer, who will be responsible to the workers as if these workers were directly employed by him (Rebong 1998).

6. Hale (1996a?) reports that if workers become organized and get pay raises, companies simply move their production site elsewhere, as was the final outcome of years of effective action by women workers in a British-owned factory in the Bataan Free Trade Zone. When the company refused to pay them the legal minimum wage in 1989, the women organized a twenty-four-hour picket and brought production to a halt. The end result was that the company moved production to another part of the country, where workers were less organized.

7. Pearson and Mitter (1993) report that in 1989 the wages of Filipino keyboard operators were one-fifth of those of equivalent employees in U.S.-based companies.

8. The "comfort women" issue is still not settled. Filipino (and other Asian) comfort women have asked for an official apology and compensation from the Japanese government for the abuse committed by its military on thousands of women during the war. The Japanese government has so far avoided officially acknowledging or taking responsibility. Instead, a private Asian Women's Fund was set up by Japanese businesses to be turned over to women claimants. The Philippine government (at least under the Ramos administration) has also refused to support Filipino comfort women openly in their claim.

9. I discuss some of these efforts in Eviota (1992, 1995); see also Matsui (1998).

10. The lower estimate is from UNICEF and ECPAT (End Child Prostitution in Asian Tourism), and the higher from *Asiaweek* (printed in Asia by *Newsweek*).

REFERENCES

Note: Today *is a newspaper published in Manila.*

Arboleda, Richard. 1997. Globalization hits labor unions hard. *Today*, September 1997.

———. 1998a. Quisumbing: No to 'labor-only' contracting. *Today*, January 7, 1998.

———. 1998b. Jobs: Where will they come from? *Today*, January 10, 1998.

———. 1998c. Layoffs triple in 1st quarter. *Today*, April 1998.

Baylosis, Karlo. 1998. Mass layoff of govt men seen. *Today*, March 29, 1998.

Bello, Walden. 1997. How to cope with economic crisis. *Today*, 1997.

Cadelina-Manar, Malu. 1998. Women at the frontlines in war versus poverty. *Today*, January 1998.

Calderon, Jo. 1996. GATT threatening RP food security? *Today*, June 1996.

De la Cruz, Erik. 1998a. 681 Companies seen closing. *Today*, March 30, 1998.

———. 1998b. Jobless rate seen rising to 9.5%. *Today*, April 1998.

De la Cruz, R. 1996. More local firms to 'downsizing.' *Today*, April 1996.

Dimaano, Tino. 1998. 50 American sex tourists land in Subic. *Today*, April 1998.

Due, Jojo. 1998. New KKK hits golf courses. *Today*, April 1998.

Elson, Diane. 1994. Uneven development and the textiles and clothing industry. In *Capitalism and development*, edited by Leslie Sklair, pp. 189–210. London: Routledge.

Eviota, Elizabeth Uy. 1992. *Political economy of gender: Women and the sexual division of labour*. London: Zed Books.

———. 1995a. Women, the economy and the state. In Shadows behind the screen: Economic restructuring and Asian women, *Asian Exchange* 2 (1): 3–17.

———. 1995b. Women, the economy and the state. In Shadows behind the screen: Economic restructuring and Asian women, *Asian Exchange* 2 (1): 19–31.

Fisheries Code does not protect fishermen. 1998. *Today*, April 1998.

GATT has failed to deliver on its promises—farmers. 1997. *Today*, October 1998.

Growth did not spell human development. 1997. *Today*.

Hale, Angela. [1996a?]. The rights of women workers in the global economy. Women Working Worldwide briefing paper. Manchester, UK.

————. [1996b?]. World trade is a women's issue. Women Working Worldwide briefing paper. Manchester, UK.

International Labour Office. 1974. *Sharing in development: A programme of employment, equity, and growth for the Philippines*. Manila: National Economic and Development Authority.

Malanes, Maurice. 1998a. Burning mining issue to eclipse polls. *Today*, April 1998.

————. 1998b. C'dillerans cry out versus threat of globalization. *Today*, April 1998.

Malig, Jose. 1997. Aetas suffer costs of globalization. *Today*, July 10–16, 1997.

Matsui, Yayori. 1998. *Women in the new Asia: From pain to power*. London: Zed Books.

Navarro, Chris. 1998. Peso fall takes toll on CL workers. *Today*, January 11, 1998.

Ocampo, Satur. 1996. The impending globalization backlash. *Today*, February 12, 1996.

Ocampo, Sonora. 1997. ASPAC sex market is expanding. *Today*, August 1997.

O'Connor, David C. 1987. Women workers and the changing international division of labor in microelectronics. In *Women, households, and the economy*, edited by Beneria Lourdes and Catharine K. Stimpson, pp. 243–66. New Brunswick, NJ: Rutgers University Press.

Oviedo, Sheila. 1998. Economy: Advancing means stepping back. *Today*, January 10, 1998.

Pearson, Ruth, and Swasti Mitter. 1993. Employment and working conditions of low-skilled information processing workers in less developed countries. *International Labour Review* 132 (1): 63.

Perante, Ceasar. 1998 Apec won't benefit countryside, environmentalists say. *Today*, November 18, 1998.

Philippine corn farmers to lose out from GATT. 1996. *Today.*

Puod, Rico. 1998. Food security: Supply can't keep up with demand. *Today*, 1998.

Rebong, Nick. 1998. Scrap labor-only contracting. *Today*, January 1998.

Reyes, Melissa. 1995. Poor Filipinos get tougher deal. *Manila Chronicle*, November 5, 1995.

Son, Johanna. 1995. Manila told to look out for its migrant workers. *Today*, November 12, 1995.

Standing, G. 1989. Global feminisation through flexible labour. *World Development* 19:1.

Tacio, Henrylito. 1997. Women rule the farms, too. *Today*, October 1997.

Talosig, Malou. 1997. Rich-poor gap grows in Aspac. *Today*, April 18, 1997.

United Nations Development Programme (UNDP). 1997. *Philippine human development report.* New York: UNDP.

World Bank. 1997a. *Everyone's miracle? Revisiting poverty and inequality in East Asia.* New York: World Bank.

———. 1997b. The maturation of the East Asia miracle. New York: World Bank.

3. The Restructuring and Privatization of Women's Industries in Nicaragua

Nancy Wiegersma

An economist, Wiegersma details the manner in which the Nicaraguan economy after the Sandinistas has been restructured to fit the agendas of the International Monetary Fund, the World Bank, and the U.S. Agency for International Development. Such restructuring has involved privatization of formerly government-run industry, as well as trade liberalization, which has led to revised tax and industrial structures and the shutdown of domestic firms. Wiegersma describes the consequences of these measures for women.

Comprising the bulk of the workforce in commerce and services at the time of the changeover from the Sandinista administration to the National Opposition Union (UNO), women were also a significant part of the industrial labor force. But structural adjustment thereafter forced them out of the formal labor market into the informal sector of production. Even with the establishment of free trade zones designed for the production of exports—in other countries resulting in the recruitment mainly of women—female employment declined in the switch from an economy with socialist features to one dominated by capitalist development.

Wiegersma trains her lenses on the marginalization of

women in the new economy, how government programs that were eliminated (health services, transportation, free noontime meals) directly affected them, and how government, business, and labor unions operated in ways that severely restricted their economic participation.

The Mercedes Free Trade Zone (*Zona Franca*; abbreviated FTZ) in the Managua region is now employing 2½ times as many workers as the (approximately ten thousand) textile and garment workers who lost their jobs during the restructuring of the garment and textile industries in Nicaragua in the early nineties. Nevertheless, if we include women's other job losses in that period in other fields where women's employment declined, such as in government offices, education, and health, the numbers of employment losses would be greater, even with the subsequent job openings in export processing. Nevertheless, employment numbers are not the only, or even the most significant, part of the story of the structural transformation from a mixed socialist-capitalist experiment under the Sandinistas to a private export-processing economy with a conservative government sponsored by the U.S. Agency for International Development (AID), the World Bank, and the International Monetary Fund.

The losses during Nicaragua's major economic restructuring and the struggles of workers versus owners in export processing in the intervening period demonstrate substantial losses of workers' rights and benefits as well as losses in community services. In addition, as we will see below, there was significant discrimination against women workers in the restructuring process. Exports from the export processing zones are now Nicaragua's leading exports, but the costs to Nicaraguan women workers of the shift from state production to this method of private production has been immense.

This chapter is a revised and updated version of an earlier article published under the title "State Policy and the Restructuring of Industries in Nicaragua," in *Women in the Age of Economic Transformation*, ed. Nahid Aslanbeigui, Steven Pressman, and Gale Summerfield (London and New York: Routledge, 1994), pp. 192–205. Reprinted by permission of Taylor and Francis.

METHODOLOGY

To compare women's overall employment position inside and outside Nicaragua's FTZ, this chapter uses an "industry study"
approach, investigating the different institutional formations, wages,
and working conditions for enterprises inside and outside the zone
in the early nineties. This is done for both state and private enterprises. An industry study was chosen in the light of the problems
encountered with alternative methods. Time-series and cross-section
approaches to the impact of export processing and industrial restructuring on workers contain inconsistencies brought about by
involving false comparisons of different sizes and types of industry
(Jenkins 1990). An industry study can specify the differences in
industry size and institutional setting in making comparisons.

Interviews and questionnaires were used to obtain information
from government officials, managers of industries, and from
workers themselves. Fifteen initial and follow-up interviews were
conducted with enterprise managers and personnel directors using
a Spanish version of a 1990 Economic Commission for Latin
America (ECLAC) study (Bishop et al. 1990).[1] Twenty initial and
fifteen follow-up interviews were also conducted with textile-garment operatives who worked in the zone as well as outside the zone
(in both formal and informal sector enterprises). The interviews
were conducted between July 1991 and July 1993.

The garment industry is a natural choice for comparing enterprises inside and outside the free trade zones because it has had a
long history. By the 1980s, Central American countries had experienced several decades of textile-garment production for domestic
and regional markets. These industries had been encouraged by
high import taxes associated with the import substitution policies of
the 1960s and 1970s and by the development of the Central American Common Market in the 1970s. Moreover, unlike electronics,
the garment industry had not previously been associated exclusively with export processing.[2] In this period, the new international

division of labor has vastly transformed the garment industry, creating new institutional structures.

BACKGROUND

The employment trends for women in Nicaragua reflect both urbanization and industrialization. Nevertheless, the majority of women who have participated in the workforce have continued to work in the service sector, employed in such jobs as domestic work and vending. In 1971, three-quarters of employed women worked in the service sector. This proportion declined to 61 percent by 1977, due to an increase in women's participation in agricultural export production and manufacturing. With limited growth in the agricultural and manufacturing sectors under the Sandinistas, the percentage of women employed in the service sector increased again, reaching 67 percent by 1985. Since 1988, structural adjustment programs (under the Sandinista and UNO governments) led to the further restructuring of the workforce. Women increasingly turned to services and the informal sector in the early nineties, away from manufacturing, as more than ten thousand industrial jobs vanished. Then, in the mid- and late nineties, with more development of the Mercedes Zone and other companies with export processing privileges, manufacturing jobs for women again increased.

During the fifties and sixties, the big surge in industrialization created job opportunities for Nicaraguan men and women alike. With the development of garment, textile, and food-processing industries, women's share in manufacturing employment grew to approximately one-fifth of the industrial workforce by 1971. Despite growth in numbers, this share remained stable until the late eighties (Pérez-Aleman et al. 1989). Although the share of women in agriculture and services shifted somewhat with the Sandinista administration and with the wartime economy, industrial employment for women was relatively stable until the structural adjustment policies of the nineties eliminated more than four thousand jobs in textiles as well as a large number in garment and other industries in the Managua region. In the period 1994 through 2000, with the rapid growth of export processing and an estimated thirty-five thousand added jobs (80 percent female), young women's employment in manufacturing has again increased (Hajewski 2000, p. 3).

Women's participation in large-scale industry, both before and after restructuring, is even more significant than these figures might suggest. Along with the development of national industry from the fifties to the seventies, an urbanized female working class emerged with specific household characteristics. Only half of all women working in manufacturing were married; one-third of them were heads of households; and 14 percent were single with no children (Pérez-Aleman et al. 1989, p. 31). News reports indicate that the percentage of single mothers in the privatized export-processing industries is even greater (70 percent) in the contemporary period (Nicaragua Network Hotline 2000, p. 5).

The civil war in the eighties encouraged women's workforce participation, but female employment in large manufacturing establishments did not increase very much because of limited opportunities. In general, large industries performed poorly under Sandinista rule, and the sexual division of labor remained fairly rigid, despite young men going off to war.

By 1985, nevertheless, one-third of females aged ten years and older were in the workforce. Twenty percent of them were in industry, 13 percent in agriculture, and the rest in services. The sectors with increasing participation during the Sandinista period were government, services, and small-scale industry. Women entered the workforce in increasing numbers during this period because a large part of the male workforce was involved in the war, more members of the family were forced to look for jobs due to the economic crisis, and there was a large increase in the number of female-headed households in the cities (Pérez-Aleman et al. 1990, pp. 1–33).

A combination of circumstances in the eighties shifted the focus of industrial enterprises to production for the domestic economy, and away from exports. Sandinista ideology favored production for the internal markets. Moreover, the U.S. trade embargo, the war, and Nicaragua's defaulting on foreign loans made international commerce very difficult. Some clothing and shoes continued to be produced for export during the eighties, but some of the plants in Nicaragua's FTZ were shifted to produce solely for the domestic economy or for the production of military uniforms.

Although the number of women in large-scale manufacturing industries did not increase substantially during Sandinista rule, working conditions changed considerably for workers in general and for women working in industry in particular. Manufacturing workers were given access to free medical care through the social security system. Employees were granted free transportation and noontime meals. Particularly important to women was the change in labor legislation that gave them paid pregnancy leave and the right to return to their jobs afterwards.

At the time of changeover from the Sandinista administration to UNO, in 1990, women made up the larger part of the workforce in commerce and government services (especially health and education). They were also a significant part of the industrial workforce. Nevertheless, the structural adjustments of the late eighties and early nineties greatly affected women's job opportunities. Vast numbers of women workers became unemployed or moved back into an already overcrowded informal sector. The hardest hit were the large-scale garment-textile industries in Managua, which employed about 10 percent of all female industrial workforce. Also affected was another 10 percent who participated in small household apparel shops and cooperatives. Nationwide, women in the garment-textile industry made up approximately one-quarter of the employed female industrial workforce.

In the depression of the early nineties, estimates of unemployment and underemployment were as high as 50 percent in the daily newspapers (these high estimates, which include underemployment, continued after the turn of the century). A social science research organization, FIDEG, put the unemployment, excluding underemployment, figure in the early nineties in the Managua area at about 20 percent and the underemployment rate at 34 percent (1992, p. 32).

At the time, a high unemployment rate was supposed to be the "medicine" that Nicaragua had to endure in order to defeat the runaway inflation that had gathered steam under the Sandinistas and during the first year of the UNO government. The managed depression was a policy that the World Bank, the IMF and the USAID insisted upon because foreign investment was impossible as long as inflation persisted. Unfortunately, many years after inflation was defeated, there were still few signs of economic growth. For the years since 1993, when our transition study was completed, Nicaraguan growth has been slow and high unemployment has been persistent.

After the Sandinistas left office, many large-scale companies were returned to their pre-1979 owners with agreements about workers' right to own 25 percent of their companies. Other industries were sold by the state to multinational corporations. Production of rum, beer, and cola, with a predominantly male workforce, was stable, as these industries did not show a strong downward turn during the recession. Unique among the large companies were the garment-textile enterprises employing large percentages of women, which were closed down in their domestic institutional form (see Table 3.1).

Table 3.1. Workers in the garment-textile industry in the Managua region

	1989	1991	1993
Export-processing zone	1,500	500	2,000
Outside the zone	4,500	2,000	500
Total	6,000	2,500	2,500

Sources: Interviews with Secretaria de La Mujer, CST labor unions, and Zona Franca management.

THE RESTRUCTURING RATIONALE

In response to international trends, restructuring of industry proceeded apace in the rest of the Caribbean and Central America during the ten years of Sandinista rule, making use of the availability of low wages throughout the region as specialization continued to subdivide markets further. Nicaraguan industries had to restructure to be incorporated into this global assembly line or global factory (Kamel 1990). Under the National Opposition Union (UNO) leadership, Nicaragua adjusted by drawing down the large textile-garment industries as well as small national firms. Shutdown orders were accompanied by decreases in import taxes for garments in 1991, encouraging imports. Increased taxes on raw materials and decreased taxes on finished goods squeezed small domestic, private industries in general and specifically affected these industries.

Adjustment led to the contradictory situation whereby the same industries that were being shut down in their national form were being constructed in the FTZ with a very different institutional structure. The economic rationale for this transition was as follows:

1. The domestic textile industry had equipment that was twenty to thirty years old and had to be replaced in any event.
2. Although textiles were still operating with old equipment in other Central American countries, they had been maintained with spare parts that were not available in Nicaragua during the blockade.[3]
3. The special tax advantages of the FTZ could bring in the investment money for the garment industry that the government and domestic capitalists could not afford.
4. There was low demand for garments and textiles in the domestic market because of a continuing depression and because used clothes from the United States were given away or sold in the eighties and early nineties, replacing a segment of the domestic market.

5. When capitalists returned to run their former companies, they chose not to upgrade facilities or produce for the domestic market. This choice was at least partly due to such social benefits as paid pregnancy leaves, which had accrued to women workers under the Sandinista government. Returning capitalists were aware that female workers then received more legal benefits than male workers outside the export processing zones.

One problem with this transition is that thousands of women lost their jobs in the old industries, but the much anticipated job openings in the new export-processing zone did not increase beyond three thousand until the mid-nineties. In addition, the new jobs did not go to women over thirty-five who were laid off, nor did they initially go to former workers who were not from the north-eastern sector of the city. Thousands of women, most of them single mothers, lost their opportunities for formal-sector jobs for years, and the informal sector was already vastly overcrowded.

RESTRUCTURING OF THE GARMENT-TEXTILE INDUSTRY AND GENDER DISCRIMINATION

The government and the unions see the textile and apparel sector as including all of the garment, textile, and shoe production factories in the Managua area. Women, whose work histories include both formal and informal sector experience (see Table 3.2), see the industry as broader, including sewing in the home and vending. On the other hand, most of these same women see the geographic limits of their labor market in narrow terms, since they must rely on public or employer-provided transportation. These two different views of reality have affected policy in various ways.

First, government advertisements have encouraged women to

**Table 3.2. Formal/informal sector shifts in worker location
(eleven reinterviewed workers with work histories)**

Code name	Age	Work history (years)	1991	1993
Anna	37	10, Enaves	Enaves	Clothes vending
Carmen	30	5, Enaves	Enaves	Velcas
Christina	49	10, Enaves 3, Conterni	Ronaco	Ronaco
Claudia	48	18, Enaves	Enaves	Unemployed
Georgina	36	1, Enaves	Clothes vending	Clothes vending
Isabel	35	Clerical work, mayor's office	Sewing/vending	Office clerk, political party
Julia	35	18, Enaves	Enaves	Velcas
Maria	40	4, Enaves	Enaves	Sporadically unemployed
Rosalia	28	8, Texnicsa 1, Tricatex 1, Enaves	Unemployed	Fortex
Ruth	38	8, Incasa (1971–78)	Clothes sewing	Clothes sewing
Sandra	35	Clothes sewing	Clothes sewing/ vending	Clothes sewing/ vending

Source: Worker interviews.
Enaves: State-operated clothing factory in the FTZ, 1979–91.
Velcas: New private factory carved out of Enaves.
Ronaco: New garment factory in the FTZ since 1991.
Fortex: Taiwanese-owned factory carved out of Enaves.
Conterni, Tricatex, Incasa: Private garment companies.
Texnicsa: Shut-down textile factory.

invest their severance pay in small shops in their neighborhoods, mistakenly assuming that these businesses did not already exist. Additional small businesses, if successful, would cut into the earnings of the already established sewers and vendors.

Secondly, even if the industries that were established in the FTZ had kept pace with those that were shut down in the city, the new jobs would not be filled with the unemployed workers from the old industries. It could not be assumed that workers from one side of the city could afford time and money for transportation or that they could relocate to the other side of the city to take advantage of the new job openings. The vast majority of workers with experience who joined the new industries were only the younger workers hired from Enaves, the former government enterprise in the FTZ (see below), and young workers from other factories located in that area. With growing zone employment in later years, increasing to twenty-six thousand in 2000, transportation arrangements were evidently made for many workers from other parts of the city (Hajewski 2000, pp. 1–2).

Shifting the formal workforce from one location in the city to another is extremely disruptive of family life, especially for women who are the family caregivers. The one worker in our study who found employment and was attempting to make the move from the northwestern part of the city to the northeastern suburbs was quite atypical. She had to leave her young children with family members as she tried to work her way through the bureaucratic maze necessary to sell her house in her barrio and purchase a house northeast of the city. Most former garment and textile workers from around the city and suburbs found it difficult to move their families from their native barrios.

The buildup of the Mercedes Zone for export production was an important part of the UNO restructuring plan for Nicaragua. In the seventies, there had been five clothing firms operating in the zone producing for the United States market. These firms were taken over by the government in the eighties and were operated by the Sandinistas under one management in an enterprise called Enaves. Production for the military and for the home market was combined with some export production during this period. Approximately two thousand workers still produced shoes, clothing, and aluminum products in 1990.

By the time of our initial interviews in 1991, Enaves was producing very little, being prepared for privatization. By the end of 1991, this enterprise was employing less than four hundred workers. Three private firms were setting up operations, but in 1991 they had few workers; hence the estimated five hundred apparel workers in the FTZ for 1991 given in Table 3.1.

In the next period, 1992–93, the new small enterprises in the zone grew larger, and the newly privatized enterprises grew rapidly, since structure and equipment already existed. The U.S. market was again opened to Nicaraguan exports, and by the middle of 1993 the FTZ's workforce had grown to twenty-five hundred. Unfortunately, this increased employment in no way made up for the workers laid off from the textile and apparel mills outside the zone.

The first large textile mill, Texnicsa, closed its doors in August 1991, letting go more than nine hundred workers. More than 70 percent of those who lost their jobs were women with children to support. The remaining domestic textile-garment factories had closed by 1993. According to Sandra Ramos of the women's secretariat of the Confederation of Sandinista Workers (CST), of the six thousand workers in this sector in 1989, only fifteen hundred still had jobs by the end of 1992 (interviews, September–November 1992). The last textile company to close, an enterprise that had originally been scheduled to remain open, Fanatex, shut its doors in 1993 while negotiating a new ownership agreement with the cotton workers and reportedly also negotiating with a Taiwanese firm (author's interviews with CST and FTZ management).

Production cooperatives and neighborhood garment makers and vendors continued operation during this period of shutdown. Every locale in Managua seems to have at least one *costurera*, or seamstress, and there are a number of sewing production cooperatives. In addition to, and sometimes in combination with, the above role, women sell clothing in their neighborhoods and at market stalls. It is reasonable to assume that this informal sector included as many garment workers as in the formal sector, even before the shutdowns. Interviews among cooperatives, sewers, and vendors showed that women with experience and reputation often made above the factory wage, even in the worst of economic times. On the other hand, the greatest poverty also exists among workers in the informal sector and newcomers into the informal sector in the depressed economic climate of 1991–93 did very poorly (worker interviews and FIDEG 1992, p. 56).

IMPACT OF PRIVATIZATION ON WORKING WOMEN

The gender bias in the transitional Nicaraguan economic program, partially a postwar phenomenon, existed in all types of industries as well as in government. With demilitarization, the few women who had worked in "male" industries such as beer, rum, cola, and petroleum during the war often lost their jobs as the soldiers came back. Moreover, the restructuring and cutbacks in government affected women in much larger percentages than men. According to Betina Reyes of the Ministry of Finance, over 70 percent of government layoffs were women (interview, July 1991). The health and education fields were hit hard, and the vacant government front offices testified to the great effects on the clerical workforce. My interviews show examples of middle-class women who, after rising to some prominence in universities and government service, were pushed aside to make room for male leadership.

When compared to the former state industries, workers in private industries in the FTZ experienced reductions in their rights and social services. The first workers to make the transition to the new regime of export production were happy about the higher hourly wages (see Table 3.3). They soon realized, however, that their real incomes had not increased, since transportation, cafeteria, and health centers were no longer a part of the services package. Another important change was that workers were no longer paid

Table 3.3. Salaries of workers in Mercedes Free Trade Zone (in cordoba, per month)

Company	Number of employees	Operators (female)	Floor supervisors (inspectors/female)*	Mechanics (male)*
1991				
Enaves	400	260–350	968	500
Pronto	114	250–370	440	—
Ronaco	70	400–620	1,500	1,400
1993				
Cresen	107	720–780	—	—
Fortex	880	450–900†	2,000	900
INCAR (Neptune)	60	750–1,000	1,500–2,000	—
Pronto	80	600	—	—
Ronaco	131	400–620	1,500	1,400
Velca	500	700–800‡	2,000	1,000

Source: Management and worker interviews.
Note: C$5 = US$1 in 1991; C$6 = US$1 in 1993.
*There is usually a strict sexual division of labor.
†C$400 for the trial (training) period.
‡Piece workers sometimes made less.

when there was a problem with the production process, such as poor raw materials or slack demand (worker interviews).

The new employers hired workers at an average age that was six years younger than in the old enterprises. Meanwhile, a new industry in the FTZ, jewelry, sought even younger workers (see Table 3.4). The new entrepreneurs thus avoided the problems of older workers, whose eyes are no longer sharp and who may have other physical disabilities. As is often customary in export processing zones, employers in Nicaragua were careful not to hire pregnant women. One manager reported that his workers had to undergo a physical examination that included a pregnancy test (manager interview).

Table 3.4. Ages of workers in Mercedes Free Trade Zone

Company	Number of workers	Workers aged 17–25 (%)	Workers aged 20–35 (%)	Workers over 35 (%)	Average age
1991					
Enaves	400	15	60	25	33
Pronto	114	65	30	5	25
Ronaco	70	30	70	—	28
1993					
Cresen	107	99	1	—	20
Fortex	880	40	40	20	25
INCAR (Neptune)	60	5	75	20	30
Pronto	80	80	20	—	25
Ronaco	131	30	70	—	28
Velca	500	20	65	15	30

Source: Management and worker interviews.

The more leisurely pace in the remaining state industries also contrasted, in 1991, with the pressure put on workers and supervisors to perform at a very rapid rate in private enterprises.[4] Rapid production is enforced by standard rates, quotas, and/or payment by piece rates. Many workers have to stay until evening in order to finish the "production standard." According to one worker in the new jewelry industry, some workers stayed up to three hours late in order to make their quotas (worker interviews).

As the FTZ developed over the period from 1991 to 1993, older female workers were laid off and replaced by the very large pool of younger women looking for work in the textile-garment industry. Three of our interviewees were among the two-thirds of Enaves employees who were not rehired by the two private firms that bought Enaves property. Meanwhile, one woman whom we had interviewed as a laid-off textile worker was hired by the Taiwanese-owned Fortex as a cutter at near the basic salary, despite her many years of experience in the textile industry.

Older women who had worked for Enaves and were not rehired entered the informal sector, sewing or taking care of grandchildren. Thirty-five years of age was the cut-off for hiring seamstresses at the new Fortex firm. Since about 30 percent of the old Enaves workers were thirty-five or older, and the new employers had a preference for younger workers, it was not surprising that two-thirds of the older workers were not rehired.[5]

LABOR UNION GENDER BIAS IN RESTRUCTURING

In this period of market adjustment and privatization, it is not just the government and businesses that seem unwilling to deal with the problems of converting and updating industries that formally employed large percentages of women—unions were also biased in their cooperation with government and businesses.

As part of the Sandinista Front, women had organized for change. The first national women's organization, later known as AMNLAE,[6] was formed in 1977. It grew in the eighties to a national membership of twenty-five thousand women, working politically to advance their social, political, and economic rights. The organization was successful in rallying women around issues such as health and day care, as well as the legal requirement of paid pregnancy leave. A women's secretariat was also set up within the CST. The secretariat was very active during the period of cutbacks in women's employment, specifically in protecting women's indemnification rights. In 1993, the organization began participating in women's labor actions in the new export-processing industries, supporting a spontaneous strike against Fortex.

The fact remains, however, that the compromises between the UNO government and the Sandinista union (CST) leadership favored men. In industries that predominantly hire men, for example the sugar industry, there were strikes and political actions across the country when settlements with former owners had disadvantaged workers. It seemed that at least partly because the textile and garment industries were "women's industries," the response of the Sandinista unions was muted. Female union members in these industries were disadvantaged for reasons indicated above and because of union leaders' assumptions about their priorities.

During the closing down of textile and garment industries in 1991 and 1992, unions appeared to react differently to job losses suffered by women and by men. Women were encouraged to leave their jobs and struggle only for severance pay, while unions struggled so that men could keep their jobs. In the beginning of 1990, 70 percent of those employed in a shoe factory in the FTZ were female (CONAPRO 1992, p. 25). In November of the same year, the factory employed mostly men (management interviews). Meanwhile, women who had been employed by the factory demonstrated for severance pay (*Barricada* 1992, p. 6).

The gender differences in the UNO-Sandinista agreements became clearer as the process of privatization progressed. Workers were supposed to receive 25 percent of the ownership of enterprises in the process, although, depending on the agreement, a larger or smaller percentage was possible. There were no women on the negotiating committee that developed the property settlements between the government and the unions, and we were not able to find any female workers who became stockholders in their enterprises in the FTZ. Enaves was sold to two private companies. Workers, primarily female, received some severance pay, but none received stocks.

CONCLUSION

Although women's job opportunities in industry throughout Latin America, and particularly in Central America, have shown significant gains in the past few decades, women in Nicaragua lost ground in the early nineties. A free-market government policy, postwar unemployment trends, and the particular economics of female industries have been factors leading to this decline.

Both the UNO government and the unions favored male workers, as the assumed family heads, in that period. A depressed economy and restructuring with gender bias significantly worsened working women's prospects. Though all female workers were adversely affected, middle-aged women suffered the most. The new industrial job openings in the export sector have been going to younger workers—and even they did not, for reasons expressed earlier, make up for the job losses in female industries.

Even when employment in the export industries reached and then exceeded the six-thousand mark in 1989, more than half of the women laid off in 1989–92 did not get jobs in this sector due to age discrimination and the inability to commute or relocate. They most likely retired early or found employment in an already overcrowded informal sector, as did the women in our sample. The most distressing loss of jobs, from a humanitarian point of view, is the joblessness at the bottom of the economic ladder. The thousands of women in the garment and textile fields, the majority of whom were single mothers, had no way to feed their children when unemployed. Many were forced to resort to prostitution (Ibarra 1992, p. 3). Women became the clear victims of Nicaragua's economic crisis and restructuring.

With the continuance of the new export-processing economic structure, nevertheless, the new, younger Nicaraguan workers have struggled in the ensuing period with the conditions of the jobs that have been available to them. Union organizing in the Mercedes Free Trade Zone has proceeded, despite continuous employer harassment, at least partly because of legal rights passed by a continuing Sandinista presence in the legislature. Struggles have centered on problems with low pay, poor working conditions, and late employer contributions to social security. There have been several rounds of struggles concerning the firing of workers engaged in union organizing.

The complaints of employees in a recent survey of workers in the zone by the Maria Elena Cuadra Women's Movement show many of the same issues that were present in 1993 are continuing. In 2000, supervisors still sought to fire anyone who became pregnant, and workers continued to be pressured to work overtime, often as much as twelve hours per day. Bathroom breaks were limited and timed, which spoke to the atmosphere of pressure that came to the FTZ with privatization and continues even now (Nicaragua Network Hotline 2000, p. 5).

In addition to local organizing and striking, unionized workers have used their connections with North American activists from the period of the U.S. war against the Sandinistas to bring the plight of fired workers to the attention of U.S. consumers at Target and Kohl's stores. After several hundred trade unionists were fired for their union activities in the FTZ in early 2000, a U.S. anti-sweatshop organization, composed of U.S. labor, student, and faith-based groups picketed these stores in 110 U.S. locations in May. Domestic Nicaraguan and international actions of this type led to some, but not all, of the workers receiving their jobs back.

Although the struggle for better conditions for Nicaraguan women workers continues, structural changes of the past decade have mostly advantaged the consumers of garments and the owners of garment industries at the expense of Third World workers. In the Nicaraguan case, these losses were more starkly seen, and more easily measured, because domestic industries that were more accommodating to the workers were shut down at the same time as export-processing industries were advanced. Women over thirty-five years of age lost their jobs, and the eventual job openings in export processing for many younger workers included many fewer benefits. The most important of these—accessible medical care, free lunch, and paid pregnancy leave—were lost to Nicaraguan women workers with restructuring.

NOTES

The author would like to thank Elizabeth Miller and Patricia Mulligan for their research assistance study and is also indebted to Carmen Diana Deere and the New England Women and Development Group for their comments on an early draft. The study was financed by a Fulbright Fellowship and a graduate research grant from Fitchburg State College, Fitchburg, Massachusetts.

1. Five of the author's interviewees, who are public officials, can be listed here: (1) Ligia Orosco, investigator for the Confederation of Sandinista Workers (CST), June 23, 1993; (2) Sandra Ramos, director of the women's secretariat of the CST, September 19 and October 24, 1991, as well as May 6, 1992; (3) Betina Reyes, management of the Ministry of Finance and originator of the government's employment reduction program in Managua, August 18, 1991; (4) Sergio Zamora, director of the FTZ in Managua and former director of the Cartago FTZ in Costa Rica, August 29 and November 15, 1991; and (5) Carlos Zuniga, public relations director of the FTZ in Managua, June 23, 1993.

2. The industry's march to a new, international industrial format began with "Operation Bootstrap" in Puerto Rico as far back as 1940 (Safa 1985, p. 8). Puerto Rico's diversification in the sixties and wage increases in the seventies diverted international investment to other countries in the region. The Caribbean Basin Initiative, begun in the eighties, did not include Nicaragua until the early nineties. Open U.S. quotas for apparel imports from Central America have recently encouraged East Asian exporters, who face filled quotas for their own countries, to invest in this region.

3. Debt, financial crisis, and a dramatic decline in terms of trade for Central American agricultural exports in the late seventies severely contracted the regional and domestic markets for industrial goods. These factors, as well as the political strife of the eighties, made the textile and garment industries unable to deal with the technological changes that have modernized the competition in other parts of the world. A 1990 CEPAL (Spanish acronym for the UN Economic Commission for Latin America) study found that with the exception of thread production in El Salvador and some computerized technology in Costa Rican textiles, Central

American industries were not well equipped to deal with 1993 import tax reductions. The majority of these plants either had to invest in modernized technology or liquidate (CEPAL 1990, pp. 18, 52, 178–79).

4. The new companies are modeled after firms in export-processing zones around the world where workers experience more health problems related to eyesight and tension.

5. This age discrimination did not hold true for inspectors, who were older in the new firms. They were more experienced workers who tended to be chosen from the forewomen and inspectors at Enaves.

6. AMNLAE refers to the Luisa Amanda Espinosa Nicaraguan Women's Association, named for the first woman Sandinista to die in the Sandinista revolution.

REFERENCES

Barricada (Managua). 1992. Exigen indemnization a COIP. April 2, p. 6.

Bishop, Myrtle, Frank Long, and Joaquin St. Cyr. 1990. *Export processing zones and women in the Caribbean.* Varadero, Cuba: United Nations Economic Commission for Latin America and the Caribbean (ECLAC).

CEPAL. 1990. *Reconservión industrial en Centroamerica* (October 8).

CONAPRO (Confederación National de Profesionales). 1992. *Radiografia del desempleo en las obreras industriales del la rama textil vestuario.* Managua: CONAPRO.

FIDEG (Fundacion International para Desafio Económico Global). 1992. *El impacto de las politicas de ajuste sobre la mujer en Nicaragua: Reflexiones de un estudio de caso.* Managua: FIDEG.

Gonzalez, David. 2000. Nicaragua's Trade Zone: Battleground for unions. *New York Times,* September 16, 2000. http://www.usleap.org/Maquilas/Nica/NTY9-16-00ReChentes.html (accessed January 13, 2004).

Hajewski, Doris. 2000. Trade Zone answers a hunger for jobs. *Milwaukee Journal Sentinel Online,* December 29, 2000. http://www.jsonline .com/bym/news/dec00/zone31122900.asp (accessed January 13, 2004).

Ibarra, E. 1992. Más obreras a la prostitución. *La Prensa* (Managua), March 27, 1992, p. 3. Also published in *Courier* (Managua) 138 (March/April 1992): 31.

Jenkins, Rhys. 1990. Comparing foreign subsidiaries and local firms in LDCs: theoretical issues and empirical evidence. *Journal of Development Studies* 26 (2): 205–28.

Kamel, Rachael. 1990. *The Global Factory.* Philadelphia: American Friends Service Committee.

Maquila Solidarity Network. 2000. Country vignettes: Nicaragua. http://www.maquilasolidarity.org/resources/maquilas/nicaragua.htm (accessed January 13, 2004).

Nicaragua Network Hotline. 2000. Study shows mistreatment of women in Free Trade Zones. Nicanet, September 11, 2000. http://www.nicanet.org/pubs/hotline0911_2000.html#topic3 (accessed January 13, 2004).

Pérez-Aleman, Paola, Diana Martinez, and Christa Widmair. 1989. *Industria genero y la mujer en Nicaragua.* Managua: Instituto Nicaraguense de la Mujer.

———. *Women in Nicaragua: A profile.* 1990. Managua: Canadian International Development Agency (CIDA).

Safa, Helen I. 1981. Runaway shops and female employment: The search for cheap labor. *Signs* 7 (2): 418–33.

———. 1985. Female employment in Puerto Rican working class. In *Women and change in Latin America,* edited by June Nash and Helen Safa, pp. 84–104. South Hadley, MA: Bergin and Garvey.

United Nations. 1989. *World survey on the role of women in development.* New York: United Nations.

———. 1991. *The world's women: Trends and statistics, 1970–1990.* New York: United Nations.

4. Six Years of NAFTA

A View from Inside the Maquiladoras

A Report by the
Border Committee of Women Workers
with a foreword by Rachael Kamel

Since the early eighties, well over a decade before the North American Free Trade Agreement (NAFTA) went into effect in 1994, workers in the maquiladora industry have been deeply concerned about their on-the-job exposures to industrial solvents and a wide variety of other toxic substances, generally without adequate safety information or protective equipment. One of the earliest examples of cross-border cooperation that we are aware of involved the translation of a warning label for a small group of electronics workers in Matamoros, at the eastern end of the Mexico-U.S. border. Over the years, cross-border collaborations on occupational and environmental health issues have grown into a complex array of trainings, shopfloor actions, "toxic tours" of border towns, and increased networking by occupational health professionals and organizers from both sides of the border.

This report was originally copublished by the American Friends Service Committee (AFSC) and the Border Committee of Women Workers (CFO) in October 1999 and is reprinted here by permission. All statistics are current as of the date of original publication. Some of the material in Kamel's introductory discussion was previously released in somewhat different form in an executive summary of the report, also reprinted by permission. The CFO wishes to acknowledge the collaboration of Ricardo Hernández, Antonio Bonifaz of the Center for Labor Information (CILAS), and Andrés Peñalosa of the Mexican Free Trade Action Network (RMALC), for helping us to understand NAFTA. We also wish to thank Rachael Kamel of the AFSC for the English translation of this report.

The maquiladoras, of course, are the foreign-(mostly U.S.-) owned assembly plants that line the Mexico-U.S. border, the only border in the world where the advanced industrial "North" directly meets the underdeveloped "South." At the latest count, more than a million workers labor in more than three thousand plants. As of the year 2000, 57 percent of them were women, down from a high of 85 percent in the mid-eighties. In this era of "free trade" and unregulated foreign investment, they are the most dynamic sector of the Mexican economy and represent the principal strategy for job creation in Mexico promoted by policy elites on both sides of the border.*

Through its Mexico-U.S. Border Program, the American Friends Service Committee (AFSC) has collaborated with maquiladora workers for more than twenty years on a broad range of labor, health, and environmental issues, as well as on initiatives geared to networking, coalition-building, and public education. As one undertaking within this broader collaboration, in the late nineties we secured modest funding to help strengthen work in occupational and environmental health by our grassroots partner organization, the Comité Fronterizo de Obreras (Border Committee of Women Workers; hereafter referred to as the CFO). The project design called for participatory diagnostic workshops to ensure that maquiladora workers themselves would play the central role in defining their most important health concerns. When these workshops took place in 1999, from one community after another, the same result came back: the most important health problem for maquiladora workers today is stress. Not toxic exposures in the workplace or community; not industrial accidents; but stress.

---

*For a comprehensive overview of maquiladora activism, see *The Maquiladora Reader: Cross-Border Organizing since NAFTA*, ed. Rachael Kamel and Anya Hoffman (Philadelphia: American Friends Service Committee, 1999).

How should we understand this completely unexpected result? It is certainly not the case that workplace health and safety problems have been alleviated or that they are no longer a source of concern to the workers; indeed, the other problems identified in the same workshop included a more familiar list of workplace health concerns, including repetitive strain injuries, inadequate protective equipment, and the like.

We believe that the best way to make sense of the identification of stress as an overriding health concern is to listen carefully to what the workers themselves have to say about how conditions inside the maquiladora plants are changing. It is in that spirit that we offer the CFO's 1999 report, "Six Years of NAFTA: A View from Inside the Maquiladoras," which comprises the bulk of this chapter. This report grew out of a monitoring project intended to gauge the impact of NAFTA at the border, which was undertaken as a joint effort by the CFO, the AFSC, and the Mexican Free Trade Action Network (RMALC, the Red Mexicana de Acción Frente al Libre Comercio). To our knowledge, it is the first such report to be authored primarily by workers themselves, and the only one that focuses on conditions inside *maquiladora plants, describing changes in the labor process itself.*

The CFO report does note one significant victory for ongoing struggles by maquiladora workers: the suspension by several major border employers of the illegal but widespread practice of compulsory pregnancy testing as a requirement for employment. This practice, which violates both Mexican law and international human rights norms, has attracted broad condemnation in both Mexico and the United States and has been documented by Human Rights Watch, with help from the CFO and other Mexican organizations. By late 1999, according to the CFO, after years of sustained pressure, several of the largest maquiladora firms had backed away from pregnancy testing.

Despite this victory, the overall panorama described by the CFO is a grim one. Over the six years described in the report, border workers endured a sharp drop in their standard of living, a marked intensification of the labor process through speed-ups and other tactics, and a sustained campaign to undermine unions, labor rights, and social protections. A major cause of stress identified by workers is the longer workdays that are part and parcel of the new "labor flexibility" touted by maquiladora management—which, for many women, means worrying every day about children who are left at home unattended. Inside the plants, calculated humiliations and abusive treatment by supervisors are the norm; the CFO also argues that the characteristic instability and high turnover of the maquiladora workforce is deliberately induced by corporate management, because "the longer workers stay on the job, the more they begin to exercise their rights." Viewed in the light of this overall assessment, the workers' conclusion that stress is their most serious health problem becomes wholly comprehensible.

The CFO report underscores why NAFTA and other "free-trade" agreements are best understood as political phenomena rather than technical matters of economic policy. Virtually none of the phenomena described by the CFO are referenced in the official printed text of NAFTA's thousand-plus pages. All, however, are central to the actual experience of life in the shadow of NAFTA. For maquiladora workers (and, in somewhat different ways, for all working people in Mexico), NAFTA opened the floodgates for a relentless assault on working conditions and labor rights.

This report also stands as a sobering reminder that despite all of the upsurge in organizing focused on "free trade" and global sweatshops, the voices least heard remain the voices of workers themselves. Cross-border alliances are indispensable, but they will never achieve their strategic potential as long as the perceptions, the interpretations, and the agenda of allies and advocates predominate over the voices of the workers, who constitute the most direct and immediate protagonists of the global factory. Such workers' voices, moreover, must be understood not only, or even principally, as sources of poignant testimony about the extremes that global corporate exploitation is reaching, but rather as our most fundamental wellspring of reflection and analysis on strategies for resisting a globalized economic order.

For us, the most important lesson of the unexpected result recounted above is that even advocates who are very deeply involved with an issue may still see it through different eyes than those who are most directly affected— in this case, workers in the maquiladora industry. As noted in the CFO report, workers at the Mexico-U.S. border have been grappling with the effects of "free trade" for more than thirty years. Their experiences and perspectives are an invaluable resource for everyone seeking to come to grips with the global economy.

—Rachael Kamel
American Friends Service Committee*

INTRODUCTION

Thirty-four Years of NAFTA

As workers in the maquiladora industry along the Mexico-U.S. border, we believe that we have been living under a free trade agreement for thirty-four years, ever since the first export-processing plants began to arrive in Mexico. Since that time these factories have enjoyed highly advantageous terms for the importation and exportation of goods and materials. The North American Free

*Grateful acknowledgment is made to Ricardo Hernández, director of AFSC's Mexico-U.S. Border Program, for ongoing collaboration in understanding and interpreting the realities of the border economy and maquiladora workers' activism.

Trade Agreement (NAFTA), signed by Mexico, Canada, and the United States, went into effect in 1994, representing a culmination of this policy of trade liberalization—for which the maquiladora industry was an important precursor. For workers, the final years of this millennium have signified a dramatic worsening of our working and living conditions.

A Big Lie

NAFTA eliminates trade barriers between our three countries. Before it was signed it was said that it would help to improve the economic situation of Mexico. To build support for NAFTA at home, the government of Carlos Salinas de Gortari (Mexican president, 1988–94) argued that Mexico would become a "First World" country. The negotiators of this agreement promised that it would bring better jobs and higher income levels to our three countries. Our experience over the past six years has shown that these promises were deceptive. NAFTA was designed to promote the interests of large corporations and the small circles of financiers and government officials who make the decisions about the economies of our three countries.

Every Advantage for the Maquiladoras

The raw materials and machinery used by the maquiladoras are imported, and the goods they produce are primarily destined for the U.S. market. Since fewer than 3 percent of their inputs come from Mexico, the maquiladoras do not stimulate the development of other small or medium-sized industries in the Mexican cities where they are located. Companies that have moved their production operations from the United States to Mexico, or local firms that subcontract with maquiladora firms, avoid paying wages that are ten to twenty times higher in their own country. In Mexico, they also enjoy exceptionally favorable treatment by the government.

The plants and industrial parks where the maquiladoras are located all benefit from utilities and infrastructure that were built by Mexico's municipal and state governments. Once they are established, maquiladoras pay no taxes on their working capital, nor do they pay Mexico's value-added tax or tariffs on imported raw materials. Over time, Mexican legislation regarding foreign investment has become continuously more relaxed, offering the maquiladoras even more incentives to establish themselves in our country.

Even after thirty-four years, the maquiladoras are not obliged to ensure that they can compensate their employees fairly and responsibly if they close down.[1] That is why there are so many fly-by-night firms with minimal assets. When they see that workers are sticking up for their rights, they shut down from one day to the next, and no one obliges them to fulfill their responsibility to compensate their employees. Ostensibly, maquiladoras operate within the same legal framework as other sectors of Mexican industry; in practice, however, Mexican labor authorities have winked as maquiladora firms have systematically violated basic rights, including the right to organize and bargain collectively, the right to profit sharing and overtime pay, and many others.[2]

The Lowest Wages, the Wealthiest Firms

In return for such favorable treatment, the maquiladoras pay the lowest wages in Mexican industry: from $28 to $45 a week, or even less, including so-called bonuses. Such wages are absolutely inadequate for covering basic family expenses. Many of the maquiladoras are subsidiaries or subcontractors of multinational firms with some of the highest profit margins in the world, which makes it even more offensive that they pay so little to their workers. We know from our own experience that huge companies such as Delphi, General Electric, Alcoa, Lucent Technologies, Panasonic, ADFlex, and many others reap enormous benefits from paying such low wages at the border (see Table 4.1). Their profits are enormous, and so we know that they can and should pay decent wages and offer working conditions that respect our human dignity.

An Unstable Source of Employment

The maquiladoras have brought jobs to our border towns. As a result, the border has not suffered as directly as the rest of the

Table 4.1. Maquiladoras and their parent firms

Maquiladora	Parent firm	Location
ADFlex	ADFlex/Innvamex	Agua Prieta
Arneses y Accesorios	Alcoa Fujikura	Ciudad Acuña
Autoindustrial de Partes	Stant Corp.	Matamoros
Carrizo Manufacturing	Salant Corp.	Piedras Negras
Custom Trim	Breed	Valle Hermoso
Delnosa	Delphi (formerly GM)	Reynosa
Deltrónicos de Matamoros	Delphi	Matamoros
Dickies	Williamson-Dickie	Piedras Negras
Dylsa	Douglas & Lomason	Ciudad Acuña
Dimmit Industries	Galey & Lord	Piedras Negras
Aparatos Eléctricos de Acuña	General Electric	Ciudad Acuña
Falcomex	Irvin Industries	Ciudad Acuña
Findlay	Finley Industries	Piedras Negras
Han Young	Hyundai	Tijuana
Kemet	Kemet Electronic Corp.	Matamoros
Carolina Processing de Mex.	Carolina Services	Ciudad Acuña
Lucent Technologies	Lucent Technologies	Reynosa
Macoelmex	Alcoa Fujikura	Piedras Negras
Maquiladora Sur	(formerly Salant)	Valle Hermoso
Mercer-Mex	Southwest Plastic Binding	Piedras Negras
Panasonic	Panasonic	Reynosa
Philips	Philips	Matamoros
Rassini de Piedras Negras	Rassini International	Piedras Negras
Sony Magnéticos de Mex.	Sony Corp. of America	Nuevo Laredo
Tenn-Mex	Tenn-Mex Inc.	Piedras Negras

country from some of the grave consequences of Mexico's various economic and financial crises, particularly the drastic rates of unemployment and underemployment. Nonetheless, these jobs— which we need and want to maintain—are not the panacea our government claims. Mexico needs a million new jobs every year; in thirty-four years, by contrast, the maquiladoras have created a total of 1.1 million jobs.

Furthermore, these jobs are highly unstable. The intensity of international competition has created substantial pressure to reduce costs and increase productivity, resulting in turn in a process of constant change inside maquiladora plants. Continual openings, closings, and sales of companies; corporate mergers; and related phenomena all mean that production operations are constantly being modified. Workers face repeated reassignments of their production lines and positions, as well as frequent layoffs and an ongoing erosion of their labor rights and gains negotiated through collective bargaining. Overall, our situation is one of perpetual insecurity in that we never know how long our jobs will last.

NAFTA: The Die Is Cast

Since long before NAFTA, the neoliberal economic policies pursued by successive Institutional Revolutionary Party (PRI) governments resulted in a sharp decline in investment in agriculture oriented to domestic consumption, a reduction in public expenditures, the privatization of growing numbers of public enterprises, and the promotion of an export-oriented economy.[3] These policies have gravely undermined Mexico's productive capacity, leading in turn to unemployment and underemployment for millions of Mexicans. Government officials have become obsessed with attracting foreign investment to the maquiladora sector, which nonetheless has failed to compensate for the overall loss of jobs. As a result, thousands of people continue to cross the border to look for work in the United States. The privatization of Mexico's national heath system, electricity, and the oil industry, to name just a few examples, are other manifestations of this neoliberal policy framework, which NAFTA has served to reaffirm and consolidate. Through NAFTA, the neoliberal approach to economic policy has been locked in.

Without Workers' Input

In the negotiations over NAFTA, the Mexican government not only accepted conditions that were injurious to both agricultural and industrial production, it also avoided addressing labor concerns. Issues such as wage levels or working conditions were not included in the negotiating agenda—to allay any fears by U.S. elites that Mexico would create obstacles to investment or that foreign firms would be met by workers' protests. Since the passage of NAFTA, the Mexican government and the official labor movement have only deepened their complicity with the investors and large corporations that own the maquiladoras.

The Labor Side Agreement

Pressure from social movements in the three NAFTA countries obliged the government negotiating teams to create a side agreement, known as the North American Agreement on Labor Cooperation (NAALC). The strongest remedy possible under NAALC is a recommendation for consultations regarding specific cases by the labor ministries of the NAFTA countries. Officially, each of the three NAFTA countries has a national administrative office (NAO) that can hear complaints against specific companies regarding violations of NAALC. In practice, however, only the U.S. NAO has pursued complaints against maquiladoras, such as those filed against Sony, Han Young, and other firms. These complaints have served to call public attention to problems in certain maquiladoras. The Mexican government, for its part, uses the mechanisms created by NAALC, such as public hearings or workshops on such topics as women and occupational health, as a smokescreen, seeking to create the impression internationally that it is enforcing its own labor laws. Real maquila workers, however, are not invited to these events.

THE END OF THE MIRAGE: SIX YEARS OF NAFTA IN THE MAQUILADORAS

Wages Take a Nosedive

In Mexican manufacturing, real wages have fallen by more than 20 percent since 1994, according to official figures. For all workers, the decline was 34 percent between 1994 and 1998. While it is true that the decline suffered by maquiladora workers has been less severe, our loss of buying power has been enormous, given the incessant increases in the cost of basic necessities. The cost of the official "market basket" of food, housing, and essential services has risen by 247 percent since 1994. Many products, including gasoline, telephone service, milk, chicken, bread, and even beans, are more expensive on the Mexican side of the border than on the U.S. side. For us, simply feeding our families is becoming more difficult every day.

It is not only that real wages have remained stagnant overall, failing to keep pace with inflation; wage levels have also come under attack wherever they rise above the threshold considered competitive by the maquiladoras. At the beginning of 1998, ceding to concerted lobbying by the maquiladora industry, Mexico's federal government imposed two-tiered wages on maquiladora workers in Matamoros, Tamaulipas, by introducing a new type of contract that gives new hires a wage of fifty pesos per day (US$38 per *week*). This was a unilateral reversal of wage levels negotiated as far back as 1982, when workers organized to win wage increases of 100 percent and a forty-hour work week. Under this two-tiered system, workers with seniority in maquiladoras like Kemet, Deltrónicos,

Philips, and many others are still paid an average of seventy to eighty dollars a week—but the companies are trying to buy them off by offering them 100 percent of their legally mandated severance packages.[4] The companies then immediately hire new employees with longer hours and the new, lower wages. In some firms, such as Autoindustrial de Partes, workers with twenty years of seniority have been offered severance payments in dollars to make voluntary resignation seem more attractive. When they seek employment in another factory, they automatically come under the new contracts: their experience and seniority are now officially worthless.

In Piedras Negras, Coahuila, the firm Carrizo Manufacturing closed its doors in April 1999 after twenty-six years of operation. After years of struggle at Carrizo, some 70 percent of the line workers earned between $60 and $110 a week. Although the shut-down was unrelated to labor costs, it did have an impact on the former Carrizo workers, who had to find jobs in other maquiladoras paying much less. In cities like Matamoros and Piedras Negras, workers with greater seniority have a great deal of experience, but they have also been debilitated by long years of working in the maquiladora industry. The companies prefer to hire very young workers, who are unaware of their labor and other human rights.

Although pay at the border is low, the maquiladoras are paying still lower wages in Mexico's interior, including in some small towns or rural hamlets not too far from the border zone. Two years ago (1997), when Dimmit, a garment manufacturer in Piedras Negras, needed to expand, it opened a factory four hours away in Monclova, Coahuila, instead of building more plants in Piedras Negras. The workers in Piedras Negras feel threatened because several production lines have been transferred to the new plant in Monclova—where Dimmit is paying between twenty-four and thirty dollars per week, 44 percent less than in Piedras Negras.

Smaller, more isolated towns are more attractive to maquiladora investors because people there will work for desperately low wages. Alcoa has also built a plant in Torreón, Coahuila, where it offers wages up to 40 percent lower than in Piedras Negras or Ciudad Acuña. A job that pays $54 to $65 a week in the latter town will pay only $22 to $30 in Torreón.

Each year, Mexico's federal government mandates increases in the minimum wage that are applicable to workers throughout the country.[5] For Mexican-owned firms, these increases serve as a benchmark for cost-of-living increases for all workers. They are disregarded, however, by most maquiladoras. In Piedras Negras, companies such as Findlay and Dickies, to name only two, simply ignore the increase, claiming that it is applicable only to the minimum wage, not to workers who are earning twice the minimum or more, which includes nearly all maquiladora workers. When the companies cannot avoid giving an increase, each firm determines the amount for itself, without discussion.

In other cases, maquiladora firms have granted wage increases in the form of a lump-sum payment. In 1998, for example, Deltrónicos offered its workers a 23 percent increase, one-fifth of which was channeled through the payroll; the remaining four-fifths was paid out up front as a lump sum. The workers accepted this arrangement because it appeared to offer them a windfall. Later, they realized that four-fifths of their "raise" was not reflected in the calculations of their pension, profit-sharing, or other benefits, a practice that is illegal in Mexico. The same maneuver was also utilized, in slightly different form, by General Electric and Alcoa in Ciudad Acuña.

To eke out their wages and provide a little extra for their families, women workers are particularly likely to supplement their income from shift work by selling sweets or other goods during their breaks; by selling their blood to blood banks on the other side of the border; by selling products at weekend flea markets; and, sometimes, by casual prostitution.

Bonuses: A Fictitious Benefit

In most cases, the "bonuses" offered by many maquiladoras are a fictitious benefit that only serves to permit the companies to manipulate their workforce into working harder. Often, up to 50 percent of a worker's take-home pay is composed of so-called bonuses—rather than these sums being integrated into a decent wage. Alcoa pays a bonus of four hundred pesos (US$[1998]47.62) to workers who have not arrived at work more than five minutes late during the month. Even the five-minute rule represents an advance; earlier, workers might lose their entire bonus by arriving a few seconds late on a single day. With three late arrivals or one absence, workers also lose the right to loans that the company offers twice a year, in amounts of $54 to $217, according to seniority. There have been cases where workers have lost their bonus because they were waiting in line at the automatic teller machine, where they receive their pay.

In Tenn-Mex, a monthly bonus of thirty dollars is paid to workers with a "clean record"—that is, to those who have not asked for time off, sick time, or permission to leave the factory for any reason, including emergencies. Those who fall ill are expected to simply endure it. Furthermore, calculations are based only on the calendar month; if a worker goes without absences from the fifteenth of one month to the fifteenth of the next, it doesn't count.

The bonus system functions as a way of pressuring workers. An absence of a single day can cause the loss not only of a monthly bonus, but also of an annual bonus, where they are given out.

Another issue concerns the legal stipulation that wages must be paid in cash, expressly prohibiting payments in merchandise or scrip. Nonetheless, most maquiladoras pay bonuses in merchandise or scrip, claiming that the workers benefit because taxes on these sums are not deducted from their paychecks. However, the companies benefit the most from these arrangements, because they register their workers with social security at a lower wage rate.[6] As a result, it is the companies whose taxes are lowered.

Some "services" provided by the maquiladoras offer a very dubious benefit to the workers. In the rural community of Los Vergeles, workers were paying four dollars a week to use transportation provided by their employer, Maquiladora Sur—an amount equivalent to 15 percent of their weekly salary of twenty-six dollars. Other benefits are discontinued at the whim of the company. In 1998, Alcoa paid a bonus of five dollars to its women workers on Mother's Day; in 1999, no such payment was made. Also in 1998, Alcoa had an on-site cafeteria, where workers had to pay for napkins and plastic forks along with their food. Even chili peppers were on sale for a nickel apiece. Practices in some maquiladoras are reminiscent of company stores that were widespread during the turn-of-the-century dictatorship of Porfirio Díaz, whose many injustices provoked the Mexican Revolution of 1910.

The annual distribution of profit-sharing benefits, though mandated by Mexico's labor code, has always been violated by the maquiladoras. Under NAFTA, many large corporations have seen huge increases in their profits. The amounts distributed as profit sharing, however, have stayed stagnant or have been subject only to insignificant increases. In the case of Deltrónicos in Matamoros, each worker received eighty-two dollars in 1998, increasing to ninety-two dollars in 1999—despite an enormous hike in profits for Delphi, the parent firm. In other cases, the maquiladoras simply fail to distribute profit-sharing payments, arguing that their operations are "cost centers" and that the company's balance sheets are not figured in Mexico.

The bad example set by foreign investors has been copied by some maquiladoras with a majority of Mexican ownership, such as Rassini. This auto parts firm, located in Piedras Negras, began as a quasi-public venture and later passed into private hands. Mexican president Ernesto Zedillo termed Rassini a "NAFTA enterprise" on its way to becoming a "global enterprise." In 1999, however, the firm paid out 50 percent less in profit sharing than in 1998. The CFO has also received reports of pregnant women who have been laid off recently.[7]

Increasing Productivity by Increasing Exploitation

Inhuman production quotas

The pace of work in the maquiladoras has always been intense. Since NAFTA went into effect, however, we have clearly perceived how the companies are defying the human limits of the workers. Extremely high production quotas make work into a forced march. We are pressured into extending our workdays and working double shifts. Although we were led to believe that NAFTA would allow the three countries of North America to share their best aspects, working conditions have not improved in Mexico; instead, they have worsened. Speed-ups take the worst toll on workers who are a little older and have worked in the maquiladoras a little longer. Only the youngest and strongest workers can withstand this intense pace of work, although they, too, suffer enormous stress.

A "new culture of work": giving more for less

Many maquiladoras are demanding higher production quotas without offering any corresponding increase in pay. In recent years this aggravated exploitation has been touted as a "new culture of work," as companies seek to manipulate workers psychologically by exhorting them to improve quality and productivity. Both have thus become obligations that the companies impose on the workers.

Cutting personnel while maintaining production

In some maquiladoras, operations that previously were performed by two, three, and even four workers are now the responsibility of a single person. In Alcoa, the functions formerly distributed among a checker, an inspector, and a line worker are now the sole responsibility of the line worker. Needless to say, the wages formerly paid to the checker and inspector are not given to the line worker, who is now doing the work of all three. Similarly, in Delnosa, a subsidiary of Delphi located in Reynosa, production lines have been changed over in the year preceding this report to "modules"; the process positions have been eliminated, and the number of operations performed by each person has increased. In addition, employees there now must work standing, rather than seated as they were before. These workers have also received no increase in pay.

Production and quality

Workers performing additional operations are expected to maintain or even increase their output—without any decline in quality. The companies reduce their costs by paying fewer salaries; the remaining workers are paid the same or even less to do more work. In textile and garment plants, such as Dimmit, the result is that individual workers are expected to increase their output by as much as 21 percent. Those who cannot comply while maintaining quality standards are called to the supervisor's office and pressured.

Involuntary overtime

In practice, throughout the maquiladora industry, workers are expected to work nine hours of overtime each week, and more if the company requires it. Mexico's labor code stipulates that workers should receive double time for up to nine hours of overtime and triple time for more. In many maquiladoras, however, these provisions of the law are not honored. Deltrónicos, Delnosa, Rassini, Mercer-Mex, and many others are continuing to pay double time above nine hours. In Findlay, in Piedras Negras, not only is overtime pay not calculated correctly, but the factory doors are locked every afternoon from 5:00 to 7:00 PM, Monday through Thursday, so that workers are effectively forced to put in two hours of overtime. A worker who does not wish to stay must ask permission and obtain signatures from as many as five people. Workers who leave without obtaining authorization are punished by a suspension without pay for up to four days. Some maquiladoras also violate the law by obligating workers to put in involuntary overtime on Saturdays or Sundays.

Supervision through tyranny

Supervision—the companies' mechanism for overseeing and speeding up production—has become harsher in recent years. Supervisors apply more intense pressure to workers, and ill treatment as well as various disciplinary and punitive measures are frequent. Supervisors act on their whims or show favoritism in giving out permission for absences or even to go to the bathroom. In General Electric in Ciudad Acuña, supervisors forbid the workers to turn their heads. In Maquiladora Sur, union personnel serve as foremen; they assist the supervisors, and the workers must obey all of these authority figures. In many cases verbal warnings are not given before sanctions or punishments are imposed.

Many companies, such as ADFlex in Agua Prieta or Alcoa in Ciudad Acuña, control bathroom breaks by using lists and badges. In Alcoa in Ciudad Acuña, workers are not allowed to leave the premises during their half-hour lunch break, which is illegal, since this half-hour is not paid by the company. Workers there have two ten-minute breaks, during which they are scolded by their supervisors if they try to eat anything on the shop floor.

"Teamwork": workers policing workers

Teamwork is another method for extracting more from workers. In many maquiladoras, such as Findlay and Dimmit, groups of ten to fifteen workers perform a complete operation. Production bonuses are given out to the entire team, not to individuals; if the team doesn't qualify, nobody receives the bonus. As a result, within each team, workers pressure each other to work harder. Since not everybody has the same level of skill, it can be difficult to meet production quotas. The team issues its own permits for bathroom breaks and makes certain other decisions, which allows managers to shield themselves behind the workers to avoid taking responsibility. When one team member is absent, the team is responsible for the same production quota, but the company keeps the missing person's pay for that day—neither the team nor the individual receive it. For all of these reasons, we consider this type of teamwork to be an abusive system.

Living with Stress

Health problems in the maquiladoras have been aggravated since the implementation of NAFTA. In the year preceding this report, the CFO has undertaken a participatory assessment of health problems in the maquiladoras. We found that the list of problems is extensive, identifying more than forty different health problems that can be divided into thirteen categories of symptoms. Of all of these, we found that the single most significant problem is stress. Allergic reactions and problems with vision emerged in second place, followed by hearing impairment and headaches. Other common ailments we identified included musculoskeletal, respiratory, reproductive, and circulatory problems; irritations of the skin; and more.

Stress, which is our top priority, is caused by many factors, including the intense pace of production imposed in the maquiladoras, arrogant treatment and sexual harassment by supervisory and management personnel, and the impact of poverty and family disintegration. Workplace hazards in the maquiladoras include not only stress but also toxic exposures and ergonomic problems. All of these are directly related to the intensified exploitation of workers that has resulted from NAFTA.

Although they deny it, the maquiladoras contribute to the health problems of their workforce. In Ciudad Acuña, with the pretext of avoiding food poisoning, Alcoa implemented a system of providing frozen meals in company cafeterias. This food is not only unpalatable, it has caused digestive problems for dozens of workers. Other working conditions with a negative health impact include poor temperature conditions, inadequate ventilation, and exposure to toxic substances and elevated noise levels without adequate protective equipment. All of these problems are common throughout the maquiladora industry. The reproductive rights of women workers continue to be violated on a daily basis by thousands of maquiladora firms that continue to impose involuntary pregnancy tests.

In addition, maquiladora firms routinely fail to report workplace accidents. Company doctors and nurses are used to conceal information from social security authorities, in order to avoid workers' compensation costs. Thousands of workers with injuries or work-related illnesses are given cursory treatment and are then pressured to return to the line. As a result, many of them develop chronic health problems.

The Maquiladoras, Our Children, and Our Communities

Our children are directly affected by the conditions fostered by the maquiladora industry. In most families, both father and mother must work, taking turns as best they can to care for their children. Child care services are scarce and inadequate; mothers must enroll their children in waiting lists that can last two years or more. Since not even two working parents are sufficient, many children must contribute to their families' income from a young age. The youngest children work in department stores, carrying bags for a tip, including during evening hours. Thousands of children as young as thirteen go to work in the maquiladoras, where their age is obscured by the massive falsification of birth certificates, a practice that is tolerated and covered up by labor authorities and maquiladora firms alike.

Over the thirty-four years preceding this report, living conditions in our communities have improved very little. Most maquiladora workers live in shantytowns that lack basic services and decent housing. The Mexican government acts as if "development" were equivalent to the construction of more international bridges or more highways. All of this infrastructure, however, is for the exclusive benefit of the companies. In several border towns, one can see clandestine discharge pipes that come from the maquiladoras, close to the workers' neighborhoods, with their inadequate water and sewer systems. The 1983 La Paz agreement between Mexico and the United States required the return of toxic industrial wastes to their country of origin. As of the year 2000, however, this agreement was superseded by NAFTA, affording less control than ever over the handling and disposition of industrial wastes. Even before the phase-out, the border environment suffered permanent damage that is not alleviated by the largely symbolic actions of publicity-conscious maquiladoras like Alcoa—which, in April 1999, was "adopting" parks in Ciudad Acuña while continuing to dispose of waste products in the open air.

The Offensive against Workers and Unions

In the name of NAFTA, the companies, aided by the Mexican government, are waging a tireless and surreptitious campaign of dirty tricks to stamp out unions in the maquiladoras. Their objective is to do away with unions altogether in those areas with the highest percentage of union representation—Matamoros, Reynosa, and Piedras Negras—or, at a minimum, to bring them under the system of "protection contracts" (company unions) that prevails in cities like Ciudad Juárez, Tijuana, and Ciudad Acuña. In Matamoros, the immediate goal is to replace the traditional Union of Laborers and

Industrial Workers (Sindicato de Jornaleros y Obreros Industriales) with a competing union, the Industrial Union of Maquiladora and Assembly Workers, which is known for being more friendly to management. However, the corporations are unlikely to stop there. In June 1999, Toyota indicated it would only open a plant in Matamoros on the condition that the workers would be represented by a company union.

Throughout the border region, the suppression of independent unions occurs with the complicity of a wide range of bodies, including official union confederations such as the CTM, CROC, and CROM;[8] local maquiladora associations; government labor authorities; and local, state, and federal government officials. The campaign of repression that has been carried out against workers at Han Young and their independent October 6 union in Tijuana, mass firings of workers at Custom Trim in Valle Hermoso when they sought to organize, and the underhanded attempts of the CTM to destroy an autonomous union at Carrizo in Piedras Negras are all examples of the suppression of labor under NAFTA. This repression has continued unchecked even when local arbitration boards or the NAO has issued rulings favorable to the workers.

Official unions in Mexico have traditionally been marked by corruption and sweetheart deals with management. Nonetheless, when they are weakened, the rank and file is directly affected, as workplace gains won in prior eras are threatened and the companies are able to exert ever greater control over the workers. At the time of this report, the official unions have failed to respond to the needs of the maquiladora rank and file, even though maquiladora workers pay between 3.07 and 5 percent of their wages in union dues. Furthermore, the official unions continue to lend their weight to the companies and the government as they seek to prevent workers from organizing. The official unions continue to say that maquiladora workers who fight for their rights are "agitators" who will "destabilize the maquiladora industry" and "scare off investors." Even when a plant has union representation, often the workers are not informed, and if they ask to see the union contract, the union representatives will not show it to them. Subcontracting is another way of evading enforcement of workers' right to organize.

The complicity among the companies, the government, and the official unions against the workers is very clear. For example, despite massive publicity, forums, and speakers, the government has taken no steps to put a stop to illegal pregnancy testing of maquiladora workers. Not only do union representatives act as foremen on production lines, union leaders distribute blacklists and act in the name of the company to fire, threaten, and seek to control the workers.

Induced Turnover and Other Deceptive Hiring Practices

The maquiladoras see a floating workforce as more advantageous, because the longer workers stay on the job, the more they begin to exercise their rights. Many companies are signing contracts with workers for only a month or two. Frequently, the companies close down operations or entire plants and then open them back up, sometimes on the same site, but with new personnel. Such "turnover" is designed to ensure that the maquiladoras can maintain total control over their workers.

In addition, labor shortages are beginning to be felt in various border cities. As a result, firms that are known among local workers to be very undesirable have to resort to other means to attract employees. The maquiladora firm Rassini, for example, has gone as far as the state of Veracruz to recruit workers for its operation in Piedras Negras, promising them work and a place to live. When they arrive, they are not given housing but are lodged in barracks equipped only with cots, with no privacy whatsoever. Workers who are not lucky enough to get a cot or a blanket sleep on the floor, with nothing. A single stove is provided for everybody. When they discover that the living and working conditions are not what they were promised, many of these workers quickly return to their homes. Sometimes, the deception is even greater. In Ciudad Acuña, maquiladoras like Falcomex, Alcoa, and Dilsa have brought people from the south of the country with promises that they will earn $110 a week, when in reality their pay will be no more than $35.

The Mirage Moves South: The "Maquilization" of Mexico

The rapid expansion of the maquiladoras into practically every state in our country has been launched without any consideration of the enormous social costs that these companies have imposed on the border over the thirty-four years leading up to this report. The maquiladoras are a mirage that promises development but delivers only poverty and exploitation. What the Mexican government does not acknowledge is that the "maquilization" of our country is going forward under conditions that are even worse than those at the border. The maquiladoras are moving like wolves into cities and small towns in the interior of Mexico, attracted by even lower labor costs than at the border and an inexperienced labor force that has had no contact with workers at the border and knows little or nothing about labor rights. In some cases, workers are not even enrolled in the social security system. In others, they live almost as slaves to the companies, whose buses arrive for them at four in the morning and bring them back at seven or eight at night.

So far, maquiladoras at the border have not been closing plants in order to move to the interior; rather, they have been expanding their operations.[9] This is occurring with many maquiladoras in Piedras Negras and Ciudad Acuña, such as Dimmit, Carrizo, Alcoa, Macoelmex, Dickies, and La Carolina. Some new maquiladoras are also arriving and setting up shop in the interior right away; examples include Vergeles, Ampliación Vergeles, and Luis Echeverría in Tamaulipas and many others in the south.

WORKERS AND THE CFO RESPOND

Every Line in Every Plant

For nineteen years before this report, the women and men of the CFO have confronted the maquiladoras, demanding our legal rights and winning many concrete gains that have improved the lives of many people. In the process, we have gained confidence, self-esteem, and new skills, and we have come to understand that we have the capacity to change our present working conditions for the better.

NAFTA has created conditions that make it more difficult for maquiladora workers to fight for our rights. Workers have less free time to spend with their families and to organize. The mirage of false promises offered by the maquiladoras means that in many zones of the interior, especially in rural areas, local residents welcome the maquiladoras with gratitude for the jobs they are bringing. On the border, we have known the maquiladoras for thirty-four years, and we are not satisfied. Here on the border, the companies face a culture of continuous, daily resistance—some of it spontaneous and much of it cultivated through many years of work by the CFO. When workers are unaware, they may respond with apathy; however, it is also true that most workers want to learn about their rights, share their experiences with others, and organize to improve their situation.

As workers in the maquiladoras, we ourselves must take responsibility for helping our fellow workers to understand that we have rights and dignity and that we must fight to put them in effect. Given the lack of support and outright repression that we face from most union leaders, labor authorities, supervisors, and maquiladora owners, our efforts to promote education and organization are based on the strength and determination that flows from every worker, every line, and every plant. Our methods of struggle span a range that includes slowdowns and other shopfloor actions, wildcats, officially recognized strikes,[10] and the creation of independent unions when desired by a majority of the workers—extending to dialogues with top executives of the maquiladoras' parent firms in the United States.

What We Have Won
(and Keep Fighting For)

- Wage increases in some maquiladoras
- Correct payment of overtime
- Payment of profit-sharing benefits that had been withheld
- An end to pregnancy testing in plants belonging to Delphi and Alcoa, among others
- No work until we are given adequate equipment, including shoes, tools, thread, raw materials, etc.
- Adequate safety equipment in some workplaces
- An end to abusive language and treatment by foremen and supervisors
- Relief in some cases from excessively high production quotas; some workers have won a say in setting fair quotas
- The ability to take the vacation time, sick leave, and breaks that we are legally owed
- Stopping management from taking away the chairs we sit in
- Teaching other workers how to identify and recognize health risks on the job
- Payment of fair settlements for injuries and for severance pay
- No tax deductions from bonuses given as prizes
- Proper treatment in social security clinics
- Publicizing on the radio unjust treatment in the maquiladoras
- Installation of ventilators and extractors in some plants
- Organization of wildcats and support for strikes for higher wages and better conditions
- Everyone on a line standing up for workers who are being abused or ill treated by supervisors or foremen
- Democratic election to local union leadership of people who

will look out for the rank and file; in some unions controlled by the CTM, nearly complete slates of local officials

- Openly confronting blacklisting by union leaders and labor authorities (since they will not publicly acknowledge the existence of the blacklist, CFO pressure has won jobs in other factories for blacklisted workers)
- Public exposure of union leaders who seek to deceive or abuse workers or misuse union funds
- Showing our husbands (and wives) and children that our cause is a just one, and winning their support for our efforts
- Helping women workers to increase their self-esteem
- Publicizing the conditions we face in the maquiladoras, in speaking tours and national and international forums in Copenhagen, Beijing, Central America, Canada, and the United States
- Testifying before the U.S. Congress and the Mexican government against inhuman working conditions and sex discrimination in the maquiladoras
- Building solidarity with other groups that support maquiladora workers, along the border and throughout Mexico
- Establishing ties and initiating ongoing alliances with unions, organizations, and networks, including the Mexican groups FAT,[11] RMALC, and CILAS, as well as the United Autoworkers, Canadian Autoworkers, United Electrical Workers, AFL-CIO, *Labor Notes*, the Interfaith Center for Corporate Responsibility, the AFSC, and many others
- Conducting dialogues with stockholders and executives of General Motors, Delphi, and Alcoa, urging them to respect our rights

The CFO and NAFTA

In its 1998 workshop on NAFTA, the CFO reached the following conclusions:

- We do not support NAFTA because we do not receive any of its benefits. On the contrary, its effects are prejudicial to us. We also oppose this agreement because it was negotiated behind our backs.
- NAFTA should be renegotiated to promote fair trade relations among Mexico, the United States, and Canada. A new treaty should assure just treatment for workers and full enforcement of the labor laws of each country.
- Mexico's labor code should be fully enforced, and the government's labor authorities as well as unions should defend the authentic interests of workers.
- We need to share information about NAFTA directly with other workers.
- We must publicize the work of the CFO more broadly.
- We will work with RMALC and other organizations in the three NAFTA countries in order to contribute to the creation of alternatives to "free trade."
- We need to influence the governments of Mexico and the United States by making the voices of workers heard regarding our situation and our proposals for change.
- We need to develop strategies that permit workers to confront NAFTA and the conditions in their factories without being fired.

The CFO believes it is necessary to fight to stop free trade agreements and economic globalization when they affect workers negatively. As a grassroots workers' organization on the Mexico-U.S. border, we intend to address the following goals:

- Educating and organizing more maquiladora workers
- Renegotiating NAFTA so that workers have a voice in its development
- Rejecting the proposed Free Trade Agreement of the Americas, and in its place adopting the Alternatives for the Americas developed by fair-trade networks of our hemisphere

- Developing international strategies for grassroots organization to combat corporate-controlled globalization
- Defending the historic gains of workers codified in Mexico's Federal Labor Law
- Working for the implementation of the conventions of the International Labor Organization
- Opposing the "Millennium Round" of the World Trade Organization (WTO), and instead evaluating the impact of WTO policies; in addition, supporting the formation of a WTO working group to explore the relationship between trade agreements and labor rights

NOTES

1. Under Mexican law, firms that close down are legally required to pay substantial severance benefits to laid-off workers, and their assets may be seized to satisfy this responsibility. It is not unusual for workers to occupy plants to ensure that machinery and other assets are not illegally removed.

2. Mexican firms are legally required to distribute 10 percent of profits among their workforce at the end of each year.

3. The PRI held a monopoly on political power in Mexico for more than seventy years. Although it is still a dominant force, its exclusive control of the government has come to an end.

4. Under Mexican law, severance payments to laid-off workers must include one month's pay, three extra days' pay for each year of seniority, and compensation for any unused vacation time. However, maquiladora workers must commonly apply pressure to receive the full benefit owed to them.

5. The official minimum wage in 1999, at the time of this report, ran between 39.4 and 41.5 pesos per day (US$4.28 to $4.51).

6. Mexico's comprehensive social insurance program, administered by the Mexican Social Security Institute, covers health care, disability, worker's compensation, and pension benefits.

7. The practice of laying off pregnant maquiladora workers to evade maternity benefits has been extensively documented by Human Rights Watch, with the assistance of the CFO and other Mexican organizations.

8. The CTM (Confederación de Trabajadores Mexicanos), or Confederation of Mexican Workers, is Mexico's largest labor confederation and the best-known in the United States. Other officially oriented confederations include the CROC (Central Regional de Obreros y Campesinos), or Regional Federation of Workers and Peasants), and the CROM (Central Revolucionario de Obreros de México), or Revolutionary Federation of Mexican Workers.

9. At the time of this report, rumors were circulating that Dimmit was planning to close its plant in Piedras Negras entirely and move operations to Monclova. [*Note:* On July 26, 2001, Galey & Lord, Dimmit's parent company, announced the simultaneous shutting down of its plants in Piedras Negras, Monclova, and Puebla. The company had started months before to move some production lines from Piedras to Monclova, but then the whole denim business segment for Galey & Lord collapsed.—Ed.] Under Mexican labor law, companies must continue to pay wages to their workers participating in strikes that are officially recognized by labor authorities.

10. Under Mexican labor law, when strikes are officially recognized by labor authorities, the company must continue to pay wages to striking workers.

11. The FAT (Frente Auténtico de Trabajo), or Authentic Labor Front, is an independent trade union confederation.

5. Maquiladoras, Migration, and Daily Life
Women and Work in the Contemporary Mexican Political Economy

Nancy Churchill

As a result of global economic restructuring, Mexico's political economy has been greatly transformed. The neoliberal economic policies that resulted in the passage of the North American Free Trade Agreement (NAFTA) between Mexico, the United States, and Canada has had a devastating impact on all aspects of Mexico's political, social, and economic life. Churchill examines two recent trends that have emerged in the wake of NAFTA: the rapid expansion of maquiladora factories and changes in the patterns of labor migration. Within this context, Churchill carefully examines the implications these changes have on women's productive and reproductive labor. More specifically, she attempts to determine the direction and form women's liberation can take in the midst of overall increasing immiseration.

Accompanying the explosion of maquiladora plants, or maquilas, has been the demand for a more flexible and feminized workforce. The increased participation of women in formal wage-earning (albeit meager) work has dramatically altered labor relations between men and women, transforming the Mexican household. Churchill argues that the increase in women's participation in pro-

ductive work has only increased their reproductive labor within the household (leading to the "double day" or "second shift"). Therefore, drawing upon the work of Henri Lefebvre, Churchill argues that the possibilities of women's liberation must be forged and articulated within the daily lives of women. Although women occupy a variety of spaces within their everyday lives, Churchill maintains that the household and reproductive labor is what binds all women together. Thus, when discussing the possibility of women's liberation, all aspects of their lives (productive and reproductive) must be carefully considered.

By detailing the manner in which Mexican women's unpaid and paid labor subsidize the global marketplace, Churchill effectively illustrates the overall connection between women's oppression and capitalist exploitation—a connection often lost or ignored in current feminist writings.

INTRODUCTION

To understand the social relations of capitalism in Latin America today, James Petras and Henry Veltmeyer suggest that we discard the catch-all concept of globalization and opt instead for "the workings of Euro-American imperialism" (1999, p. 31). This assigns both origin and agency to the many practices and processes we keep hearing and reading about, such as privatization, structural adjustment, and economic development, reconceptualizing their dynamic, so that *privatization* becomes "the purchase and takeover of public and state assets," *structural adjustment* consists of "the removal of restrictions on foreign investment, the liberalization of markets, and the deregulation of private enterprise," and *economic*

The author would like to thank Leigh Binford, Nancy Chance, Gloria Salgado, and Susanne Soederberg for their close readings and comments on earlier versions of this article. All translations from Spanish are mine.

development includes a whole series of "policies designed to increase the rate of profit on invested capital" (ibid., p. 32). Only by "discarding the euphemistic, imprecise and obfuscating language and discourse that have come into fashion" can we reclaim the class analysis so integral to our comprehension of the implications of global change for workers experiencing these processes of capitalist imperialism firsthand (ibid., p. 33; see also Henwood 1995).

Rather than discard the concept of globalization entirely, Joachim Hirsch asks whether the changes in the regime of accumulation and regulation characteristic of contemporary capitalism constitute a "historical structural modification" (1996, p. 86). The previous regime, the Fordist, relied upon an accumulation strategy based on mass production, salaried labor, and the development of internal markets for goods. The Fordist state promoted unionization of the labor force, the welfare state, and the institutionalization of a social pact between big labor and capital. This "golden age" of capitalism ended in the 1970s, when production stagnated and the incompatibility between capital's profit-making capacity and the welfare state came to a head. What is now called globalization, says Hirsch, is an emerging regime of flexible accumulation and regulation that calls for further advances in technologized production, the destruction of the capital-labor pact, and most importantly, the breaking down of national boundaries for production and marketing. The "vast political strategy" known as neoliberalism ensures that these economic processes flower under the protection of the state (Hirsch 1996, pp. 88–89).

While debate continues over the existence, nature, and effects of globalization, capitalist social relations—and in particular, the division of labor—have long been "global" in nature, with severe repercussions for those who labor in economies subordinate to the dictates of international lending agencies, foreign banks, and a highly mobile capital constantly in search of cheaper labor.[1] Given that only a portion of the working class is employed at any given place and time, those whose labor power cannot be absorbed in production continue to constitute what Karl Marx ([1867] 1967) termed the surplus population, the reserve from which capital draws the "redundant" worker into the active workforce in order to foster competition and drive down wages.

Flexible accumulation has intensified capital's tendency to incorporate the surplus labor of unemployed men, women, children, and even the elderly, as well as racially and politically oppressed groups. To further sharpen competition among current and potential workers, capital manipulates the division of labor to locate each differentially. For example, the gendered division of labor, which Kathryn Ward calls "capitalist patriarchy" (1988, p. 18), is an ideology that places men in production outside the home and relegates women to the realm of reproductive enterprise within it. Women's labor is thus devalued as nonproductive and constituted as a reserve that can be called upon to compete with or discipline male workers (see also Saffioti 1978).

In what follows I examine the implications of increasingly globalized social relations for women, work, and daily life in the contemporary Mexican political economy. Because Mexico is a complex nation with a vast number of regional geographies and economies that defy summary and facile categorizations, I wish to focus on two discrete but interrelated economic trends that are intensifying under the neoliberal policies propelled by the North American Free Trade Agreement (NAFTA) among Mexico, the United States, and Canada, both affecting women and their work inside and outside the home. These trends are the growth in the maquiladora industry, export-based assembly plants controlled by transnational corporations, and the expansion of international labor migration and its extension into regions with few antecedents.

As women enter the paid labor force in substantial numbers and both men and women continue to migrate in search of employment, daily life in Mexico is undergoing constant transformation. Women are experiencing an intensification of the "double day," working in production outside the household while the gender division of labor continues to assign them primary responsibility for reproductive activity within it. And once the neoliberal Mexican state began pulling back from the sphere of social welfare, women had to mobilize to restore such critical services as education, health care, and child care; when unsuccessful, they had to manage to replace them in the home, laboring a triple day to care for the elderly, the sick, and the young. All of these changes have implications for the reproduction of both class and gender relations in contemporary Mexico.

NAFTA, THE MEXICAN POLITICAL ECONOMY, AND WOMEN'S LABOR

Petras and Veltmeyer (1999) posit the origins of the "imperial order" in Latin America in capital's reaction to the social reforms enacted by progressive governments in the sixties and seventies. The thrust of these policies was to protect national economies, foster public education, and put in place health care and pensions for large sectors of the working class. By the eighties, the International Monetary Fund and the World Bank began demanding reversal of those trends. In Mexico, claim Helene Hirata, Michel Husson, and Martha Roldán (1995), the shift from import substitution to export-oriented production was fundamental in tying the country's economic future more closely to the United States, a process that culminated in the 1992 NAFTA treaty. Kathryn Kopinak agrees: this "continental economic integration was stimulated by a debt-ridden Mexican government, which in the early 1980s, attempted to transform maquiladoras into permanent industrial bases by encouraging more capital intensive operations and devaluing the peso to cheapen labor" (1994, p. 142).

The United States was forced to the treaty table to sign NAFTA with Mexico and Canada due to what Ricardo Grinspun and Maxwell A. Cameron identify as cutthroat global competition from a "unified Europe and a more assertive Japan" (1994a, p. 16), a decline in U.S. political and economic hegemony, and the shift to a regimen of flexible accumulation. As they see it, the U.S. goal is to "maintain 'international competitiveness' [through] . . . regressive competition with other 'cheap labor havens,' which results in lowered wages, coerced trade unions, and lax enforcement of labor and environmental regulations" (Grinspun and Cameron 1995, p. 45).

The official pronouncements on NAFTA claimed that it would stimulate production and consumption in all three nations through the free movement of commodities across national boundaries and by enhancing employment (and therefore earnings) opportunities, particularly in Mexico. Since 1989, U.S. capital had established industries and businesses in nonreserved areas of production in Mexico, but with further reductions in import-export taxes and tariffs, the economic invasion intensified. Productive infrastructure moved deeper into Mexican territory.

NAFTA has succeeded in producing what James M. Cypher identifies as a "disarticulated" Mexican economy (2001, p. 16). Industrial growth is now led by the maquiladora sector, which does not promote "spillover effects for the rest of the economy" (ibid., p. 28). Nor, says Cypher, has there been any "sustained effort to enhance production chains and create links between export-oriented activities and the domestic economy" (p. 18). Mexico is at best "able to obtain badly needed jobs at abysmal wage rates where a 'flexible' labor regime and a lack of solid union representation leaves workers vulnerable to occupational hazards, speeding, and the exercise of arbitrary managerial power." At the same time, the agricultural sector of the economy has been neglected. Thomas J. Kelly notes that rural producers who for decades had been heavily dependent on government subsidies and infusions of credit were "extremely vulnerable to the fiscal austerity and policy changes that occurred during liberalization" (2001, p. 90).

Social relations in Mexico are characteristic of the "Euro-American imperialism" discussed by Petras and Veltmeyer, which features a "direct assault on the working class, attacking its organization and negotiating capacity, [as well as indirectly assaulting] state-legislated social benefits to further undermine the capacity of labor to participate in any productivity gains" (1999, p. 43). They note that today the flexible accumulation regime and labor regulation "give capital . . . more freedom to hire, fire, and use labor as needed; and to render labor more flexible—that is, disposed to accept wages offered under free market conditions and to submit to the new management model of its relation to capital and the organization of production" (ibid., p. 46). The search for cheap labor has incorporated more and more women into capitalist production in assembly plants owned by transnational capital. And as maquiladora plants locate to small cities and periurban areas, they draw upon those rural populations seeking relief from the lacerating poverty that has accompanied the collapse of small, family-based agricultural production.

Stinging devaluations of the peso in 1982 and again in 1994 rocked the Mexican economy, pushing many precariously positioned middle-class families downward toward the "popular classes," Mexican shorthand for the working class and the poor. These periodic crises, which most people tend to read as one long, unforgiving trajectory, thrust Mexican women into the labor force in record numbers. Although reliable statistics are hard to come by, the trend is clear: in 1970, only 17 percent of women over the age of twelve worked, while in 1995, this number grew to 35 percent (Lagunes 1997, p. 7; García and de Oliveira 1998, p. 226). In 1997, 36.8 percent of Mexican women participated in the labor force (Hernández 2000, p. 119). Although differences exist by class, age, educational level, and rural versus urban residence, the trend holds overall (García and de Oliveira 1998). The National Institute of Geographical and Information Statistics reports 77 percent of all males and 36 percent of all females working outside the household during the year 2000 (INEGI 2002, p. 317).

It is interesting to note that while female labor force participation has been rising, the figures for males have decreased: while 88.2 percent of Mexican men worked in 1950, only 78 percent were employed in the early nineties (Hernández 2000, p. 119). Clara Judisman, economist and member of the Advisory Board on Women and Development for the Interamerican Development Bank, claims that one of the important factors leading to women's increased participation in income-earning activity was that the privatization policy of the Salinas administration left thousands of formal sector workers jobless, most of them male (cited in Del Valle 1997, p. 5). The wave of unemployment that accompanied this aspect of structural adjustment also led men to abandon their families, increasing the numbers of female-headed households. Now estimated to comprise close to 18 percent of all Mexican families, many of these women and their children have been pushed into poverty (Román 1997, p. 48; see also Del Valle 1997, p. 5). NAFTA has failed to correct these ills, claims Paul Cooney (2001, pp. 58–59): today, an estimated two-thirds of Mexicans are either unemployed or underemployed, and over 40 percent of Mexican families live in poverty.[2]

Before entering into a discussion of the trends affecting female labor in the contemporary political economy, we must remind ourselves that women have long engaged in productive labor in Mexico, both inside and outside the home, and there have always been exceptions to the rule of the patriarchal household governed by the male head (see Chassen-López 1994; Fowler-Salamini 1994; Dore 1997). However, the hegemonic discourse of male dominance supports the sexual division of labor that assigns responsibility for domestic and family-related labor to female members of domestic groups, while males are expected to work in remunerative or self-employed labor to earn the family wage (Selby, Murphy, and Lorenzen 1990; García and de Oliveira 1998; Coubès 2000). Among Mexico City's popular classes, notes anthropologist Larissa Lomnitz (1994), it is still the norm for men to work in wage labor or engage in petty commodity production, in both cases bearing the public face of the household, while women, children, and the elderly are removed from view as they labor in and around the home.

Researchers Guadalupe López Hernández, Cecilia Loría Saviñon, and Julie Pérez Cervera report that 99.6 percent of Mexican women who labor outside the household work an average of 42.6 hours a week within it. Only 56 percent of men do domestic tasks, and when they do, it is for an average of only 7.3 hours per week (statistics cited in Blanco 1998, p. 8). At the same time, women contribute income to one-third of Mexican households, more income than males in one in five households, and are the only income earners in one in ten (Román 1997, p. 48). Even those women, children, and elderly who work primarily in the household go beyond the realm of simple reproduction, producing commodities and services in order to ensure sufficient cash income and material resources to house, feed, and clothe the domestic group.[3]

In the next two sections, I discuss the history of maquiladoras and labor migration, the social relations of production prevalent in each distinct sphere, and some of the ways in which changes in women's active employment in production outside the home affects the daily lives of working women and their families, or the sphere of reproduction. I then examine the importance of the informal sector of the economy, the principal economic terrain open to women of the popular classes, who lack the education and family connections available to the small middle class and even smaller bourgeoisie.

MAQUILADORA ASSEMBLY PLANTS

Maquiladoras are predominantly export-oriented assembly plants whose social relations of production in Mexico consist of the hiring of Mexican labor by foreign capital and its national collaborators. The origins of today's maquiladora factories are located in the Mexican government's Depression-era attempts to stimulate the development of industry along the U.S.-Mexico frontier. Between 1942 and 1964, the flow of Mexican workers looking to enroll in the temporary, but legal, migrant worker program in the United States swelled the population of border towns. Thus, when the U.S. Border Industrialization Program sought in 1965 to take advantage of unemployed Mexican labor by establishing export-production factories on the Mexican side of the international boundary, capital profited from an existing urban infrastructure (Fernández-Kelly 1983). By the late seventies, says María Patricia Fernández-Kelly, Mexico was at the forefront "of countries taking part in labor-intensive offshore manufacturing for the U.S. market" (1983, p. 34).

Cooney (2001) attributes growth spurts in the maquiladora industry in the seventies, mid-eighties, and post-NAFTA period to the competitive advantage given to U.S. capital due to changes in laws governing plant ownership, tariffs, and repatriation of profits, in exchange for which the Mexican government receives foreign exchange with which to pay its debt, one of the highest among developing nations, and employment for formerly rural populations. Though 90 percent of the plants are located along the U.S.-Mexico border, the number of maquiladoras in the interior has doubled in recent years (Urrutia 1998, p. 35). In the central state of Puebla, for example, the small cities of Tehuacán, Tezuitlán, and San Martín Texmelucan are burgeoning with migrants in search of factory jobs. Seven hundred textile factories located in the state's four largest cities hire workers to sew pre-cut pieces into garments destined for the foreign market, generating over one hundred thousand jobs statewide. The small city of Tehuacán holds four hundred of these factories, with 90 percent of the product shipped to and sold in the United States. In this fast-growing urban zone, the maquiladoras employ forty thousand people in assembly plants and another twenty-five thousand in related industries (Olivares 1997, pp. 4–5).

The number of maquiladora plants nationwide increased from 620 in 1980 to 2,411 in 1996, with an increase of 14 percent during 1995 alone. The number of workers also increased: from close to 120,000 in 1980 to over 750,000 in 1996 (*La Jornada* 1997, p. 22) and 800,000 by the end of 1997 (Urrutia 1998, p. 35). These industries now account for 25 percent of Mexico's industrial sector and are said by some researchers to be the only type of industry undergoing expansion (Urrutia 1998; Steinsleger 1998, p. 39). The more than four hundred maquiladoras in and around the border city of Ciudad Juárez, for example, employ over two hundred thousand workers, almost a quarter of all maquiladora employees in the country. Some 60 percent of these are women earning minimal wages, as low as twenty-six U.S. dollars a week (Wright 2001, p. 133; Nathan 1999, p. 5). Official statistics from which most figures are culled are incomplete because many maquiladora operations are clandestine workshops located in homes in order to avoid taxes, payment of social security benefits, and just treatment of workers (Olivares 1997, p. 4).

Since their inception, the offshore export assembly plants in Mexico have preferred to hire young women, roughly aged sixteen to twenty-five. Capital bases its hiring preferences on patriarchal conceptions of women as more docile, adaptable, easily disciplined, and unlikely to unite in struggle for better wages and benefits. Young women are preferred over older women because they are said to be healthier and thus capable of laboring long hours under unsanitary and unsafe conditions. However, the pattern varies according to the composition of the labor force and the type of manufactory. Tiano found that the single women preferred in all maquiladoras gravitated toward the better working conditions in electronics plants, while less appealing apparel factories had to hire older women and mothers to round out their workforces. In any case, child rearing must not interfere with work attendance and performance, and in some firms women are given pregnancy tests at the time of job application (Tiano 1994, p. 74). A constant source of preoccupation for all women, regardless of age or marital status, is the potential for sexual harassment by male supervisors.

Despite the steady demand for a large supply of cheap labor, turnover in maquiladora factories is high. This is not surprising, given the working conditions that can only be described as hyper-exploitation, recalling those described by Friedrich Engels ([1845]

1968) in Manchester, England, during the Industrial Revolution. In fact, Marx's chapter, "The Working-Day," in the first volume of *Capital* is pertinent for understanding the labor practices found in maquiladoras. He describes the attempt by capital to extract greater surplus value during production by implementing a host of practices including longer hours, no overtime pay, the denial of or shortened meal times, increasing hours to fill "special" orders, shift work, and the use of the time and labor of existing workers to train new recruits (Marx [1867] 1967, pp. 222–86). Although the working conditions detailed in virtually all of the contemporary research on maquiladoras echo those discussed by Marx (see Fernández-Kelley 1983; Iglesias Prieto 1997; Cravey 1998), it is important to stress, as does Devon G. Peña (1997), that circumstances vary widely, depending on the nationality of the company's owners, the type of manufacture (e.g., textiles, electronics, auto parts), and the level of technological development in individual factories.

Both Fernández-Kelly (1983) and Iglesias Prieto (1997) maintain that fierce competition for jobs makes workers more willing to endure difficult conditions, at least in the short run. Even when hourly or daily wages are the norm, women must meet production quotas to earn this base pay, and are then induced to work for the extra pay doled out for pieces produced over and above the daily quota. Since wages are, in Peña's words, "uncomfortably close to subsistence levels" (1997, p. 56), there is an incentive for women to speed up their work in order to surpass quotas and earn the bonus. This is not always an easy undertaking, as Fernández-Kelly notes in her description of the labor process in one factory, where workers were linked to one another in "a rigidly structured chain" (1983, p. 120). If a stitcher is reliant on a thread cutter, and the latter works more slowly, the stitcher cannot maintain her output and loses the extra pay. Relations among workers in such stressful work environments can quickly escalate from irritation to hostility. And when tempers flare over the work pace, they can spill over into other areas, such as the volume level on the radio (Olivares 1997).

Researchers working in Puebla and Tlaxcala factories report the lack of the most rudimentary health and safety practices, including ventilation and the provision of simple face masks to prevent the inhalation of the millions of tiny fibers that fill the air in textile factories (Olivares 1997; Arzate Rivera 2001).[4] Toxic chemicals are another health hazard left uncontrolled to the detriment of labor (Iglesias Prieto 1997). Fernández-Kelly (1983) reports the use of metal folding chairs for sewing machine operators, a practice that contributed to back problems. In some factories, women work all day while standing, producing not only back pain but also swollen feet (Olivares 1997).

The pace in maquiladoras is fast and pressured. The din can be deafening. Peña describes how "the noise coming from the conveyor belts; soldering decks, various pneumatic tools, jig bores, and lathes; and clattering components is nonstop. . . . You can feel," he recalls, "the entire complex of building and machinery pulse and vibrate through your body" (1997, p. 55). Many women work under these conditions from early morning well into the evening, with only half an hour for lunch. With supervisors constantly hovering over the production lines, the only time that women can relax a bit and chat among themselves is when the higher-ups leave the shop floor (Olivares 1997).

Unionization drives have become more frequent, but few have been successful. Capital uses competition among workers to stave off union organizing and municipal police forces to suppress strikes and sit-ins when the threat of competition proves ineffective. In Mexico, as in other countries that promote export-oriented production and free trade zones, the state works hand in glove with capital (Martínez and Urrutia 1998).

Given the competition for wage labor among the surplus population, it is easy to replace discontented workers. Those who complain are fired and sometimes blacklisted in other factories. Women are not only replaced by other women, but in some cases by children, and more recently, by men. The latter trend is related to the serious male employment crisis resulting from repeated economic downturns and structural adjustment policies since the early eighties, as well as the militarization of the U.S.-Mexico border (García, Blanco, and Pacheco 1999). Under such circumstances, men are willing to accept low wages and poor working conditions, at least in the short run. However, this apparent trend may harden over time with changes in the maquiladora sector of the Mexican economy. World Trade Organization researcher Alfredo Hualde notes that the maquiladora industry has undergone technological innovation in order to increase productivity and as a result has begun demanding skilled labor (cited in Urrutia 1998, p. 35), which is translated as "male" in what Peña terms a system of "gender-based occupational segregation" (1997, p. 258). Though hard data on the changing demographics of maquiladora employment is sketchy, it seems to suggest that men are "disproportionately present in technical, repair, maintenance, group-chief, and supervisory positions" and that engineers, supervisors, and managers are "overwhelmingly" male (Peña 1997, pp. 258–59). Melissa Wright details the social construction of women as "untrainable subjects" (2001, p. 135), a discourse that serves to rationalize management's pigeonholing of women in low-skilled, dead-end jobs. High turnover is blamed on women's lack of ambition and loyalty to the company, rather than poor working conditions and low pay.

Despite the negative picture painted by researchers and workers alike, women continue to flock to maquiladoras and other factories. As García, Blanco, and Pacheco point out (1999), the sexual division of labor has historically created conditions that disadvantage women when they do enter the labor force. Women are paid less than men, since it is assumed that men are providing for their families, because the sexual division of labor assigns women to housework and child-rearing. Women tend to be less skilled and educated, thus unprepared for higher-paying, skilled employment (see also Becerril and López Amador 1998; García and de Oliveira 1998; González Marín 1998b). Women of the popular classes seek jobs in maquiladoras because the pay is higher than that often earned in jobs traditionally reserved for them—domestic labor and other types of informal sector work. Some offer much-needed medical benefits and social security. Women also look for factory work because they tend to have lower education levels than men, and many maquiladoras are willing to accept their lack of credentials and train them on the job. And they prefer the factory setting because workers in small, household-based production units labor under even worse conditions and pay rates, given the family-based nature of operations.

Full-time work outside the household by women whose primary responsibility continues to be socially defined as attending to family produces dissonance in the daily lives of female workers, their husbands, and their children. As the many researchers who have worked in this area have documented, mothers and wives must rise before the rest of the family to prepare meals and get children ready for school before they report to the factory. They press older children, especially females, into service as well, placing them in charge of picking up younger children from school and preparing simple meals while waiting for their mothers to arrive, exhausted from the "first" workday, but ready to assume the responsibilities of the so-called second shift. Although some research suggests that Mexican husbands are contributing more time to household tasks, the sexual division of labor in domestic groups remains firmly in place (Cravey 1998; García and de Oliveira 1998).

Weekends, for those lucky enough to have five- instead of six-day workweeks, are spent washing, ironing, cleaning the house, buying food, running errands, and trying to find some time to relax before work begins again on Monday morning. Any family emergency causes further complications for women whose time is stretched to the limits. Added to the poor housing and sanitary conditions and irregularities in public services experienced by Mexico's urban popular classes, maquiladora employment complicates women's lives as much as it contributes to their economic survival (Iglesias Prieto 1997; Fernández-Kelly 1983; Tiano 1994).

Single women who are not heads of households and are therefore confined to the same work and child-rearing routines as their married counterparts may lead less problematic personal lives but are subject to more difficult interpersonal relationships on what Nathan characterizes as a "highly sexualized" shop floor (1999, p. 27). A conventional feminine appearance, defined by youth, slimness, and the wearing of short skirts and high heels, conflates an attractive appearance with a "good worker," a designation that arouses contradictory reactions of desire and competition on the part of males, some of them supervisors. The resultant flirting and "cat calling," says Nathan, cannot help but "[spill] out of the plants during time off" (1999, p. 27), forcing young, female workers to contend with the resultant social reprobation that attends economic independence and expressions of personal liberty on the part of Mexican women (see also Wright 2001).[5]

MIGRATION

The international migration of workers and rural agriculturalists has been a trend since the last quarter of the nineteenth century, when Mexicans provided a great deal of the sweat labor for the construction of U.S. railroads, worked in northern Illinois steel mills, and subsidized California agriculture and the southern Texas brick industry (Durand 1994; Cook 1998). Within Mexican national boundaries, migrants from rural areas swelled the population of Mexico City and other urban areas in the 1950s and 1960s and migrated to large-scale, agro-industrial zones to harvest sugar, coffee, and the winter fruits and vegetables that stock U.S. supermarkets (Durand 1994). Indeed, migration within Mexico has greatly exceeded international migration, although the gap is narrowing. According to Corona Vázquez (1993, p. 752), interstate migration was ten times greater than international migration in 1970, decreasing to four times greater in 1990. Mexico City, the nation's principal post–World War II migrant destination, now expels more people than it attracts.

These population movements are symptomatic of the ongoing economic crisis and neoliberal reorganization discussed in the introduction to this article. Mexico's large cities no longer provide the seemingly limitless labor markets that formerly sheltered, albeit precariously, migrants drawn from rural areas. Reduced government budgets, a decline in the purchasing power of 90 percent of the population, and a massive influx of imports have destroyed much domestic industry and led to a reduction in formal-sector employment and the growth of precarious, informal-sector work. The rural crisis, which began well before the current wave of neoliberalism, has been exacerbated further by the 1992 reversal of land reform, practical elimination of government credit and technical assistance for small peasants, and NAFTA-driven competition with U.S. and Canadian grain farmers, who, contrary to free market ideologies, are heavily subsidized by their respective governments.

The social characteristics, source areas, and destinations of Mexican migrants have altered in response. Not surprisingly, women are being drawn increasingly into migratory labor or at least find their domestic routines altered as males leave in growing numbers for *el norte*, the colloquial term for the United States. Jorge Durand characterizes contemporary Mexican international migration as "preponderantly rural but progressively urban, preponderantly male but progressively female" (1994, p. 51).

The growing presence of women among international migrants cannot be attributed solely to economic necessity. Two additional factors play important roles: first, the legalization of almost two million Mexican residents in the United States through the 1986 Immigrant Reform and Control Act, better known as the Simpson-Rodino Law, which promoted family reunification (Donato 1993); second, the consolidation of migrant networks between sending and receiving areas, which reduce both cost and the risk for undocumented persons to move long distances and across international borders (Massey, Goldring, and Durand 1994). By the late seventies such networks had developed in many rural communities of the western Mexican states of Michoacán, Jalisco, Guanajuato, and Zacatecas. As Puebla, Guerrero, Oaxaca and other states of the center and south responded to the crisis with international migration in the eighties and nineties, social networks developed rapidly, leading to a process that Binford refers to as "accelerated migration" (1998). For instance, the first international migrant left the Nahuatl-speaking community of Zoyatla, Puebla, in 1978, and within twenty years fully half the adult population, including a quarter of adult females, had traveled at least once to the United States (Binford 1998, p. 13).

The estimated 200,000 Mexicans in and around New York City illustrate another feature of Mexico-U.S. immigration—the increasing geographic dispersal of migrants within the United States. Historically Mexicans concentrated in rural, and to a lesser degree urban, areas from Texas to California, where they were overwhelmingly employed in agriculture (Jones 1984). Although the southwest United States remains the favored destination, Mexican migrants, both male and female, reside in every state in the continental United States, including Alaska. Reversing the earlier trend, a majority of migrants now reside in urban areas, where they staff both small factories whose owners lack the capital and contacts to move offshore and the low-wage urban service industries that enable middle-class urban- and suburbanites to maintain their lifestyles during a period of stagnant wages (Smith 1998).

Mexican female migrants concentrate in low-wage factory work (domestic sweatshops, often off the books) and clean the houses and care for the children of middle-class families, making it easier for educated Anglo females to pursue professional careers. Those who legalize their status experience some occupational mobility, although "private household cleaners and servants," "textile sewing machine operators," and "janitors" are among the most frequent job categories of female migrants who obtained green cards under Simpson-Rodino (Powers, Selzer, and Shi 1998, pp. 1028–29).

Since 1986, however, U.S. immigration policy has hardened. Recent immigrants confront a hostile social climate and, unable to openly seek formal-sector employment, will likely be confined to the most precarious informal sector and off-the-book jobs. Only by reducing their expenses to the minimum—crowding eight to ten people into cheap apartments and sleeping in shifts—are restaurant workers, janitors, gardeners, and housekeepers, earning two or three hundred dollars weekly, able to send a quarter of their salaries home to Mexico.

Women who remain in Mexico enable male migration, performing childcare and domestic chores in what some authors refer to as "bi-national families," while working on the farm and earning money through wage labor, petty commerce, or the production of artisan goods (Proctor and Preibisch 2000). Women's unpaid labor in Mexico subsidizes U.S. and Canadian capitalists, who set wages below the level required for the reproduction of the individual worker, without concern for the worker's household obligations. Mexican women often realize productive and reproductive responsibilities under the watchful eye of their mothers-in-law, into whose care they are committed during their husband's absence. The added economic responsibilities and social pressures, which include raising children in the absence of their fathers, often generate conflict within immediate and extended families (D'Aubeterre Buznego 2000; Castañeda Salgado 2000). The inability or failure of males to send money to support the household (because of job instability, the need to pay back the "coyote" who guided the migrant across the border, or a lack of iron discipline), severed relations when males establish second households in the United States, children alienated from their fathers, jealousy manifest at long distance, and the "remittance" of AIDS and other diseases are among the serious problems that counterbalance the stories of success in virtually every community history of migration.

Reactions to the migratory experience are gendered. Some international female migrants, having seen the benefit of laws that provide relative protections for women, become more active advocates for their rights when they return home. Luin Goldring (1996) notes that long-term male migrants tend to idealize the home community and plot their eventual return, whereas many women, having become accustomed to greater freedom of thought and movement in the United States relative to Mexico, do everything possible to inhibit the plan's realization (see also Espinosa 1998). Still, not all women migrants share these sentiments. The poor, undocumented Mexican male migrants encountered by Victoria Malkin (1999) in New Rochelle, New York, attempt to reproduce customary patterns of male dominance by controlling the social relations and movements of their wives and lovers, sometimes confining them in apartments under lock and key. In contrast to those interviewed by Goldring, these women dream of returning to Mexico, where they at least have the support of family members in their struggles with abusive spouses.

One consequence of male international migration is the entry of their wives into the labor force in search of wage income to support their families until such time as the migrant begins sending money. In rural areas, women and their children serve as agricultural day laborers: surveys conducted in agro-industrial regions of five states indicate decreased numbers of child workers and increased numbers of adult male and especially female workers, many entering the labor market for the first time (Barrón and Hernández Trujillo 2000). In urban areas, women enter the "informal sector" of the economy as street vendors and domestic workers.

THE GROWTH IN THE "INFORMAL SECTOR"

The catch-all concept of the "informal sector" is used to group all economic activity that falls outside the dynamic of the "formal," or modern, technologically sophisticated, and capitalized sector (Connolly 1985; Bueno 1990; González Marín 1998b). It includes a myriad of income-earning activities that share few characteristics other than their precarious nature, such as domestic labor, processed-food vending, home-based petty commodity production, and ambulant sales. Generalization appears to be an impossible undertaking, so most researchers on the subject confine themselves to synchronic studies of one informal economic activity in one location, examining the labor process in detail (Bueno 1993). As Patricia Connolly points out, it is still "difficult to derive any common characteristic, apart from unfavourable labour conditions, from which an overall theoretical categorization could be construed" (1985, p. 72). Rather than recognize the informal sector as an outgrowth of the limits to full employment under capitalism, says Connolly, this category is manipulated in government statistics to disguise unemployment as employment by claiming that individuals choose to work outside the bounds of regular salaries, hours, benefits, and taxes for personal reasons.

The informal sector has long served as an economic space available to urban working-class women, given the possibility of combining reproductive household tasks, primarily child care, and food preparation with income earning. In urban zones in neoliberal Mexico, however, it has become the means by which an estimated 44 percent of the economically active population earns its living (Gómez Flores 1999, p. 24). As noted above, the structural adjustment policies implemented to stabilize the economy following the crisis of 1994–95 resulted in massive layoffs in male formal-sector employment, which in turn thrust both men and women into the informal sector (Del Valle 1997, Cooney 2001). An assessment of NAFTA's toll after three years in operation indicated that salaries had regressed, the number of unemployed workers had doubled, nonsalaried employment had risen to 34.9 percent, and child labor was on the rise (Muñoz and Calderón 1997, p. 19). Victor M. Godínez concludes that "unemployment and underemployment continue to be [Mexico's] . . . principal economic and social problem" (1999, p. 26).

In order to compensate for income lost as a result of spousal migration or unemployment, or as a domestic group strategy designed to enhance reproductive potential, urban working-class women apply their considerable skills to provide low-cost products and services. Domestic work is a common source of income for this group, always a "necessity" among the upper classes and now desired by middle-class working women who wish to escape the burden of the double day. Young, single women from rural towns are the preferred recruits for live-in domestic work in the homes of the bourgeoisie, whereas the economically pressed middle classes can afford to hire a domestic worker from a poor urban neighborhood or a periurban town only one or two days a week. Salaries are situated well below the cost of reproduction, and the exploitation of women's labor power is not only (or in all cases) class-based but gendered as well, by women of higher socioeconomic positions who accept the patriarchal discourse that assigns women responsibility for the household.

Another common informal sector earnings strategy is petty commodity production, particularly food processing and vending. The urban Mexican meal pattern supplies ample opportunity for women preparing foods for sale at distinct hours of the day. In the mornings, tamale vendors are in profusion around worksites, as are women selling candies, sodas, juices, and snacks outside schools. In the evenings, women set up tables on the sidewalks and in the doorways of apartment buildings and sell local dishes to regular customers. This type of work is viable for mothers of young children, who can clean, shop, and wash during the morning and prepare food for sale during the afternoon and evening. For start-up one need only purchase raw foods and fuel, and perhaps a small table and brazier. Food vending is also attractive because there is no need for transportation, and police are unlikely to raid unlicensed sales sites. Women can thus work in a safe and familiar environment. However, returns are low, since women selling in poor neighborhoods cannot charge much for their labor and products.

Still another option is ambulant sales, a general category that includes a myriad of social relations involving two or more links in a vending chain. Female vendors comprise the last link, purchasing items such as towels, socks, or sweatsuits from an intermediary. Actual practices run the gamut, from entire families selling flowers in the median dividers of heavily trafficked boulevards to women who pay a monthly quota to a vendor organization that grants her the right to occupy space on a particular street. Those who do not join an organization that provides them with some protection from periodic police raids run the risk of being persecuted and beaten and having their products confiscated. Unlicensed vending is illegal, and municipal authorities prefer that vendors buy or rent stalls in the public markets created for this purpose. Vendors who cannot afford stalls or who do not want to be tied to a single location either pay for protection or remain mobile all day in order to avoid police harassment. Like other informal sector workers, street vending is attractive to women because they can work around household tasks and children's school schedules, selling when they have time.

CHANGING SOCIAL RELATIONS IN "EVERYDAY LIFE": PROSPECTS FOR LIBERATION

The quickening of these trends ripples throughout the Mexican political economy, affecting social relations at what Lourdes Benería and Martha Roldán have dubbed "the crossroads of class and gender" (1987). At that intersection, argues Ward, "gender inequality increases when the processes of the capitalist world-system and underdevelopment interact with local forms of male dominance over women" (1988, p. 18). If we agree with her that "capitalist patriarchy . . . uses gender as a basic category in the economic system" (ibid.), then researchers must weave together analyses of class exploitation and gender oppression in order to comprehend the nature of unequal social relations and assess the possibilities for righting them. It is easier, however, to analyze the nature of class and gender oppression than it is to speculate on the possibility of women's liberation in any one or all of the spheres in which they struggle.

As the global reach of U.S. capital strengthens its hold on the Mexican political economy, it contributes to the reconfiguration of Mexican society. Whether women go to work in maquiladoras, migrate, remain behind when their male partners "go north," or work as domestics or ambulant vendors, they and their families experience often tumultuous changes in the social relations of production and reproduction that reverberate throughout all the spaces of everyday life. Researchers have dedicated themselves to the local study of these complex changes, the results of which can be found in the prolific literature on gender, work, migration, NAFTA, maquiladoras, and family relations.[6] Here I want to reflect on movements of resistance from the bottom up. How might they be generated, enacted, and maintained?

Though Henri Lefebvre's work does not focus primarily on gender oppression, his theorization of daily life provides some useful conceptual tools for examining the possibilities for liberation in a general sense. Lefebvre maintains that capitalist social relations are reproduced in the space of daily life, which for him include the worksite as well as the household and the streets and parks of the neighborhood. Predominant among these relations is alienation: as workers we are estranged not only from the means of production—our labor power and its products—but, just as importantly, from recognition of our own human needs and desires. I propose that since the social spaces in which alienation manifests itself are multiple, we might begin moving toward consciousness of that estrangement and its causes in any one of the spheres of daily life, from the classic location of class-based struggle, the factory, to the locus of more intimate oppression within the household. Although

Lefebvre's proposals are less rigorous in terms of how such struggles might begin to take form, as well as how class-based consciousness is mediated by gender, race, age, or ethnicity, he recognizes the importance of individual awareness, which leads to collective resistance. Given the small number of viable national and international class-based movements in today's global neoliberal political economy, Lefebvre's suggestions speak to the local and to the importance of oppression deriving from patriarchy and racism (Lefebvre 1978, 1994; see also Shields 1999).

Since the daily life of all Mexican women is reproduced in the space and time of the household, the street, and increasingly the workplace, it might be around struggles in any or all of these places that women's interests coalesce. Despite the fact that maquiladora workers have organized unions, they continue to be fiercely opposed by transnational capital and host governments. Migrants who reach the United States disperse; the partners that remain behind cope with economic difficulties through kin-based networks or operationalize income-gaining strategies through the informal sector. The disparate nature of informal-sector employment in terms of worksites, pay/earnings, and organization of production makes it unlikely that these workers will unite as workers, except within similar occupational groupings. To be sure, ambulant vendors join organizations that resist local governments' attempts to force them into controlled spaces, such as public markets, and domestic workers have formed urban, national, and even international organizations to improve labor conditions and wages. But as critics have noted, this is not a segment of the economy whose workers share natural affinities based on sector-wide characteristics, nor is the source of their exploitation easily identifiable.

In an interesting case study of three Mexican working-class women involved in struggles over urban land and public services in the capital city, Alejandra Massolo (1982) explains the movements' dynamics in terms of women's roles as reproducers of labor power. In one of the cases cited, the first phase in the struggle for housing required families to join forces with others and, en masse, illegally occupy vacant urban land and fight for the right to remain. The second phase developed when male domestic group members returned to work, leaving the responsibility for sorting out the legal issues concerning land tenure to their wives. In order to accomplish these goals, the women collectivized reproduction by setting up community kitchens and child care facilities so that some women's labor could be freed for the necessary, daily confrontation with government authorities. Once the residents were relatively secure in their new homes, the third phase began, in which women fought for the public services necessary for the continued reproduction of the working class as a whole, such as drinking water, paved streets, and public transportation and lighting. During this prolonged struggle, women become aware of their dual oppression: first, by the state, which assumes capital's responsibility to provide the public services necessary for the reproduction of labor, and secondly by their husbands, who complained when their wives' political activities took them out of the household and into the streets.

This example signals the likelihood that women's struggles for liberation will congeal around reproductive issues, because the unequal relations of capital are reproduced in the space of the household, the space assigned to all Mexican women, regardless of class, in their everyday life. In the case of the testimonies presented by Massolo (1982), women's perceptions of the nature of both class-based and gender oppression took shape in the same crucible—their prolonged struggle for housing and services.

The increasing numbers of women wage laborers who directly experience the exploitation of their labor power by capital in their everyday lives at the workplace are likely to develop consciousness of class oppression before that of gender. However, the lower wages and lack of benefits common to female employment, their firing and replacement by male workers, and the overwhelming nature of the double day can lead to awareness of the dual but tied nature of women's oppression. For migrants and women left behind by spouses and partners, the question of how consciousness develops is less clear, but it has everything to do with women venturing outside the household. What is certain is that liberation will not come about only with the unionization of the factory or the raising of wages, for the space of daily life colonized by the capitalist patriarchy goes beyond these boundaries. Once female workers leave the factory and return to their households, they experience exploitation again, by male members of the household—to the benefit of capital, to be sure, but also to the benefit of their husbands and sons, who can rest while women begin their second and, in some cases, third shifts.

NOTES

1. An extended discussion of the debates on globalization in contemporary Latin America can be found in *Latin American Perspectives* 127, vol. 29, no. 6 (2002).

2. Here Cooney cites unemployment figures reported in La Botz (1997).

3. In "Urban Women's Work in Three Social Strata," Lomnitz elaborates on productive activity not always recognized as such, noting that "women help their husbands in their small family enterprises as unpaid family laborers, have their own food-preparation enterprises, do washing for middle-class people, pick up scrap metal or paper to resell, and raise animals such as pigs or bird stock. Children shine shoes, carry water, wash cars, sell chewing gum at street lights, and collect food. They also help care of animals raised by households, deliver tortillas made for sale by their mothers, and take care of their brothers and sisters when their mothers go out to work. Old people carry water, sit long hours in front of tables selling peanuts or candies, and help women take care of children" (1994, p. 63). Similarly, the research of Mercedes González de la Rocha emphasizes the "social base" of the household, the organization of which "serves as the basis for survival and reproduction in urban contexts" (1995, p. 13). Her long-term research in Guadalajara neighborhoods leads

González de la Rocha to conclude that as economic crises endanger that capacity, women's salaries have become even more important at the level of nutrition, health, and education.

4. In one Puebla factory described in Olivares (1997), workers must provide their own face masks or do without.

5. Both Nathan (1999) and Wright (2001) discuss the murders of almost two hundred young women in the environs of Ciudad Juárez, many of whom were maquiladora workers. They attribute the apparent lack of attention by government authorities to pervasive class and gender ideologies that, in Wright's words, craft "the Mexican woman as a figure whose value can be extracted from her," at which point she becomes disposable (2001, p. 142).

6. To record just a few of the recent Mexican contributions to this literature, see González et al. (1995), Alatorre et al. (1994), and González Marín (1998a).

REFERENCES

Alatorre, Javier, Gloria Careaga, Clara Judisman, Vania Salles, Cecilia Talamante, and John Townsend. 1994. *Las mujeres en la pobreza.* Mexico City: Colegio de México.

Arzate Rivera, Xochitl. 2001. Mujeres y salud laboral en las maquiladoras de ropa del área de influencia del parque industrial Xiloxoxtla. Master's thesis, Universidad Autónoma de Tlaxcala.

Barrón Pérez, María Antonieta, and José Manuel Hernández Trujillo. 2000. Cambios en la migración interna en México: Las nómadas del nuevo milenio. Paper presented at the Twenty-second Congress of the Latin American Studies Association, Miami, FL, March 16–18.

Becerril, Lilia, and María de Jesús López Amador. 1998. La mujer trabajadora: Sus condiciones de instrucción y capacitación. In *Mitos y realidades del mundo laboral y familiar de las mujeres mexicanas,* edited by María Luisa González Marín, pp. 65–89. Mexico City: Siglo Veintiuno Editores.

Benería, Lourdes, and Martha Roldán. 1987. *The crossroads of class and gender: Industrial homework, subcontracting, and household dynamics in Mexico City.* Chicago: University of Chicago Press.

Binford, Leigh. 1998. Accelerated migration between Puebla and the United States. Paper presented at the Mexican Migration to New York conference, Barnard College and New York University, New York, October 16–17.

Binford, Leigh, and María Eugenia D'Aubeterre Buznego, eds. 2000. *Conflictos migratorios transnacionales y respuestas comunitarias.* Puebla, Mexico: Benemérita Universidad Autónoma de Puebla and Consejo de Población.

Blanco, José. 1998. Familias con futuro. *La Jornada* (Mexico City), April 28, 1998, p. 8.

Bueno, Carmen. 1993. Los estudios del sector informal en México. In *Antropología y ciudad,* edited by Margarita Estrada, Raúl Nieto, Eduardo Nivón, and Mariángela Rodríguez, pp. 125–35. Mexico City: Centro de Investigaciones y Estudios Superiores de Antropología Social and Universidad Autónoma Metropolitana, Unidad Itztapalapa.

Bueno, María del Carmen. 1990. ¿Es la venta de comida una actividad marginal en la dinámica de la ciudad de México? In *Crisis, conflicto y sobreviviencia: Estudios sobre la sociedad urbana en México,* edited by Guillermo de la Peña, Juan Manuel Durán, Agustín Escobar, and Javier García de Alba, pp. 139–50. Guadalajara: Universidad de Guadalajara and Centro de Investigaciones Estudios Superiores en Antropología Social.

Castañeda Salgado, Martha Patricia. 2000. Conyugalidad y violencia: Reflexiones sobre el ejercicio del derecho femenino a la denuncia legal en una localidad expulsora de migrantes. In Binford and D'Aubeterre 2000, pp. 97–114.

Chassen-López, Francie R. 1994. "Cheaper than machines": Women and agriculture in Porfirian Oaxaca, 1880–1922. In Fowler-Salamini and Vaughn 1994, pp. 27–50.

Connolly, Patricia. 1985. The politics of the informal sector: A critique. In *Beyond employment: Household, gender, and subsistence,* edited by Nanneke Redclift and Enzo Mingione, pp. 55–91. Oxford: Basil Blackwell.

Cook, Scott. 1998. *Mexican brick culture in the building of Texas, 1800s–1980s.* College Station: Texas A & M University Press.

Cooney, Paul. 2001. The Mexican crisis and the maquiladora boom. *Latin American Perspectives* 118, vol. 28 (3): 55–83.

Corona Vázquez, Rodolfo. 1993. Migración permanente interestatal e internacional. *Comercio Exterior* 43 (8): 750–62.

Coubès, Marie-Laure. 2000. Trayectorias laborales femeninas en México: Evolución en las cuatro últimas décadas. Paper presented at the Twenty-second Congress of the Latin American Studies Association, Miami, FL, March 16–18.

Cravey, Altha J. 1998. *Women and work in Mexico's maquiladoras.* Lanham, MD: Rowman & Littlefield.

Cypher, James M. 2001. Developing disarticulation within the Mexican economy. *Latin American Perspectives* 118, vol. 28 (3): 11–37.

D'Aubeterre Buznego, María Eugenia. 2000. Arbitraje y adjudicación de conflictos conyugales en una comunidad de transmigrantes originarios del estado de Puebla. In Binford and D'Aubeterre 2000, pp. 115–44.

Del Valle, Sonia. 1997. Las PAE aumentaron la carga de trabajo feminine. *Doble Jornada*, special insert in *La Jornada* (Mexico City), August 4, 1997, p. 5.

Donato, Katherine M. 1993. Current trends and patterns of female migration: Evidence from Mexico. *International Migration Review* 27 (4): 748–71.

Dore, Elizabeth. 1997. The holy family: Imagined households in Latin American history. In *Gender politics in Latin America: Debates in theory and practice*, edited by Elizabeth Dore, pp. 101–17. New York: Monthly Review Press.

Durand, Jorge. 1994. *Más allá de la linea: Patrones migratorios entre México y Estados Unidos.* Mexico City: Fondo de Cultura y las Artes.

Engels, Friedrich. [1845] 1968. *The condition of the working class in England.* Stanford, CA: Stanford University Press.

Espinosa, Victor. 1998. *El dilema del retorno.* Zamora, Mexico: Colegio de Michoacán.

Fernández-Kelly, María Patricia. 1983. *For we are sold, I and my people: Women and industry in Mexico's frontier.* Albany: State University of New York Press.

Fowler-Salamini, Heather. 1994. Gender, work, and coffee in Córdoba, Veracruz, 1850–1910. In Fowler-Salamini and Vaughn 1994, pp. 51–73.

Fowler-Salamini, Heather, and Mary Kay Vaughn, eds. 1994. *Women of the Mexican countryside, 1850–1990.* Tucson: University of Arizona Press.

García, Brígida, Mercedes Blanco, and Edith Pacheco. 1999. Género y trabajo extradoméstico. In *Mujer, género y población en México,* edited by Brígida García, pp. 273–316. Mexico City: Colegio de México and Sociedad Mexicana de Demografía.

García, Brígida, and Orlandina de Oliveira. 1998. *Trabajo femenino y vida familiar en México.* Mexico City: Colegio de México.

Godínez, Victor M. 1999. Las cuentas del empleo. *La Jornada,* May 19, 1999, p. 26.

Goldring, Luin. 1996. Gendered memory: Constructions of rurality among Mexican transnational migrants. In *Creating the countryside: The politics of rural and environmental discourse,* edited by E. Melanie DuPuis and Peter Vandergeest, pp. 303–29. Philadelphia: Temple University Press.

Gómez Flores, Laura. 1999. El sector informal abarcará 44% del empleo urbano. *La Jornada* (Mexico City), June 7, 1999, p. 24.

González, Soledad, Olivia Ruiz, Laura Velasco, and Ofelia Wood, eds. 1995. *Mujeres, migración y maquila en la frontera norte.* Mexico City: Colegio de México and Colegio de la Frontera Norte.

González de la Rocha, Mercedes. 1995. The urban family and poverty in Latin America. *Latin American Perspectives* 85, vol. 22 (2): 12–31.

González Marín, María Luisa, ed. 1998a. *Los mercados del trabajo femeninos: Tendencias recientes.* Mexico City: Universidad Nacional Autónoma de México.

———. 1998b. El trabajo femenino en el sector informal. In González Marín 1998a, pp. 15–47.

Grinspun, Ricardo, and Maxwell A. Cameron. 1994a. The political economy of North American integration: Diverse perspectives, converging criticisms. In Grinspun and Cameron 1994b, pp. 3–25. New York: St. Martin's Press.

———, eds. 1994b. *The political economy of North American free trade.* New York: St. Martin's Press.

———. 1995. Mexico: The wages of trade. In Rosen and McFadyen 1995, pp. 39–53.

Henwood, Doug. 1995. Clinton's trade policy. In Rosen and McFadyen 1995, pp. 27–38.

Hernández Licona, Gonzalo. 2000. El empleo en México en el siglo XXI. *El Cotidiano* (Mexico City) 100 (16): 117–28.

Hirata, Helene, Michel Husson, and Martha Roldán. 1995. Reestructuraciones productivas y cambios en la división sexual del trabajo y del empleo: Argentina, Brasil y México. *Sociología del Trabajo*, no. 24: 75–97.

Hirsch, Joachim. 1996. *Globalización, capital y estado.* Mexico City: Universidad Autónoma de México.

Iglesias Prieto, Norma. 1997. *Beautiful flowers of the maquiladora.* Austin: University of Texas Press.

INEGI (National Institute of Geographic and Information Statistics). 2002. *Mujeres y hombres 2002.* Aguascalientes, Mexico: INEGI.

Jones, Richard C. 1984. Micro-patterns of undocumented migration between Mexico and the U.S. In *Patterns of undocumented migration: Mexico and the United States,* edited by Richard C. Jones, pp. 33–57. Boston: Rowman and Allanheld.

Kelly, Thomas J. 2001. Neoliberal reforms and rural poverty. *Latin American Perspectives* 118, vol. 28 (3): 84–103.

Kopinak, Kathryn. 1994. The maquiladorization of the Mexican economy. In Grinspun and Cameron 1994b, pp. 141–61.

La Botz, Dan. 1997. Mexico at a turning point, part 2: Deeper crisis and blocked reforms. *Against the Current* 12 (January–February): 31–35.

Lagunes, Lucia. 1997. Insólita cotidiana. *Doble Jornada,* special insert to *La Jornada* (Mexico City), August 4, 1997, p. 7.

La Jornada. 1997. Las maquiladoras. May 12, p. 22.

Lefebvre, Henri. 1978. *De lo rural a lo urbano.* Barcelona: Ediciones Peninsulares.

———. 1994. *Everyday life in the modern world.* New Brunswick, NJ: Transaction.

Lomnitz, Larissa. 1994. Urban women's work in three social strata: The informal economy of social networks and social capital. In *Color, class, and country: Experiences of gender,* edited by Gay Young and Bette J. Dickerson, pp. 53–69. London: Zed Books.

Malkin, Victoria. 1999. La reproducción de las relaciones de género en la comunidad de migrantes mexicanos en New Rochelle, Nueva York.

In *Fronteras fragmentadas*, edited by Gail Mummert, pp. 475–96. Zamora, Mexico: Colegio de Michoacán.

Martínez, Fabiola, and Alonso Urrutia. 1998. Exigen centrales obreras revisar el TLC y el acuerdo laboral. *La Jornada* (Mexico City), January 24, 1998, p. 47.

Marx, Karl. [1867] 1967. *Capital*. Vol. 1. New York: International.

Massey, Douglas S., Luin Goldring, and Jorge Durand. 1994. Continuities in transnational migration: An analysis of nineteen Mexican communities. *American Journal of Sociology* 99 (6): 1492–1533.

Massolo, Alejandra. 1982. *Por amor y coraje: Mujeres en movimientos urbanos de la ciudad de México*. Mexico City: Colegio de México.

Muñoz, Patricia, and Judith Calderón. 1997. Salarios y empleo, afectados por el TLC. *La Jornada* (Mexico City), April 29, 1997, p. 19.

Nathan, Debbie. 1999. Work, sex, and danger in Ciudad Juárez. *NACLA* 33 (3): 24–30.

Olivares, Patricia. 1997. Las costureras—muy mal pagadas—son el soporte de la economía en talleres clandestinos. *La Jornada* (Mexico City), November 3, 1997, pp. 4–5.

Peña, Devon G. 1997. *The terror of the machine: Technology, work, gender, and ecology on the U.S.-Mexico border*. Austin, TX: Center for Mexican American Studies.

Petras, James, and Henry Veltmeyer. 1999. Latin America at the end of the millennium. *Monthly Review* 51 (3): 31–52.

Powers, Mary G., William Selzer, and Jing Shi. 1998. Gender differences in the occupational status of undocumented immigrants in the United States: Experience before and after legalization. *International Migration Review* 32 (4): 1015–46.

Proctor, Sharon, and Kerry Preibisch. 2000. Emerging patterns in rural Mexico: Experiences from two regions. Paper presented at the Twenty-second Congress of the Latin American Studies Association, Miami, FL, March 16–18.

Román, José Antonio. 1997. Dirigidos por mujeres, casi 3.4 milliones de hogares: Conapro. *La Jornada* (Mexico City), May 15, 1997, p. 48.

Rosen, Fred, and Dierdre McFadyen, eds. 1995. *Free trade and economic restructuring in Latin America*. New York: Monthly Review Press.

Saffioti, Heleieth I. B. 1978. *Women in class society*. New York and London: Monthly Review Press.

Selby, Henry, Arthur D. Murphy, and Stephen A. Lorenzen. 1990. *The Mexican urban household: Organizing for self-defense*. Austin: University of Texas Press.

Shields, Rob. 1999. *Lefebvre, love, and struggle: Spatial dialectics*. London: Routledge.

Smith, Robert. 1998. Mexicans in New York: Membership and incorporation in a new immigrant community. In *Latinos in New York: Communities in transition*, edited by Gabriel Haslip-Viera and Sherriel L. Baver, pp. 57–103. Notre Dame, IN: University of Notre Dame Press.

Steinsleger, José. 1998. Las madres de la maquila. *La Jornada* (Mexico City), May 19, 1998, p. 39.

Tiano, Susan. 1994. *Patriarchy on the line: Labor, gender, and ideology in the Mexican maquila industry*. Philadelphia: Temple University Press.

Urrutia, Alonso. 1998. Generan maquiladoras 800 mil plazas. *La Jornada* (Mexico City), April 12, 1998, p. 35.

Ward, Kathryn B. 1988. Women in the global economy. In *Women and work: An annual review*. Vol. 3, edited by Barbara A. Gutek, Ann H. Stromberg, and Laurie Larwood, pp. 17–48. Newbury Park, CA: Sage.

Wright, Melissa W. 2001. The dialectics of still life: Murder, women, and maquiladoras. In *Millennial capitalism and the culture of neoliberalism*, edited by Jean Comaroff and John L. Comaroff, pp. 125–45. Durham, NC, and London: Duke University Press.

6. Haitian Women in the New World Order

April Ane Knutson

Today the poorest country in the Western hemisphere, Haiti's glorious history as the first black republic in the world and the first to rid itself of slavery has been sadly obscured. Knutson highlights this notable feature of Haiti's past and its independence from French rule in 1804, explaining how this example of self-emancipation resulted in Haiti's economic isolation by Western powers, including the United States. It was not until after the Civil War when slave labor was freed in the United States that the latter could begin investing in Haiti. Invaded and occupied by the United States from 1915 to 1934 and again in 1994, Haiti today bears all the marks of a nation that has been subjected to maldevelopment.

Knutson's essay focuses on the ways in which women, traditionally producers and merchants, are made to bear the burden of an International Monetary Fund–mandated policy of neoliberalism that ultimately favors U.S. corporations. Constituting 90 percent of workers in clothing assembly plants, women are notoriously under- paid at two dollars for eight hours' work. Those in the informal sector of production struggle for survival by vending staples, such as rice, that are imported from the

United States. Under pressure to grow mangoes and coffee to pay its foreign debt, Haiti imports rice from North Carolina. In the second half of the article, Knutson shifts from the socioeconomic to the cultural arena, drawing out examples from literary works to show how their themes serve to reflect preoccupying questions: of identity, of language, and of neocolonialism.

INTRODUCTION

The women of Haiti are a source of dirt-cheap labor for multinational corporations. With the support and frequent intervention of the U.S. military machine, U.S. corporations have plundered the resources and impoverished the people of this tiny island nation, which is by far the poorest country in the Western Hemisphere. Yannick Etienne, a leading trade union organizer for the largely female workforce in the assembly plants in Port-au-Prince, notes that the Haitian bourgeoisie and the U.S. occupation force have the same objectives: "That is to preserve the old social order, impose a neoliberal order, and block popular demands for the fundamental transformation of Haiti" (cited in Coughlin 1999, p. 20).

To fully appreciate Etienne's analysis of the goals of U.S. imperialism working hand in glove with the Haitian bourgeoisie, it is necessary to briefly review the history of Haiti before examining the current situation, especially the economic conditions in which women workers—and women labor organizers like Yannick Etienne—play a key role. The analysis of the economy includes a look at the growing informal economic sector, as well as the operations of U.S. corporations in Haiti. After an examination of IMF policies toward Haiti, contrasting models of alternative development proposed and partially enacted by the Lavalas movement are shown. In discussing the Lavalas movement, we will also look at its language of revolution and the role women played in the movement. To better understand the cultural consequences of the economic devastation of Haiti, it is enlightening to review Haitian literature, especially novels written by women under the U.S. occupations of Haiti, during both the first occupation (1915–1934) and the contemporary occupation, which began in 1994. Finally, we will briefly sketch the current economic and political situation in Haiti.

HISTORY

Haiti has a glorious and tragic history. The first black republic in the world and the first population to emancipate itself from slavery and colonial rule, Haiti became an independent state in 1804. Isolated by its former colonial masters, the French, and shunned by all other Western powers, including the United States, Haiti struggled for survival as markets for its sugar, coffee, and indigo were cut off. In the last years of the eighteenth century, just before the French Revolution and the Haitian War of Emancipation and Independence, Haiti (then known as the French colony Saint Domingue) produced three-fourths of the world's sugar and two-thirds of the world's coffee (James 1989, pp. 45–46; Farmer 1994, pp. 62–63). This unprecedented productivity gave France enormous wealth; in fact, Haiti produced more wealth than all the British colonies in the Western Hemisphere combined.

This wealth was created by slave labor on large plantations, with both men and women working in the vast fields of sugar cane. A small number of slaves, both men and women, worked in the mansions of the French owners. These relatively privileged slaves lived longer lives and in some cases learned to read and write French, as did Toussaint Louverture, the leader of the revolution. The house slaves, both men and women, were active in resistance to the worst abuses of slavery, often poisoning particularly brutal owners. Both men and women slaves were brutally tortured if suspected of acts of resistance or if caught while trying to flee the plantation. Even pregnant women were mercilessly beaten, though a hole was dug to shield her swollen belly as she lay face down on the ground to receive her punishment.

On the eve of the August 1791 insurrection, there were 452,000 slaves in Haiti, more than two-thirds of whom had been born in Africa (James 1989, p. 56). C. L. R. James has vividly described the rigors of the plantation system of production, under which one-third of the labor force died every three years (1989, chap. 1). Some slaves, mostly men, escaped to the mountains, where they formed maroon communities. Some women joined them, and they began reproducing. James estimates that there were at least three thousand fugitive slaves by 1751, the year of the first rebellion, led by the maroon chief Mackandal (ibid., p. 20). By 1791, the maroons and the slaves had found ways to communicate with each other and to organize the revolution that began on the night of August 22, after a voodoo ceremony led by Boukman, a high priest and headman of a plantation near Cap Haïtien, then called Le Cap François, the colonial capital. Immediately following the ceremony, maroons and slaves began to destroy the plantations around Le Cap. "In a few days one-half of the famous North Plain was a flaming ruin" (ibid., p. 88), and within four years, the slaves, with the collaboration of the maroons and the free mulattos, had control of the whole colony. Toussaint Louverture, who had become the general of the armies of liberation in the fall of 1791, proclaimed himself governor of Saint Domingue in 1796.

That such an oppressed, enslaved working class succeeded in emancipating itself caused panic among imperialist powers and capitalist owners of the means of production around the world. The Colonial Pact, under which colonies provided raw materials at very low prices to the developed capitalist world, had been broken (Luc 1976, p. 31). Furthermore, the slave system of production had been successfully challenged. In 1804, of course, slavery was firmly established on all the other islands of the Caribbean: British,

French, and Spanish possessions alike. And slavery was still the mode of production in the southern United States. The United States was not just pleasing its allies by refusing to recognize and trade with Haiti; economic interest compelled the U.S. government to prevent contact between slaves in the South and self-emancipated men and women of African descent in Haiti.

A century later, after the U.S. Civil War and the emancipation of African American labor, the United States felt free to deal with Haiti, and U.S. companies began to invest in Haiti, buying up large tracts of land for cultivation of sugar and bananas. Luc, citing Lenin, notes that imperialist policy changed at the end of the nineteenth century, when the exportation of capital, rather than the export of goods, became primary. Luc asserts that Haiti was particularly attractive to U.S. capitalists because they were investing in a place close to home where they could maximize their profits. As early as 1910, U.S. corporations began buying up land at ridiculously low prices in order to set up banana plantations (ibid., p. 32).

When peasants began organizing to regain possession of the land, the United States declared an "unstable situation" that threatened the security of the Caribbean. Soon U.S. troops invaded and occupied Haiti, an occupation that lasted from 1915 to 1934. As many as fifteen thousand political leaders and organizers were murdered by U.S. troops in the initial stages of the invasion and occupation (ibid., pp. 97–98). During this brutal imperialist siege, in 1918, a young Franklin Delano Roosevelt, then undersecretary of the navy, wrote a new constitution for the people of Haiti (ibid., p. 93). This ensured continuing U.S. control of the political situation and wide-open access to the land and labor of Haiti for U.S. corporations.

ECONOMIC DOMINATION
AND SUPEREXPLOITATION
OF WOMEN WORKERS

Micheline Labelle has studied the multiple economic consequences of the first U.S. occupation. First of all, German and French capitalist investments were eliminated. In agriculture, there was a consolidation of the great landed properties, especially on the plains, where U.S. companies secured a monopoly in the production of sugar, bananas, and other fruits, as well as sisal. Peasants were dispossessed, and forced labor on roads was reinstated. The expropriation of peasant land brought about the break-up of the peasant class; the proletarization of agricultural and seasonal labor; migrations by both men and women to the Dominican Republic and Cuba, which served the interests of international capital on those islands, for Haitian labor was the cheapest; and the lumpenproletarization of the masses in the cities, especially Port-au-Prince (Labelle 1978, p. 59).

On the eve of the second U.S. military occupation of Haiti, in 1994, U.S. companies were by far the largest investors in Haiti, with a total amount estimated at $120 million, constituting 90 percent of all foreign investment. There are sixty-six U.S. companies that have set up clothing assembly plants in Haiti (National Labor Committee Education Fund, cited in Black 1994). Yannick Etienne, an organizer for Batay Ouvriye, the union for clothing assembly workers, described these plants during visits to the United States to gain support for her union. In October 1999, in a presentation at the Resource Center for the Americas in Minneapolis, she said that there were around one hundred assembly factories in Port-au-Prince that export products, mostly cheap apparel sold in Walmart and K-Mart. Disney products are also assembled in Haiti, notably the Pocahontas dolls.

The Haitian workers who sew clothing together (e.g., sewing sleeves on T-shirts) are overwhelmingly female, at least 90 percent.

Etienne says that employers think men are too militant. Many women workers are recent arrivals in the capital city, having left the rural areas because the land is less productive and can no longer support a family. Most left school after the eighth grade; their only employment possibilities are as maids or factory workers. They work without a contract; they don't know their salary; and they are not informed of any rights. Most earn two dollars a day for eight hours of work. They can earn as much as five dollars a day for piece work, for example, sewing two hundred dozen collars on boys' shirts, but for that they must work much longer than eight hours.

These are miserable wages, way below poverty level in the United States; but for Haitian women, these are good wages in a country where the average annual income is under three hundred dollars—that is, less than a dollar a day. In a country where the official unemployment figures stand at 68 percent, women in these U.S. off-shore assembly plants feel lucky to be employed. They put up with a complete lack of benefits and security, as well as improper ventilation or lighting. Since they have no electrical lighting at home and live with their children in hovels on streets that have become open sewers, their working conditions probably seem pretty good.

According to Yannick Etienne, the U.S. embassy characterizes these assembly enterprises as important to the development of Haiti. Yet these enterprises contribute to Haiti's trade deficit and pay no taxes or tariffs under the "in transit" provisions of the Reagan-era Caribbean Basin Initiative. The presence of these enterprises in Haiti is doing nothing to help the society as a whole: creating no tax base to help provide education, medical care, and other basic services; no revenues to repair the infrastructure of crumbling roads and overwhelmed sanitation systems; nor to undertake a modern electrification program. With the rapid influx of millions to Port-au-Prince and other urban centers, the city streets are filled with garbage, animal waste, and human excrement. In both Port-au-Prince and Cap Haïtien, the population has tripled in the last five years. As more and more impoverished people leave the country-side, the agricultural base continues to deteriorate. The U.S. corporations that do take an interest in agriculture are of course encouraging production for export, not production for self-sufficiency, and thus are not promoting sustainable agriculture. Deforestation and erosion continue as the peasants who have not yet left the land cut trees for fuel and to fashion into charcoal, a cash commodity sold by vendors throughout Haiti.

THE INFORMAL ECONOMIC SECTOR

Vendors of charcoal, produce, used clothes, soap, and other household necessities make up the informal sector of production, a system of survival for the millions of formally unemployed in Haiti. According to Melinda Miles, writing for the newsweekly *Haiti Progress*, "the informal economy in Haiti is a direct result of the policies and programs that have been forced on the country by the government of the United States and the international financial institutions, most notably the International Monetary Fund" (1999). Miles states that plans to make Haiti the "Taiwan of the Caribbean" began in the eighties, when loans were made with the conditions of setting up export-oriented industries, such as the clothing assembly plants. At the same time, used U.S. goods were dumped on Haiti. Writing in *The Nation*, Dan Coughlin calculates that "in 1998, U.S. firms exported more than 16.5 million pounds of used clothes to Haiti and just about everybody wears them" (1999, p. 20). Miles describes the street scene in Port-au-Prince:

> Walking through downtown Port-au-Prince's boulevards is a lot like walking through a yard sale in North American suburbia. Everywhere you look you see second-hand clothes, and piles of old shoes and leather belts. These items, used and thrown away by consumers in the U.S., are what constitutes the majority of the merchandise in Haiti's informal economy. They undercut local

products and cause tailors and shoe makers to lose their liveli-hoods. These now unemployed skilled craftspeople find them-selves peddling lower quality products. The informal economy in Haiti has really become a viscous [*sic*] cycle—the very items keeping the unemployed alive through "informal" labor were what cost them their jobs in the first place.

The same chaotic, desperate street scene is played out in Cap Haïtien, the second-largest city, whose population, like that of Port-au-Prince, has tripled in recent years. At the break of dawn, women and young girls, balancing huge baskets filled with garage-sale merchandise on their heads, leave tumbledown shacks by the sea and walk the filthy streets in search of a spot on a strategic corner of downtown Cap. Once situated, they unpack their baskets, display their merchandise, staying out in the heat all day until the sun begins to set or (rarely) until they have sold all their goods. They use their small sales revenue to buy food for the evening meal (usu-ally rice and beans) on the way home to their waiting children. They also have to buy water. Everyone drinks Culligan water in Haiti—there is *no* safe drinking water.

INTERNATIONAL MONETARY FUND POLICIES

The rice that these women vendors of the informal sector purchase with the money they earned by selling used clothes is also dumped in Haiti. Rather than encouraging the cultivation of rice and other essential foodstuffs, the new world order insists that Haiti import rice from the United States. As participant and translator for a Pastors for Peace delegation to Haiti in January 1997, I interviewed Father Jean Yves Urifyé, a teacher in the Petit Séminaire (a Catholic middle school for boys) in Port-au-Prince and founder of the first Creole newspaper in Haiti, *Libète*. Urifyé believes strongly that

Haiti should not be dependent on imported food, that it should instead be embarking on a project to grow four times more rice; however, with pressure from the IMF, Haiti is growing more mangoes and coffee for export and importing rice from North Carolina, from distributors with ties to North Carolina senator Jesse Helms.

Father Urifyé also discussed the slaughter of Haitian Creole pigs and the importation of pigs from Iowa. Under the direction of USAID officials in Haiti, who claimed to have detected an outbreak of African swine fever, more than six hundred thousand Haitian pigs were killed in 1978. This was a devastating blow to the peasants' livelihood, for, as many rural organizers told us, the pigs were a family's savings account, used to barter for essential items and a source of food if crops failed. The peasants were never compensated for the slaughtered pigs; rather, they were expected to purchase, house, and feed huge white pigs from Iowa that could not scavenge for food as the little black Creole pigs had done; in addition, the imported pigs needed to be protected from the burning tropical sun. Since the people could not afford to purchase and raise these pigs, pork production became an industry in Haiti, controlled by U.S. corporations. And the internal migration from the rural areas to Port-au-Prince and other urban areas began in earnest.

This first slaughter of pigs was executed under the Duvalier *fils* regime (Baby Doc), but when we met with representatives of the Assemblée Popilaire Nationale (APN), the largest peasant organization, in Plaisance in January 1997, they claimed that similar schemes to force people off the land were being carried out under the Préval administration. Creole pigs, reintroduced to Haiti from Jamaica, were being vaccinated against swine fever, and many were dying from the shots. Others were getting sick from pesticide sprays being used under USAID programs. People on the land just don't have enough to eat, we were told. Their staple food was yams, and often that was all they ate, having lost their small plots of land where they grew beans and other legumes during the coup of 1991 that removed Aristide from power. Most peasants now work for large landowners, cultivating cash crops for export—bananas, sugar, and tobacco.

ALTERNATIVE DEVELOPMENT MODELS

A visit with Moïse Jean-Charles, the mayor of Milot, a small town in the Département du Nord, not far from Cap Haïtien, acquainted us with an alternative rural development model. Here the people resisted the takeover of land during the coup and won. Supported by a militant peasant organization whose leader had just been elected mayor, the people liberated the land not only from the military but also from the corporations that controlled the production. Jean-Charles asserted that women took a leading role in the peasant organization and the liberation efforts, especially during the initial terror of the 1991 coup, because the male leaders were forced underground. Women remain active and some are still in top leadership positions, directing the alternative development of the land. Now, instead of growing sugar and tobacco for export, the people are growing rice and corn for consumption. People are not hungry, and children are not dying of malnutrition in Milot, Jean-Charles said. During the Duvalier regime, five or six children died every day in Milot from hunger and disease. Milot has a public health center funded by Canada yet privatized by military commanders during the coup. When Jean-Charles became mayor, the town took control of the clinic and opened its doors, providing free services and medications to the poor.

Milot is an isolated island of progressive reform amidst an ocean of stagnation, corruption, and misery. The Lavalas movement, headed by Jean-Bertrand Aristide, had proposed an alternative model of development for the whole country that would have transformed Haiti into a participatory democracy following a basic-needs or growth-with-equity model of economic development. Opération Lavalas, the political movement that elected Aristide in 1990, published concrete proposals for change: *La chance qui passe* (The Chance That Is Passing By) and *La chance à prendre* (The Chance to Take) (Dupuy 1997, p. 93). The titles indicate the movement's awareness of the necessity to act quickly, to seize the moment to enact sweeping reforms. The Lavalas Project was presented to the International Monetary Fund in April 1991. Implementation of the program was to take place during the five years of Aristide's term of office, but the coup d'état ended this government after only seven months. Nevertheless, significant reforms were enacted.

Paul Farmer succinctly itemizes the problems facing the Lavalas government: "the worst health indices in the hemisphere, a moribund economy, widespread illiteracy, landlessness, the exploitation of workers, unemployment, ecological devastation, a bloated and ineffective public administration, and, most of all, the entrenched gangsterism and drug trafficking closely linked to the army" (1994, p. 167). Farmer then proceeds to detail the enormous accomplishments of those few months of democratic reform government. An adult literacy campaign was immediately launched throughout the country. Public health became a priority, with the restructuring of major hospitals and the creation of a Ministry of Health. A program of land distribution was begun, with allocation of fallow lands to peasant families. Official ombudsmen were appointed to settle land disputes, while the position of *chèf de section* was dissolved. This reform was hailed by the rural masses as a revolutionary change, for the section chiefs had long abused human rights in their crushing of any challenge to their absolute power to determine land rights and use. Aristide also initiated other measures for agrarian reform, including expanded credits and loans for peasants and programs for reforestation and other means to halt erosion of the soil. Perhaps the most controversial reform—and the one most opposed by the Haitian bourgeoisie and U.S. corporations—was raising the minimum wage from fifteen to twenty-five gourdes a day—still less than three dollars (Farmer 1994, pp. 167–69).

In his speech before the United Nations on September 25, 1991, just five days before the coup d'état that toppled his government, Aristide outlined ten democratic commandments, including the right to eat and the right to a job, and enunciated the principles of his administration: "justice, participation, and openness" (Dupuy 1997, p. 94). He maintained that the three necessary conditions for a participatory democracy were decentralization of the government, a massive literacy campaign, and agrarian reform.

The growth-with-equity approach to development proposed by Aristide and the Lavalas movement was not a program for socialism. In fact, according to Alex Dupuy, it was a moderate reform program, within the framework of capitalism, which respected private property. But it did challenge the World Bank model:

> The basic-needs approach begins by redefining development in class terms since it assumes that the development process is not neutral vis-à-vis the class interests it primarily serves. In contrast to the World Bank's free trade model, which clearly promotes the interests of foreign capital and the domestic dominant classes, the growth-with-equity model gives preeminence to satisfying the basic needs of the majority—the peasants, workers, women, unemployed, poor, and small traders and entrepreneurs. It is they who bear the heaviest burdens of underdevelopment and poverty in the Caribbean region. (1997, p. 95)

LANGUAGE AND REVOLUTIONARY CHANGE

As Dupuy analyzes in detail, Aristide's rhetoric was often much more confrontational, even revolutionary, than the programs submitted to the parliament and the international finance institutions. For instance, in speeches to his supporters, Aristide often referred to the International Monetary Fund (*Fond Monétaire International* in French and Creole) as the *Front de Misère Internationale* (the Front for International Misery) (Dupuy 1997, p. 121). This rhetoric signaled a collision course with the IMF and international capital, while his ministers were trying to gain acceptance of a compromise program for reform. Aristide's public discourse was always radical, whether on the newly organized Creole radio stations, at public rallies, or in the homilies he delivered in his church in the worst slum in the Western Hemisphere, Cité Soleil. "Yon sèl nou fèb. Ansam nou fò. Ansanm ansam nou se lavalas." (Alone we are weak. Together we are strong. All together we are *lavalas*.)

The Lavalas movement's very name was radical: first, because it was a Creole word that became a political force and later a (brief-lived) reality in a country whose public discourse had always been in French; second, because it signified a cleansing flood that would sweep away all the criminal, corrupt institutions and practices of the Duvalier era. Right after Baby Doc fled to France aboard a U.S. military jet, the popular organizations called for a *dechoukaj*, an uprooting of the entrenched powers, particularly the terrorist thugs of the National Security Police, known as the *Tontons Macoutes*. In Creole, this signifies bogeyman, for "Uncle" Macoute appeared often in children's fairy tales as the ogrelike figure who roamed around at night carrying a bag on his shoulder stuffed with children stolen from their homes. Duvalier's security forces usually came at night to people's homes and carried away young trade unionists, peasant organizers, dissidents, and community activists. To this day, the *Tontons Macoutes* have not been completely uprooted, nor washed away. Many of their leaders took part in the 1991 coup against Aristide's Lavalas government, and some of the rank and file are in the newly organized national police force, trained by the U.S. military occupation force, and are engaged in drug trafficking (Coughlin 1999, pp. 21–22). One of the principal demands of the popular organizations—and of Préval's government—is that the United States turn over the 150,000 pages of documents seized from the Haitian army and FRAPH death squad offices during the initial stages of the 1994 invasion and occupation. The Clinton administration refused to release these documents to Haitian parliamentary and judiciary authorities who want to hold hearings and start trials of those responsible for the coup and the three years of violence and terror. The U.S. ambassador to Haiti told the Pastors for Peace delegation that the release of the documents would compromise U.S. security and intelligence operations (interview with William Swing, U.S. embassy, January 29, 1997).

WOMEN'S ROLE IN THE REVOLUTIONARY STRUGGLE

Despite the violent overthrow of the Lavalas government and the military occupation by the giant bully neighbor to the north, Haitian people continue to organize and struggle. They are proud of their historic achievements and vow to fulfill what they see as their historic destiny—establishing a free, progressive Afro-Caribbean society. Women have been active in the latest struggles to uproot tyranny and corruption. In his 1992 book, *Théologie et politique* (Theology and Politics), Jean-Bertrand Aristide devotes the last section to a praise of women. Without women's participation, he emphasizes over and over again, the whole Lavalas campaign would not have been possible.

Aristide begins his homage to women by discussing an apparent contradiction: the celibacy of his state as a Catholic priest kept him in a masculine world, but life put him in contact with a feminine world, for women are the majority participants at religious ceremonies and celebrations. He soon realized the potential and talents that women possessed for inspiring and leading a political movement, and he encouraged them to lead people from the church out into the street. Many of the commentators on the revolutionary Creole radio programs were women community leaders (Aristide 1992, pp. 117–20). Young women were particularly active in forming and sustaining neighborhood organizations among the youth, such as *Solidarite ant Jèn* (ibid., p. 123).

Aristide, always mindful of symbolic imagery on public occasions, chose a peasant woman to play a key role in his historic inauguration on February 7, 1991. Alex Dupuy describes and interprets the scene: "To symbolize that things had changed and that henceforth the poor and excluded masses would be included and made a priority, the new president chose a peasant woman to put the presidential sash on him. The next morning, President Aristide served breakfast to hundreds of homeless people and street kids invited to the National Palace. There is little doubt that for the wealthy Haitian elite, who abhor the common Haitian people, these two gestures alone justified all their hatred of Aristide" (1997, p. 110).

In *Théologie et politique*, Aristide praises not only the political contributions of women but also their key economic role. His choice of a peasant woman to install the presidential sash may have reflected his understanding that women are the backbone of the Haitian economy, toiling on the land to feed the people. Women are both producers and merchants, he writes, and then evokes the popular figure of Haitian folklore, *Madanm Sara*, the trader who transports foodstuffs and other essential products from one region of Haiti to another (Aristide 1992, p. 127). David Nicholls defines Madam Sara as "the agent that establishes contact between urban consumers and rural producers" and describes a typical business trip of this key economic player: buying avocados, poultry, pork, and syrup in Marbial; selling this produce in Jacmel, where she buys oranges, rice, maize, and beans; selling those products in Port-au-Prince, where she buys cloth, clothing, soap, and hardware; selling all this in the rural areas north and west of the capital; then returning to the peninsula to start the cycle over again (1985, p. 126). Women, Nicholls confirms, dominate the vegetable and fruit markets in all trading areas and handle the family cash (ibid., p. 126).

HAITIAN LITERATURE:
PORTRAITS OF STRONG WOMEN
AND VICTIMS

In a recently (1994) published collection of short stories titled *Tante Résia et les dieux* (Aunt Résia and the Gods), Yanick Lahens, a teacher, editor, and director of cultural programs, gives us a rich portrait of the woman trader. Tante Résia is an independent woman, who travels freely all over Haiti and into the Dominican Republic and other Caribbean nations to gather goods to sell in her store in Acul du Nord, a seacoast town in the north of Haiti. Her store is a neighborhood gathering place, where people come not only to buy much-needed goods but also to renew social and cultural ties. Tante Résia helps the community to preserve the customs of their ancestors and to organize voodoo ceremonies. She has also hidden political organizers and schoolteachers targeted by the Duvalier regime.

Haitian literature of the twentieth century reflects the beauty and horror of this land and her people's history. At the beginning of the century, on the eve of the first U.S. occupation, Jean Price Mars founded a literary journal called *La Revue des Griots*, dedicated to the rediscovery and revalorization of the oral tradition of Haitian culture. Up to this time, most Haitian literature had been a pale imitation of French literature, as only the writings of the Paris-educated elite were published. *Griot* refers to the traditional African storyteller, the historian of the tribe. At about the same time, Jacques Roumain, agricultural engineer, ethnologist, political activist, and founder of the Haitian Communist Party, began publishing intensely political poetry committed to social progress and the independence of Haiti. His most famous work, the novel *Gouverneurs de la Rosée* (published in English as *Masters of the Dew*), is an epic account of the struggle of Haitian peasants against poverty and superstition to regain control of their land and their lives. When the hero is killed, it is a woman, his lover and the mother of his child, who leads the people to find water and build canals to bring life to their dying fields.

Novels written during the first U.S. occupation reveal the effects of U.S. control of the land and the people, both physical and psychological domination. As Myrian Chancy writes, "The occupation changed Haitian literature which had not up to that point textually engaged its northern neighbor" (1997, p. 17). Many writers were radicalized by this first-hand experience with colonization and devalorization.

Two of the more notable writers of this period were women: Virgile Valcin and Annie Desroy. Valcin published novels and poetry and founded a feminist journal, *Voix des femmes* (Women's Voices). Desroy wrote plays, two of which were produced under the U.S. occupation, and four novels. Valcin's novel, *La blanche négresse* (The White Negress), recounts the history of a light-skinned French-Haitian woman who marries an American during the occupation; he is horrified when he discovers her African ancestry. The novel reveals the heightened racism brought by the U.S. occupation, when questions of race trumped class: the heroine's privileged class status in Haitian society—and all the social, cultural, and educational advantages she enjoyed—were suddenly wiped out by the fact that she was black.

In his collection of selected essays titled *Racism, Imperialism, and Peace*, Herbert Aptheker demonstrates that eras of imperialist conquest in U.S. history coincide with eras of increased racist repression in the colony and at home. The mass lynchings of African American males in the South occurred right after the U.S. victory in the Spanish-American War and the annexation of Puerto Rico and the Philippines (1987, p. 136).

Annie Desroy's novel *Le joug* (The Yoke), published in 1934, examines in a more complex fashion the effects of the U.S. occupation on the Haitian psyche. Through the lives of two couples, one American and the other Haitian, Desroy traces the dynamics of racial, sexual, and class oppression during the occupation. Through the character of an American officer, Harry Murray, who considers himself a liberal protector of the Haitian people and can hardly wait to be taken to a voodoo ceremony, Desroy exposes the exoticism and profound condescension of the U.S. fascination with Haitian culture. Moreover, Desroy demonstrates that class and racial privilege exists side by side with a sexist ideology that posits Haitian women as erotic creatures who respond to acts of violence.

Under the current occupation, women are again writing the most trenchant testimonies of the noxious effects of U.S. troops on their soil. Some of these women writers are now publishing in Haiti. Haiti now has several publishing houses, so Haitian writers are no longer dependent on French editors for publication of their works.

Yanick Lahens, whose character Tante Résia has already been described, was born in Haiti and educated in France, but unlike many of the Haitian intelligentsia and cultural workers, she returned to Haiti after completing her degree in literature and stayed in Haiti. She has worked as a teacher, an editor, and director of cultural programs on Haitian radio. She has also published several important articles on Caribbean literature.

Lahens has written a second collection of short stories, issued by a Haitian publishing house in Port-au-Prince in 1999. In these stories, U.S. influence is clear, and U.S. soldiers are key players in the dramas. The first story, "Le désastre banal" (The Banal Disaster), recounts the coming-of-age story of the teenaged girl Mirna, one of seven children in a desperately poor family in Port-au-Prince. Mirna sees the coming of the U.S. soldiers as her opportunity to acquire the clothes and makeup she sees in old-fashioned magazines stolen from secondhand stores: "pour elle, cette occupation serait un cadeau de destin" (for her, this occupation would be a gift of destiny) (Lahens 1999, p. 20). She begins dating U.S. soldiers; one of them, fifty-year-old William, takes her to a hotel by the sea, where she has sex for the first time. In the bathroom, Mirna "chercha plus tard à renouer les fils épars de son esprit" [later tried to stitch together the separated threads of her spirit]. Thinking of the dirty, smelly streets of her neighborhood, of her brothers and sisters always underfoot, of the absence of hope and privacy in her home, she is able to swallow the nausea she felt after sex with William and walk back to his bed wearing a mask "that would replace her face for the rest of her life."

Lahens entitles this story "The Banal Disaster" to imply that it is commonplace and perhaps of little interest compared to tales of terror and massacre. But it is nevertheless a disaster, devastating for the very reason that it is common that young women are selling their bodies and souls for a chance to wear a pretty dress and sleep in a luxurious bedroom.

The title story of this collection, "La petite corruption" (Small Corruption) is a fast-paced thriller that reveals the noxious effects of the U.S. culture of drugs and violence on a group of young Haitian men who have been caught up in drug deals, robbery, murder, and gang warfare.

The last story of the collection is perhaps the most interesting, from both a thematic and structural point of view. "Une histoire américaine" (An American Story) recounts the travels to the southern United States of a young Haitian woman who had escaped the violence of the Duvalier regime to study in New York City. There she met a civil rights activist from Alabama, a law student, who urged her to come with him on a tour of the South to speak to church groups and youth groups organizing for equality. The year is 1963. The story, told in the first person by the young Haitian woman Jocelyne, chronicles the difficulties and humiliations of traveling through the South, where blacks were not served in restaurants and could not stay in hotels. Every morning, before leaving one city, they must pack enough to eat and drink for the day's drive to the city of the next speaking engagement, where they will stay in the home of local organizers. In Birmingham, one of the organizers of the meeting at which they speak is slain later that night by a white mob. These episodes alternate with italicized passages of Jocelyne's memories of her adolescence in Haiti, where her first boyfriend is forced underground by the *Tonton Macoutes*. Textually, the message is clear: in the 1960s, political terror was practiced both in Haiti and in the United States, and the system that supported the Duvalier regime fosters racism, political repression, and terror at home.

As with all emerging literatures, the literature of Haiti raises questions of identity, memory, and language. Colonialism gobbled up territory and minds, eradicating culture, language, identity. Who are we? Who were we? Who will we become? And in what language should we express our experience? Lahens intersperses her stories with phrases in Creole, as does a second woman writer publishing in Haiti today, Jan J. Dominique, whose *Mémoire d'une amnésique* (Memoir of an Amnesiac) was published in 1984. She is a journalist with Radio Haiti and is the daughter of Haiti's most famous journalist, Jean Dominique, described by Amy Wilentz as "a tireless militant for democracy and a man who never kept silent" (2000). Her memoir is composed of alternating chapters, with two alternating narrative voices: one the author's, the other that of a woman named Paul. Preceding both narratives is a tale about a little boy who refuses to drink his milk until one day, out of desperation, his mother yells, "If you don't drink it, the Americans will take you away!" The little boy rushes out on the balcony and cries to the U.S. soldiers in the streets below, "No! No! Don't hurt me, Americans! I'll be good! I'll drink my milk!" Dominique is deliberately playing on the bogeyman story, told in many cultures to frighten children into obeying adults. But in Haiti, the bogeyman is *Tonton Macoute*, so the connection between U.S. domination and Duvalier terror is clear.

Soon after the publication of Lahens's *La petite corruption*, a letter appeared in one of Haiti's newspapers, *Le Nouvelliste*, under the heading "Littérature." The writer was a young working woman with the wonderful name Josiane Louverture, who lives in Carrefour-feuilles, a poor neighborhood in Port-au-Prince. She said she had never written to a newspaper before; in fact, she had never written before to anyone she didn't know personally, but she had to communicate with Lahens to tell her how much she appreciated her book. She wrote that she was not able to go to the university and that her schoolteachers had made her hate literature by only talking about dead writers. She has been working at odd jobs and sinking lower and lower and thought she must have forgotten everything she learned in school. But by chance, she discovered *La petite corruption*, and she was attracted to it because the author was a woman. She wants to express her gratitude for a book that taught her to love to read and reread and to think again and again about what she has read. She was afraid at first that she would be bored by the politics, but she came to like it. "Your book has done me so much good," she concludes. "There are certain stories that resemble my life a bit too much. Know that you have made a reader of me."

How gratified Yanick Lahens must feel! This is surely recompense for the hard choices she has made to stay in Haiti, to teach, work, and write under such difficult circumstances. So often, in discussing postcolonial literature, the question arises, who is the reader? And too often, the answer is the former or neocolonial master—especially when this literature is usually published in the capital of the former or neocolonial power and rarely available to the postcolonial population. In the unique case of Haiti, there is a population that threw off the shackles of colonialism and slavery nearly two centuries ago, long before the emerging nations of Africa, but it is a population that was alienated from a literature that for more than a century merely imitated French form and substance with almost no reference to Haitian reality. That changed with Price Mars and Roumain in the early years of the twentieth century, but their works, though centered in Haiti, were published in France, and the majority of the population was illiterate. Now, it seems, with Lahens leading the way, important works of necessarily political literature will be published in Haiti and will be read by young workers who will recognize their own lives and begin to understand the imperialist system that is oppressing them.

THE HAITIAN DIASPORA: INTELLECTUAL EXPATRIATES AND ECONOMIC REFUGEES

The Haitian diaspora has produced many important writers, though they are read more in their adopted countries, usually French-speaking Canada, than in Haiti. The first Haitian American author who writes in English, interspersed with Creole phrases, is a woman, Edwidge Danticat, who has been living in Brooklyn, New York, since the age of twelve. She has published a collection of short stories titled *Kric? Krac!* (1995) and two novels, *Breath, Eyes, Memory* (1994) and *The Farming of Bones* (1998). The first novel chronicles the journeys back and forth between Haiti and Brooklyn of a young Haitian American woman in search of her identity and the meaning of her mother's nightmare memories of rape and torture under the Duvalier regime. Although the narrator fully recognizes and relates the racism of the U.S. treatment of Haitian refugees, the direct support that the United States gave to the Duvalier regime is not mentioned.

The Farming of Bones is a historical novel of the 1937 slaughter of Haitian immigrant workers in the Dominican Republic by General Trujillo. The story is presented through the voice and perspective of a young Haitian woman working as a maid in the Dominican Republic, whose friends are Haitian sugarcane workers in the fields owned by her master. The text of the novel does not indicate the U.S. support of the Trujillo regime, but the inside covers reproduce letters written in French by the Haitian president Vincent to the Haitian foreign secretary, who was in New York at the time, asking him to secure U.S. help to stop the massacre. The United States did nothing. Danticat notes that these letters can be found in the Franklin Delano Roosevelt Library. However, these letters are not reproduced in the paperback edition of the novel, and Danticat's reference to them and to the FDR Library are expunged from the acknowledgments.

Displaced Haitian peasants, both men and women, no longer able to make a living on the land that is no longer theirs, are again going to the Dominican Republic as migrant farm workers. In fact, the Préval administration encouraged mass seasonal emigration to the Dominican Republic as a way to lower the unemployment rate in Haiti and to ease the stress on the infrastructure of Port-au-Prince and other cities. In a study of the exodus of Haitian peasants to Cuba and the Dominican Republic in the first decades of the twentieth century, Nicolas Hogar, a secretary to the Haitian ambassador in Washington, found a dramatic increase in emigrants at the time of the first U.S. occupation. In 1914, only 117 Haitians emigrated in search of farm work; in 1915, the first year of the occupation, 2490 left Haiti, and in 1916, 4878 Haitians left home, a land that was no longer theirs (Hogar [1955?], p. 189). Now, during the second U.S. occupation, Haitians are certainly not encouraged to go to Cuba; in fact, such seasonal migration would be prohibited by the terms of the U.S. embargo against Cuba. However, U.S. agricultural corporations in the Dominican Republic welcome Haitian *brazeros* to work on their lands for very low wages.

CURRENT POLITICAL AND ECONOMIC SITUATION

Current conditions in Haiti are even more dismal than in 1999, when the trade union organizer Yannick Etienne toured the United States to educate activists about the desperate situation in Haiti and to plead for aid. Even though Aristide and his party Lavalas Family handily won the presidential and legislative elections in November of 2000, his government has been recognized neither by the other political parties in Haiti, the ruling elite, nor the United States. The Caribbean Community (Caricom) has urged the end of economic sanctions and the release of loans from the IMF. Samuel Insanally of Guyana stated at a meeting of Caricom on February 7, 2002,

"Finally, let me say that the Caribbean, in dealing with the Haitian issue, felt that the government of that country should be given access to funds to help build the democratic pillars which the international community is demanding that it provide. The actions taken by President Aristide are in the right direction, and the release of the cut funds would assist in building, rebuilding democracy in Haiti" (quoted in *Haiti Report*, February 22, 2002). In the absence of funds for much-needed development projects to improve transportation, hygiene, public health, and education, Haitians will sink ever deeper into misery. In early February 2002, the IMF Board expressed "deep concern about the continued decline in per capita income and persistence of widespread poverty, the increase in the fiscal deficit and central bank financing, and the accumulation of external debt arrears" (quoted in *Haiti Report*, February 22, 2002).

It is hard to imagine a "continued decline in per capita income" in a country that already had the lowest per capita income, by far, in the Western Hemisphere. The internal migrations from the barren countryside to the filthy cities is continuing, the informal economic sector is expanding, and the miserable jobs offered by U.S. firms in offshore assembly plants must look even better to women desperate to feed, house, and clothe their children. The United States must be held accountable for the dire situation spawned by military occupations, brutal puppet regimes, and corporations who pay no taxes on value created by the labor of Haitian women.

CONCLUSION

Despite its unique beginning as the first black republic, comprised of the only self-emancipated slave population in world history, Haiti today faces problems similar to those of other so-called Third World countries. These countries are not merely underdeveloped; they have been deliberately maldeveloped by colonial masters, capitalist investors, imperialist armies of occupation, and "First World" financial institutions, notably the International Monetary Fund. The strategies of maldevelopment strip the land of natural resources; force people off the land and into sweatshops in the cities; deprive the people of education, health care, transportation, and sanitation; prevent them from organizing to improve their working conditions; and undermine, even topple, democratically elected progressive governments. Like other Afro-Caribbean nations and formerly colonized peoples around the world, Haitians have learned that the road to true independence is long and rocky, but they still hope that one day justice will prevail. Women such as trade unionist Yannick Etienne and writer Yanick Lahens are working to educate and organize their sisters and brothers for the struggles ahead.

REFERENCES

Aptheker, Herbert. 1987. *Racism, imperialism, and peace*. Minneapolis: MEP Publications.

Aristide, Jean-Bertrand. 1992. *Théologie et politique* (Theology and politics). Montreal: CIDIHCA.

Black, Eric. 1994. Questions and answers concerning U.S. in Haiti. *Star Tribune* (Minneapolis), October 1, 1994.

Chancy, Myriam J. A. 1997. Ayiti çé ter glissé: L'occupation américaine en Haïti et l'émergence de voix féminines en littérature (Virgile Valcin et Annie Desroy) [The American occupation in Haiti and the emergence of feminine voices in literature]. In *Elles écrivent des Antilles* (Women write about the Caribbean), edited by Suzanne Rinne and Joëlle Vitiello, pp. 17–36. Paris: L'Harmattan.

Coughlin, Dan. 1999. Haitian lament: Killing me softly. *Nation*, March 1, 1999.

Danticat, Edwidge. 1994. *Breath, eyes, memory*. New York: Vintage Contemporaries.

———. 1995. *Kric? Krac!* New York: Soho Press.

———. 1998. *The farming of bones*. New York: Soho Press.

Dominique, Jan J. 1984. *Mémoire d'une amnésique* (Memoir of an amnesiac). Port-au-Prince: Deschamps.

Dupuy, Alex. 1997. *Haiti in the new world order: The limits of the democratic revolution*. Boulder, CO: Westview Press.

Farmer, Paul. 1994. *The uses of Haiti*. Monroe, ME: Common Courage Press.

Haiti Reborn/Quixote Center. 2002. *Haiti Report*. February 22, 2002.

Hogar, Nicolas. [1955?]. *L'occupation américaine d'Haïti* (The American occupation of Haiti). Madrid[?].

James, C. L. R. 1989. *The black Jacobins*. New York: Random House.

Knutson, April Ane. 1999. "Reflections of U.S. imperialism in Haitian literature. *Nature, Society, and Thought* 12 (1): 115–24.

Labelle, Micheline. 1978. *Idéologie de couleur et classes sociales en Haïti* (Color ideology and social classes in Haiti). Montreal: Presses de l'Université de Montréal.

Lahens, Yanick. 1994. *Tante Résia et les dieux* (Aunt Résia and the gods). Paris: L'Harmattan.

———. 1999. *La petite corruption* (Small corruption). Port-au-Prince: Editions Mémoire.

Louverture, Josiane. 1999. Letter to Yanick Lahens. *Le Nouvelliste* (Port-au-Prince, Haiti), July 2–4.

Luc, Jean. 1976. *Structures économiques et lutte nationale populaire en Haïti* (Economic structures and the national popular struggle in Haiti). Montreal: Editions Nouvelle Optique.

Miles, Melinda. 1999. For debt relief without conditions. *Haïti Progrès* 17 (32) (October–November). http://www.haitiprogres.com/1999/sm991027/Eng1027.htm (accessed March 10, 2004).

Nicholls, David. 1985. *Haiti in Caribbean context: Ethnicity, economy, and revolt*. New York: St. Martin's Press.

Wilentz, Amy. 2000. Chaos and death swirling around Haiti. *Star Tribune* (Minneapolis), April 12, 2000.

7. Internationalization of Capital and the Trade in Asian Women
The Case of "Foreign Brides" in Taiwan

Hsiao-Chuan Hsia

The contemporary mail-order bride industry is generally known to involve men in the industrialized North seeking brides from poor nations in the South, a practice that stems from and mirrors international power relations. In this empirical study, Hsia draws attention to the marriage trade within the South itself. She locates its emergence in the particular ways that capitalism has developed that have installed Taiwan as the economic superior of neighboring Southeast Asian countries such as Indonesia, Vietnam, the Philippines, and Thailand.

Using a variety of sources and methodologies—official and media reports, participant observation, and indepth interviews—Hsia's readings of the more intimate personal data surrounding "commodified transnational marriages" remains linked throughout to a macroanalysis of capitalism and the theory of uneven development. Thus her view of "foreign brides" in Taiwan, while defined as an aspect of immigration, goes beyond the traditional "push-pull" framework of mainstream social science.

This article, then, devotes considerable space to the expansion of capital in Taiwan and the foregoing relations of dependency with its neighbors, whose economic devel-

opment was forced into either stagnation or collapse. The author states that it was precisely when Taiwan's outward-bound investment speeded up after 1987 that the phenomenon of Taiwanese men marrying Southeast Asian women began to take form and thrive. Thrown against this backdrop, it becomes clear how "marriage immigration" cannot but acquire its peculiar feature of gender inequality while simultaneously functioning to bolster the systemic inequalities that were its source.

In her interviews, Hsia gives her subjects the opportunities to talk about their marriages. We learn that Taiwanese men seeking foreign brides are agricultural and industrial workers whose low social status and limited time for socialization make them unattractive grooms for Taiwanese women. Foreign brides, on the other hand, explain their presence in Taiwan as a result of unstable economic and political conditions at home. Because these marriages are contracted as coping strategies for both parties, notions of a resulting "global village" are immediately eliminated. Instead, prevailing negative stereotypes in Taiwan about foreign brides are extended to their countries of origin and used as explanations for their failure to develop.

THE PHENOMENON

In recent years, paralleled with the impending threat of the General Agreement on Tariffs and Trade and the World Trade Organization to the agricultural economy and the exodus of labor-intensive industry, thousands of Taiwanese peasants and working-class men have been leaving the countryside in search of brides. Led by marriage brokers, they are transported to modern international airports, where their humble glances are immediately seized by an alien

The original English version of this paper was presented at the annual meeting of the American Sociological Association, August 12–16, 2000, in Washington, DC.

combination of luxurious lounges, complex and wordy immigration forms, and expressionless customs bureaucrats. Experiences like this are rare in their lives. Meanwhile, across the South Pacific, marriage brokers and matchmakers weave in and out of communities on the margins of cities and rural areas in Indonesia, Vietnam, and other Southeast Asian countries, encouraging young women to meet the men they hope to introduce. During the meetings, the men cast their anxious, searching glances, while the women act shyly and the matchmakers confidently try to sew the two together into a couple. Days later, the engagement ceremony is held. The men return to Taiwan to wait several months up to a year for their "foreign brides" to arrive.[1] Transnational marriages of this type require a long time and a large sum of money, many times half of the savings of a family from rural Taiwan. If a man successfully marries a woman, he must pay the broker a sum between US$10,000 and $15,000, only 10 percent of which goes to the bride's family as a dowry. Still, a dowry of this size is a considerable sum to families in Southeast Asian nations where wages are low.

This is not a new phenomenon. In the early eighties, men from rural areas in Taiwan began marrying brides from Thailand and the Philippines. By the end of the decade, the Taiwanese government stopped issuing visas to single women from Southeast Asia, since several women were caught engaging in prostitution after coming to Taiwan on tourist visas. Since then, Taiwanese men who want to marry foreign brides have to go to Southeast Asia. Since the early nineties, Indonesia has become the primary source of foreign brides in Taiwan. In each of the past few years, more than two thousand women from Indonesia have left their homes, heading to their imagined "prosperous paradise"—Taiwan. In order to reduce the number of Indonesian brides, the Taipei Economic and Trade Office in Indonesia slowed processing of visas for these women, making them even more anxious for their required interview for a visa to Taiwan. Many Indonesian brokers have therefore become impatient with the Taiwan government's slow pace and have increasingly matched Indonesian women with Hong Kong men instead; meanwhile, Taiwanese brokers have begun to turn their attention toward women in Vietnam, Cambodia, and other countries.

THE PROBLEMATIQUE

In Taiwan, "foreign brides" refer to Southeast Asian women married to Taiwanese men. In the media, such women are often portrayed as uneducated and from poor families, while their husbands are viewed as socially undesirable and thus incapable of finding Taiwanese brides. Their marriages are usually regarded simply as "trade marriages" by the media and are viewed as a source of social problems (Hsia 1997).

The idea that their marriages are a function of "trade" contributes to nothing but strengthening the stereotypes of "foreign brides" in Taiwan. Transnational marriages between the Taiwanese and Southeast Asians must be understood in the context of a larger process, not as an isolated phenomenon. In the United States, pictures of mail-order brides from Asia, Eastern Europe, and Russia are printed up in catalogs (Lai 1992; Glodava and Onizuka 1994), and the importation of women from the Philippines to Japan, Australia, and the former West Germany for marriage has become an issue of debate (Aguilar 1987; Cooke 1986; del Rosario 1994; Sato 1989). In patriarchal marriages, women have been regarded primarily as tools for reproduction for centuries. Situations of women from the peripheral countries in the world system are even more devastating—some being sold as sex commodities, others having to rely on transnational marriages as a way out of poverty. The foreign bride phenomenon in Taiwan also needs to be examined in this global context.

These types of transnational marriages are very different from those resulting from immigration, study abroad, and work. They involve not only women and men of different nationalities and cultures, but also marriage brokers and trade relations between the countries involved. In order to distinguish from other forms of trans-national marriages, I use "commodified transnational marriages" to refer to the "foreign bride" and "mail-order bride" phenomena.[2]

Commodified transnational marriages have existed for several decades. At the end of World War II, U.S. and European soldiers brought home many women from Third World countries. Still, there has been little systematic research into this widespread phe-nomenon. Little research on transnational marriages discusses the differences between commodified and noncommodified marriages, either completely ignoring the issue of the trade in brides (e.g., Brewer 1982; Rhee 1988; Rho 1989; Rousselle 1993), or confusing them with other types of transnational marriages (Donato 1988).

The phenomenon of foreign brides in Taiwan is most similar to that of mail-order brides in other countries. Most research into mail-order brides assumes it is a social problem and adopts a sympathetic attitude toward the women, describing in detail their unfortunate fate. However, this research often falls into the trap of constructing the women as "exotic others." For instance, in *Mail-Order Brides: Women for Sale*, Glodava and Onizuka strongly criticize common Western stereotypes of Asian women as "subservient, exotic man-pleasing creatures" (1994, p. 38), while at the same time uncon-sciously adopting other Western stereotypes. When analyzing the vio-lence these women face in the process of being "selected" as a mail-order bride, the authors posit that the women are "traditional" and therefore unwilling to forsake marriage or question whether their hus-bands deserve their respect and love. Being therapists themselves, Glodava and Onizuka are especially concerned that mail-order brides are not willing to seek help and professional therapy, because Asian values dictate them to be deferent to authority and have harmony within relationships (ibid., p. 109). This discourse implies that Asian women are the victims of Asian culture, and in order to become lib-erated, they must forsake their traditional culture and accept Western individualism. Their table titled "Asian Cross-Cultural Values and Assumptions Regarding Philosophy of Life and Implications for

Therapy" (ibid., p. 111) best depicts their position on cultural differences. This table dichotomizes values into "Asian/Pacific" versus "Western." In the Asian/Pacific column, characteristic values include suppression of individuality, fatalism, rigidity of role and status, and deference to authority, whereas in the Western column, the characteristics are independence, mastery of one's own fate, flexibility of role and status, and challenger of authority. By contrasting the "Asian" and the "Western" values and focusing on the "problems" Asian women have suffered, their cultural beliefs are established as the cause of their suffering; Asian cultures are thus depicted as inferior "others" that need the salvation of "Western" individualism.

Gender is the main axis of most studies, but the authors often establish those participating in these transnational marriages as distinguished from the rest of the population—they are the products of the "premodern" or "traditional" sexist values that have been left behind in the process of "modernization" (Sato 1989; Glodava and Onizuka 1994). Men who marry mail-order brides are constructed as "evil-doers" (e.g., del Rosario 1994). Sexism is definitely an important issue of commodified transnational marriages. However, scholars often only view the men as patriarchal actors, while dismissing their marginalized status in society, thus unwittingly perpetuating an existing classist image: only less-educated peasants and blue-collar men are so sexist (e.g., Cooke 1986) that they do not understand the true meaning of "modern" marriage.

Studies that view commodified transnational marriages as a social problem, or even an individual problem, lack a macroanalytical framework. Other studies, on the other hand, focus on structural trends and stress the unequal relationship between developed and underdeveloped countries as the root cause. One such study is "Women in the Political Economy of the Philippines" (Aguilar 1987) in which the author describes the parallel between prostitutes and mail-order brides, both of which are the results of U.S. colonialism. On the one hand, the Philippines' economic dependence on the United States leads to unemployment, inflation, and widespread hunger, forcing many Filipino women to become prostitutes or mail-order brides out of financial needs. On the other hand, U.S. cultural colonialism has created romantic fantasies of betrothal to tall, light-skinned American men. Aguilar takes on the historical viewpoint of U.S. colonialism and concretely examines how colonialism distorts and remakes gender relations, reminding us of the pitfalls of an essentialist feminist theory of gender.

However, we also need to realize that commodified transnational marriages do not only occur between the Philippines and the United States. The push (e.g., unemployment) and pull (e.g., job opportunities) of countries that export brides (such as the Philippines) and countries that import them (such as the United States) is insufficient to explain the global phenomenon of commodified transnational marriages. We need a broader theoretical overview to understand them. Furthermore, a structural discourse provides us with a broader view of the issues but often overlooks the voices of the men and women involved. The issues of how the structural forces are processed by the agents and thus localized in their everyday lives have not been thoroughly examined.

This article will construct an analytical framework of commodified transnational marriages that is understood within a larger, international politico-economic structure and will at the same time discuss how actors within the structure search for solutions and react and interpret their surroundings. I will also show how actor's choices in turn reinforce the international politico-economic structure. To prevent taking on too theoretical a tone, I will limit the scope of research to foreign brides in Taiwan, which in the future may serve as a foundation for further theoretical developments.

RESEARCH METHODS

The foreign bride phenomenon involves various complicated issues. However, not much research has been done regarding this important phenomenon. I have therefore explored many methods, including document and media analyses, participant observation in Taiwan and Southeast Asia, life-story–telling, and most importantly, participatory research based on a literacy program for foreign brides.

This is a long-term study that began in May 1994 and continues to the present time. In 1994 and 1995, my fieldwork focused on transnational marriages between Taiwanese men and Indonesian women; since 1995, I have included marriages involving women from Vietnam, Cambodia, the Philippines, and Thailand.

In the course of spending time with foreign brides, it came to my attention that the inability to write Chinese or speak Mandarin is a primary barrier these women encounter in their everyday lives; thus I offered free classes in Chinese for the few Indonesian brides to whom I was closest. Later I expanded this program to the whole community and then to other areas. On July 30, 1995, the opening class of the literacy program for foreign brides was held. This literacy program was the first in Taiwan designed exclusively for this demographic.

Written Documents

Two types of documents are analyzed in this study: official reports and media reports. The official reports include Taiwan's governmental plans to develop trade relationships with Southeast Asian countries and various related statistics, the rules of regulating the immigration of foreign brides, the evaluation of foreign bride phenomena, and related statistics. Media reports related to foreign bride issues from newspapers, television news, and magazines in the period from 1988 to 1996 are analyzed.

Participant Observation

The participant observation took place in several locations— Taiwan, Indonesia, Vietnam, and the Philippines—and in different settings—visa interviews, matchmaking meetings, and social gatherings of Taiwanese men and Southeast Asian women.

The Taipei Economic and Trade Office (hereafter referred to as TETO) requires that a Taiwanese man and his foreign bride be interviewed at the TETO office before the bride's visa to Taiwan can be granted. I observed interactions in the TETO lobby while Taiwanese men and Southeast Asian women were waiting to be called upon, as well as interactions during the interview process.

In Indonesia and Vietnam, I observed interactions among matchmakers, parents, Taiwanese men, and Southeast Asian women, both in the matchmaking meetings themselves, and before as well as after the meetings. In addition, while visiting the hometowns of the foreign brides, I observed how local people perceive the phenomenon of women of their ethnicity marrying Taiwanese men.

Taiwanese men and their families gathered at the matchmaker's home while waiting for the brides to come to Taiwan; some of them continued to do so even after their brides arrived. They would attend each other's wedding or other parties, such as the celebration of the birth of a baby. I have participated in many of these gatherings and have written detailed notes after the participant observation.

In-Depth Interviews

Marriage is a collective activity, rather than being restricted to the two partners, in the context of Chinese and many other Asian cultures. To avoid the pitfall of methodological individualism, in-depth interviews were not restricted to the marital partners; rather, they included the marital partners, their families, matchmakers, marriage brokers, and involved governmental agents.

I also conducted semistructured interviews with Taiwanese government officials regarding their perceptions of transnational marriages. They were very comfortable with tape recorders and would ask me to stop recording if the issue was sensitive, reminding me to record again at "appropriate" times. The foreign brides, on the other hand, felt uncomfortable with formal interviews, so I only conducted informal interviews with them at the earlier stage of this research. Since the literacy program served to foster mutual trust and rapport, they gradually felt more comfortable with formal interviews.

Participatory Research

Participatory research related to this phenomenon is a part of the community movement I have been involved in.[3] The applied methods are therefore geared to empower the researched subjects, who have been marginalized in the mainstream society. The goal of the literacy program for foreign brides is to enhance interaction and dialogue and to enable them to organize themselves. Many candid opinions of the foreign brides were revealed in the literacy program.

INTERNATIONALIZATION OF CAPITAL AND "MARRIAGE IMMIGRATION"

Commodified transnational marriages such as mail-order brides and foreign brides in fact compose one particular form of female immigration (del Rosario 1994). In order to understand this global phenomenon, one needs an analytical framework that provides more than "push-pull forces." Cheng and Bonacich (1984) critiqued earlier migration theory for only examining the "push" of exporting countries and "pull" of importing countries without supplying an overarching theoretical framework. They established a chart of the relationship between immigration and capitalist development, positing that labor immigration is a product of capitalist development. This article draws on that of Cheng and Bonacich and posits commodified transnational marriages found in mail-order brides and foreign brides as a type of "marriage immigration," analyzing the situations of the relationship between marriage immigration and capitalist development since the eighties (see fig. 7.1). This analytic

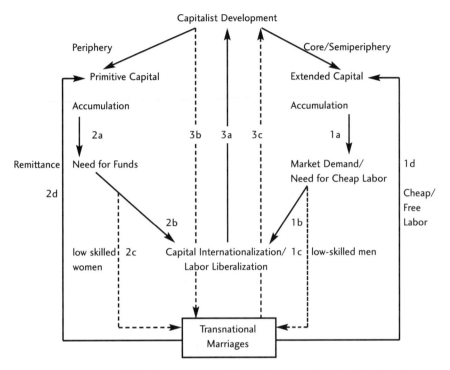

Figure 7.1. Commodified transnational marriages and capitalist development since the eighties. Note that there are numerous factors involved in capital accumulation, but this chart only shows those factors related to the international division of labor: markets and cheap labor in the core and semiperiphery, as well as funds in the periphery.

framework is a result of empirical research rather than theoretical assumption. In the following paragraphs, I will briefly explain the framework, illustrating it further later on with empirical data.

Capitalist development has resulted in unequal development and led to a division of labor among core, semiperipheral, and peripheral states. Capital from core states such as the United States, Japan, and the European Union began to invest in Malaysia, Thailand, and Indonesia in the eighties in search of new markets and investment outlets, greatly expanding production in those regions. Taiwan, South Korea, and other "newly industrialized economies" began extending their economies into Southeast Asia, becoming semiperipheral states by exploiting peripheral states.

One of the key characteristics of capitalist development in core and semiperipheral states is the expansion of capital accumulation. Methods of expanded capital accumulation include finding new markets and lowering labor costs (1a). In order to secure the sources of cheap labor, developed capitalist states have two approaches: importing cheaper labor from the periphery and exporting productive capital to the source of cheaper labor in the periphery. To open up markets and investment opportunities in the periphery, the core uses international trade and financial organizations to force the periphery to accept investment and engage in trade (1b). Being at the initial stages of capitalist development, peripheral countries are often faced with the collective pressure of core countries and their agents (the IMF, World Bank, etc.) and are forced to further distort the domestic distribution of resources in order to come up with funds for capital accumulation in a bid to develop a capitalist economy (2a). This distorted development takes two forms: the periphery opens up its borders to dominant states, accepting foreign investment and working to create a better foreign-investment climate, or it exports laborers pushed out of a bankrupt agricultural sector, which serves to reduce unemployment pressures and earns much-needed foreign currency, thereby contributing to capital accumulation (2b). These pressures have contributed to capital internationalization as well as labor liberalization and have led to further capitalist development (3a).

Capital internationalization and labor liberalization in the semiperiphery have led to large-scale plant closures and unemployment. At the same time, the core and semiperiphery have imported a great number of migrant workers to replace more expensive local low-skilled and unskilled workers. This has put further pressure on local agricultural and industrial workers, who find it even more difficult to survive in the domestic labor market. Because of a patriarchal marriage structure, in which men are expected to be of a higher social status than their wives, male agricultural workers and blue-collar workers find it hard to compete in the domestic marriage market (1c). A similar trend is found in the periphery, where the original agricultural economy is bankrupt and where foreign capital prevents the development of domestic industry, further driving down the conditions of local workers. As a result, many laborers are forced to find work in the labor markets of more developed countries. This also has an effect on the interaction of men and women in marriage markets: the deteriorating economic condition of men in the periphery forces women to search for husbands in the core and semiperiphery (2c). The development of global capital and liberal labor markets has led to the formation of marriage brokers, who operate between the core/semiperiphery and the periphery, spurring on the creation of marriage immigration.

The process of marriage immigration involves a number of exchanges and affects the core, semiperiphery, and periphery in several ways. For the core and semiperiphery, foreign brides provide unpaid household labor, childbearing, and child-rearing, thereby stabilizing the reproduction of a pool of cheap labor. Foreign brides also serve directly as a new source of cheaper laborers in these countries (1d). For peripheral countries, document and travel fees as well as remittances collected from women from peripheral countries benefit primitive accumulation (2d).

In sum, the phenomenon of foreign brides brings together men and women who have been marginalized in core, semiperipheral, and peripheral societies by capitalist development in order to survive. This integration of people from different societies is not a voluntary alliance, however, and should not be romanticized into the realization of a "global village." The phenomenon of marriage immigration is not only the product of capitalist development but also concretely manifests the abstract structure of international political economy in interpersonal relationships (3b). Unequal relationships between societies are thus realized in everyday life, and the minute details and conflicts that arise in marriages are often interpreted by members of core and semiperipheral societies as problems endemic to people from peripheral societies, which are then used to explain the underdevelopment of those countries. In other words, the historical and dynamic dimensions of capitalist development are sedimented to become an irreversible process, thereby strengthening the very process of capitalist development (3c).

The dynamic process of capitalist development mentioned above has occurred at varying historical stages and has appeared in different forms. The foreign bride phenomenon in Taiwan serves as a concrete example of the relationship between the development of the international division of labor and commodified transnational marriages.

FORMATION OF DEPENDENT RELATIONS BETWEEN TAIWAN AND SOUTHEAST ASIA

An official at the Taipei Economic and Trade Office (TETO) in Indonesia commented, "Long before the government announced its 'March South' policy, Taiwanese businessmen had been investing in Southeast Asia; so did the Taiwanese men who came here for wives." Businessmen from Taiwan had been investing in "less developed" countries near Taiwan many years before former president Lee Teng-Hui announced his "March South" policy in 1994, encouraging capitalists from Taiwan to invest in Southeast Asia. In fact, Taiwan is currently shifting from a low-wage, labor intensive phase characteristic of "underdeveloped" nations to a high-wage, capital-intensive phase often seen in "developed" countries.

Taiwanese capital began seeking outlets in 1984, but outward-bound capital investment began to grow rapidly after 1987, when the government in Taiwan relaxed restrictions on outward-bound investment (Sung 1993). In 1990, Taiwan's investment in Southeast Asia (36.6 percent out of the total investment to other countries) was greater than that in the United States (27.6 percent), and Southeast Asia became the region receiving the most investment from Taiwan. In 1992, mainland China became the favored location of investment by Taiwanese capitalists, and in 1993 investment in China overtook investment in Southeast Asia. Southeast Asia has remained, however, an important investment destination for local capitalists (see Table 7.1).

In terms of value of foreign trade, bilateral trade between Taiwan and ASEAN member countries reached US$12.51 billion in 1991. In 1995, one year after the "Outlines of Strengthening Trade and Investment with Southeast Asia," serving as the guide for the March South policy, was released, bilateral trade between Taiwan and ASEAN reached US$25.34 billion, at a 26.3 percent growth rate from the previous year. Trade continued to grow between 1991 and 1997, rising at an annual average of 15.8 percent (see Table 7.2) during those years. Statistics from the Ministry of Finance show that Southeast Asia is now Taiwan's fourth-largest export market, behind the United States, Hong Kong, and the European

Table 7.1. Taiwanese investments in the United States, Southeast Asia, and mainland China

Year	Investment (%)		
	United States	Southeast Asia	Mainland China
1952–1986	60.0	26.3	—
1990	27.6	36.6	—
1991	16.3	39.3	9.5
1992	17.0	27.3	21.8
1993	10.9	8.9	65.6
1994	5.6	15.4	37.3
1995	10.1	13.3	44.6
1996	7.8	17.3	36.3
1997	12.1	14.2	35.8

Source: Investment Commission, Ministry of Economic Affairs, Taiwan.
Note: Southeast Asia includes Singapore, Thailand, Malaysia, Indonesia, the Philippines, and Vietnam.

Table 7.2. Taiwanese investment in Southeast Asia in the nineties (in US$100 millions)

Type	1991	1992	1993	1994	1995	1996	1997
Trade volume	125.1	146.1	163.0	200.6	253.4	264.5	294.3
Yearly growth rate	—	16.8	11.6	23.1	26.3	4.4	11.3
Singapore	38.5	42.0	47.5	57.7	73.6	73.6	80.5
Vietnam	2.3	4.0	6.5	9.6	12.8	14.9	16.9
Thailand	20.3	26.3	29.9	35.5	45.3	44.6	44.9
Malaysia	28.7	34.3	36.1	45.5	58.5	65.2	72.7
Indonesia	24.3	26.2	29.1	35.4	40.2	38.4	43.2
Philippines	10.8	13.2	13.9	16.8	22.8	27.7	36.2

Source: Statistics Department, Ministry of Finance, Taiwan.
Note: Southeast Asia includes Singapore, Thailand, Malaysia, Indonesia, the Philippines, and Vietnam.

Union, as well as Taiwan's fourth-largest source of imports, behind the United States, Japan, and the European Union.

Taiwan's economy has gradually entered what Immanuel Waller-stein has termed the "world system," following the increased global character of capitalism in Taiwan. Taiwan is no longer merely a major importer and exporter of goods but now also an exporter of capital (Sung 1993; Peng 1990). By the mid-eighties, Taiwan had begun investing in Southeast Asia, following investments by the United States, Japan, and Europe, to use its cheaper labor and raw materials for expanded production. An international hierarchy of labor developed between Taiwan and Southeast Asian countries (excluding Singapore), and Taiwan began to attain semiperipheral status. Relative to Taiwan, Southeast Asian countries (excluding Singapore) were thereby placed in a peripheral status (Sung 1993).

With wages rising, and pressure from environmental concerns increasing, labor-intensive and highly polluting industries began to leave Taiwan for destinations in Southeast Asia with greater reserves of labor and lower environmental standards (Sung 1993; interview with TETO officials in Indonesia 1994). Taiwan gradually became

Southeast Asia's primary source of foreign capital, surpassing Japan to become the greatest capital investor in the Philippines (in 1987), Thailand (1988), Malaysia (1989), and Indonesia (1990) (Sung 1993). In Indonesia, Taiwanese accumulated investments ranked second by 1994, only behind Japan (TETO in Jakarta 1994a). Vietnam began to allow foreign investment in 1988, and Taiwan held the number one foreign-investor rank there for several years before giving it up to Singapore in 1994 (CETRA in Ho Chi Minh City 1999).

Southeast Asian countries have at the same time released many special incentives to attract foreign investment. For instance, to finish its sixth economic plan (REPLEITA VI), the Indonesian government passed new regulations widening the scope of foreign investment. In 1994, Government Regulation 20 lifted the restrictions on minimum investment, loosened the regulations on foreign holding and time limits on transference of stock rights, and expanded areas for foreign investment. In addition, the Indonesian government announced changes in 1994 regarding industrial, agricultural, and commercial regulations, lowering tariff rates on 739 classes of goods (TETO in Jakarta 1994a).

As mentioned above, even the socialist republic Vietnam was forced to open up its market in 1988 due to the expansion and penetration of global capitalism. In 1987, the Vietnamese government issued its first Foreign Investment Law, serving as the guideline for foreign investment. This law encouraged export-oriented foreign investment over that targeted at the domestic market; tax reductions and grace periods were the main types of incentive. For instance, foreign-investment projects that export 100 percent of the products and that are established in export-processing zones could enjoy up to four years of tax-free status and a 50 percent tax reduction for another four years. High-tech industries were also eligible for up to eight years of tax-free status (CETRA in Ho Chi Minh City 1999).

From 1986 to 1991, Taiwanese investment in Southeast Asia was concentrated in Thailand and Malaysia, where the infrastructures were more advanced. The Philippines also attracted a significant amount of Taiwan's investment, and Taiwan became the Philippines' largest foreign investor in 1989. In 1991, however, the unstable political and social situation in the Philippines drove away investment from Taiwan. Taiwan's investment in Indonesia began in 1988, and an Investment Guarantee Agreement was signed between the Taiwanese and Indonesian governments in December 1991, spurring further investment, with a rise from US$158 million to US$618 million in 1990 and a jump to US$1.057 billion in 1991 (Sung 1993). After Vietnam opened its doors to foreign investment in 1988, Taiwan's China External Trade Development Council (CETRA) sent a delegation to Vietnam and established an office in 1990. Many Taiwanese investors applied for investment permits to Vietnam between 1992 and 1993 (interview with CETRA officer in Ho Chi Minh City 1999). Taiwan and Vietnam signed an Investment Guarantee Agreement in 1994 and a reciprocal agreement to lower tariffs in 1998. The two governments also concluded agricultural and labor export agreements in May 1999. All of these agreements have further encouraged Taiwanese firms to invest in Vietnam (CETRA in Ho Chi Minh City 1999). According to the Ministry of Planning and Investment in Vietnam, Taiwan now ranks first in total investment. Taiwan's accumulated investment in Vietnam is US$5.96 billion as of 2003.

DISTORTED DEVELOPMENT AND THE FORMATION OF "MARRIAGE IMMIGRATION"

A clear international division of labor has developed between Taiwan and Southeast Asia. Taiwan gradually began to take on the characteristics of a semiperipheral state after it became increasingly incorporated in the world capitalist system in the eighties, when Taiwan began to exploit Southeast Asia and other peripheral countries. At the same time, globalization began to push liberalization, privatization, and deregulation, resulting in distorted development in Southeast Asian countries and a great number of agricultural and industrial laborers in distress. The poverty created by globalization was not as serious in Taiwan, but agriculture in Taiwan was clearly hollowed out by the twin forces of continued urbanization and industrialization, as well as the recent international pressure on agriculture. Low-skilled workers have also been affected by the increasing threats of liberalization. These agricultural and industrial laborers found survival increasingly difficult and fell into an extremely disadvantaged position in Taiwan's domestic marriage market.

Meanwhile, capitalist globalization has resulted in large-scale rural bankruptcy and unemployment in Southeast Asia, forcing many workers to travel to developed countries for survival. With the encouragement of matchmakers familiar with both Taiwan and Southeast Asia, "marriage immigration" has emerged.

Taiwanese investment in Southeast Asia and the trend of Taiwanese men marrying Southeast Asian women grew in tandem.[4] As previously mentioned, Taiwanese investment in Southeast Asia began to grow between 1986 and 1991, mainly concentrated in Thailand, Malaysia, and the Philippines. According to matchmakers and media reports, foreign brides from Thailand and the Philippines began coming to Taiwan in the mid-eighties. There were few brides from Malaysia, most likely because of that country's relative wealth. An Indonesian matchmaker commented, "Next to Singapore, Malaysia is probably the most well-off Southeast Asian country. There are many women from Indonesia who marry men in Malaysia." According to the statistics from the Ministry of Economic Affairs, Taiwanese investment in Indonesia did not really begin until 1991, which was also the year the number of Indonesian brides dramatically increased. According to an official at TETO in Indonesia, the number of women marrying Taiwanese men began to significantly grow in 1991.

As Vietnam and Cambodia have relaxed restrictions on foreign investment, Taiwanese men have begun to travel to those nations to find brides. According to marriage brokers, since 1993, Indonesian women have had to wait for months to even a year to get their visa granted; thus more and more Taiwanese men turn to Vietnam instead. That was also the same year that Taiwanese investment is Vietnam significantly increased (statistics from the Ministry of Economic Affairs, Taiwan). Unfortunately, the Taiwanese government kept no figures of the total number of foreign brides until 1994. The limited statistics can still show the high correlation between Taiwanese investment in Southeast Asia and the influx of "foreign brides" from those countries. Table 7.3 shows that after Taiwanese investment in Vietnam grew significantly following the signing of an investment agreement in 1994, the number of brides from Vietnam grew rapidly in 1995, to 2.7 times the number of the previous year.

The relations of dependency between Taiwan and Southeast Asia have become the context of commodified transnational marriages between the countries. However, not all Taiwanese men need to go to Southeast Asia to find brides. And not all Southeast Asian women wish to marry men in Taiwan or other countries. The following sections will analyze the unequal domestic development in Taiwan and Southeast Asia and the relationship between this unequal development and the phenomenon of marriage immigration.

Table 7.3. Approved marriages between Taiwanese (ROC) nationals and citizens from Southeast Asia

Year	Indonesia	Malaysia	Philippines	Thailand	Vietnam	Total
1994	2,247	55	1,183	870	530	4,899
1995	2,409	86	1,757	1,301	1,969	7,574
1996	2,950	73	2,085	1,973	4,113	11,212
1997	2,464	96	2,128	2,211	9,060	16,009
1998	2,331	102	544	1,173	4,644	8,879
1999 (through July)	1,787	58	321	693	3,362	6,267
Total	14,188	470	8,018	8,221	23,678	54,850

Source: Spouse visa applications approved by the Bureau of Consular Affairs, Ministry of Foreign Affairs, Taiwan.

Taiwan

Taiwan's economic development policies after the successful land reform of the fifties have been characterized as sacrificing agriculture for industry. The end of the sixties was the "spring" for industry in Taiwan, but the "autumn" for agriculture. The most important and characteristic strategies are "import substitution industrialization" and "export-oriented industrialization." The role of agriculture under this plan was to provide a surplus for extraction in industry, cheap labor, and a market for locally produced industrial goods. In other words, the ultimate goal of the government's agricultural development policy was to squeeze the fruits of agricultural labor in the interests of industrialization and overall economic growth. The function of agriculture is always to develop industry, whereas industry never plays a role in developing agriculture.

Two aspects of the agricultural sector felt the squeeze: (1) agricultural products and labor forces and (2) agricultural capital. The first was to lower agricultural prices in order to lower production costs in industry, thereby lowering labor reproduction costs. It also forced agricultural workers to urban areas in search of work. The second type, mediated through agricultural capital, occurred when the government raised taxes on industrial inputs needed for agriculture, including fertilizer, farm tools, etc., which drew out excess capital from agriculture and transferred it to the industrial sector (Hsiao 1981). Moreover, since the mid-eighties, the government in Taiwan has gradually liberalized the import of foreign agricultural products in exchange for entry into GATT and later the WTO. This has further depressed agriculture in Taiwan. The wide gap between industrial and agricultural workers in Taiwan has formed what Michael Lipton described as an "urban-industrial bias" (1976). Simply put, Taiwan's farmers have been victims of Taiwan's "economic miracle" since its inception.

Taiwan's developmental-policy bias toward industry and urban areas meant that farmers have become more and more dependent on income from nonfarming sources. Official statistics show that the ratio of per capita income in farming to nonfarming in 1986 was 0.72. The hard life of rural living coupled with the high wages and modern lifestyle in the cities drew many agriculture workers, particularly young people, to urban areas. The results of a survey reported by Chu show the sense of victimhood of Taiwan's agricultural workers: approximately 50 percent of farmers feel that the income gap in Taiwan is very large (1990).

The long-standing government policy of supporting industry by sacrificing agriculture had led most rural youth to the cities. Even if young people prefer to stay in the farm, their parents would do everything necessary just to push them away, because they foresee no prospects. The story of A-Ching illustrates the difficult situation of a young man returning to his hometown: "After I got out of the army, I worked in a nursery in Kaohsiung. The job was my dream, since my parents raised flowers for a living. I wanted to make a living out of my strength and the land. You know, life in the cities is hard for someone from the countryside like myself. But my parents said that I shouldn't do anything that involves dirt. They called me several times a day to tell me to change jobs, and I was going crazy under their pressure. But I could handle it. I took their advice, quit my job in the nursery, and got a job in the florist as a delivery boy. I was still working with flowers! Ha!"[5] A-Ching's parents' reactions vividly reflect farmers' hopelessness in farming. A-Ching fully understands his parents' feelings: "Don't think that farmers are below other people; they're very proud people. They don't want others to look down on them, and they are afraid that other people will say that their children are deadbeats and can't make a living in the cities. I know that in their hearts they want me to go back, since they're getting old and they need help around the house as well as companionship."

Capital flight from Taiwan began after the mid-eighties, resulting in the closure of many factories and widespread unemployment in Taiwan. The government also began importing migrant workers, further exacerbating unemployment among domestic workers.

Many urban workers who had moved from rural areas could no longer stay in the cities and returned to the countryside to find work in the informal sector.

After working for the florist for a while, A-Ching's parents told him he should find a "real job." So A-Ching finally severed all his ties with the earth and went to work in a car parts factory. Unfortunately, after working there for less than a year, the plant was shut down and moved to Southeast Asia like many other factories in the mid-eighties. A-Ching, unemployed, had to go home. His parents had to accept the fact that A-Ching was going to help them on the family's plot of land.

Youth like A-Ching, who were forced back to rural areas after the mideighties, appeared to be failures. Suffering from the agriculture decline in the process of industrialization, urbanization, and internationalization, those men staying on the farm or forced back to the countryside because of urban unemployment are disadvantaged not only economically but also symbolically. They are viewed as "men without future," as most people in the countryside believe that they only return home if they are unable to "make it" in the cities. Even women staying in rural areas are not willing to "marry down" to men living in the same locales, for fear of the hardship of agricultural work.

Unlike the stereotypical man who is unable to find a wife, A-Ching looks very strong and handsome. He made the following comments about his decision to marry a wife from Indonesia: "I had had girlfriends when I was living in the city. But I was young then and never really thought about marriage. When I got back to the countryside, it was nearly impossible to find a girlfriend. Who would be willing to give up their comfortable city life and spend their days in hardship with me?"

A-Ching was not alone in his woes. His neighbor A-Chie was in a similar situation. A-Chie worked in the city and had gone out with several women, but all left him after he brought them home to see his parents in the countryside. They didn't want to be with someone who came from a farming family. A-Chie's parents very much wanted grandchildren, so they contacted a matchmaker and eventually convinced A-Chie to marry an Indonesian woman. His parents felt remorse for the difficulty their son had finding a bride: "What's wrong with people from the countryside? The boys from the sticks are the best. Why do women treat them so badly? We're strong, and we don't care about what other people think. If [A-Chie] can't find a bride, then we'll go to Indonesia!"

In addition to the rural men, blue-collar workers also have similar difficulty in finding women to marry. The three-shift work schedules greatly limit their social lives. They do not necessarily have low income, but their social status is relatively marginalized under the prevailing urban middle-class values.

Fu-Hsin has been working in a chemical factory ever since he finished his service in the army. He was in his late thirties and had a stable income but never a girlfriend, when he finally decided to go to Indonesia for a bride under his father's pressure. When asked why he had never had a girlfriend, he responded with a humble smile: "We have three shifts and the schedule is rotated. It's basically like you don't have time to be social with friends. After work, all you want to do is go home and sleep. You know, it takes time to have a girlfriend—you need to be social. I don't even have enough time to sleep. After all, when I have a day off, everyone else is at work; when they have a day off on weekends, I am at work. How could I have a date?" I asked Fu-Hsin why he didn't work less overtime, so he could have more time for a social life. He said, "Before, I just wanted to make more money. Later, business was bad and it was very hard to find a stable job. You don't know when the factory is going to be shut down. Whenever your boss gives you overtime, you just have to take it. Otherwise, you might get fired."

Statistics show that most men who marry foreign brides come from the lower rungs of the socioeconomic ladder in Taiwan, mostly from agricultural counties or counties outlying major metropolitan regions. Statistics from the Bureau of Police Administration, Ministry of Interior Affairs, show that the majority of foreign brides holding Alien Residency Certificates are located in Taipei County (13.7 percent), followed by Taoyuan County (12.8 percent), Pingtung County (11.1 percent), Changhua County (7.0 percent), Kaohsiung County (6.7 percent), Yunlin County (6.2 percent), Taichung County (5.9 percent), and Kaohsiung City (5.8 percent). Of the counties listed above, Pingtung, Changhua, and Yunlin are agricultural counties, while Taoyuan, Kaohsiung, and Taichung are mixed industrial-agricultural counties. Within Taipei County, most foreign brides are located in Panchiao, Hsintien, Hsinchuang, Sanchung, Tucheng, Shulin, and Chungho, where most residents are involved in the industrial sector. In Kaohsiung County, the most concentrated regions include Chienchen and Hsiaokang, which are predominantly industrial, and Sanmin, whose residents are mostly immigrants from the agricultural regions.

Breaking down the statistics by occupation again shows that the majority of men who marry Southeast Asian brides are either industrial or agricultural workers. In a sample of two hundred applications for foreign brides obtained from the TETO in Indonesia, 17.2 percent of applicants were farmers, 16.5 percent farmed but also did other work on a casual basis (including cement, carpentry), 54.3 percent worked in low-skill industrial jobs (lathe operators, electronics industry, moving business, etc.), and only 12 percent were in business for themselves (own a small stall selling goods or food). Most of the full-time farmers planted high-value cash crops including fruit and tea, which are highly affected by the imports since liberalization, while part-time farmers had to take on other work during the slack time in their farming work in order to make ends meet.

Furthermore, most men who marry foreign brides are between thirty and forty years old. Based on data collected from TETO in Indonesia, of Taiwanese men marrying Indonesian women in 1993, 27.7 percent were between the age of 20 and 30, 55.5 percent were between 31 and 40, and 16.8 percent were 41 and over. Statistics from the Taipei Economic and Cultural Office in Vietnam show that of the 2,972 men marrying Vietnamese women from January to June in 1999, 18.1 percent were between the age of 20 and 30, 60.3 percent were between 31 and 40, and 21.5 percent were 41 and over. For this age group of rural men (born right before or in the early sixties, when Taiwan's economy began to take off, and reaching marriage age when Taiwanese capital began leaving the island), Taiwan's economic development not only led to their economic marginalization but also marginalization in the domestic marriage market.

Southeast Asia

Colonialism and Underdevelopment

Southeast Asia's development must be understood alongside the development of imperialism. There are different opinions about the origins of imperialism, which are beyond the scope of this paper. Most authors agree, however, that its origins are related to crises in the development of capitalism. That is, imperialism is one way that capitalism temporarily solves its internal contradictions. There is another set of theories about capitalist crises, but most agree that the fall in the profit rate drives capitalists to lower their investment. This further leads to unemployment and a drop in consumption, which are in turn harmful to further capitalist development (Cheng and Bonacich 1984). Therefore, capitalism is constantly in search of cheaper labor and natural resources, as well as markets for goods produced in capitalist countries.

Southeast Asia was confronted by imperialism at an early date. After World War II, anticolonial movements sprang up in many Southeast Asian countries, demanding political independence. Despite later independence, the development of Southeast Asia was still highly influenced by the region's colonial history and Western imperialism. Many scholars also believe that the World Bank, IMF, and other Bretton Woods organizations have in fact extended imperialist development in Southeast Asia and contributed to continued capitalist accumulation in the region.

Western imperialism has long sought after the rich natural resources in Southeast Asia. Indonesia's large land area, for instance, including more than seventeen hundred islands, holds rich oil, tin, gold, and other mineral deposits. Its rich soil produces rubber, pepper, gambier, palms, cocoa, coffee, rice, sugar, and other agricultural products. The Dutch colonized Indonesia for 340 years, and Japan briefly occupied the country during World War II. Indonesia declared independence at the end of the war, but the Dutch government did not recognize the declaration until 1949.

Under colonialism, however, Indonesia's rich natural resources led to underdevelopment. The country was turned into a natural resource provider for the colonizers, preventing the development of a local industrial sector, and failing to contribute to the wealth of the Indonesian people (Aas 1980; Knight 1982). After independence, Indonesia remained caught in the colonial development model, continuing to rely on exporting raw materials for foreign currency. Indonesia's high dependency on international markets meant that large fluctuations in the prices of raw materials seriously affected Indonesia's chances of earning foreign currency and even threatened to derail the country's economic development.

For instance, oil became Indonesia's prime foreign currency earner after 1969, accounting for 82 percent of Indonesia's foreign earnings in the early eighties. The price of oil plummeted between 1982 and 1985, seriously crippling Indonesia's economy. The government was forced to borrow to meet its payments, and foreign debt skyrocketed. The average economic growth was below 4 percent during these years (TETO in Jakarta 1995).

Oil markets remained depressed after 1985, and the Indonesian government began to promote export-oriented light industry. The government canceled taxes on the import of raw materials for export industries, lowered import tariffs, liberalized import restrictions, widened the scope of industries that allowed foreign investment, and simplified import customs procedures. To lower the country's dependency on petroleum and natural gas, the government encouraged nonpetroleum manufacturing industries, especially the textile, shoe, and wood products industries (TETO in Jakarta 1995).

The Indonesian government shifted between market and planned economic policies in the seventies and eighties. By the mid-eighties, the government owned over two hundred enterprises, including tea plantations and steel furnaces. Once Indonesia was no longer able to depend on petroleum sales for foreign currency, the government clearly shifted toward a market-oriented economic policy, stopped subsidizing local industry, and began deregulating its economy in 1986 when the price of oil dropped sharply (Robertson-Snape 1999).

The government's market-oriented economic policies did not lead to a burst of economic development, however. Indonesia undertook its first five-year plan in 1969 and experienced an average yearly growth of 7.3 percent until 1974. Economic growth hit a yearly average of 7.5 percent during the second five-year plan from 1974 to 1979. During the third five-year plan, from 1979 to 1984, growth slowed to 6 percent. The government began to encourage foreign investment during the country's fourth five-year plan, but economic growth continued to slow to 5.1 percent. The start of the fifth five-year plan in 1990 saw a growth rate of 6.2 percent, and economic growth returned again to 6.2 percent by 1993 (TETO in Jakarta 1994b).

In sum, Indonesia inherited a dependent market economy from its colonial period, which forced it to adopt a different economic strategy to earn foreign currency to repay its foreign debt after it could no longer depend on petroleum and natural gas exports. Indonesia's official foreign debt reached US$73.6 billion in 1993, but the country only had US$12.1 billion in foreign reserves.

Chossudovsky (1997) contends that Third World countries' foreign debt consigns them to continually finding new ways of repayment. This limits the development of Third World countries and leads to economic bankruptcy, social instability, ethnic conflict, and even civil war. Since the debt crisis in the early eighties, international monopoly capital has pursued a strategy of liberalization to increase its profits, break down barriers throughout the world, and allow multinational corporations to grow. The Bretton Woods organizations have played a crucial role in this reorganization of the global economy.

Internationalization of Capital and the Woes of the Working Masses

"Globalization" should not be romanticized into the realization of an ideal "global village." Globalization in fact entails privatization, deregulation, and liberalization, which means unemployment, hunger, disease, and a threat to survival for the vast majority of laborers. The "bitter medicine" of the Bretton Woods institutions—structural adjustment programs (SAPs)—appears to help economic development in developing countries in Southeast Asia. The financial crisis that started in Thailand in 1997 exploded the myth of the sixties that Southeast Asian countries could sustain economic growth. Waves of criticism of the neoliberal development models have arisen (e.g., Dixon 1999).

Harsh criticism points out that the World Bank and IMF have driven hundreds of millions of people into poverty in the guise of offering loans to developing countries and promising a boost in development by carrying out SAPs (Chossudovsky 1997). Structural Adjustment Programs include reductions in medical, education, and social welfare spending; privatization of state-owned enterprises; and tax hikes. Deregulation, liberalization, and privatization are also the policy goals pursued by APEC, the WTO, and other international organizations. These policies have led to outbreaks of diseases in many developing countries. The World Bank's goal included eradicating poverty and protecting the environment, but ironically it still funds massive construction projects such as large dams, which speed up environmental destruction and displace millions of people.

It is the conscious plan of the IMF and World Bank to keep the economies of Southeast Asian countries both export-oriented and import-dependent, as well as to integrate light industry in those countries into the global production system of multinational corporations. This has subjected these countries to the volatility of international markets and also increased international competition among developing countries, forcing them to raise their concessions to foreign capital and lower labor costs.

In the agricultural sector, liberalization policy has destroyed the self-sufficient system and led to the bankruptcy of farming areas. To take the Philippines as an example, the neoliberal policies adopted included crop conversion and land conversion. Around 3.1 million of 5 million hectares of corn and rice fields were converted to the production of cash crops, or used to raise animals for export. By 1996, 300,000 hectares of prime agricultural land were rezoned as high-class residential areas, golf courses, recreation centers, and industrial land, in conjunction with the government's policy weighted toward foreign investment and industrial parks. According to estimates produced by Kilusang Magbubukid ng Pilipinas (KMP, a national alliance of farmers in the Philippines), the nation's neoliberal policies have led to widespread rural bankruptcy, forcing the Philippines to import many agricultural products, even rice, the nation's staple grain. It is estimated that by 2005, the Philippines will have to import 239,000 metric tons of rice each year, even though the nation was previously self-sufficient in producing this staple (Center for Women's Resources 1998).

The large-scale transfer of land away from agricultural and rural bankruptcy has driven millions of rural residents into urban areas. Many unable to find employment end up in urban ghettos. A large portion finds work in the low-wage, labor-intensive informal sector, forcing them to put up with poor labor conditions. The Philippine government has adopted a "no union, no strike" policy to attract foreign investment, allowing employers to worsen labor conditions and lower environmental standards with impunity. The utter lack of public facilities in urban ghettos prevents the flood of people from rural areas from finding a respite from rural bankruptcy and unemployment (Largoza-Maza 1996).

Now let us turn to Vietnam. Eighty percent of Vietnam's population is classified as farmers (CETRA in Ho Chi Minh City 1999). The World Bank and the UN's Food and Agriculture Organization helped Vietnam draft a series of agricultural reforms beginning in 1986, leading Vietnam to abandon its policy of grain self-sufficiency, encouraging farmers to "specialize" in "high-value" crops tailored for their regions and destined for export. Even areas suited for growing rice such as the Mekong delta have been advised to switch to cash crops. This has led to the overcropping of coffee, cassava, cotton, cashew nuts, and other crops, further depressing rural areas already hard hit by the plummeting of world commodity prices and high costs for imported farm inputs. The state policy of regional specialization has led to a ridiculous situation: although grain exports at costs below international prices, there are still grain shortages in areas that had switched to cash crops, while rice oversupplies obtain in the Mekong delta (Chossudovsky 1997).

The complete deregulation of grain markets and dismantling of state grain companies led to regional grain shortages and drove up the price of grain. Famine affected not only food-deficit areas but also major regions, including urban areas and even the Mekong delta, that consistently ran grain surpluses. A report produced by the World Bank (1993a) stated that the daily caloric intake of 25.3 percent of adults at the Mekong delta was below eighteen hundred calories. In urban areas, the devaluation of the Vietnamese currency and cancellation of subsidies and price controls sent the price of staple grains skyrocketing. Coupled with unemployment, malnutrition spread quickly.

Land conversion in Vietnam also led to rural bankruptcy. Many farmers in the Red River and the Mekong delta areas were driven off the land. Under the guidance of the World Bank, Vietnam passed the Land Law in 1993, allowing farmers to freely "transfer" land, or put it up as collateral. Many farmers lost their land after they were unable to pay their debts, leading to the concentration of land into a few hands, particularly in the south following the reemergence of usury and land tenancy. Many state farms were converted into joint-venture plantations that hired permanent and seasonal workers. The number of farmers who had lost their land continued to grow. Some found work as seasonal workers, and others were forced into urban areas for work.

Those who are pushed out of rural areas can hardly find work in urban areas or in factories, because the industrial sector is also in deep trouble. The policy to attract foreign investment in the end crowded out many local firms, forcing them to cut their workforce and close plants down. Combined with a labor "flexibilization" policy, many workers were forced into the informal sector, earning a living at a piece or part-time rate that was much lower than in the formal sector. Official statistics from the Philippine government state that the unemployment rate is 10.23 percent for women and 8.16 percent for men, but the statistics count each person working more than an hour a day as employed. The actual number of unemployed should therefore be much higher.

The serious unemployment in the Philippines and the government's labor export policy drove tens of thousands of Filipinos to work abroad each year. The government established the "Philippine Overseas Employment Administration" to search out areas where Filipino workers are needed. Statistics show that 654,022 workers from the Philippines left in search of work in 1995 alone. Remittance from migrant workers is the largest source of foreign currency for the Philippines, and there are an estimated 7.2 million Filipinos now working abroad. Official government statistics indicate that migrant workers remitted US$1.67 billion in foreign currency in the first quarter of 1996 alone (Largoza-Maza 1996).

To take Vietnam as a further example, what on the surface appeared to be "free" market mechanisms and "economic reforms" have seriously damaged Vietnam's productive capacity. By the end of 1994, 5,000 out of 12,300 state enterprises had been shut down. Regulations passed regarding the state enterprises in 1990 further eroded Vietnam's industrial base. Between 1991 and 1992, four thousand state enterprises closed their doors (Chossudovsky 1997).

A reorganization of Vietnam's state banking and financial institutions allowed the government to close down local cooperatives and freeze medium-term loans to domestic producers, sending the interest rate on short-term loans up to 35 percent in 1994. The IMF banned the government from providing the state or an incipient private sector with budget support, yet at the same time requested the government to give tax holidays and exemptions to foreign investors while continuing to impose taxes on state-owned enterprises to 40 to 50 percent. The so-called reforms served to destabilize Vietnam's industrial base, and heavy industries including petroleum, mining, cement, and steel came increasingly under the control of foreign companies. The lowering of Vietnam's tariffs further allowed imported goods to replace domestically produced products, squeezing domestic industry (Chossudovsky 1997).

Under conditions set down by the IMF, SAPs require the cutdown of public investment and restricts the investment to limited areas. For instance, Vietnam has not received any war reparations payments, but Hanoi has been forced to accept the foreign debt incurred by the southern Saigon regime during the Vietnam War as a precondition for the "normalization" of relations with First World countries and the lifting of the U.S. embargo. The IMF has also requested that the Vietnam government repay more than US$140 million in debt borrowed by the Saigon regime as a condition for further loans from the IMF. The SAP that Vietnam undertook later in the eighties had devastating consequences: many clinics closed down, and the country experienced regional famines affecting a quarter of the population. After four years of "reforms," the malaria death rate increased threefold (Chossudovsky 1997).

Public investment sharply dropped after the government started to introduce reforms. Between 1985 and 1993 (World Bank 1993b), the ratio of government capital expenditure to overall GDP fell from 8.2 percent to 3.1 percent, a fall of 63 percent. The decline was most marked in agriculture and forestry, falling from 1.0 percent to 0.1 percent of the GDP, a 90 percent decline. Government spending in industry and construction fell from 2.7 percent to 0.1 percent of GDP, a 96 percent decline. Under pressure from Bretton Woods institutions, Vietnam was no longer able to allocate national resources for public infrastructure projects. Creditors had become the "brokers" of public investment projects, and the World Bank's Public Investment Program put control over what public project was best suited to Vietnam and what should be funded by the "donor community."

The negative influence of Vietnam's reforms was clearly seen in the deteriorating conditions of education. From 1954 to 1972, the enrollment for primary- and middle-school children grew sevenfold in northern Vietnam. When North and South Vietnam unified in 1975, the government undertook a literacy drive in the south. Statistics from UNESCO show that the literacy rate (90 percent) and school enrollment rate in the south were among the highest in Southeast Asia. The economic reforms systematically cut the national budget for education, lowering teachers' wages and raising school fees (including occupational schools, and affecting all levels of education), eroding the educational system. Statistics from Vietnam's Ministry of Education show that after three years of economic reforms, nearly seven hundred fifty thousand school-age children were forced to leave school. Education, which had previously been guaranteed by the state, was now a commodity.

Transnational Marriage as a Way Out

Under the sway of distorted development, farmers and workers in the Philippines, Indonesia, Vietnam, and other Southeast Asian countries were increasingly squeezed economically and were forced to find work abroad. For women in Southeast Asia, they could choose to find work outside of their native countries or escape their economic plight through transnational marriages.

A-Hsuei, from Indonesia, is a typical example. She worked

overseas before she married her Taiwanese husband. As the eldest daughter in the family, A-Hsuei had to take care of brothers and sisters ever since she was little. She worked in Singapore as a maid for two years. Compared to what she earned in Indonesia, the wage in Singapore was a fortune. One day, she got a letter from her mother in Kalimantan, asking her to come home. It turned out that her mother wanted her to get married, because she was worried that A-Hsuei would spend too much time working abroad and would forget about marriage. A neighbor introduced her to a Taiwanese man, and A-Hsuei's mother took it as a great opportunity. "I thought I would never get married," said A-Hsuei. "I was thinking of working overseas for a few years and saving some more money to open a small shop at home. But my mom was really worried about my marriage. So, I thought, I would not want her to worry, and I decided to marry in Taiwan."

A-Fang came from a small island in Indonesia. She grew up in a family of eight in a small straw house. Her family was too poor to let her finish primary school. She left home for Jakarta at sixteen, working at a store, sending home her salary to support her younger brother's education. One day, her boss asked her to "see a man," which she later realized was a matchmaking meeting with a Taiwanese man. She went home and could not make up her mind. "Taiwan is so far away. I didn't know what it looked like. I was very afraid. I thought about it for many days and got really bad headaches." Finally, A-Fang decided in favor of marriage: "People are poor in Indonesia. I thought that if I married a Taiwanese, I could help my family build a cement house." Recalling her days in Indonesia, A-fang said, "We didn't have any lights at night, and sometimes we didn't know where the next meal was going to come from." A-fang's mother did not want to see her daughter leave, but supported her decision, saying, "It doesn't matter which country women go to, it's never their home whatever family they marry into. I just hope that my daughter can marry a good man and that their children have better lives than she did. We were too poor to send her to school. Her life will be better if she can get married and move abroad—it doesn't matter to which country."

After A-Fang arrived in Taiwan, she hoped to help her younger sister find a husband as well, but her sister did not want to get married to someone so far away and only wanted to work in Taiwan to send money home. The family was unable to afford the broker's fee, however. Several years later, after the financial crisis of 1997 and the subsequent political unrest in Indonesia, her sister changed her mind and began to search for a husband in Taiwan.

Tsui-Hua, from Vietnam, was lucky compared to A-Fang, because she was able to finish high school. When she was little, her family was not rich, but the rice they grew could at least feed the family of seven. Schools did not cost much. Tsui-Hua's eldest sister is the primary support of the family. It is hard to believe that her slim body can endure the hardship of the rice fields. She said, "Life is different now. Everything takes money. The rice we grew can only feed us and can't make money for other needs." Tsui-Hua's sister talked about Tsui-Hua's marriage: "It is good to get married in Taiwan. She doesn't have to work so hard like us here." Her remarks seem mixed with envy and frustration. The interpreter accompanying me asked her, "Do you want to marry in Taiwan as well?" Tsui-Hua's sister looked at her mother beside her and nodded.

Almost all foreign brides I have interviewed expressed the hardship back home as the primary reason for their decision to marry in Taiwan. Even the few foreign brides with better-off family backgrounds also pointed out that under the unstable economic and political conditions in their home countries, life is unpredictable and that they therefore hoped to find a better and more stable life for their children by marrying abroad.

The Development of Marriage Brokers

The relationship between Taiwan's export of capital and the phenomenon of foreign brides can be further explored through the different types of marriage brokers that developed. The first type is the staff of Taiwanese investors who once worked in Southeast Asia and only later became brokers. In the town of Meinung in Kaohsiung County, for example, the marriage broker Chi-Wen is the eldest son of a farming family. His younger brothers and sisters all moved to the cities, and he was the only one left home taking care of the family farm. The falling price of rice forced him to plant mushrooms as a cash crop. Later, a Taiwanese businessman who owned a mushroom canning facility in Indonesia needed someone who understood mushroom-growing techniques. He found Chi-Wen, employed him for two years, and replaced him with cheaper labor from Indonesia. Chi-Wen then returned to Meinung. A neighbor's son, in his late thirties, was still unmarried. The father was worried and talked with Chi-Wen on his return. Chi-Wen then contacted some of his Chinese friends in Indonesia and found a bride for his neighbor. The news spread in the community, others began to ask Chi-Wen to help them find brides from Indonesia, and Chi-Wen began his job as a marriage broker.

The second type of marriage broker is the transnational married couple. With their social networks built up in both Taiwan and Southeast Asia, they are perfect for the role. To take Mei-Hua as an example, after she was married for two years to a Taiwanese man, her husband's relative asked her to find a bride for his son; hence, she started life as a marriage broker. Mei-Hua's mother worked as a matchmaker in Indonesia, finding appropriate women for match-making meetings, and her sister also helped arrange accommodations, make schedules, and assist with paperwork.

The third type is the professional marriage broker company, most of which are Taiwanese businessmen who have investments in Southeast Asia. Knowing the high profits of working as marriage brokers, they often start part-time and eventually turn their brokerage into a full-time business. In Vietnam, the office of one marriage broker used to be a small factory owned by a Taiwanese businessman. The businessman used his connections through the workers he hired to begin his marriage brokering. Another broker in Indonesia said that he runs a factory in Indonesia but the business did not turn out to make the profits he expected. To make more, he started a marriage agency, and the profits from the marriage agency had become higher than his factory. At first, the agency depended on occasional introduction of women by a Chinese-Indonesian worker in his factory; later on, as the business increased, this Chinese Indonesian worker and his family became the full-time staff of the marriage agency, responsible for introducing women, driving them around, taking care of papers, and offering their family room as the place for matchmaking meetings. The Taiwanese businessman then focused on running the office in Taiwan to attract Taiwanese men to go to Indonesia for brides.

Southeast Asian women themselves account for the fourth broker type. Many Filipino domestic and factory workers meet Taiwanese men while working in Taiwan. The law forbids migrant workers from marrying while working in Taiwan; they must first return home and then apply to come to Taiwan on a marriage visa. Jenny is a typical example. She was hired as a domestic helper in Taiwan but actually worked at the employer's family business. The employer's truck driver was forty years old and still unmarried. The employer matched Jenny with the driver. She returned to the Philippines and asked a marriage agent to process the paperwork, and she came back to Taiwan with a marriage visa. Jenny said she knew many Filipino women married Taiwanese men the same way she did. Since they learn some Chinese while working in Taiwan, many Taiwanese men prefer them to other Southeast Asian women who cannot understand Chinese.

Of the four types of marriage brokers listed above, the first three are the result of Taiwanese foreign investment, while the fourth is the result of Taiwan's labor importation policy. This further demonstrates that the "marriage immigration" phenomenon in Taiwan is closely linked to trade and investment between Taiwan and Southeast Asia.

CONTRIBUTION OF TRANSNATIONAL MARRIAGES TO CAPITAL INTERNATIONALIZATION

Transnational marriages strengthen the internationalization of capital (1d, 2d, and 3c in figure 7.1) by (1) stabilizing the reproduction of cheap domestic labor in core and semiperipheral states, as well as by offering a new source of cheap labor; (2) enhancing the primitive accumulation of capital in the peripheral countries; and (3) personalizing the abstract international division of labor.

Transnational marriages are one way to ensure reproduction of the agricultural and working classes in Taiwan, and also continue to provide a new source of cheap labor to Taiwan's labor market. The Japanese government has set up various channels to help rural men find foreign brides to maintain labor reproduction in rural areas (Sato 1989). The government in Taiwan has not taken an active role in this respect, but the effect on Taiwan's labor market is the same. Based on interviews I conducted with transnational married couples, 95 percent of couples had children within the first one to two years of marriage. Many men who married foreign brides also said that if they had not had the pressure to carry on their family line, they would have been unlikely to marry a foreign wife (Hsia 1997).

In addition to undertaking domestic work and raising children, foreign brides also take on productive work while in Taiwan. A survey by the Hung-Yi Travel Agency showed that 10.3 percent of brides from Vietnam worked, making an average NT$14,810 (US$460) a month, a salary lower than Taiwan's minimum wage. Based on extensive interviews, I found that 32 percent of foreign brides worked for wages, in electronics and textile factories as well as household put-out work. Most employment was low-skill, low-wage work. To take a small factory as an example, the owner married a Chinese Indonesian more than ten years ago, who unfortunately died in a car accident. He then married another young Chinese Indonesian. The factory hires all Indonesian women who are married to the local men nearby, and his new Indonesian wife has become the factory manager. Foreign brides who live in rural areas mostly work on the farm, helping to reduce the problem of a lack of agricultural labor. When A-Fang was newly married, her aging parents-in-law still worked on the farm every day. A-Fang was curious about farming, on the one hand, because her own family in Indonesia was too poor to own any land. On the other hand, she felt anxious about farming, because she knew that as the wife of the eldest son, she would have to take over the hard work. In 1994, when A-Fang was still new in Meinung, she complained to me, "I go to the farm watching my parents-in-law work everyday. I feel dizzy just watching them. I had never seen it before in Indonesia. It is so hard growing tobacco. My parents-in-law are so old and they still have to work on the farm. I want to help them, but I don't know how to do it. I go to the field everyday, and the sun burns me. What will I do after they pass on the land to us?" Having now lived in Taiwan for six years, A-Fang has two children. At first, her main responsibility was to take care of the children and cook for the whole family. Two years ago, her father-in-law decided to divide the family property, and consequently A-Fang and her husband have to take care of the farm themselves. A-Fang got used to it very quickly; the neighbors jokingly call her "the youngest tobacco farmer in Meinung."[6]

Moreover, commodified transnational marriages greatly increase the foreign remittances sent to the homes of the brides. In Vietnam, according to an information sheet issued by the Taipei Economic and Cultural Office in Ho Chi Minh City in September 1991, it costs US$150 and US$15 to apply for a marriage license and passport, respectively, while the Foreign Affairs office in Ho Chi Minh City charges US$12 per document for certificates of marriage eligibility and birth certificates. Notarization of each of these documents costs another US$0.40, and the couple must undergo a US$52 health checkup in the hospital. Further, the groom must pay a dowry of between US$2,000 and $3,000 to the bride's family, as well as around US$500 to the matchmaker. It costs about US$20–

25 to stay a night in a hotel in Ho Chi Minh City. If the groom stays for a week to take care of the paperwork, then, everything included, he must pay around US$3,500 to marry his bride. As of July 1999, 23,678 women from Vietnam successfully applied for marriage licenses from Taiwan. Estimating outlays of US$3,500 for each woman, that comes to a total of US$82.7 million, a significant source of foreign revenue for Vietnam.

In addition to the expenditures the groom pays abroad to marry, foreign brides also remit considerable funds back to their home countries. Reports have stated that Taiwan remits the equivalent of US$3,200 to Indonesia each day (Napitupulu and Kaliailatu 1995). Also, transnational marriages have increased the consumption of Taiwanese men in Southeast Asia. According to a survey by the Hung-Yi Travel Agency, brides from Vietnam return home on average 1.6 times a year. If every time the Vietnamese woman spends US$500, the 23,678 Vietnamese brides have contributed more than US$18.9 million in Vietnam in one year.

The effect of transnational marriages on consumption in Southeast Asia can also be seen from Indonesia's revisions of its anti-Chinese policy. In August 1994, the government relaxed its restriction on the display of Chinese characters in public places in order to increase the number of Chinese-speaking tourists. In recent years, many Chinese tourists from Taiwan and other locations have traveled to Indonesia, along with capital from overseas Chinese. Statistics from the Indonesian Tourist Bureau in Taipei show that three hundred thousand Taiwanese tourists traveled to Indonesia in 1993, ranking Taiwan fifth behind Japan, Germany, the United States, and Australia in the number of tourists. Indonesia's airlines were previously banned from using the Chinese language (including Chinese subtitles) or displaying Chinese magazines, and ethnic Chinese stewardesses were forced to speak in Indonesian. The increasing number of tourists from Taiwan led the government to relax the language restrictions, for the influx of funds has contributed to Indonesia's economic development. The government also allowed

Chinese tourists to fly to the airports of Surabaya and Medan (Central Daily News, International Division, August 6, 1994).

THE PERSONALIZATION AND ENGENDERING OF THE INTERNATIONAL DIVISION OF LABOR

The structural phenomena of capital internationalization and the international division of labor analyzed in political economy have the strongest impact on the working class. The working class often feels increasing difficulty in survival but rarely realizes that the reason is tied to the poverty of their nation or linked to the international division of labor. The development of transnational marriages transforms what appeared abstract into a relationship between real people.

Capital internationalization has led to distorted development, but we should not overlook the resistance of actors in this system. A-Ching, A-Fang, and many others like them are all active in finding solutions to their problems. Transnational marriages are the result of the resistance of marginalized laborers in core and peripheral countries. For men from Taiwan, transnational marriage is a way for them to solve the problem of carrying on their family line, while for the women, it is a way of escaping poverty.

This "merging" of the marginalized in two societies is not automatically an alliance, however, and should not be seen as an ideal realization of the "global village" concept. Commodified transnational marriages are a product of capitalist development and inscribe abstract international relations of political economy as unequal social relations.

Taiwan's mainstream media and official discourse assume that foreign brides use the pretext of marriage to come to Taiwan for money and in doing so create social problems (Hsia 1997). Based on interviews and observations, I have seen how the media's negative reporting has influenced the way that families and friends of foreign brides view the women. At the earlier stages of marriage, the families and groom often worry that the bride will run away or steal money. Taiwan's immigration rules state that foreign brides must leave Taiwan after their first six months of residence there. Women often use the opportunity to return to their home countries, often becoming a crucial moment for the success or failure of the marriage. Before returning home to Indonesia, Shei-Fen's mother-in-law reminded her, "You should hurry back; otherwise people will begin to talk about you." She only went home for a week, but neighbors began to ask, "Has your daughter-in-law come back?" The mother-in-law was angry. "It was like they were watching some kind of play, just waiting to laugh at us!" The mother-in-law was also worried that the new bride would run away as many people had said, and sighed, "It's hard to have a foreign bride as a daughter-in-law. You don't know if she's sincere or not. What if she runs away?" Anytime that the foreign bride wants to leave home or remit money to her family abroad, it strengthens the stereotype of these women popularized by the media. Shu-Hsien's first husband died, and she had a child in Vietnam. After she married her Taiwanese husband, she started to send money back to Vietnam to raise the child, which began a long-standing argument with her husband. Shu-Hsien later decided to return to Vietnam and did not contact her husband in Taiwan. Her husband and his family and friends concluded this problem, "You see, it's just like what they say in the papers! She just came to Taiwan for money."

Even if the foreign brides "perform well" and act as the paragon of new brides, it is still hard to shake the preconceptions held by their husband and families. For them, "good" foreign brides are the exceptions. A happily married man said, "My wife is great, and she gets along with my family well. But other people might not have the same luck [with foreign brides]. I've heard stories about women who run away." The force of real experiences with foreign brides is not enough to overpower their image created by the media.

There is often friction in transnational marriages that leads to conflict, that in turn strengthens discrimination against Third World countries stemming from Taiwan's economic prowess. For instance, when questioned about high fees, a matchmaker retorted by saying that, "There are a lot of procedures and you have to give 'red envelops' to [bribe] officials if you want to hurry things up. You know how it is in underdeveloped countries. Everyone wants money. Ha!" Furthermore, because foreign brides often send money home, which can be a burden to the agricultural and working-class families of their husbands, which are not wealthy to begin with. This is often a source of conflict. I have met many husbands of foreign brides who do not view their wives' desire to send money home as a result of Third World poverty. Instead, they blame the women and interpret it as the essential characteristics of the foreign brides, saying, "You see, they just come to Taiwan for money."

I have accompanied Taiwanese men and their families numerous times to Indonesia and Vietnam to meet prospective brides or to visit the families of their wives. Often the men and families reveal their explanation of the poverty of Southeast Asian countries through casual comments. During one such trip in Jakarta, the family and I visited a park with a large lawn. The mother of the Taiwanese man cried out, "What a waste of land! If this were in Taiwan, someone would have planted crops on that land long ago." The other companions from Taiwan all agreed, and someone else added, "When I arrived at my wife's home, the living room was empty, without even a chair. If it were Taiwan, even if the family didn't have money for furniture, they would have piled some stones up to make a chair." Another added, "The people here are poor because they're lazy. The land here is so fertile; how can they not make money?" The minute differences perceived by people from core countries are interpreted as problems resulting from the essence of people from the periphery. Even things as mundane as taking a shower often become issues that lead to conflicts. Many husbands and families of foreign brides complain that the women take showers three times a day, seeing this as a wasteful practice: "They just don't know how to save money. No wonder they are so undeveloped."

This essentialism is thus used to explain the underdevelopment of the periphery, ignoring the historical and dynamic relationship between the periphery and capitalism, instead viewing it as inevitable. Guided by this framework, the unequal division of labor between core/semiperipheral and peripheral states constructs the personal and gender relations among those involved in transnational marriages, that is, the personalization and engendering of the international division of labor.

CONCLUSION

The "foreign bride" phenomenon is not restricted to Taiwan but is a global phenomenon where women from underdeveloped countries move to more developed countries. This essay has attempted to view commodified transnational marriages as a product of capitalist development. Capitalism has led to an international division of labor among core, semiperiphery and periphery, as well as distorted domestic development. Commodified transnational marriages are marriages across national boundaries between people marginalized by this distorted development. The marriages are people's solutions to problems resulting from capital internationalization and labor liberalization. This in turn feeds back into the international division of labor and contributes to further capitalist development.

Some scholars contend that the influx of a large number of foreign brides has contributed to a more pluralistic society in Taiwan, turning the island into a "global village." These transnational marriages do not, however, lead to local internationalization, as transnational marriages crystallize an unequal international division of labor into personal relationships. We can therefore boldly assert that transnational marriages are the deepest state of capital internationalization. Commodified transnational marriages link together the men and women most seriously affected by unequal development. The marriages are the flip side of capital internationalization. These transnational marriages also add an understanding and acceptance of the international division of labor into people's stock of knowledge, as well as among interpersonal relationships. "Local internationalization" will only come about as a result of the purposeful raising of mass consciousness undertaken by a social movement. Furthermore, this social movement cannot be achieved merely by emphasizing the importance of "multiculturalism"; it needs to be enlightened by political economic analyses to pinpoint the formation process of unequal status and treatment among different cultures.

Furthermore, for feminists, commodified transnational marriages make us aware that globalization forces gender issues to be understood in the context of class and capitalist development. When men from relatively wealthy countries are threatened by a rising feminist consciousness, international capital flows allow them access to poorer regions to maintain their patriarchal relationships. It is similar to the trends where capitalists move to poorer regions when they are threatened by rising workers' demands for better conditions. This phenomenon signals us that in the context of capitalist globalization, isolated feminism shall never succeed, and international solidarity is necessary. Moreover, feminists with a global vision must openly criticize the internationalization of capital, rather than follow the flow of neoliberalism.

NOTES

1. The term "foreign bride," common parlance in Taiwan, reflects the discrimination experienced by Third World women in that country. I use the term in quotes to remind readers that it is ideologically charged.

2. I do not intend to define "commodification" or "commodified transnational marriages" in this paper, since it would involve additional complicated analyses beyond the scope of this article.

3. For more details and discussion of the literacy program and related issues of participatory research, please see Hsia and Chung 1998 as well as my dissertation (Hsia 1997).

4. In addition to Southeast Asian women, many Taiwanese men marry women from mainland China, a trend that is closely linked to Taiwan's investment in China and thus fits in the analytical framework of this paper. Since cross-strait restrictions add another dimension to this type of transnational marriage (such as yearly quotas), this paper focuses solely on foreign brides from Southeast Asia.

5. Pseudonyms are used to protect the privacy of interviewees. All quotes have been translated to English by the author.

6. Like other farming areas, Meinung has experienced serious aging problems, as most young people have left for the cities. Although the expression "the youngest tobacco farmer in Meinung" is not based on scientific fact, it fully indicates the problem of an older labor force in the rural areas.

REFERENCES

Aas, Svein. 1980. The relevance of Chayanov's macro theory of Java. In *Peasants in history: Essays in honour of Daniel Thorner*, edited by E. J. Hobsbawm et al., pp. 221–49. Calcutta: Oxford University Press.

Aguilar, Delia D. 1987. Women in the political economy of the Philippines. *Alternatives* 12:511–26.

Brewer, Brooke Lilla. 1982. Interracial marriage: American men who marry Korean women. PhD diss., Syracuse University.

Center for Women's Resources. 1998. *Worsening poverty and intensified exploitation: The situation of women under the Philippines 2000 of Ramos administration*. Quezon City, Philippines: Center for Women's Resources.

CETRA in Ho Chi Minh City. 1999. *How to establish a business base in Vietnam*. Ho Chi Minh City: CETRA.

Cheng, Lucie, and Edna Bonacich, eds. 1984. *Labor migration under capitalism: Asian workers in the United States before World War II*. Berkeley and Los Angeles: University of California Press, 1984.

Chossudovsky, Michel. 1997. *The globalization of poverty*. Penang, Malaysia: Third World Network.

Chu, Hi-Yuan. 1990. *The report of the Taiwan Social Change Survey* [in Chinese]. Taipei: Institute of Ethnology, Academia Sinica.

Chung, Yung-Feng. 1996. Siciology and activism: The Meinung anti-dam movement, 1992–1994. Master's thesis, University of Florida.

Cooke, Fadzilah M. 1986. Australian-Filipino marriages in the 1980s: The myth and the reality. Research Paper 37 of the Center for the Study of Australian-Asian Relations, the School of Modern Asian Studies, Griffith University, Australia.

Del Rosario, Virginia O. 1994. Lifting the smokescreen: Dynamics of mail-order bride migration from the Philippines. PhD diss., Institute of Social Studies, The Hague.

Dixon, Chris. 1999. The developmental implications of the Pacific Asian crises: The Thai experience. *Third World Quarterly* 20 (2): 439–52.

Donato, K. Mary. 1988. The feminization of immigration: Variability in the sex composition of U.S. immigrants. PhD diss., State University of New York at Stony Brook.

GABRIELA Women's Update (Quezon City, Philippines) 8 (1) (1998).

Glodava, Mila, and Richard Onizuka. 1994. *Mail-order brides: Women for sale*. Fort Collins, CO: Alaken.

Hsia, Hsiao-Chuan. 1997. Selfing and othering in the "foreign bride" phenomenon—a study of class, gender, and ethnicity in the transnational marriages between Taiwanese men and Indonesian women. PhD diss., University of Florida.

Hsia, Hsiao-Chuan, and Yung-Feng Chung. 1998. Participatory research: A way for empowerment and an invitation for the power game of reality production. Paper presented at the annual meeting of the American Sociological Association, August 21–25, San Francisco.

Hsiao, H. H. Michael. 1981. *Government agricultural strategies in Taiwan and South Korea: A macro-sociological assessment* [in Chinese]. Taipei: Institute of Ethnology, Academia Sinica.

Knight, G. R. 1982. Capitalism and commodity production in Java. In *Capitalism and colonial production*, edited by Hamza Alavi et al., pp. 119–59. London: Croom Helm.

Lai, Tracy. 1992. Asian American women: Not for sale. In *Race, class, and gender: An anthology*, compiled by Margaret L. Anderson and Patricia Hill Collins. Belmont, CA: Wadsworth.

Largoza-Maza, Liza. 1996. The impact of imperialist globalization: Displacement, commodification, and modern-day slavery of women. Paper presented at Workshop on Women and Globalization, November 23, Quezon City, Philippines.

Lipton, Michael. 1976. *Why poor people stay poor*. Cambridge: Harvard University Press.

Napitupulu, Sarluhut, and Toeti Kaliailatu. 1995. From Singkawang looking for love [in Indonesian]. *Gatra Magazine* 30.

Peng, Huai-En. 1990. *The politico-economic analysis of Taiwan development* [in Chinese]. Taipei: Fung-Yun-Lun-Tan.

Rhee, Siyon Yoo. 1988. Korean and Vietnamese outmarriage: Characteristics and implications. PhD diss., University of California, Los Angeles.

Rho, Jung Ja. 1989. Multiple factors contributing to marital satisfaction in Korean-American marriages and correlations with three dimensions of family life satisfaction. PhD diss., Kansas State University.

Robertson-Snape, Fiona. 1999. Corruption, collusion, and nepotism in Indonesia. *Third World Quarterly* 20 (3): 589–602.

Rousselle, Ann. 1993. Effects of international intermarriage on family functioning and the identity and attachment behavior of children. PhD diss., State University of New York at Buffalo.

Sato, Takao, ed. 1989. *Farming villages and international marriages* [in Japanese]. Tokyo: Nihon Hyoronsha.

Shaffir, William B., and Robert A. Stebbins, eds. 1991. *Experiencing fieldwork: An inside view of qualitative research*. Newbury Park, CA: Sage.

Sung, Cheng-Chao. 1993. The emerging dependent economic relations between Taiwan and ASEAN-4 [in Chinese]. *Taiwan Economy* 203:16–36.

Taipei Economic and Trade Office in Jakarta. 1994a. *Monthly report of economy and trade—Indonesia* (June) [in Chinese]. Jakarta: TETO.

———. 1994b *Overseas Chinese and Indonesia* [in Chinese]. Jakarta: TETO.

———. 1995. *Basic data on investment in Indonesia* [in Chinese]. Jakarta: TETO.

World Bank. 1993a. *Viet Nam: Population, health, and nutrition review*. Washington, DC: World Bank.

———. 1993b. *Viet Nam: Transition to market economy*. Washington, DC: World Bank.

8. Globalization in Living Color

Women of Color Living under and over the "New World Order"

Grace Chang

Chang's paper examines globalization as it affects women—those who suffer first and worst under the destructive spread of global capitalism. It looks at the consequences of so-called development and free trade in Third World nations in terms of women's losses in status, freedoms, safety, and education, as well as their diminished access to the basic needs of food, housing, and health care. It reveals the relationship between domestic welfare "reform" in First World nations and structural adjustment as imposed on indebted nations of the Third World. It explores the parallels and interconnections between those phenomena in rendering Third World women as a superexploitable labor pool, vulnerable to being trafficked and ultimately coerced into low-wage service work in First World "host" countries.

Ironically, migrant women from the Third World absorb the cost of structural adjustment in their home countries as well as "host" countries, where they meet the demand for low-wage care workers in First World nations dismantling already limited social supports. In short, the paper examines the engineering of Third World women's migration to the United States and other First

230

World countries, their coercion into exploitative and low-wage service work through the use of debt and "development" policies abroad as well as through restrictive immigration and welfare policies in these receiving countries. Finally, it explores how women around the world are mobilizing in alternative workers' and community organizations to resist and pose viable alternatives to this globalization of poverty.

The title of this article reflects a number of important principles in my analysis of globalization. The first is that people of color, and especially poor women of color, throughout the world are those who suffer first and worst under globalization. This perspective looks at the consequences of "development" and free trade as assaults on the survival of women of color, as losses by women in status, freedom, safety, education, and access to the basic needs of food, water, housing, and health care. The second principle is that women of color, as the first victims of globalization, are also the primary leaders in fighting back, in resisting this "new world order." That is, women of color do not merely suffer *under*, but struggle, survive and forge resistance *over* globalization. The third principle is that this "new world order" is not new but in fact a continuing manifestation of neoimperialist projects into the twenty-first century that have previously gone under the banners of "development," "modernization," and "growth."

During the United Nations Decade for the Advancement of Women (1976–1985), "women in development" (WID) programs were hailed as the great hope for Third World women's liberation from both poverty and patriarchy. This was to be achieved through the spread of Western institutions and Third World women's increased participation in these institutions, including the Western educational system, a "modernized" workforce, and emphasis on the individual (Nader 1989, p. 329). At the close of the decade for women, Gita Sen and Caren Grown wrote that the main failure of

WID programs was the implicit assumption that Third World women suffer only from "insufficient participation in an otherwise benevolent process of growth and development." Many feminists of color have questioned the beneficence of development for people in the Third World, especially women (see Grown and Sen 1987, p. 15; Beneria and Sen 1981). Vandana Shiva captured this perfectly in her naming of the violence of development against nature and women in the Third World as "maldevelopment" (1989). As women of color, we must continually name and reframe globalization as the racist, sexist, imperialist enterprise of maldevelopment that it is.

In an International Women's Day radio program, Ethel Long Scott of the Women's Economic Agenda Project remarked that we must talk about globalization in its proper terms, as the *globalization of poverty*—that is, the creation, perpetuation, and exacerbation of poverty worldwide. Moreover, she cautioned listeners not to think of the ravages of globalization as being confined to "over there" in the Third World, but to examine its impact here at home, in our own communities of color (Scott 2001). Scott raised an important point often missing from the debates surrounding globalization—that it is not only those in the Third World, but those in the "Third World within" First World countries who share these conditions and thus must be central to the struggles against this globalization of poverty.[1]

Betita Martinez articulated this for many of us so profoundly in her critically needed statement, "Where was the Color in Seattle?" (2000). She quotes Jinee Kim, Korean-American youth organizer from the San Francisco Bay area, who observed after the Battle of Seattle against the WTO in 1999 that missing from the action were those people most drastically impacted by globalization. Kim said, "We have to work with people who may not know the word 'globalization' but they live globalization."

Like Martinez and Kim, many members of communities of color have registered the need for the central participation and leadership of people of color in the largely white antiglobalization movement. They point out that this movement has largely failed to address the concerns of people of color, often putting "the environment" before human rights, as if people of color were second-class citizens to all other living creatures. As Kristyn Joy of the Northwest Labor and Employment Law Office (LELO) puts it, "When World Trade Organization (WTO) protest groups made the Sea Turtle the symbol of opposition to global economic policy, local Seattle activists and organizers from communities of color, immigrant rights groups, and women's organizations stepped forward to reframe the debate" (2000, p. 12). Women of color and immigrant women understand that the mascot at the Battle of Seattle, instead of the sea turtle, could well have been an immigrant woman domestic worker, garment worker, sex worker, or child laborer.

One of the largest features and gravest impacts of globalization is the displacement of women from the Third World, the disruption of their families, and their forced migration to the First World to serve other people's families and fill other people's pockets. While many people understand U.S. military interventions around the world that cause migration, fewer people understand the impact of U.S. and First World *economic* interventions in compelling migration, especially women's migration from the Third World to the First World for work, indeed for survival. Women of color and immigrant women understand all too well these effects of globalization in creating the massive migrations in which they have been forced to leave their homes and families.

TESTIMONIES ON LIVING UNDER GLOBALIZATION

At the Fourth World Non-Governmental Organizations (NGO) Forum on Women, held in China in 1995, women from Africa, Latin America, the Middle East, and Asia echoed the same truth in their testimonies: global economic restructuring, embodied in structural adjustment programs (hereafter referred to as SAPs), strikes poor women of color around the world the hardest, rendering them most vulnerable to exploitation both at home and in the global labor market. Since the 1980s, the World Bank, the International Monetary Fund, and other international financial institutions (IFIs) based in the First World have routinely prescribed structural adjustment policies to the governments of indebted countries as preconditions for loans. These prescriptions have included cutting government expenditures on social programs, slashing wages, liberalizing imports, opening markets to foreign investment, expanding exports, devaluing local currency, and privatizing state enterprises. While SAPs are ostensibly intended to promote efficiency and sustained economic growth in the "adjusting" country, in reality they function to open up developing nations' economies and peoples to imperialist exploitation.

Women consistently reported increasing poverty and rapidly deteriorating nutrition, health, and work conditions, trends that have emerged as a direct result of SAPs. When wages and food subsidies are cut, women as wives and mothers adjust household budgets often at the expense of their own and their children's nutrition. As public health care and education vanishes, women suffer from lack of prenatal care and become nurses to ill family members at home, and girls are the first to be kept from school to help at home or to go to work. When export-oriented agriculture is encouraged, indeed coerced, peasant families are evicted from their lands to make room for corporate farms, and women become seasonal workers in the fields or in processing areas. Many women are forced to find work in the service industry, in manufacturing, or in home work producing garments for export (Sparr 1994). When women take on these extra burdens and are still unable to sustain their families, many have no other viable option but to leave their families and migrate in search of work. As women have been displaced from their lands and homes under structural adjustment, women who were once small farmers have been forced to do home work, to migrate to the cities to work in manufacturing and the electronic industry, or to migrate overseas to do nursing, domestic work, sex work, or "entertainment" (testimony of representative from the International Organization of Prostitutes, GABRIELA Workshop, September 3, 1995).

Women's accounts of the consequences of structural adjustment are remarkably similar in every context. For example, in a workshop on the impact of SAPs on women (September 2, 1995), Fatima, an organizer from rural India, spoke of the particular hardships women face, as those most affected by cuts in social programs and the first to be displaced from their farmland. She reported that lands in India formerly used to produce rice have been rapidly converted to shrimp farms and orange orchards. While rice has always been a staple for local consumption, shrimp is purely a cash crop for export to Japan, and oranges for export to the United States for orange juice. In her community, peasant women assembled in front of bulldozers to try to prevent these lands from being taken over, but without success (see also Shiva 2000).

At the same workshop, Eileen Fernandez, an organizer from Malaysia, observed, "We are adjusting with no limits to capital mobilizing everywhere. Malaysia has used all of the SAP principles, including privatization of services and deregulation of land acquisition." Fernandez reported that in Malaysia, land once held by small farmers has also been shifted to shrimp cultivation, while in Sri Lanka, peasants see their lands being taken up to cultivate strawberries for export to other countries. Peasant women from the Philippines at a GABRIELA workshop the following day also testified that under SAPs, they have had to relinquish all the profits of their labor to landlords and that lands once used to grow rice, corn, and coffee have been converted to growing orchids and "other exotic flowers that you can't eat" for export. Lands not used for growing export commodities are "developed" instead into golf courses and luxury hotels, strictly for tourists' enjoyment (see also *The Golf War* 2000).

In each of these countries, women bear the brunt of SAP-induced poverty daily through lack of healthcare, housing, water, and food. Rural Filipino women such as Merceditas Cruz have reported going without power for four to eight hours each day and coping with little or no water (Migration and the Globalizing Economy workshop, September 6, 1995). Urban women from the Philippines reported working an average eighteen-hour day doing domestic work and laundry work outside their homes as well as begging, while men face increasing unemployment rates. Their children are most often on the street, rather than in school, and many families are becoming homeless with the high price of housing and the demolition of houses under development. Families may eat only once or twice a day because they can't afford more, and most go without health care, since the public hospitals demand payment up front and prescription medicines are prohibitively expensive (testimony of caregiver, Organization of Free and United women, GABRIELA workshop 1995). Similarly, a rural organizer from India reported (at an Impacts of SAPs workshop, September 2, 1995) that prices for essential medicines have gone up 600 percent since the onset of SAPs, severely reducing Indian women's access to proper healthcare.

Marlene Kanwati, a woman from Egypt—typically considered a "medium developing country"—testified that IMF-dictated SAPs in her country have also resulted in food shortages and even the first occurrence of deaths from starvation in recent Egyptian history. Egyptian women report that hardships from frozen wages and taxes increased in order for the government to pay its debts (e.g., sales taxes of 18 percent on food and clothes). The end of free education and health services has been most devastating to women and girls, with girls being kept home from school, sent to work, and married off earlier. While previously girls in Egypt were educated at levels comparable to boys, now 66 percent are illiterate, and only 50 percent of girls continue to high school. Finally, there has been a growing trend of early pregnancy, with no prenatal or postnatal care (testimony from workshop on Effects of the International Economic System on Women, September 4, 1995).

Since the 1995 NGO Forum, women of color from around the world have spoken about these continuing trends of the effects of globalization on their lives in no uncertain terms.[2] They report the persistence of the most devastating impact of globalization on their ability to support their children and families in the form of increased assaults on their reproductive rights. In other words, globalization threatens the very survival of people of color by hindering the ability of women of color to reproduce and maintain their families and communities. In 1999, prior to the Seattle protests against the WTO, LELO, a multiracial community and labor organization, recognized the need for education to build awareness of these issues and the linkages between workers' struggles in the United States and workers' struggles abroad. Through LELO other grassroots groups were brought together, including the Seattle Young People's Project, Ustawi, the Committee against the Repression in Mexico, the Community Coalition for Environmental Justice, and the Washington Alliance for Immigrant and Refugee Justice, to form the Workers' Voices Coalition. The coalition sponsored eight women labor rights organizers from Third World countries to participate in the WTO activities and a post-WTO conference, "Women and Immigrant Workers in the Global Economy." Cindy Domingo, founder of the Workers' Voices Coalition, explained at the conference the intention behind meeting and gathering the testimony of the participating women: "[T]he words of these women—workers, mothers, organizers, leaders, and activists—can continue to affect our views on globalization and corporate-sponsored trade policies. Their contribution to the currently one-sided debate on globalization is necessary to ensure that the citizens of the world hear firsthand why the trade policies authorized by WTO leaders in no way improve living and working conditions for workers in developing countries, or for those of us in metropolitan countries, in particular women workers."

One participant, Amparo Reyes, is an organizer with the Border Committee of Women Workers (CFO; see chap. 4), educating women workers about the effects of NAFTA and free trade policies. Reyes has worked in maquiladoras in Mexico since she was eighteen years old and currently works at an electronics plant assembling parts for Ford cars. She testified:

> It has been some time now that neoliberal economic policies, imposed by the "priista" government, have abandoned the drive for agricultural production, reduced public spending, and accelerated privatization, creating an economy based on exportation. . . . Consequently, 14 million Mexican workers are unemployed or under-employed. The government, in its desire to attract foreign investments, has created low-quality jobs for Mexican workers, jobs that far from compensate for those lost as a result of NAFTA. The wages in the NAFTA-supported maquilas are poor and this is why thousands of immigrants cross the border looking for work in the United States. (cited in LELO and Workers' Voices Coalition 1999, p. 6)

Reyes explained that privatization of social security, electrical energy, oil, and education under a neoliberal economic policy has resulted in lower wages for workers, with drastic impacts on families. For example, in the maquilas, workers are paid between twenty-five and forty dollars per week, insufficient wages to raise a family. As a result, Reyes reported, many children are forced to enter the labor force to help support their families, working in supermarkets as clerks during day or night shifts and, once they reach the age of thirteen, they begin to work in the maquiladoras, using false birth certificates. "This child labor is tolerated and even enforced by authorities and the companies themselves," Reyes said.

Reyes also reported that in the majority of Mexican families, both mothers and fathers have had to work in the attempt to support their families but "even with both parents working, paying for a child's education is virtually impossible because of low wages." In addition, day care facilities are scarce and insufficient and often require waiting lists of two years or more for those parents who choose this option. Reyes said, "Bad working conditions and the intensity of the work provokes great stress, and families, working twelve to fourteen hours a day, are starting to disintegrate."

Reyes's account of the destruction of Mexican families is particularly disturbing in light of the well-documented abuses of women's reproductive rights in the maquiladoras and Free Trade Zones of Mexico and Central America.[3] For example, the National Labor Committee (NLC) reports that in Honduras, in factories where garments are sewn and exported for major U.S. labels, young women workers are routinely injected with the contraceptive Depro Provera to prevent pregnancies, which might delay production. Workers are often purposefully misinformed that they are being given tetanus shots, or they are given contraceptive pills with no medical supervision or education about the drugs. Women told the NLC that in the past, workers were forced to get the injections or else face suspension without pay (*Corporate Crime Reporter* 1998).

Women are thus "doubly" vulnerable under global economic restructuring, subject to worker and human rights abuses in their roles in both productive and reproductive labor.

Another sponsored participant at the Workers' Voices Coalition conference, Altagracia Batista, a former Free Trade Zone worker from the Dominican Republic, spoke to these particular dangers to women under globalization in the intensified feminization of poverty: "We are already feeling the effects of a rising cost of living, as our basic food staples become more expensive, as well as the recent increase in fuel. . . . Many of the services offered by private companies are already inaccessible to the majority of the population due to the high costs of private goods. Women are disproportionately affected by privatization because they are often the major consumers of these services. Let us recall that women head 49 percent of households, and most of these women are not organized" (cited in LELO and Workers' Voices Coalition 1999, pp.

14–15). At home, Batista leads the Women's Coordinating Committee of Cibao, a federation of sixty women's rights organizations. Batista called for Dominican women workers to devise "our own regional alternatives, amidst the threat of globalization, a force that has been imposed upon us, working to divide and exclude us, condemning us to death" (ibid.).

Cenen Bagon, another participant at the post-WTO conference, addressed the hypocrisy of WTO leaders and Michael Moore, then WTO director-general, specifically. She recalled Moore's address to the International Confederation of Free Trade Unions, in which he said, "There is also a darker side to the backlash against globalization. For some, the attacks on economic openness are part of a broader assault on internationalism, on foreigners, immigration, a more pluralistic and integrated world." Bagon, who works with Filipino and other immigrant women workers in Canada through the Vancouver Committee for Domestic Workers and Caregivers Rights, countered sharply:

> Mr. Moore and others like him, in his ideological dogma, forget to add, and I'm sure it's quite intentional, that what we are against are the realities brought about by trade authored by the backers of capitalist globalization. . . . And if these so-called leaders are really looking for indicators of whether their programs are truly creating economic improvements, they should look beyond the country's balance of payment and budget deficits and analyze how women are affected by these programs. . . . Supporters of Structural Adjustment Programs should visit the night life in Japan, Hong Kong, and certain places in Canada and listen to the stories of Filipino and other women who unknowingly left their countries as entertainers and ended up being prostituted by their recruiters. They should also listen to the stories of domestic workers who left not only their countries . . . but their families and their own children, as well, to care for other women's children and households. (cited in LELO and Workers' Voices Coalition 1999, pp. 16–17)

Bagon calls for "leaders" to view the migration of women forced to leave their homelands and families because of the ravages of SAPs as true indicators of the impact of global economic restructuring. Extending on this, the experiences of immigrant women workers can serve not only as a measure of the effects but also as true indicators of the *intentions* of SAPs and other neoliberal economic policies. The sheer magnitude of women's migration—with millions of Third World women leaving their homes each year to work as servants, service workers, and sex workers in the United States, Canada, Europe, the Middle East, and Japan—urges us to examine this phenomenon and view it not merely as an effect of globalization but as a calculated feature of global economic restructuring.

In other words, it is important to understand these economic interventions in Third World nations, embodied in SAPs and free trade policies, as deliberate. They facilitate the extraction of resources, especially labor or people, from the Third World and their importation into the First World. In effect, they support a trade or traffic in migrant women workers and their exploitation at both ends of the "trade route." This trade or forced migration is orchestrated through economic interventions compelling migration from the Third World, then coupled with welfare, labor, and immigration policies in the First World channeling these migrant women workers into service work at poverty wages in "host" or receiving countries.

For example, in the United States, domestic forms of structural adjustment, including privatization and cutbacks in health care, as well as the continued lack of subsidized child care, contribute to an expanded demand among dual-career middle-class households for workers in child care, elder care, home health care, and housekeeping. The slashing of benefits and social services under "welfare reform" helps to guarantee that this demand is met by a pool of migrant women readily available to serve as cheap labor. The dismantling of public supports in the United States in general, and the stringent denial of benefits and services to immigrants in particular, act in tandem with structural adjustment in the Third World to force migrant women into low-wage service work in the United States.

Migrant women workers from indebted nations are kept pliable not only by the dependence of their families on remittances sent home but also by severe restrictions on immigrant access to almost all forms of assistance in the United States. Their vulnerability is further reinforced by immigration policies in First World countries explicitly designed to recruit migrant women as contract laborers or temporary workers, yet deny them any of the protections and rights afforded to citizens. This phenomenon is readily apparent in the cases of both U.S. and Canadian immigration policy structured to ensure a ready supply of women workers available to do nursing aide, home care, domestic, child care, and elder care work at low wages and under conditions most citizens would not accept.

"FILIPINOS FOR THE WORLD"

The massive migration of women from the Philippines to all corners of the First World illustrates clearly how structural adjustment imposed on the Philippines, combines with welfare and immigration policy in First World receiving countries to make the global traffic in Filipino women an explicit government practice and highly profitable industry on both ends of the "trade route." The Philippine Department of Labor and Employment states that every day, over two thousand people are estimated to leave the Philippines in search of work. Currently there are over eight million Filipino migrant workers in over 186 countries, and an estimated 65 percent of these are women (Filipino Nurses Support Group 2001). A Philippine government agency called the Philippine Overseas Employment Administration (POEA) deploys hundreds of thousands of women workers each year.[4]

Confining the analysis for the moment only to the benefits of this trade to the Philippine government and capital, the numbers are staggering. One woman migrating to Canada reported paying 1,900 pesos ($150 Canadian) at the embassy in the Philippines, 1,500 pesos for a medical exam, and 5,000 pesos to the POEA—typical bureaucratic expenses paid for migrating from the Philippines (testimony of Pamela, cited in Philippine Women Centre [PWC] of British Columbia 2000, p. 20). Moreover, the remittances sent home to families by overseas Filipino workers infuse into the economy what amounts to the Philippines' largest source of foreign currency, far more than income from sugar and mineral exports. While the absolute numbers are remarkable, taken in context they are particularly telling. In 1994, for example, remittances from overseas workers were estimated at $3 billion officially, reported as channeled through the Central Bank of the Philippines, and $6 to $7 billion through informal channels. This represented 3.4 percent of the gross domestic product, or the entire interest payment on the country's foreign debt that year (*PAID!* editorial 1995).[5] In 2001, the officially recorded remittances were estimated at $6.23 billion, with over half, $3.3 billion, sent home by Filipinos working in the United States and Canada.[6]

Current Philippine president Gloria Macapagal-Arroyo has launched a program to celebrate and further institutionalize this exportation of Filipino workers for profit, calling it "Filipinos for the World." Arroyo, unaffectionately referred to as GMA, persists in glorifying these migrant workers, following a long line of Philippine officials, who once called the women in particular the country's "modern heroes." In more crass economic terms than ever before, GMA now calls them "overseas Philippine investors" and "internationally shared resources" (cited in E. Farrales 2002). She is promoting her new labor export plan, announced in June of 2002, as a push to have 100 million overseas Filipinos serving others across the globe. Arroyo's program will certainly serve her interests well. As one observer remarked incisively at the Link Arms, Raise Fists: U.S. out of the Philippines Now! North American Conference of 2002, Arroyo seeks not only the remittances from the migrant

workers but also their absentee ballots to keep her in office and bolster her unstable position. She wants not only the dollars but also the
eight million Filipinos abroad in her pocket at election time.

Arroyo was the keynote speaker at the first Global Filipino
Community Networking Convention, San Francisco, August
31–September 1, 2002, promoting her labor export plan "unveiled"
that year. How do we reconcile these grand schemes with the recent
deportation of sixty-three Filipinos (fifty-nine men and four
women) from the United States, transported in shackles by airplane
on June 24, 2002? The deportees were reported to have been
shackled throughout the flight, forced to eat with their faces in their
plates and to use the bathrooms with the doors open while security
guards stood by outside (Bis 2002). Only a few spoke out in
defense of these people's dignity, protesting the poor treatment of
those who were not criminals, not terrorists, but trying to work to
maintain families and survive in the United States (Villaviray 2002;
Puno 2002). It seems clear that this shameful event is seen as just
one cost of "business as usual" between the United States and the
Philippines, one of its best sources of human labor importation, in
the context of so-called homeland security.

The benefits of this business as usual to receiving countries
such as the United States and Canada are also painfully obvious. It
is particularly useful to examine the experiences of Filipino women
trained as nurses who migrate to work in the United States and in
Canada. In each context, they are used to provide cheap yet skilled
labor, and they also serve to further the neoliberal agenda of privatizing health care. Also, in each case, immigration policy is structured to keep these trained workers underemployed and de-skilled,
in exploitative situations closely resembling indentured servitude
and debt bondage. In 1989, an estimated thirty thousand new nurses
graduated from 132 nursing schools in the Philippines, and 65 percent of these new graduates left the country (Bush 1995, p. 540). It
is estimated that there are one hundred thousand registered nurses
in the Philippines, but almost none actually reside in the country.

The Philippine Women Centre (PWC) of British Columbia, a group of Filipino-Canadian women working to educate, organize, and mobilize Filipino women migrant workers in Canada, identifies this phenomenon as the "commodification of the nursing profession in the Philippines." The group observes that nursing training is promoted as the "quick route to work abroad" rather than to serve the needs of Filipinos; thus Filipino women nurses are seen as "exportable commodities" (2000, p. 10). A survey of members of the group revealed that 77 percent of participants studied nursing with the specific intention of going abroad, and 62 percent took an entrance exam allowing foreigners to practice nursing in the United States (ibid., p. 16).

Ninotchka Rosca of GABRIELA Network USA has observed the ironic history of Filipino nurses in the United States. In the eighties, the United States experienced a drastic shortage of nurses because the nursing profession was so poorly paid, with salaries at about twenty thousand dollars a year. With few U.S. citizens going into nursing or willing to do this work at such low wages, many Jamaican and Filipino women immigrated to fill these positions, entering through special temporary worker visas specifically for foreign-trained nurses.[7] With the downsizing in healthcare, many of those same nurses who have dedicated their services here for decades are now finding themselves as expendable as new immigrants. Hospitals seek to reduce costs by firing their most experienced, and thus highest-paid, nurses. Rosca suggests that U.S. hospitals and the healthcare industry would collapse without Filipina nurses and remarked: "We take care of everybody else's weaker members of society, while we let our own society go to hell" (telephone interview, April 29, 1996).

In Canada, the fate and the function of migrant Filipino nurses are much the same or perhaps worse. I have argued elsewhere that exclusion from both welfare benefits and workers' rights through U.S. immigration policy makes immigrant women workers available for, indeed unable to refuse, low-wage service work in the

United States. In Canada, the connection between this labor control and immigration policy is even more explicit because of the use of both Canadian immigration policy and nursing accreditation policy to prevent foreign-trained nurses from being able to practice nursing for many years after arriving in Canada. In tandem, the policies serve to exclude immigrant nurses from their professions and channel them into low-paid care work as nannies or domestic and "home support" workers. The Live-in Caregiver Program, or LCP, is the immigration policy through which the vast majority of Filipino women migrants enter Canada and become trapped in this low-wage care work.

Established in 1992 to facilitate the importation of primarily Filipino women, the program provides that a Canadian employer (either an individual or an employment agency) may apply through the Canadian Employment Office for a prospective employee after showing that an attempt was made to find a Canadian to do the job. The applicant must be in good health and must have two years of postsecondary education, six months of formal training, or twelve months' experience in caregiving work. Once matched with an employer, she must notify the Ministry of Citizenship and Immigration if she wishes to change employers. After two years of live-in work, a nanny can apply for landed-immigrant status, but during those two years she is considered a temporary migrant. Three years after applying for landed-immigrant status, she can become a Canadian citizen (PWC 2000, p. 11).

The PWC of British Columbia undertook a community-based, participatory action research project, interviewing thirty Filipino nurses who had entered through the Live-in Caregiver Program and were doing domestic work in Canada. Cecilia Diocson, founding chair of the PWC, says the interviews revealed that women with up to fifteen years' experience in nursing in operating rooms, cancer units, and other nursing work were becoming de-skilled while working as nannies and "home support" workers (telephone interview, August 2002). Others were indeed using their skills, working around the clock performing nursing tasks, but were not recognized or compensated as such. Many of the workers' tasks included doing heavy lifting, transferring, personal care duties, and administering medications and tube feeding for elderly, ill or disabled clients. One woman, Mary Jane, reported, "Because of the LCP requirements, we become responsible for our employers twenty-four hours a day, but we are only paid for eight hours, with no overtime pay. For some of us, we accompany our employers to the hospital and even sleep at our employer's bedside at the hospital" (cited in S. Farrales 2001, p. 51).

Many of those interviewed did not realize when they migrated that they would not be doing nursing after entering through the LCP; many believed that they would be doing nursing in private homes or caring for disabled children. Moreover, many did not know that working as a nanny would mean so much labor demanded of them beyond caring for children. For example, Pamela, a registered nurse in the Philippines who left behind three children to seek work in Vancouver, said:

> I thought being a nanny, as the dictionary says, is child's nurse. In the Philippines, a yaya (Tagalog for nanny) works for the kids only, right? They don't do other jobs in the house. They just change the kids, feed them and put them to bed. . . . When I came here, I was shocked. I said, why is it a package? Three children in a big house, 5 bedrooms, 1½ baths and 3 living rooms. . . . I feel like I'm going to die. My female employer didn't work. She stays at home. Then, she said that I'm not clean enough. I told her that I have to prioritize the work and I asked her, what's more important, the kids or cleaning? . . . It was so hard I quit. (cited in PWC 2000, p. 19)

Once Pamela quit, her former employer refused to give her a reference, nanny agencies would not accept her, and she decided to advertise for a job caring for the elderly. Several prospective employers answered the ad looking only for a caregiver willing to provide sexual services. After several such experiences and trying to work as a nanny for one more family, she found a job caring for a single woman.

Pamela is supporting her husband, who is a student, and her three children in the Philippines by sending $150 (Canadian), a quarter of her wages, each month. She spoke of the hardships of being separated from her family, and her doubts and fears about reuniting: "I'm confused whether I should get my family or not. The separation is really hard for me, but I also think if my family is here, my husband and I have to chip in. I fear that communication will be through messages on the refrigerator. . . . We don't see each other any more. That's why sometimes I feel that maybe it's better for them to stay in the Philippines because they write to me and there's an attachment still. Here, it seems that you're not really intact" (ibid., p. 20).

Mary Jane, another Filipino nurse working as a nanny, reflected on the pain of the separation from her children and the great financial hardship of maintaining contact: "My children are now five and eight. I spent so much money on the long distance because sometimes when I call, my child will say, 'Mommy I still want to sing.' You know, you didn't see your child for four years and she will tell you she wants to sing, you cannot say no. . . . I said I will call everyday so that [my youngest child] will not forget my voice. I only stopped calling because my phone bill is over five hundred dollars." For these women, the agony of being separated from their own children is surely not diminished by caring for their employers' children.

For many of the women interviewed, the hope of eventually being able to bring their families to join them in Canada influenced them to stay working in unhappy and often abusive situations, in order to fulfill the two-year live-in work requirement of the LCP as quickly as possible. The policy prohibits them from earning any extra income to supplement their low wages as caregivers. The law stipulates explicitly that "working for anyone other than the employer named on the employment authorization is illegal" and that unauthorized employment will not count to satisfy the two-year employment requirement to apply for permanent residence (Canada Immigration Code 1999, cited in PWC 2000, p. 29). Thus, women are effectively kept bonded to the employers named on their original LCP employment authorization—at whatever wages and conditions the employer chooses to provide. As Pamela reports, "Filipinos are abused because they are pressured to stay with the twenty-four-month requirement. . . . You stay because it's not that easy to find an employer. And you get exploited and we are highly educated. . . . That's really racism."

In addition to these barriers that essentially lock trained nurses into nanny and home support work for at least two years, migrant Filipino women face more hurdles in trying to gain accreditation to practice nursing even after they have served their two-year live-in requirement. Applicants must take English tests that are irrelevant and extremely costly, about $208 Canadian or US$410. According to Leah Diana, a registered nurse and volunteer with the Filipino Nurses Support Group (FNSG) in Vancouver, Filipino nurses are usually educated in English, have worked in English in the Philippines and elsewhere, and have already passed mandatory English interviews prior to coming to Canada. Diana says, "The English tests required are only based on the racist assumption that people of colour can't speak English." Clearly, too, it functions as a means of preventing Filipino nurses from being able to practice nursing, receive fair compensation, or advance professionally.

Even if women are able to overcome these barriers and become accredited, many are convinced to stay in caregiving jobs by "hints" by immigration officials that they may have trouble gaining landed immigrant status if they leave. Josie, a member of the FNSG who managed to receive her accreditation, reported, "I was told by an immigration official that if I leave the LCP and practice nursing, I will be denied landed-immigrant status. I am angered that for another year, Canada Immigration forces me into modern-day slavery instead of allowing me to contribute my skills and expertise to the health care system" (cited in *Kapitbisig* 2001). All of these barriers are particularly outrageous when viewed in the context of Canada's recognized nursing shortage. A Canadian Nurses' Association study showed that there will be a shortage of 59,000 to 113,000 registered nurses in Canada by the year 2011 (cited in S. Farrales 2001, p. 51).

Dr. Lynn Farrales, then chair of the PWC, observes that the LCP program functions simply to bring in women who are educated and trained nurses to do domestic work, live-in childcare and private home-care for the disabled and elderly for less than minimum wage. Farrales says: "Canada, a country without a national day care program and a health care system moving towards increased privatization, has established in the LCP a means of importing highly educated and skilled workers to fulfill the need for flexible and cheap labour in the spheres of child care and health care. The economic and social consequences of the LCP have been devastating for Filipino women. They are highly exploited, oppressed, and de-skilled. Despite being highly educated, many are trapped in minimum wage jobs after completion of the LCP, and are effectively legislated into poverty" (2001, p. 42). Moreover, Dr. Farrales notes that these negative impacts extend to the next generations of Filipino youth as well, including the effects of years of separation of mothers and children, and the systemic racism inherent in the Canadian institutions that Filipino-Canadian youth encounter. As Filipino youths drop out of high schools at high rates, they join their mothers in the service sector working for low wages also, and the Canadian government achieves what Farrales calls the "commodification of the migration of the entire family as a package deal of cheap labor" (ibid.). Meanwhile, ironically, with rapidly privatizing health care and the continuing nursing shortage in the public sector, health care becomes inaccessible for working-class Canadians, including Filipino nurses and their families.

These women workers are well aware that the Canadian government's aim in the LCP is to exclude them from the nursing profession, rendering them de-skilled, underemployed, and thus available—indeed, unable to refuse—to do other care work for low wages. As Gemma Gambito, a member of FNSG who graduated from nursing school in the Philippines in 1993 and came to Canada in 1997 under the LCP, says, "Our presence in Canada is used to drive down the wages of Canadian nurses and health care workers. Once completing our temporary work contract and becoming landed immigrants, many become home support workers, nursing aides, or continue to do domestic work for low wages. A pool of highly skilled yet low-paid health workers has been created by the Canadian government's LCP" (Gambito 2001, p. 61). Thus, the Canadian government provides middle- and upper-class Canadian citizens with quality, low-cost, in-home child care and health care, literally at the expense of Filipino women workers and their families, who cannot afford these services for themselves.

Filipino migrant workers also understand how the Philippine government profits from and thus plays a calculated role in this trade in Filipino women. The following statement of the PWC reflects this clear analysis of the complicity of the Philippine government now and historically in this trade:

> The migration and commodification of Filipinos is sanctioned by official Philippine government policy. Known as the Labour Export Policy (LEP), this scheme of systematically exporting labour is part of the Structural Adjustment Programs (SAPs) imposed by the IMF and World Bank as conditionalities for borrowing. Ultimately, the LEP and SAPs are part of the neoliberal policies of the globalization agenda. The LEP seeks to alleviate the continuing problems of massive unemployment, trade deficits, foreign debt, and social unrest. First adopted by the dictatorship of Ferdinand Marcos in the 1970s, labour export has remained a key part of the so-called development plans of successive Philippine governments. . . . The government relies upon the remittances of these migrants to prop up the economy and pay

off the massive foreign debt owed to the IMF and the World Bank. Instead of selling coconuts and sugar, the Philippine government is now engaged in the sophisticated practice of selling its own people to industrialized countries. (2000, p. 7)

This statement reflects these women's clear recognition that the Labour Export Policy, an official Philippine government policy, is part and parcel of the SAPs that wreak havoc on their lives and force them to migrate in the first place. The LEP institutionalizes the exportation of Filipino women to other countries for cheap labor and effectively guarantees remittances from these migrant women workers used in paying off the foreign debt.

WOMEN TURNING THE "NEW WORLD ORDER" UPSIDE DOWN

Carol de Leon is now program coordinator for the Women Workers' Project at CAAAV: Organizing Asian Communities in the Bronx, New York. She grew up in the Philippines, where she was a youth activist until she left in 1987 to work abroad as a nanny. In a telephone interview conducted in August 2002, she recalled that when she was in Hong Kong, she applied to go to Canada, but it did not materialize, and this was probably fortunate. She explains that in the mid-eighties, the Canadian government was "very lenient, inviting people to come into the country, so at the time it was so easy to find an employer and go to Canada." But, de Leon observes, in the nineties, the Canadian government instituted requirements such as an educational background check for two to three years of college education. She comments, "It seems very appealing to go to Canada when you are in other countries . . . for a Third World woman to go there—but in reality that structure is not well implemented. When you go there, you'll end up working for a family for two or three years, and if you are being exploited, you can't leave while applying for a change in status. So the employer has all of the control, because the worker will end up staying anyway." De Leon knows that she is lucky not to be speaking from the experience of being trapped as a live-in caregiver in Canada. Although some aspects of her initial experiences in the United States were very similar, she was able not only to escape these exploitative situations herself but also is now organizing other women like her to mobilize against the common abuses they have faced.

De Leon says that here in the United States, although there is no program for domestic workers like the Canadian LCP, there is a formal legal structure for au pairs. These are for young students coming from Europe, so that employers can hire them through agencies and arrange for them to have connections to church and school here, she says. But for Third World women working for corporate executives, de Leon says, "you don't get a working permit, you just get a visa that is tied to an employer." She recalls that in her case, she had a contract to work as a live-in nanny for a family, and on her papers it said, "personal servant to American family," adding "I really hated that." She started working a few months after arriving here in Ardsley, a suburb of New York City, with "people and weather that were strange to me." Her job conditions were "a nightmare—I did everything from waking up the children, giving them breakfast, walking the dog, shoveling the snow, and cleaning the house." She worked from 6:30 AM to 9 PM and had only one day off a week. After a year, she asked for another day, seeing that others had two days off. Her employer, who worked for the Philip Morris corporation, said that he had seen in Hong Kong the common practice that allowed only one day off, and he refused on that basis.

She took the initiative to call the Department of Labor, to find out about the minimum wage and overtime pay and asked her employer to adjust her salary. Again, her employer said that the contract they signed was based on earnings in Hong Kong, but de Leon pointed out that she couldn't support herself here on those wages. When she asked for overtime, saying she understood the law limited the workday to eight hours, her employers demanded to know where she was getting this information. After telling them that her source was the Department of Labor, they still refused, then gave her a twenty-five-dollar raise. De Leon calculated that her earnings then amounted to two dollars an hour, at a time when the minimum wage was four dollars. After that, de Leon decided that she wanted to leave, but she encountered the typical tactics of exploitative household employers: "When I told them that I'd rather leave, they said I couldn't break the contract. I said that in a contract, either party can break the contract if you are not happy, so I'm giving you two weeks notice. They insisted that I couldn't do it and tried to manipulate me, asking where I was going, if I was going back to my country. To me, that's an implication that I was going to starve! I told her that it's none of her business."

Ultimately, though, de Leon decided to stay "because I signed a contract to work for two years—the reality is that I felt I was legally trafficked." She remarks that women who are brought here by executives or diplomats have no way to network with others and no assistance from employers to find a community. Instead, she observes, workers are discouraged from this and deliberately isolated in the suburbs, where they "don't have contact with other nannies, not even in the park." De Leon explains, "Without other people giving me support, I decided to stay and finish my contract and just survive," recalling that this was what happened to her in Hong Kong also. Finally, she was able to leave the job and found a live-out job from 11 AM to 7 PM that allowed her to start going to the park: "That's when I realized that in this industry the majority of workers are women from the Third World. Also, because of a lack of standards, women are subject to abuse and exploitation, working long hours, even when they're sick. And a lot of women who are here with families are even forced to terminate pregnancies. After eight years, I met people from CAAAV. They were handing out fliers in the park. I approached them, they took my number, and the next week I met with them and ended up going to weekly meetings."

Now de Leon leads the Women Workers' Project, which holds monthly meetings to improve working and living conditions among women in the domestic-work industry. The project members began drafting standard guidelines and a pay scale to make recommendations for how much should be paid per child, for housekeeping tasks, etc., using the contract de Leon had from Hong Kong as a model:

> We started looking at the industry and realized that we had to be strategic about it, doing outreach with women from other ethnicities, and women really embraced it. We did a survey in 2000 in parks, indoor playgrounds, and train stations, to see the conditions of women—who gets minimum wage, overtime pay, sick days, holidays. One woman who was being sponsored was forced to work six days a week, over forty-four hours. She wanted to have one day to go to church. She started asking and showing papers from the Labor Department, and her employers were furious. Employers will try all their ways to not follow the regulations.

De Leon remarks on the lack of regulations on the industry to begin with: "We're not even protected from sexual harassment or any other abuses." Moreover, she notes that employers try many different tactics, including using race, to divide household workers. For example, they make comparisons and say women from the Philippines are "better than from other countries, to create tensions between workers." Meanwhile, she says, "they discriminate against us because of race, language, and immigration status."

Domestic Workers United, a project sponsored by CAAAV and Andolan, a South Asian workers' group, is pushing now for legislation that de Leon's group drafted. Led by a steering committee composed mostly of women from the Caribbean, they used their research to design a standard contract and approached the New York City Council to pass a new law regulating the industry. Essentially, it will regulate the Department of Consumer Affairs, which licenses the employment agencies recruiting and placing domestic workers. Seventy-five percent of domestic workers get their jobs through these agencies, which ought to serve to protect these workers' rights, yet, de Leon says, when a worker has an abusive employer and calls her agency, "they advise you to stay for at least three or four months because they want to receive their fees from the employers." Otherwise, the agency will have to give the money back or provide another employee without a fee. De Leon explains, "So what we are asking for is a code of conduct, so that the agency provides a contract with your work conditions, including minimum wage, two weeks paid vacation, etc., and the agency should enforce it."

The group introduced the bill in March 2002 and had a hearing in May with the chair of the Committee on Labor, providing supporting testimony. De Leon says that it was "difficult to read [the chair], but he told us they would study and consider the issue and indicated that if it passes, it will protect everyone, including the undocumented." Some supporters, like Councilwoman Gail Brewer, have said it should be easy to pass because there is no money involved, or won't cost the city anything. De Leon says the group is still worried because "we don't know if it's going to pass, and lots of council members are on vacation"; so they planned to stage a citywide action on October 5, starting with a rally at Washington Square Park and a march to City Hall. They planned to wear gloves and aprons, just as they did when they introduced the bill.

De Leon comments that their demands are in some ways modest and in others revolutionary: "The bill is very basic—how we should be treated, working conditions, minimum wage, overtime pay, legal holidays, and sick days—but really, we want to turn the industry upside down and change the notions that immigrant workers are lazy and uneducated. Because it relates to history, because this country inherited this industry through American slavery and ideas that this is women's work, etc. We're calling for respect and recognition for women in this industry." While it is working to turn these structures and notions on their heads, the project also provides training courses for nannies on child care and psychology, on doing CPR (for a certificate from the Red Cross), and on negotiating with employers. Every week, they have a small action in the park, to make sure that all workers are aware of the proposed legislation and know about the citywide march. De Leon says that even though the press has covered it, most women don't have time to read the paper to learn about it. "We want to make sure that everyone knows this is happening," she says, so they put posters in visible places and do outreach with certain members as point people for particular parks. She recalls the enthusiasm when they started circulating the draft of the guidelines in the parks: "Women were very excited—they said it should have happened a long time ago."

Cindy Domingo and members of the Workers' Voices Coalition, Cecilia Diocson and her comrades in the Philippine Women Centre, Carol de Leon and her sisters in Domestic Workers United, and many others allied in these struggles are in the process of making what should have happened long ago happen now. They are making these revolutionary changes in the face of what they all know is surely "not new" under globalization. With this knowledge, all of these women have demonstrated, in living color, that women of color around the world have been and will continue to be the leaders in forging a radical "new world order" of our own.

NOTES

1. See, for example, Third World Within (2000), p. 17. Cindy Domingo, founder of the Workers' Voices Coalition, called for seizing the moment after the Battle of Seattle in 1999: "We saw the profound deterioration in the conditions of immigrant and women workers worldwide as a direct result of free trade policies, globalization, and privatization. In the United States, immigrant workers have become scapegoats for the failures of the global economy because U.S. workers don't see their interests as one and the same with workers in Latin America, Asia, or Africa. The WTO coming to our city gave us a once-in-a-lifetime opportunity to draw links between conditions faced by working people in developing

countries and those faced by immigrants and people of color in the United States" (cited in Joy 2000, p. 12).

2. See Sandrasagra (2000) and Tauli-Corpuz (2000) on two women's conferences, the "Roundtable Discussion on the Economic, Social, and Political Impacts of the Southeast Asian Financial Crisis," Manila, April 12–14, 1998, and "Rural and Indigenous Women Speak Out on the Impact of Globalisation," Chiangmai, Thailand, May 22–25, 1998.

3. Also, in the Philippines, 60 to 80 percent of the workers in export-processing zones (EPZs) are women, often young, single women who work for low wages under deplorable conditions. In some cases, they are subjected to virginity tests, or their families are made to sign agreements that they will not allow their daughters to become pregnant or to join a union. Many of the Filipino workers laid off in recent years are women workers in the EPZs, who often go into the informal sectors of the Philippine economy, including prostitution. The Philippines has the highest number of prostitutes in Southeast Asia—six hundred thousand, according to the International Labor Organization (cited in GABRIELA Philippines 1999). See also Ninotchka Rosca (2000).

4. This number does not include women who are trafficked or illegally recruited, women who migrate for marriage, or students or tourists who eventually become undocumented workers (Kanlungan Center Foundation from POEA and Department of Labor and Employment statistics, 1995); see Vincent (1996). Other authors address more extensively trafficking in women for the sex work, entertainment, and mail-order bride industries; see, e.g., Rosca (1995), Kim (1984), Global Fund for Women.

5. By comparison, workers from Mexico—one of the leading countries in receipt of remittances from its citizens working in the United States—send home more than $9.3 billion a year, almost half of the $23 billion sent by all Latin American and Caribbean overseas workers to their home countries. As is true of all the poorest Latin American countries, remittances exceed all international aid and increase by an average of 11 percent each year. Remittances are Mexico's third largest source of income, following oil exports and tourism.

6. POEA figures for 2001; see reports at http://poea.gov.ph.

7. In 1988, the Filipina Nurses Organization fought for the Nursing

Relief Act in the United States, which provided some rights and stability to H-1 nurses, granting nurses permanent residency after five years of living in the United States and working in the nursing profession. Prior to the passage of this act, H-1 nurses had to go home after five years and could return only after one year's residence in their home countries. Only after this absence could they apply to have their H-1 visas renewed. For more on U.S. government programs to recruit nurses as temporary workers under H-1 visas, see Chang (2000), pp. 131–32.

REFERENCES

Beneria, Lourdes, and Gita Sen. 1981. Accumulation, reproduction, and women's role in economic development: Boserup revisited. *Signs* 7 (2): 279–98.

Bis, Richard. 2002. Paper presented at Link Arms, Raise Fists: U.S. out of the Philippines Now! North American Conference, San Francisco, July 6–7.

Bush, Barbara. 1995. The Rockefeller agenda for American/Philippines nursing relations. *Western Journal of Nursing* 17 (5).

Chang, Grace. 2000. *Disposable domestics: Immigrant women workers in the global economy*. Boston: South End Press.

Corporate Crime Reporter. 1998. Young women in Honduran Free Trade Zone injected with Depo Provera, National Labor Committee alleges. November 23, 1998. http://www.citinv.it/associazioni/CNMS/archivio/lavoro/honduran_ftz.html (accessed March 10, 2004).

Farrales, Ethel. 2002. Paper presented at Link Arms, Raise Fists: U.S. out of the Philippines Now! North American Conference, San Francisco, July 6–7.

Farrales, Lynn. 2001. The feminization of labour migration. In *Advancing the rights and welfare of non-practicing Filipino and other foreign-trained nurses*. Vancouver, BC: Filipino Nurses Support Group.

Farrales, Sheila. 2001. The use of Filipino nurses in the scheme to privatize health care. In *Advancing the rights and welfare of non-practicing Filipino and other foreign-trained nurses*. Vancouver, BC: Filipino Nurses Support Group.

Filipino Nurses Support Group. 2001. Contextualizing the presence of Filipino nurses in British Columbia. Paper read at the conference titled Advancing the Rights and Welfare of Non-practicing Filipino and Other Foreign-trained Nurses, Burnaby, BC, December 7–9.

GABRIELA Philippines. 1999. *Report to the UN Special Rapporteur on Violence against Women.* N.p.: GABRIELA.

Gambito, Gemma. 2001. In *Advancing the rights and welfare of non-practicing Filipino and other foreign-trained nurses.* Vancouver, BC: Filipino Nurses Support Group.

Global Fund for Women. *Sisters and daughters betrayed: The trafficking of women and girls and the fight to end it.* VHS. Produced by Chela Blitt. San Francisco: Global Fund for Women.

Golf War, The. 2000. VHS. Directed by Jen Schradie and Matt DeVries. Produced by Anthill Productions, Highland Mills, NY.

Grown, Caren, and Gita Sen. 1987. *Development crises and alternative visions: Third world women's perspectives.* New York: Monthly Review Press.

Joy, Kristyn. 2000. Gender, immigration, and the WTO. *Network News* (National Network for Immigrant and Refugee Rights), winter 2000.

Kapitbisig: A Newsletter of the Filipino Nurses Support Group. 2001. Filipino nurses trapped by the Live-in Caregiver Program. Vol. 2 (3).

Kim, Elaine. 1984. Sex tourism in Asia: A reflection of political and economic equality. *Critical Perspectives of Third World America* 2 (1) (fall): 215–31.

LELO and Workers' Voices Coalition. 1999. *Voices of working women.* Proceedings of conference titled Beyond the WTO: Conference on Women and Immigration in the Global Economy, Seattle, WA, December 4, 1999. N.p.: LELO.

Martinez, Elizabeth (Betita). 2000. Where was the color in Seattle? Looking for reasons why the Great Battle was so white. *Colorlines* 3 (1) (spring): 11.

Nader, Laura. 1989. Orientalism, occidentalism, and the control of women. *Cultural Dynamics* 2 (3).

PAID! (People against Immoral Debt). 1995. Flor Contemplaion: Victim of mismanaged economy. Editorial. April 1995, p. 20. Newsletter of the Freedom from Debt Coalition.

Philippine Women Centre (PWC) of British Columbia. 2000. *Filipino nurses doing domestic work in Canada: A stalled development.* Vancouver, BC: PWC of British Columbia.

Puno, Ricardo V., Jr. 2002. Viewpoint: Handcuffing Filipino deportees is ok? Editorial. *Manila Times*, June 26, 2002.

Rosca, Ninotchka. 1995. The Philippines' shameful export. *Nation*, April 17, pp. 523–25.

———. 2000. The genesis of the Philippine sex trade. Unpublished paper, Philippine Women Centre of Ontario.

Sandrasagra, Mithre J. 2000. Globalisation heightening gender inequalities. *IPS Daily Journal*, October 11, 2000, pp. 3–4.

Scott, Ethel Long. 2001. Interview by Andrea Lewis. KPFA Radio morning show.

Shiva, Vandana. 1989. *Staying alive: Women, ecology, and development.* London: Zed Books.

———. 2000. *Stolen harvest: The hijacking of the global food supply.* Boston: South End Press.

Sparr, Pamela. 1994. *Mortgaging women's lives: Feminist critiques of structural adjustment.* London and Atlantic Highlands, NJ: Zed Books.

Tauli-Corpuz, Victoria. 2000. Asia-Pacific women grapple with financial crisis and globalisation. *IPS Daily Journal*, October 10, 2000.

Third World Within. 2000. Women, race, and work. Special issue, *CAAAV Voice* 10 (4) (fall): 17.

Villaviray, Johnna. 2002. 63 Filipino U.S. deportees arrive at Clark. *Manila Times*, June 26, 2002.

Vincent, Isabel. 1996. Canada beckons cream of nannies: Much-sought Filipinas prefer work conditions. *Globe and Mail*, January 20, 1996, pp. A1, A6.

9. Who Needs Yehudi Menuhin?

Costs and Impact of Migration

Bridget Anderson

In her examination of domestic labor in the European Union, Anderson argues that we must understand this form of work within the realm of social reproduction. That is, the contributions domestic workers make in their "host" countries go far beyond a strict economic understanding and extend into the realm of social relations. Not only does the reproductive work performed by migrant domestic workers in private households reproduce people, but it also reproduces consumers, lifestyles, and the status of the employers. By conceptualizing domestic work in terms of social reproduction Anderson is able to reveal that migrant domestic workers (who at this historical moment are overwhelmingly female) not only sell their labor power, but their entire personhood.

Anderson supplements her insightful thesis with concrete examples drawn from her involvement with Kalayaan—a support group for migrant domestic workers based in London. Using the analytic lens of social reproduction analysis, she goes on to examine the issues and barriers currently facing domestic workers as they begin to mobilize and organize for their rights. What makes Kalayaan unique is its dedication to broad-based

*campaigns at a grassroots level that incorporate the par-
ticipation and experiences of migrant workers of many
nationalities. Anderson's essay adds a much-needed
dimension to understanding the highly complex nature of
domestic work.*

We cannot measure the impact that Yehudi Menuhin (as an immigrant) had on those who heard his music, or were taught by him:
but he clearly had an impact.

—Stephen Glover et al.,
Migration: An Economic and Social Analysis (2001)

So observes an analysis of migration published by the U.K.
Home Office. In the context of my own work on migrant
domestic workers in the European Union, this set me to thinking
about the enormous impact this secret labor force has on Europe.
Although themselves hidden, the effects of their labor and their presence—economically, socially, and culturally, are everywhere
apparent. How many of those smart politicians, senior executives,
and newscasters who appear on our television sets night after night
have had their shirts and blouses ironed by migrant women? As with
Yehudi Menuhin, migrant domestic workers contribute something
more than can be captured in economic terms. We need to turn to
ideas of social reproduction, "the fleshy, messy, and indeterminate
stuff of everyday life" (Katz 2001, p. 709), to understand the ways in
which they are integrated into European societies: how the transnational, globalized economy is brought into the home, not just in the
goods consumed there, but in the organizing of reproductive labor.

But we must also recognize that this situation is not unique to
Europe and North America: poor migrant women and girls as
domestic workers are a feature of homes throughout the world,
whether moving across international borders or from rural to urban
areas. As the market relentlessly expands, more and more women
have little choice but to move in order to survive. As the market

relentlessly penetrates the organizing of social reproduction, historically, culturally, and geographically specific processes are increasingly commercialized.

THE TROUBLING RELATION OF DOMESTIC LABOR TO CAPITALISM

The relation of reproductive labor to capitalist production has been the subject of significant debate. Engels distinguished between productive and reproductive labor, the latter being "the production of human beings themselves, the propagation of the species." Some have argued that housewives are, together with peasants, capitalism's subsistence producers, since they reproduce labor power for capital without compensation (Bennholdt-Thomsen 1981). This labor power is differentiated (by gender, caste, class, etc.), but the notion of "production of human beings themselves" goes beyond the production of differentiated workers (and requires more than domestic labor). Domestic work—mental, physical, and emotional labor—is reproductive work, and reproductive work is not confined to the maintenance of physical bodies: people are social, cultural, and ideological beings, not just units of labor, and reproductive labor is not organized exclusively for the labor market, although market forces affect it.[1]

Under capitalism, human beings' social relations find expression and are mediated by patterns of consumption. Reproductive labor, then, not only produces workers; it also produces *consumers* of the products of capitalism, consumers from the cradle (cot or basket? Bed or crib?) to the grave (marble or granite? Embossed or engraved?). Domestic labor both enables and reproduces patterns of consumption. While much attention has been paid to the importance of paid care work, domestic work is not only about care work—it is also cleaning houses, dusting, polishing, ironing, etc. The servicing of lifestyles and consumer goods that would be difficult (if not impossible) to sustain if the other household members were to attempt to do the work themselves—and that household members might not bother to do at all if they had to do it themselves—is an important component of paid domestic work: "Every day I am cleaning for my madam, one riding shoes, two walking shoes, house shoes, that is every day, just for one person. . . . Plus the children, that is one rubber and one shoes for everyday school, that is another two. Fourteen shoes every day. My time is already finished. . . . You will be wondering why she has so many bathrobes, one silk and two cotton. I say, 'Why madam has so many bathrobe?' Every day you have to hang up. Every day you have to press the back because it is crumpled" (Filipina working in Paris, cited in Anderson 2000, pp. 16–17).

Here I am reminded of another observation in the Home Office publication quoted above, noting that the dominance of migrants in low-paid, insecure, "unskilled" sectors does not disadvantage "natives," since "if migrants do not fill these jobs they simply go unfilled or uncreated in the first place" (Glover et al. 2001, para. 6.33). The confinement of tasks to those merely necessary for individual survival would enable most productive workers to service themselves. We do not *have* to live in tidy, dusted homes nor wear ironed clothes. Madam (the consumer) does not *have* to have so many bathrobes in the same sense in which Madam (the "productive worker") maybe has to have her children cared for. While we need to accommodate the raising of children, the distribution and preparation of food, basic cleanliness, and hygiene in order to survive individually and as a species, domestic work is also concerned with the reproduction of lifestyle and, crucially, of status—nobody has to have stripped pine floorboards, hand-wash only silk shirts, and dust-gathering ornaments; they all create domestic work, but they affirm the status of the household, its class, and its access to resources of finance and personnel.

These two functions cannot be disentangled. Reproduction and production are both distinct and intimately related. As labor is socially produced and the organization of homes and kin demonstrates one's position within wider social relations, so the actual doing of the work—who does what job, when and where, and indeed if it is done at all—is a crucial part of its purpose. The relations of social reproduction are "both the medium and the message of social reproduction" (Katz 2001, p. 714). Moreover, as Peck puts it, "the boundary between the spheres of production and reproduction is porous" (Peck 1996, p. 38), for such categories, along with the public and private with which they are twinned, are socially produced and imagined; they are not real.

COMMODIFICATION AND DOMESTIC LABOR— A "WIN-WIN" SITUATION?

Given the unrecognized contribution that domestic work in private households, overwhelmingly performed by women, makes to capitalist economies, could one not argue that paying for domestic work is a step forward, that this recognizes that this is labor and that it has value? Moreover, if a hard-pressed working mother in Europe (and current social and economic structures ensure that there are plenty of these) employs a migrant worker who not only needs the money, but also perhaps the chance to leave a violent husband or a militarized province, is this not a satisfactory and mutually beneficial solution to both their problems?

It is important to recognize the complexity of global and local economic and social forces at work in the national and international migration of women. The impact of structural adjustment policies; of histories of colonialism, imperialism, and patriarchy; of national debt; of the growth of agribusiness; and so on can get lost in microstudies. But women are not simply flotsam on the immense forces that these generate; migration to work in domestic service can represent an opportunity to be creatively grasped, and it is important neither to overromanticize nor to victimize those who might be seizing such opportunities to escape poverty or violence, or to see the world. My suspicion of an approach (the "win-win" approach) that argues both female employer and worker benefit from the commodification of domestic labor emanates in part from the ease with which it lets middle-class employers off the hook. As Janet Momsen, editor of an international collection of case studies on domestic work commented in the preface to her volume, "As mothers and employers we cope with feelings of guilt and ambivalence. . . . Studies of domestic service . . . demand . . . reflexivity on the part of the researcher. If the maid is perceived or defined as having some form of 'otherness,' then we are so defining ourselves and have to struggle with feelings of sisterhood, guilt, and dependence in relation to the worker" (Momsen 1999, p. xiii). This is not just true of researchers but of policy-makers, politicians, activists, trade unionists, and so on. It is these groups that have easiest access to the fora where these debates are not only articulated but also responded to, both theoretically and empirically.[2] It can lead to calls to "professionalize" domestic work, to adopt models of organizing and hierarchizing labor from the productive sphere. These models can seem strangely inappropriate—how does one professionalize dusting, for example? Moreover, professionalization is most easily accomplished in the caring sector, and caring, particularly of the young, is often the "respectable" end of domestic labor (after all, Lady Diana was a nanny before she married a prince). This approach then leaves other workers (and doubtless this will be where migrants congregate) to languish as unskilled. I'm unconvinced that professionalization can be equated with respecting domestic labor and those workers who do it.

The forces of patriarchy and capitalism are such that anyway this win-win approach is not adequate even as a descriptive model. Reproductive labor is often not regarded as work at all. The borders between paid and unpaid domestic labor are extremely nebulous. Take au pairs for instance, constructed by immigration laws in

Europe and in the United States, not as domestic workers but as visitors on "cultural exchange," paid not a wage but "pocket money," and not working but "helping" in the house. In practice, au pairs' experiences are often very different: they complain of working excessive hours for minimal money (and sometimes nothing at all). "Host families" opt for au pairs because it is a cheap and socially acceptable form of childcare, not because they want to give a young woman the opportunity for cultural exchange.

When domestic labor is bought, it is not usually bought in the formal economy. In September 2000 the European Parliament held a public hearing on "Regulating Domestic Help in the Informal Sector," in which it discussed the Smet Report. This noted that "domestic workers who are paid but not declared . . . have a considerable impact on the black economy. This form of work, which is hidden and not easily quantifiable, provides a significant proportion of women with a source of income which is not subject to any form of state control" (Smet 2000, p. 5). Paying for domestic work does not in itself bring it unproblematically into the "productive sphere" since it is still often within the informal economy. And then there is the question of exactly what is being bought. I have argued elsewhere that since the logic of social reproduction is such that the employment of a domestic worker reinscribes gendered, classed, and racialized roles, then what is being purchased is not simply labor power, but "personhood," i.e., it is not only that silver gets polished, but that silver gets polished *by a certain "type" of woman*.[3] The "win-win" approach ignores the relations of power and the conflicts of interest that are intrinsic in the domestic worker–employer relationship (Anderson 2000).

Analyzing paid domestic labor is incredibly complex—there is no quick fix. The social relations surrounding domestic labor vary all over the world, and let's be clear that even when they are not commodified, they can be abusive and unjust. The relations of reproduction are as complex as those of production. Moreover, while some may want women back at home being wives and mothers, placidly facilitating male productivity (or activism!), I am not one of them. But, at the moment, these are the two choices that many women are presented with—which is why many migrant domestic workers themselves employ domestic workers to take on "their" responsibilities while they are away or else ask a (female) relative to do this work unpaid. Nevertheless, it is important, while respecting analytical complexity on the one hand and the reality of women's lives on the other, to use insights from both to inform action and ways forward. What, then, are the issues posed for organizing domestic workers if one takes this social reproduction analysis?

KALAYAAN: A CASE STUDY IN ORGANIZING MIGRANT DOMESTIC WORKERS

To examine this question I will draw on my experiences with Kalayaan, a London-based support organization for migrant domestic workers that I have been involved with since its inception in 1987. Kalayaan provides advice and support to migrant domestic workers and also campaigns with them on immigration and employment matters. It works very closely with the United Workers' Association (UWA), a self-help group of migrant domestic workers comprising some four thousand members from over thirty-five different countries, 90 percent of them women. All its members were undocumented until winning regularization after over ten years of campaigning.

It is important to be clear, since I'm going to be talking about new challenges and conditions, that domestic workers in private households throughout the world have a long history of organizing, in their own organizations, in trade unions, and in migrants' associations (see Chaney and Castro 1984; Cock 1989; Anderson 2000). Just to give one historical example, Domestic Workers Industrial Union IWW Local No. 113, a Wobblies union, specially trained members to wear down the nerves of their employers in order to teach them how to treat their workers: "Speak gently to your cook from now on unless you wish to prepare the meals for your family and scrub the kitchen floor. Because cross and undesirable mistresses are going to be black listed by the union. . . . There will be a long list including every employer of house servants in Denver. And opposite each name, its owner's character will be described without mincing words" (cited in van Raaphorst 1988, p. 191).

Though recognizing that workers are reproducing the status of their employer and that the employer is "buying" more than the worker's labor power, Kalayaan nevertheless emphasizes the importance of the employment contract—both literally and figuratively. The employment contract acknowledges the existence of an employment relation—that the employee is performing *work* and is not in a feudal, quasi-familial, or bonded relation to her employer. It also sets certain standards, minimum wages, maximum hours, rights to holiday and other pay, and delineated tasks. Of course, many employment contracts do no such thing, and in fact workers who want to leave their employers often find that employers threaten them with contract and claim that they are breaking contractual obligations.[4] In the informal sector, where workers are theoretically able to withdraw their labor at a moment's notice, keeping labor—particularly when it is badly paid and "flexible"—can be very difficult. Employers will maximize mechanisms of coercion and control, including immigration status and contract, while if workers attempt to enforce such contractual obligations, the response is typically, "Adel, I think the contract is only paper. The most important thing is the one between us" (employer in Barcelona, cited in Anderson 2000, p. 166).

The existence of an employment contract is beneficial, but as with any worker, the contents of such contracts need to be heavily scrutinized. Moreover, as Adelle Blackett (2000) has so forcefully argued, this is not a job like any other but requires specific legislation. One must recognize the defining impact that living in has on workers. Most obviously, if one loses one's job, one also loses one's home, but more broadly a contract must protect the employee, not only as a worker but also as an individual who has a right to private space, to be a person. There are also very specific issues with mechanisms of contract negotiation and implementation, which often are very unsuitable for domestic workers in private households. Enforcement mechanisms are designed for workers in the public sphere, and the primary means to vindicate rights is through work-initiated lawsuits, but there are numerous formal and informal obstacles for domestic workers to enter such processes.

Kalayaan recognizes that a contract, its existence, negotiation, and enforcement, is not enough. A contract by itself does not adequately express the mechanisms of power of the employers of domestic workers, particularly when they are live-in. The limitations set by a contract will not adequately limit the power of the employer over a migrant woman or man, particularly if the worker is undocumented. Working as a caregiver in a highly personalized environment often draws the worker herself into intense personal, socially durable relationships, furthering and embedding dependence and questions of autonomy. So to take a "benevolent" example, she might choose to use her day off to take the little boy she cares for to a much-anticipated birthday party, because she knows the parents will not take him. Such complex social relations are very difficult to deal with under contract. Though this situation clearly leaves the worker open to working excessive hours for no pay, we cannot ignore the fact that labor is a social as well as an economic process. In some cases women will make a decision to work with a family who offers lower wages precisely because they feel they are "nice," "easy to live with," or treat them "as part of the family." We must be wary of dismissing this as "false consciousness." Human beings desire social and personal relations: university professors may opt to stay with a department where they are lower paid and work harder but operate in a more friendly environment. Many are the voluntary workers and activists who work late into the night because of a sense of responsibility to a client group, sustained by camaraderie. Of course, the social and economic relations governing these situations are very different. I would argue absolutely that migrant domestic workers in private households, isolated in their employment, often far from home and with very limited choices, are far more vulnerable to exploitation as a consequence of this desire for and pleasure in human relations. And this is precisely why reiterating the importance of a contract must go together with enabling people to make informed choices, to set boundaries, and to recognize when their interests inevitably conflict and if they might ever coincide with the employing family. This requires complex and multilayered organizing work that takes into account both the individual situation of the worker and the more general context of the work.

But such requirements are not restricted to the organizing of migrant domestic labor. The informal sector and nontraditional forms of employment such as part-time work, home work, contract work, and telecommuting pose clear challenges to organizing. There are issues around isolation and insecurity of employment, but there is also the fact that the regulation of workers' protection has been focused on the legal concept of the employment relationship based on a distinction between dependent workers and self-employed persons. The rise in the informal sector has brought about confusion with regard to this concept: the employment relationship may be disguised as a relationship with a different legal nature (civil, commercial, familial, etc.), as a short-term relationship that is actually a stable and indefinite relationship (as in persistent renewal of short-term contracts), or as a relationship with an intermediary or agent rather than an employer. There may also be objective ambiguity of employment relationships. Domestic workers in private households may in this sense be seen as archetypal "new workers," and analyzing their labor relations and exploring ways of organizing them may in the long run prove very beneficial to other workers. The old agenda of the labor movement was set by "normal" workers—typically white and male, with a full-time job for a specific employer and limited individual resources, but with the potential for collective action. And certainly not undocumented. But such normal workers are increasingly aberrations; part-time, self-employment, short-term, casual, agency work, and unemployment—this is the fabric of the labor market. Some of the issues that domestic workers have long struggled against are now confronting workers more generally. For example, being constantly "on call," available at any time to labor for an employer, has been a complaint of live-in domestic workers for generations. In the United Kingdom now we are experiencing "zero-hours" contracts, where the employee must be available but is paid only if called to work—in practice, exactly the same phenomenon. Some trade unions are beginning to wake up to these challenges and the tremendous opportunities and potential offered by organizing migrants both with and without legal status, but there is much, and broader, work to be done.

Campaigns in support of migrant domestic workers require community-based organizing and fostering of alliances as well as an internationalism that is practically and theoretically committed to antiracism. Having a constructive means of combating racism, communalism, and chauvinistic nationalism, both within the broader society and within progressive organizations, is extremely important to organizing, particularly when working with migrant communities. Kalayaan and UWA are unusual organisations in a U.K. context in that they organize and work with domestic workers from many nationalities. In the United Kingdom migrants and refugees typically self-organize along lines of country of origin or ethnicity. Moreover, settled communities who may have won certain rights at no small cost to themselves, often dissociate themselves very sharply from "illegal" immigrants, asylum seekers, and others whom they feel will give the community a bad name. As one worker from the Ivory Coast in Kalayaan put it, "The other groups from Ivory Coast are for refugees, they are not interested in me, they will look down, especially if you are undocumented. For what would I go to another place?" The construction of such boundaries encouraged UWA to form what was, for the United Kingdom, a new type of migrants' organization, based first and foremost on legal status and type of employment, working as an undocumented migrant domestic worker. At first commonality was emphasized, and in particular the identification of the impact of legal status on migrants' experiences. This enabled domestic workers of many different nationalities to work together for a common aim. So workers shared experiences across boundaries (of nationality, country of reception, of the private) with a view to identifying common problems.

However, "migrant domestic worker" is not some homogenized category. People have very different experiences and expectations, and these differences are partly structured by individual, household, and broader social factors in their country of origin. But most crucially, domestic workers' employment typically depends on the commodification of some stereotyped national or racialized identity (Anderson 2000). Employers of domestic workers will usually stipulate a particular nationality on the basis that "Filipinas are good with children" or "Sri Lankans are hard workers," or they will state that they do not want workers from a certain group (usually African or Muslim women). Rates of pay vary among nationalities, and different nationalities are competing with each other for jobs often purely on the basis of their nationality. In the United Kingdom, employees in the private household are explicitly excluded from coverage by the race and sex discrimination acts and can be legally discriminated against on the grounds of color or nationality. By overemphasizing what migrant domestic workers shared, the organizations risked alienating a significant proportion of the more marginalized women, particularly since those who are relatively better off in this highly segmented labor market also tend to find it easier to participate in activities—because days off are more determined, because they speak English, because they are more likely to live in central London, and so on. Concerted efforts have been made at an organizational level to allow for differential access to employment and services and the different needs of different groups. This entails recognizing the relations and power among different national groups within the organization. In February 2001, I observed a woman complain that she had not been greeted by a group of Indians when she entered the office, which she felt was because she was African. Jasmin, from India, argued that people often want simply to be among friends and to speak their own language, but she conceded that "we are in a racist country" and so must be sensitive to how such choices might be perceived. The response: "So give me your telephone number, and I will phone you." This kind of organizing is not easy, but it is extremely important for migrant domestic workers because of the reproduction of racialized hierarchies that is in the nature of their employment relations.

CONCLUSIONS

Paid domestic labor is often presented as an issue of personal morality (rather like paid sex). The market and its workings are amoral and are to be applauded except when it enters certain sacrosanct and female areas. I have often noticed how *men* respond to my presentations with glee, because in some sense they feel I'm "showing" the middle-class feminists. The privileges of patriarchy shield many of them from acknowledging their dependence on reproductive labor, managed by wives, mothers, and au pairs. But what needs to be acknowledged is not a question of personal morality; it is that we are all woven into structures of privilege and want, justice and injustice, and privileged women and men must recognize that one cannot simply disavow structural advantages—just as, to a far greater extent, one cannot disavow structural disadvantages.

I repeat, there is much work to be done. At theoretical and empirical levels, we need to engage with the processes of social reproduction. It is by making visible these relations in our daily practices and by organizing and empowering the most marginalized that we can begin to develop the capacity to challenge the currently multiple reactionary relations of social reproduction. We must dare to imagine a world where social reproduction is a positive force, where human interdependence is a source of strength, not weakness. Such imaginings require a leap that takes us way beyond the "win-win" approach—perhaps our imagination can be facilitated by listening to the music of Yehudi Menuhin.

NOTES

1. Moreover, the private household is not the only site of reproductive work, and domestic labor is not the only form of reproductive labor. Not all of this labor is contracted across a market or across the same market: the sectors of the media, of education, of marketing, and so on. But in most societies currently, the household is a vitally important site, not just for the maintenance of physical bodies but also for the reproduction of people.

2. This shouldn't be dismissed as a minor point. When I met the president of the South African Domestic Workers' Union in 2000, she told me that ANC employers can be as exploitative as any other and described that cabinet members would phone her up on the basis of old times in the struggle asking, "Comrade, I need someone to work in my home." "Not comrade," she retorts, "that was before. Now you are an employer."

3. It's important to recognize that domestic workers are not necessarily female; this is historically, geographically, and socially contingent.

4. An interesting case in point is the Standard Employment Contract issued by the Philippine embassy in the United Kingdom. This contract is extremely onerous, requiring in clause 5, for example, that "the Worker is expected at all times to observe proper decorum and shall be courteous, polite, and respectful to her Employer and members of his/her family. The Worker shall also observe the Code of Discipline for Filipino Workers and abide by the laws of the United Kingdom and respect its customs and traditions." In fact, the contract itself does not abide by the laws of the United Kingdom and is in contravention of European legislation since, for example, the hours set out (ten hours per day, six days per week) are well in excess of those set out by the European Working Time Directive.

REFERENCES

Anderson, Bridget. 2000. *Doing the dirty work? The global politics of domestic labour*. London: Zed Books.

Bennholdt-Thomsen, V. 1981. Subsistence production and extended reproduction. In *Of marriage and the market: Women's subordination in international perspective*, edited by K. Young et al., pp. 16–29. London: CSE Books.

Blackett, Adelle. 2000. *Making domestic work visible: The case for specific regulation*. Geneva: International Labour Organisation.

Chaney, E., and M. Castro, eds. 1984. *Muchachas no more: Household workers in Latin America and the Caribbean*. Philadelphia: Temple University Press.

Cock, Jacqueline. 1989. *Maids and madams: Domestic workers under apartheid*. London: Women's Press.

Glover, Stephen, et al. 2001. *Migration: An economic and social analysis*. RDS Occasional Paper 67. London: Home Office.

Katz, Cindi. 2001. Vagabond capitalism and the necessity of social reproduction. *Antipode* 33 (4): 708–27.

Momsen, Janet, ed. 1999. *Gender, migration and domestic service*. London: Routledge.

Peck, Jamie. 1996. *Workplace: The social regulation of labour markets*. New York: Guildford.

Smet, Miet. 2000. Report on regulating domestic help in the informal sector. Report presented to the European Parliament's Committee on Women's Rights and Equal Opportunities.

Van Raaphorst, Donna. 1988. *Union maids not wanted*. New York: Praeger.

10. South African Women

Narratives of Struggle and Exile

Thelma Ravell-Pinto

Globalization, Ravell-Pinto states at the outset, was the chief impediment to national liberation in South Africa. Rich minerals and other natural resources of the country, not to speak of its cheap labor, made it very attractive to foreign investors. Consequently it was not until the mid-eighties that the United States and Europe finally withdrew support for the apartheid regime. Ravell-Pinto contends that national liberation sets the terms upon which feminism in South Africa must be comprehended. Unfortunately, the part played by black South African women against apartheid has been both underestimated and misinterpreted, because conventional history, for a variety of reasons, has simply ignored women. Moreover, white feminists, when writing about black women, are often unable to take the virulence of racism adequately into account. They cannot understand, for instance, why black women resisted apartheid but appear to accept a rigid gender division of labor.

Ravell-Pinto tries to fill in the gender gaps in history by providing a historical overview of the pass system, its implications for women whose service as domestics in white households it was meant to procure, and the cam-

paigns women waged to fight against its institution. She brings into view the participation of women in the formative meetings of the African National Congress and details their own independent efforts in the antiapartheid struggle, including peaceful means such as mass protests and the gathering of signatures for petitions. These events resulted in the imprisonment of large numbers of women and ended in fatalities resulting from police brutality.

Claiming women's narratives—autobiographies, novels, short stories, poems, and plays—as a rich source of information about black African women's roles in the making of history, Ravell-Pinto cites works by women and shows how these can subvert the way conventional history is transcribed. She notes, however, that because black women do not have access to resources, their narratives continue to be mediated by white women writers. She seizes the opportunity to demonstrate the power of the personal narrative by interspersing her essay with "interludes." These interludes (in italics) recount anecdotes about her parents' confrontation with apartheid and her own experience as an exile.

African feminism owes its origins to different dynamics than those that generate Western feminism. It has largely been shaped by African women's resistance to Western hegemony and its legacy within African culture.

— Gwendolyn Mikell, *African Feminism* (1997)

INTRODUCTION

Globalization tends to empower hegemonic communities and structures. South Africa, a recent member of the global community of

---

The original form of this paper was presented at the Seminar on African Women's Narratives, held by the Japan Center for Area Studies, National Museum of Ethnology, Osaka, Japan, in 2000. Reprinted by permission.

democratic nations, is a good example of how this worked. The apartheid politics prior to 1994, which excluded more than 80 percent of the population from participation in the national political arena, made South Africa an international pariah. However, the strategic position of South Africa geographically, coupled with its mineral and other natural resources made the country an attractive partner to Western hegemonic nations. It is therefore not surprising that it took until the mid-eighties for the United States and European nations to withdraw some of the massive economic, military, and political support to this racist minority regime. What muddied the waters was the South African regime's family ties to Europeans; this made the declaration and enforcement of a total (i.e., economic, academic, political, and cultural) boycott of South Africa extremely problematic for European politicians. Not only did the question of kinship to the oppressors play a role, but the apartheid regime was also a haven of cheap black labor. This significantly lowered production costs and made South Africa an international investor's heaven. Even after the declaration of an international boycott, many companies managed to maintain clandestine relations with South Africa.

Western hegemonic interests in South Africa, therefore, made the struggle for liberation extremely complex and protracted, and globalization constituted a stumbling block. The overwhelming burden of the liberation struggle rested mainly on the shoulders of the oppressed population, a situation that made it virtually impossible for women to focus primarily on issues relating to women. The liberation of black South African women became an integral part of the struggle for national liberation.

Women have played a very important role in the South African liberation struggle, not only as mothers, wives, and daughters but also as active participants in the process of change. Their contributions have not always been given the place they deserve because historians have only examined conventional historical sources and ignored women's narratives as sources. According to Tony Bennett,

history "constitutes a particular form of social regulation of statements of the past," and it draws on "social processes whose relations with other social practices are historically variable and contingent (1990, p. 42). For Fredric Jameson it is "not a text, not a narrative, master or otherwise, but . . . as an absent cause, it is
inaccessible to us except in textual form" (1983, p. 35). However,
black South African women's narratives navigate between history
and literature, producing literary texts in order to rewrite history.
Women's narratives, such as *Mother to Mother* by Sindiwe Magona
(1998), reconstitute the collective experience of oppression and
violence, approached through the life of one individual. The historical perspective overlaps with the narrative text and is a site for
political and ideological subversion. The literary imagination can in
this way restore black women, especially, to the history from which
they have been systematically erased. History and literature can
thus enable us to reread, rewrite, and reconfigure the African
woman as an agent of history.

South African women's resistance to apartheid legislation is
often made synonymous to their resistance to the imposition of
passes for women. Some white feminists point to a major discrep-
ancy between black women's public protest and their domestic subjugation. Black South African women have had to enter the public
domain in order to protect the very existence of their families.
There was a concerted effort by the South African government of
the time to systematically eradicate black families. It is therefore
disturbing when well-meaning and otherwise solid white feminist
academics (like Julia Wells, for example), see black women's
resistance to state-imposed restrictions as contradictory to their
apparent acceptance of family structures in which they do not enjoy
complete agency: "While the women effectively resisted oppression from a ruthlessly coercive state, they were at the same time
defending the primacy of their roles as mothers and homemakers.
Racial oppression was tackled while traditional gender-defined
roles were reinforced" (Wells 1993, p. 1).

This view is, however, not shared by Shamim Meer, founding member of both *Speak* magazine and *Agenda: A Journal on Women and Gender.* In an anthology of women's contributions to *Speak,* published between 1982 and 1994, Meer comes to very different conclusions. She shows how gender relations were manifested in the thinking of black South African women:

> When we started *Speak*, we often heard comments that ideas of women's liberation were foreign to African tradition and culture. That these ideas were Western and bourgeois, and had nothing to do with the struggles of black, working-class women in South Africa. But the more we talked and listened to women in communities and factories, the more this was proved wrong.
>
> Whenever women came together it was clear that it was these very personal struggles that held us back. Women in communities talked in their women's groups about difficulties in getting to meetings because of husbands who expected meals on time. Women in trade unions talked of similar problems. Women's time was not their own time. . . . Trade-union women raised issues such as sharing housework and child care with men, sexual harassment from male comrades, and the traditional attitudes of men and women. Women talked about violence in the form of rape and beatings by men.
>
> Women spent a lot of time talking about such personal problems because these [*sic*] are important. (1998, p. 96)

Moreover, in her anthology she shows how women were in the forefront of the struggle against traditional practices such as *labola* (bride price) and polygamy, both of which were hostile to women. It is precisely the psychological impact of racist and structural oppression on all areas of the lives of black women that seem to be consistently underestimated by some white feminists. This inability of hegemonic feminism to be inclusive of cultural and political *difference* can lead to profound misunderstanding and hostility. Beverly Guy-Sheftall's definition of African American feminism is more appropriate and attractive to black South African women: "I use the term 'feminist' to capture the emancipatory vision and acts of resistance among the diverse group of African American women who attempt in their writings to articulate their understanding of the complex nature of black womanhood, the interlocking nature of oppressions black women suffer, and the necessity of sustained struggle in their quest for self-definition, the liberation of black people, and gender equality. Some also express solidarity with other women and people of color engaged in local and global struggles for liberation" (1995, p. xiv).

Feminism can only be used as a global concept if it truly represents the variety and diversity among women crossculturally, interculturally, and transnationally.

HISTORICAL OVERVIEW

Apartheid is often erroneously marked by the year the Nationalist Party came to power in 1948; however, the pass system dates back to the beginning of the nineteenth century. In 1809 the Caledon Code was introduced in the Cape Colony to limit the movement of the Khoisan servants; it was expanded in 1828 with the emancipation of slaves (Wells 1993, p. 5). The pass laws were used to tie black workers to their masters in perpetual servitude and prevent them from free access to other employment. Ordinance 50 of 1828, however, was intended to improve the conditions of the Khoisan and other free persons. This gradually led to a vision of a nonracial franchise that developed in the Cape. A black African elite began to emerge all over South Africa, composed of teachers, ministers of religion, interpreters, clerks, traders, editors, farmers, and craftsmen. However, the white Afrikaner farmers' trek from the Cape, also known as the Great Trek, challenged this development. The Afrikaners trekked inland to escape the antislavery legislation and avoid paying taxes levied by the Cape Colony. It was among their ranks that white nationalism could show its ugly head.

With the emergence of an educated black elite, there was a need for newspapers in African languages to keep the people informed, especially about new legislation passed concerning their rights. The first newspapers in an African language were printed as early as 1844. In 1876, Rev. Elijah Makiwane became the first African editor of the newspaper *Isigidmi Sama Xosa* (Xhosa Messenger; Rosenthal [1949?], pp. 2–13). John Tengo Jabavu succeeded him as the new editor in 1881; he was symbolic for the new political awareness among Africans. In 1888, J. T. Jabavu became the editor of the first newspaper in Xhosa, *Imvu Zebantsundu* (Opinion of the Brown People; Wilson and Thompson 1975, p. 74). He used the African vote as a lever to influence political opinion.

A Native Education Association had been formed in 1882. It attacked the pass laws as a burden for "civilized natives." The pass laws remained on the books right through the nineteenth century, and with the discovery of diamonds in 1867 and gold in 1886, it took on new characteristics. In *We Now Demand*, Julia Wells posits that the imposition of passes for black women was mainly caused by the economic needs of white society, although she expresses this differently: "[They used means] both coercive—aimed at forcing the unemployed into wage labour—and exclusive by hypothetically preventing or discouraging those who refused to become employed from entering the urban or mining areas. Africans who were not working for white employers now became the special target of pass legislation. . . . Passless Africans could face fines, imprisonment, forced labour, or expulsion from the area until such time as they contracted employment" (Rosenthal [1949?], pp. 5–6).

Before 1890, black women were not covered by the pass laws, but as their labor was required they became targets for new legislation. Wells's analysis of passes for women understates both the significance of the ideology of racism that prevailed even at that time and how this was built into, and maybe itself became, the most important element of all the legislation enacted by the South African government. Mahmood Mamdani compares racism in

South Africa to the "native question" in the other colonial territories in Africa: "That is why it takes a shift of focus from the labor question to the native question to underline that which is African and unexceptional in the South African experience. That commonality, I argue, lies not in the political economy but in the form of the state: the bifurcated state . . . (which) tried to keep apart forcibly that which socioeconomic processes tended to bring together freely: the urban and the rural, one ethnicity and another" (1996, p. 28). He emphasizes the similarities in the way in which the colonial authorities imposed their rule. Mamdani sees the interethnic rivalries and wars that followed independence in many African states as a direct result of this ideological manipulation.

The first demonstrations against passes occurred in the Orange Free State in 1913. This is described by Wells as related to a special group of urbanized African women "more nearly [resembling] the eighteenth-century Cape, where trekboers and their Khoikhoi or slave servants shared a common way of life" (1993, p. 15). However, the slave-owner's way of life and the slave's way of life cannot be equated. Furthermore, the Orange Free State has always been the most harshly segregated and oppressive state in South Africa; at the time, it had discriminatory legislation not yet prevalent in the rest of the country.

In 1938, my parents went on a tour of South Africa by train. They had just stopped at Bloemfontein station (in the Orange Free State) and were happy to get new refreshments. They were traveling with three young children, and the dining facilities for blacks on the trains were all but adequate. Happy to have reached a big station, my mother alighted for some boiling water and coffee. Having been given both of the above in her own containers, she discovered that the coffee was black. Viewing this as an accidental oversight, she asked for some milk for the coffee. The vendor, shocked by this unexpected request, brusquely told her to pay and leave.

It took only a split second for my mother to realize that the black-

ness of the coffee had political connotations. When this dawned on her, she absolutely refused to pay unless she was given milk, and she offered to return the coffee. This, she realized, was out of the question, as her container was considered "black" and thus unclean. It was a taboo for white people to share utensils with black people.

The assistant at the little window was completely overwhelmed by my mother's refusal to pay, for, as he repeatedly told her "black people drink black milk here [i.e., in the Orange Free State]." My mother's insistence on "white" milk seemed to violate this tacit agreement and made him uncertain and agitated. He was confused by her refusal to comply with a perfectly normal request. The manager was called on my mother's insistence, and he grudgingly instructed the still-bewildered shop assistant to give "the woman" some milk. Needless to say, he must have been very happy to see the train depart so that he could revert back to the accepted practice of "black milk."

While the Cape Colony provided clear guidelines for educated Africans in the form of limited participation in common citizenship, namely the vote, the Transvaal and the Orange Free State established constitutional barriers. Their central policy was based on the perceived fundamental inequality between whites and blacks. The crown colony of Natal, which was to become the fourth province, "entered the Union [in] 1910 with a tradition of differentiation and arguments of segregation which, when allied to the policies of the ex-republics [i.e., Transvaal and the Orange Free State] succeeded in confining and then eliminating the Cape tradition" (Walshe 1970, pp. 1–10).

In 1891, the Waaihoek Location in the Orange Free State was created to remove the squatters. A formal set of location regulations was enacted as early as 1893, based on the principle that blacks (this applied to both males and females) not working for whites were undesirable. The Anglo-Boer war (also called the South African War) forced huge numbers of people into the towns. From a commercial center of about four thousand people in 1890, Bloemfontein's population increased more than tenfold (Orange River Colony 1904, Table X, p. 16). The Orange River Census showed that the urban population of Bloemfontein consisted of mainly local women, while a large number of the men who came to the area had come in from the rural areas. About 50 percent of all black females in Bloemfontein worked as domestic servants in white households. However, because of the low pay and poor working conditions, they actively looked for other forms of employment. They became wives of standholders or worked in the informal sector as professional cake decorators, dressmakers, or laundry women for whites (Wells 1993, pp. 22–28).

Women's passes were already instituted in the free states in the 1890s, and their petitions and lobbying were of no avail. For a short time during and after the war, black people thought that the British, who had won the war, would be more liberal with regard to their "native policy," and the pass system would be abolished. However, with the South African Act of 1910, the four provinces united to form the Union of South Africa. The British unequivocally surrendered the whole of South Africa to the whites, and the native policies of the respective provinces remained intact. When these intentions became apparent, black leaders came together at the South African Native Convention in Bloemfontein in 1909. They sent a delegation to London to put their case to the British king. They also petitioned the colonial secretary and the governor of the Orange River Colony, but all was in vain.

The Bloemfontein municipal authorities argued that passes for black women were necessary to stop them from engaging in prostitution and brewing beer illegally. However, as Wells points out, the main purpose of passes for African women was to get them into domestic service in white households. According to the 1904 census report, 81 percent of all female prisoners were domestic workers. As Wells states, "Clearly, Free States Whites found disobedient servants far more threatening to the social order than either brewers or prostitutes" (1993, p. 30). Women fought against the imposition of passes, as it put their lives at jeopardy on various levels. They not only became the targets for white men who exchanged passes for sexual favors, but they also became easy victims for the police (black and white), who sexually harassed them. After the formation of the Union, the Native Vigilance Association petitioned the new minister of finance and native affairs. They stressed that passes imposed both physical abuse and additional financial burdens on women.

In 1902 the African People's Organization (APO) was formed. It had a predominately so-called Colored membership (i.e., one of mixed ancestry: African, Asian, and European), and from 1905 on was headed by Dr. Abdurahman, a member of the Cape Provincial Council. The APO sought contact with African leaders, contributed to the expenses of African delegates to London in 1909, and advocated passive resistance for all groups, Africans, Coloreds, and Indians. In the north, in the Orange River Colony, the Native Vigilance Association was founded, later becoming the Orange River Colony Congress. They argued for the extension of the Cape Colony rights in the whole Union, especially with regard to passes for women (South African Native Affairs Commission 1903–1909, pp. 369–78).

In the first years after the formation of the Union of South Africa, it became clear that there was serious cause for concern about the position of Africans. Seme, a lawyer who had studied in the United States and in Britain, took the initiative to convene a Union-wide conference on January 8, 1912, inviting African intellectuals and chiefs. This led to the formation of the South African Native National Congress (SANNC), later to be renamed the African National Congress. The Reverend John L. Dube became the first president, with Seme as treasurer and Solomon Plaatje as the secretary (Walshe 1970, pp. 33–35). There are no records that reveal women's political participation in the SANNC's inaugural meeting, even though women obviously attended as caterers, hostesses, and interested observers. Women circulated a petition

throughout the towns and villages of the Orange Free State and
an all-female delegation to Cape Town to see the ministe ₋₁
finance and native affairs, Henry Burton. With the assistance of
Walter Rubusana and Senator W. P. Schreiner, six women were
granted an audience. They submitted their petition, containing five
thousand signatures (see "Petition to Louis Botha" 1912).

Women were not members but sympathizers of the Congress;
thus the executive council of the Free State Congress petitioned the
prime minister on their behalf. In May 1913, as a result of the
arrests of many more women, a mass meeting was held in the Waaihoek location. Two hundred women marched through the center of
town, demanding to see the mayor. In a meeting with the mayor the
next day, the women were told that passes were the responsibility
of the Union government. Dissatisfied, they decided to surround the
police station of Waaihoek. Eighty women were arrested and put on
trial the next morning. Six hundred women marched through
Bloemfontein in support of these women and counteracted police
attacks by hitting the police with sticks. The Free State unrest of
1913 led to the formation of the Bantu Women's League, with
Charlotte Maxeke as their first president. In July, six hundred
women handed their passes to the deputy mayor of Bloemfontein,
and so many women had been arrested that they had to be sent to
other prisons. Charlotte Maxeke also led a delegation of women to
see the prime minister, Louis Botha, who promised to seek redress
for women's passes. At this stage, the Bantu Women's League was
a support structure for the Congress movement.

It is interesting to note in the case of Bloemfontein that the
imposition of passes for African women was directly related to the
actions of white women. In 1910, white citizens had complained
about not being able to get domestic workers at a reasonable price
any longer. As a result of the influence of these whites on municipal policy, the Free State Municipality moved toward harsher
enforcement of the pass laws, which manifested itself in various
ways. In order to force black women into domestic service, the

municipality instituted harsher control of the payment of the location tax. When even this failed, the whites called a public meeting to discuss the "acute native servant problem." As women continued their campaigns against passes in the Orange Free State and refused to buy passes in the face of imprisonment, whites had their own protests: "The situation in Winburg became especially volatile when angry whites proposed that all passless black women be imprisoned in the town, rather than arrested only six at a time—the capacity of the local jail. Black men responded by threatening a general strike of the entire black workforce, and even white women protested the possible loss of all their domestic servants at once" (Wells 1993, p. 45).

It was women who had mobilized black political movements and black newspapers, receiving much publicity. Both Sol Plaatje and Dr. Abdurahman spoke out regarding the treatment received by black women in prison. At the APO annual meeting in Kimberley, Dr. Abdurahman attacked the condition of black women as a modern form of slavery. Katie Louw from Bloemfontein attended the conference and read out reports on the women's struggle. Women's activities were reported in the local and national papers. Although the police reduced the active harassment, the laws on the books remained unchanged. The needs of the white urban housewives, however, finally prevailed.

The Land Act of 1913 and the subsequent Land and Trust Act of 1936 removed African voters from the common voters' role. Africans were consigned to 13.8 percent of the land, which was designated as Reserve Areas for Africans; this prohibited them from buying land and owning property in the rest of South Africa (Rodgers 1980, p. 10). For the women who lived in the Reserve Areas, influx control exacted some of the most extreme forms of punishment. They were not allowed to join their husbands if these husbands were termed "migrant workers." These women were left behind in the rural areas and did not get to see their husbands for years. These "widows in the Reserves" (Ntantala 1957) had to care for their children, the elderly and infirm, and those people the South African government termed "superfluous appendages" in the urban areas. Women who were in gainful employment in the cities were severely restricted. Their children were not allowed in the urban areas. Women's responses to the harsh treatment meted out to them have been documented variously in many publications (e.g., Cock 1980 and Magona 1990).

For the first time I am a mother to my child. I carried my other children for nine months. I fed them with my milk to make them strong. But even as they made me happy, they made me sad. I knew I must send them away.

My first born Sipho was just eleven months when the inspector came. They gave me 24 hours to take him to my sister. I can still hear him crying. He didn't understand.

For me the saddest thing in my life was to take my children on the train and come back without them. For Matshepo it was even worse. She took Teboho home. A month later her baby was dead. (Matlanyane Sexwale 1994, pp. 12, 13, 72)

Black women who lived in the townships on the basis of their marriage to a man who had residential rights enjoyed an equally tenuous existence. They were dependents of their husbands while the latter were gainfully employed. If their husbands lost their jobs, divorced them, or died, the wives lost their houses and residential permits. For, as Luckhardt and Wall state, "Women serving no purpose for the White economy are discarded, unable to live with their husbands except perhaps during the annual two-week holiday allowed to migrant workers. They fight for survival in the barren reserves, eking out a miserable existence from what little land is available, supplemented only by the meager earnings sent by their husbands. Kwashiorkor and other diseases associated with malnutrition are widespread and death from starvation, particularly among children, is common" (Luckhardt and Wall 1980, pp. 298–99).

Though women remained active and vigilant, they could not prevent legislation. The Bantu Women's League had been replaced by the ANC Women's League through a resolution passed in 1943. The skills women learned in the "Defiance Campaign" gave birth to a new generation of politically active women like Lilian Ngoye, Martha Mahlokoane, Florence Matomela, and many others. The founding of the Federation of South African Women (FSAW) in 1954 facilitated a national organization of women under a Charter of Women's Aims (Bernstein 1985, p. 86). This was the first time that women formulated their particular position within the liberation movement and focused on their roles as women.

The FSAW broadened the struggle to include the rights of women as workers as well as mothers and wives. This feminist women's association was structurally linked to the broad liberation movement representing the ANC, the Congress of Democrats, the South African Indian Congress, and the Colored People's Congress.

The women in all these organizations automatically became members of the FSAW. It is worth mentioning that during this period the Black Sash, an all white women's organization, had been organizing silent protests against the imposition of passes for African women. But as an all-white organization, their actions remained restricted to one racial group demonstrating for another racial group. This was problematic because it removed agency from black women. In 1955, the first major national multiracial demonstration against passes was organized. It was attended by more than two thousand women from all walks of life. What started as a peaceful demonstration became a huge antipass movement:

> When Helen Joseph and Lilian Ngoyi left their homes at 4:45 AM on the morning of 27 October 1955, neither knew what to expect. Ngoyi left her burial book, bankbook, and other papers with her mother, not knowing if she would be coming back. But as they

drove the forty miles to Pretoria, they saw trainloads of singing, shouting women on their way to the demonstration. Even the refusal of ticket agents to sell tickets for Pretoria had not deterred the women. Many simply walked to the next station and requested tickets for an intermediate destination and then paid the extra fare to Pretoria once on board. (Wells 1993, p. 110)

The police took no action against the delegates, who delivered the piles of written protests while the women outside sang freedom songs. When the strength of the women became apparent, the husbands and fathers, in particular, realized that the apartheid authorities would have no hesitation about beating, brutalizing, and imprisoning the leaders in order to intimidate the members of the movement. But as Yawitch explains, "Action by women was fundamental. For women are conceptualized as being the center of stability and security. The arrest of the women radicalized the men, and in the case of the white men, rioting by African women was perceived as a threat to the entire social structure and to all order" (1980, p. 215).

During the ensuing months, networks developed, and at the Transvaal Women's Day Conference on March 11, 1956, more than two thousand women showed up. All over the country, authorities had to deal with demonstrations and processions of women protesting the pass system. A major demonstration was planned for August 9, 1956. The leadership of the ANC was hesitant, however, because they feared that women would be arrested. Nevertheless, on August 9 twenty thousand women converged on Pretoria despite the threats of the police. All of these women crowded into the amphitheater in front of the Union Buildings in Pretoria. Lilian Ngoyi led the delegation of eight to the prime minister, but he would not receive them.

This great Pretoria march was a turning point in the women's struggle. It radicalized both the women themselves and the Congress alliance. After the democratic elections in 1994, August 9 became an official holiday, South African Women's Day, in recognition of the important contribution of women to the general liberation struggle.

The issuing of passes continued nonetheless. The first women's passes issued in 1956 were to women in the rural areas. At this stage, the ANC and the FSAW were in competition over the issue of who should be organizing women and whether it was advisable to continue in the same manner or whether the women should return to their former tactics of passive resistance. Men in the Congress movement had become involved in the antipass movement, and mass arrests continued. In Johannesburg, large numbers of women had to go into wage labor in order to pay taxes. During an antipass campaign organized by the Pan African Congress (PAC) at the police station at Sharpeville on March 21, 1960, the police opened fire on unarmed demonstrators. They killed sixty-nine women, men, and children and injured many others. This massacre marked the end of the nonviolent struggle in South Africa. The government responded with the Unlawful Organizations Act (1960), which banned the ANC and the PAC and effectively forced the liberation movement underground. The General Laws Amendment Acts (1962, 1963, and 1965) gave sabotage a very wide definition and gave the police the authority to detain people in solitary confinement, first for 90 days and later for 180 days. The repressive laws aimed at controlling and silencing the black population had a gender-specific impact; it caused an estimated one-third of all African households in the urban areas and two-thirds in the Bantustans to become female-headed (Budlender 1999).

I have early memories of traveling to Cape Town with my mother on a Saturday in the early fifties in one of those "trackless" trams that ran only on the suburban line to Cape Town. They had a very special sound I have not heard anywhere since. I remember the Old Drill Hall, where the big public meetings were held. I was too small to understand the politics, but I felt the tensions and enthusiasm of the people handing out flyers and engaging the passers-by in debates about upcoming legislation. I remember hundreds of multi-colored people milling around each other in the halls. In the fifties, we still thought that apartheid would be over in a few years' time. I remember my mother assuring us that we would see the new South Africa soon—that we had history on our side.

My mother and some other union officials came to our house to discuss strategies. They were trying to set up a trade union at the local fireworks factory. We were not allowed to listen to these big people talking, but the walls were not thick enough. They had to plan and organize a strike at the fireworks factory. Here my mother did the work of a white man but got the pay of a black woman. She had to teach her boss about the chemical formulae and how to run a department. She realized that as a white man, he had to appear to be in charge. I remember the tension and excitement in the family when my mother was arrested with the other union officials. They had to go to trial for organizing an "illegal" strike.

I remember the fundraisers and how we as children helped. Our "farm" was a good venue for big barbecues. We had a big, enclosed yard with lots of space to have fires and an outside band to play music. This was an opportunity for people to have fun and engage in a lot of political interaction at the same time. In this way they raised enough funds to pay the lawyers' fees. I remember the treason trial and the conversations that my parents had about the misinformation in the newspapers. We were apprehensive, yet all this time we thought that this could not possibly last.

I remember the Sharpeville massacre in 1960. We traveled past Nyanga, the black location in Cape Town every day on our way to high school. We saw the people who had been evicted by the police sitting outside with their bundles and their babies in the cold Cape Town winter rain. They were waiting to be picked up on a government truck. I remember the police coming to check for "passes" in the bus queue where we waited to get the "Crossroads" bus after school.

The police regularly beat up grown women with babies on their backs. I remember the feeling of nausea as we stood around in small groups whispering our outrage. I remember my father listening to our anguished stories and giving us sweets from his jacket pocket.

I remember Sharpeville. I was a teenager in high school preparing for matriculation finals that year. There were fewer girls in our class, and I would have liked to concentrate only on the academic work, but politics intruded. Politics always intruded. I was old enough to understand the shock and horror that reverberated around the country at the killing of unarmed women, men, and children. South Africa had no television, and the radio news was censored.

I remember our school bus passing along the border of Nyanga, completely surrounded by the South African army trucks and heavily armed soldiers. We lived in shocked silenced and anticipation. Then came the banning of all political organizations. We were reduced to whispering and looking around us for possible informers.

WOMEN'S WRITINGS

The documenting of black women's stories is an ongoing process. Much of South African women's narratives seek to rewrite the construction of South African reality as it has been portrayed through conventional history. The narrative text is a site of political and ideological subversion. Literature enables us to explore a different version of South African history. The successful artistic documentation of the indices of injustice and exploitation helps us to understand this history. As we reread women's stories—autobiographies, plays, shorter or longer fiction or poetry—we gain insight into a new process of history-making. However, most black women still lack the basic means to record their own narratives, as well as financial resources and educational facilities. Thus many stories of black women are still mediated through the perspective of white female narrators. This is a complicated process, as it involves several ideologically complex issues.

In a country like South Africa, where communication across

color lines continues to be complicated, who is telling the story and who is writing it becomes pertinent. The (hidden) agenda of the compiler/editor and the context in which the narration occurs are significant. A recent example of this can be found in the recording of the stories of black women who testified to the Truth Commission as narrated in *Country of My Skull* by Antjie Krog. These narratives are embedded in the Afrikaner master narrative; thus, even in their own narratives, these women are marginalized.

Another ideological question is whether the actual taping occurs in the house of the madam or in a neutral space. The language of the narration and the identity of the translator are pertinent as well. The educational level of the translator influences the content and quality of the narration. Most whites recording the stories of African women do not speak African languages and are dependent on "free translation" by other Africans. These are only a few of the problem areas. Many of those who are privileged with access to knowledge-making structures in South Africa have been and are still the same people who were actually involved in the deliberate silencing of black women's voices.

Thus we have to distinguish between self-representation and reportage by others. Although both have ideological problems, the latter has a greater chance of misrepresentation. In the case of white narrators telling the stories of black women (very often their domestic servants), the degrees of mediation and the extent to which the text will be counter-hegemonic may be problematic. If the "I" who speaks has to use a different language, we could ask ourselves whether the text is properly understood. Some examples of white women recording the experiences of black women include *Die Swerfjare van Poppie Nongema*, written by Elsa Joubert (1978); *The Calling of Katie Makanya: A Memoir of South Africa*, by Margaret McCord (1995); *Zulu Woman: The Life Story of Christina Sibiya*, told by Rebecca Hourwich Reyher ([1948] 1999) to mention but a few. These texts seldom escape the imprint of white patronage. Very often both the white writers and the black female narrators have an inadequate grasp of the workings of hegemony. A notable exception is Beata Lipman, who published the anthology *We Make Freedom: Women in South Africa* (1984), in which she records interviews with black and white women. She appears cognizant of her whiteness and the advantages it affords her.

Too few black women are writing or have written autobiographies; *Drawn in Colour* (1960) and *The Ochre People* (1963) by Noni Jabavu remained the only ones for a long time. Here, too, the educational opportunities and social status Noni Jabavu enjoyed as the daughter of D. D. T. Jabavu and the granddaughter of John Tengu Jabavu (see above) played an important role. Her father, D. D. T. Jabavu, studied at Yale University and became one of the first African lecturers to teach at the University College of Fort Hare (Walshe 1970).

If we adhere to conventional genre categories, it is possible to list all the autobiographies by black South African women rather quickly: *A Window on Soweto*, by Joyce Sikakane (1977); *Call Me Woman*, by Ellen Kuzwayo (1985); *Part of My Soul Went*, by Winnie Mandela (1985); *Makeba*, by Miriam Makeba with James Hall (1987); and *Across Boundaries*, by Mamphela Ramphele (1997). However, if all literature is autobiographical (and all autobiography is literature) in some measure, we can include many more works.

There is another subgenre, which covers the testimonies of workers, mostly semiliterate or illiterate black women, which is worth mentioning here. The problem with this type of work remains the focus and influence of the researcher and how this detracts from the empowerment of the women concerned. The following texts are not uniform; sometimes it is obvious that the respondents do not understand that certain statements or attitudes actually contribute to further stereotyping. However, many texts focus on the suffering and effects of oppression on these women: *The Story of Mboma*, by Mboma Dladla as told to Kathy Bond (1979), and *The Women of Phokeng: Consciousness, Life Strategy, and Migrancy in South Africa, 1900–1983*, by Belinda Bozzoli and Mmantho Nkotsoe (1991). Other publications consist mainly of anthologies comprising autobiographical sketches: *Working Women: A Portrait of South Africa's Black Women Workers*, by Lesley Lawson and Helene Perold (1985); *We Came to Town*, edited by Caroline Kerfoot (1985); *A Talent for Tomorrow: Life Stories of South African Servants* by Suzanne Gordon (1985); *Vukani Makhosikazi* (Women Awake): *South African Women Speak*, compiled by Jane Barret et al. (1985); *Simbambene* (We Work Together): *The Voices of Women at Mboza*, by Hanlie Griesel (1987); and *Women Speak*, edited by Shamim Meer (1998).

Many novels by women give insight into historical processes as they affect women's lives. A novel like *Mother to Mother*, by Sindiwe Magona (a fictional account of the killing of the American Amy Biehl in Guguleto, Cape Town) has historical value not only because it is based on a historical incident but also because of the context. This incident gives valuable insight into the lives of urban blacks under the apartheid system. The novel shows how seemingly innocent and well-meaning Africans became brutalized by a system geared to the destruction of black life and livelihood in South Africa. There are many other examples, of which I will mention but a few: *A Question of Power*, by Bessie Head (1974); *Muriel at Metropolitan*, by Miriam Tlali (1975); *Cross of Gold*, by Lauretta Ngcobo (1981); *You Can't Get Lost in Cape Town* (1987) and *David's Story* (2001), by Zoe Wicomb; *Daughters of the Twilight*, by Farida Karodia (1986); *To My Children's Children*, by Sindiwe Magona (1990); *Die Storie van Monica Peters*, by E. K. M. Dido (1996); and *Have You Seen Zandile?* a play by Gcina Mhlophe et al. (1988). This list is by no means exhaustive. Historians will have to read both the written versions of the oral narratives in books such as Lipman's *We Make Freedom* and *Women in South Africa*, compiled by Seageng Tsikang and Dinah Lefakane (1988), as well as the poetry written by South African women. A few prominent published women poets include Gladys Thomas, Blossom Pegram,

Jennifer Davids, and Lindiwe Mabuza. The works of many women remain unpublished, and some have not had the courage to even submit these to publishers, for, as the Vietnamese filmmaker and scholar Trinh T. Minh-ha posits, "The world's earliest archives or libraries were the memories of women. Patiently transmitted from mouth to ear, body to body, hand to hand. In the process of story-telling, speaking and listening refer to realities that do not involve just the imagination" (1989, p. 121).

It was the first time that my children would be in Africa even though Africa had permeated their lives in Holland. Rayner was twelve, and Mondli four. Rayner still remembered that South Africa refused him a visa when he was eight and when his brother was a few months old. His granny had sent airline tickets. She thought that because his father had been allowed to visit his very ill mother for two weeks, we would be allowed in, too. We applied for visas at the embassy in The Hague, thinking that a mother with two small children could not possibly pose any serious political threat. We received an official letter saying that we had been refused entry into South Africa; no reasons were given for this refusal. This letter traumatized him. What did they think he would do?

I tried to get a visa again in 1980 when I visited Zimbabwe as a consultant on a fact-finding mission. This time my mother had flown up from Cape Town and urged me to try again. Zimbabwe had no embassy, just a trade mission, and my mother was convinced that they would allow me in for two weeks. I can still hear her say to me: "How can they refuse you entry into your own country?" The official at the desk wanted me to explain why I had previously been refused entry. When I informed him that no reasons were given, he appeared offended by my response. He retorted angrily, "I don't like your attitude!" and stamped "Entry Refused" across my Dutch passport.

We were excited about the trip to Zimbabwe in 1981, because we had been sent out by a Dutch organization to set up an educa-

tional center for ex-combatant women. This was one of the projects I had submitted the year before during a fact-finding mission to Zimbabwe. The women had already been settled on the farm but without adequate organizational or educational structures. My husband and I had originally been hesitant about relocating because it meant uprooting the entire family. Having been convinced that it was really urgent, we ended up postponing our commitments. For my husband, it actually meant giving up his job. This was going to be an opportunity to participate in this brand-new African democracy and maybe to see some family members. We were excited about finally going to live in Africa again. We saw this as a dress rehearsal for the return to our own country.

We arrived at Salisbury (now Harare) airport in the late afternoon of Friday, July 31, 1981. We had to change planes in Nairobi, Kenya, and wait at the airport for six hours. Our airline, KLM, flew from Amsterdam to Johannesburg via Nairobi and then from Johannesburg to Salisbury. As we were not allowed entry into South Africa, we had to disembark in Kenya. By the time we reached Zimbabwe we had been traveling for almost twenty-four hours. My niece, Geraldine, a member of the ANC unit in Zimbabwe, had promised to meet us at the airport. We saw her waving as we stepped down on the tarmac. We were elated and overwhelmed to see her mother, my eldest sister Cynthia, with her. This now really felt like a homecoming. Neither my sister nor Geraldine had ever seen Rayner or Mondli, so we were all very excited about this family reunion.

Our destination was Melfort farm, forty kilometers north of Salisbury, so we decided to have dinner first. However, the big station wagon was so full of luggage that it seemed foolish to just leave it parked on the side of the road while we went into a restaurant. Geraldine called her chief to find out whether we could all come to their residence for dinner. Joe Gqabi, the ANC's chief representative in Zimbabwe, welcomed us enthusiastically. He was also the chief of intelligence and a member of the ANC's National Executive Council.

We arrived at the house in the suburb of Ashdown Park just as it was getting dark and parked our car next to Joe Gqabi's car in the enclosure. Geraldine and Kobalo, the co-resident, immediately noticed that the outside lights were not working. While we prepared the dinner of fried chicken, Kobalo and the boys tried to fix the lights, which served as a security precaution. I distinctly recall my sense of unease about the children being outside in the dark.

We had a happy and cheerful dinner, talking and toasting on meetings and reunions and singing "Nkosi Síkelel'i-Afrika" while we took pictures of this "homecoming." Cynthia had come up from Cape Town to spend a few days with Geraldine. We were happily reunited with our family and compatriots and made plans for the year ahead. Little did we know that this was a "last supper" for Joe, whose assassins were just biding their time outside. When we were ready to leave, Joe picked Mondli up in his arms to give him a farewell hug, and I remember him saying, "What is a big boy like you doing with a bear?" Those were the last words I remembered.

Cynthia decided to accompany us to Melfort for a few days so that we could catch up on some of the news. We left Joe standing in the enclosed yard, ready to leave, too—he did not sleep at the house because he knew that it was not safe. Six months earlier, on February 24, there had been an attempt on his life. I remember how dark it was with no streetlights once we left Salisbury. We arrived at Melfort at about 8:30.

It was a huge, old-fashioned, eight-room farmhouse with an enormous lounge and a patio that opened to a big swimming pool. The floodlights and siren reminded us of this country's recent history. It was clear that the previous owner felt that this was a war zone. We had tea and made plans for the next day. Geraldine and Kobalo left around 11 PM. James and the boys retired immediately, while Cynthia and I stayed up to catch up on the lost years.

When I opened my eyes the next morning, Geraldine was standing in our bedroom. I must have slept so deeply that I did not hear James letting her in. Her first sentence changed our entire stay in Zimbabwe. She looked subdued and spoke softly, and I remember wondering why she was there so early. The words "they assassinated Joe last night" sounded matter of fact, but we all suddenly jumped in shock and horror. I felt my skin crawl.

On their return from Melfort, they found him beside his car. The car was riddled with bullets, and his body looked like a sieve. This was not an assassination; it was overkill. They reported the killing to the minister of state first, because he was a friend. He came to the house with them, and then only did they alert the police. They suspected that the police could be involved somehow, because the old Rhodesian police had close ties with the apartheid government.

This, then, was our homecoming! I thought I could protect the children from this news, but it was on the radio and the television the next day. Cynthia dressed hastily and left with Geraldine, as so many things had to be arranged. Joe Gqabi's wife, who worked as a nurse in Botswana, still had to be told. As it turned out, she had already heard the news of her husband's assassination on the radio.

We were hardly up and dressed when two detectives arrived at the house to interview us. We were the last people to see Joe Gqabi alive, and James's hat was found at the scene of the crime. We suddenly became witnesses, even suspects, in a murder investigation. The experience was surreal. They only wanted to question me and not James, who had been with us all the time. It slowly became obvious that they had ulterior motives: they were interested in my relationship with Geraldine and when we had planned this trip. To say that this was a nightmare would be an understatement. The same detectives came back the next day and interrogated me about the sequence of events and tried to intimidate me. It felt like being back in South Africa again. Slowly I realized that the detectives did not behave like South Africans—they were South Africans! How did the police in independent Zimbabwe come to have South Africans running the investigation into a political assassination? It was much later that we found out that Varkevisser, the head of the Joe Gqabi investigation team, was working for the South

African Security Forces. Before this news broke, though, he returned to South Africa.

The reality of our situation dawned rather abruptly. We were in a war zone and not safe from the South African authorities; Dutch passports were insufficient protection against submachine gun bullets and bombs. The beautiful full glass wall of our bedroom suddenly became a deathtrap, and the car had to be checked for suspicious contraptions every morning before the children were driven to school. This turned out to be a real homecoming—we had to watch our backs and were unsafe even in our home.

On August 24 we went to a surprise twenty-first birthday party for Geraldine. The surprise, however, was on us. She failed to turn up for her own birthday party because she had been arrested as a suspect in Joe Gqabi's murder that very morning. Nobody knew where she was held and how to get to see her. What we did not know was that she was kept in solitary confinement in the maximum-security prison. She was only released seventeen days later. This was all part of an elaborate setup by which they tried to discredit Geraldine and the ANC. Geraldine's own story about the circumstances of her detention would require another chapter. Varkevisser is living somewhere in South Africa today and has not appeared before the Truth and Reconciliation Commission.

Our arrival in Zimbabwe may have saved Geraldine's life. The killers could not have anticipated the events of the early evening, because our visit to the house in Ashdown Park was unplanned. The evidence available to the TRC suggests that Joe Gqabi had been killed by a hit squad acting on the evidence supplied by South African agents inside Zimbabwe's Central Intelligence Organization. Some time after the murder, Colin Evans and Philip Hartlebury were arrested and charged with spying for South Africa. The Truth and Reconciliation Commission's official report stated that Joe Gqabi was assassinated by South African agents operating in collusion with a group of Zimbabwean agents.

Working in Zimbabwe as a consultant for a European develop-

ment agency opened my eyes to the way in which feminism had penetrated and influenced aid organizations. However, this was still an imperialistic and hegemonic feminism. I had to mediate between Western concepts of feminism and the particular African form of feminism. The aspirations of Zimbabwean female ex-combatants were far removed from what was defined as feminist in Western Europe. They were on the cutting edge of different and often intersecting ideologies and identities. It became clear that the construction of feminism that worked in a particular region had to be cognizant of the needs of the women concerned. Zimbabwean women had to address definitions of femaleness and femininity in the context of their traditional culture.

Having been to war to help in the liberation of their country did not exonerate these ex-combatants from the burdens of femaleness in this strongly patriarchal society. They discovered what European and American women experienced after World War II: society expected them to return to their former domestic roles. Traditional societies everywhere are conservative, and Zimbabwe was no different. This made the return of these women to their rural communities problematic. Thus any educational program had to be geared to making women independent and self-reliant. They had to become economically independent and learn to cope with the problems of reintegration.

We knew that we were not safe in frontline states as long as apartheid South Africa could cross the national border and assassinate political activists at will. We lived through many moments of terror not only in Zimbabwe but also in Mozambique. After the independence of Mozambique in 1975, the South African government supported a rebel faction, Renamo, which attacked the new government. Renamo tried to destabilize and undermine the government of Mozambique and to terrorize the people. Our visit to Mozambique was directly linked to the activities of this rebel group.

When we left the Netherlands to work in Zimbabwe, we were informed that it would be expedient to bring a car from Europe; our *work at the center would require travel to Harare and other cities regularly. Shipping a car to landlocked Zimbabwe, however, left few choices to us. We were not allowed into South Africa, so Durban was out of the question. The port of Beira in Mozambique was our only option, as we could have the car sent to Zimbabwe by rail.*

We could not have anticipated that Renamo rebels would blow up the bridge over the Pungwe River. This made the only railroad transport between the port of Beira and Zimbabwe impossible. Our only option was to fly to Beira and drive the car back ourselves. We put this off as long as possible, but finally, we received notification from the Port of Beira that they could no longer assume any responsibility for the car; it was parked in an open yard. As we prepared for the trip to Beira we realized the dangers involved in driving through Mozambique even in the daylight hours. Frequent reports of ambushes after dark told us that even though Frelimo, the national army, patrolled the roads, they were unable to be everywhere. We left the boys with friends in Harare to be picked up by my mother.

The release of the car and fuel rations detained us longer than we intended. We were fortunate that we were staying with friends, as the hotels did not have any food. We managed to get some food for the trip and bought bags of mangoes on the road when we left. We had worked out that if we left early enough we would be able to reach the border before 6:00 PM, when the border post closed for the night. As we approached the Pungwe, we were horrified to see a long line of trucks and cars waiting ahead of us. All the vehicles had to be pulled across this fairly narrow stretch of water with a hand-operated ferry. Just driving onto this ferry required considerable skill and nerves of steel. The wheels had to be driven onto narrow planks, which seemed neither wide enough nor strong enough to hold the weight of the vehicles. When we had finally crossed after many hours of waiting, we realized that we would never make the border post before dark, as we promised our children.

There were no gas stations or motels along the road, and

driving into the villages with this conspicuous new car seemed equally unsafe. The only option we had was to drive as far as we could and then see what was ahead. Needless to say, we were terrified. There were no telephones, no restaurants, and no street lights—only the dark road and the possibility of a Renamo ambush. We knew that when the sun went down around 6 PM it would be dark: no twilight, just all-encompassing darkness. We talked to each other to keep our spirits up and hoped for the best. We had at least another two hours' drive ahead of us when the darkness closed in. We had been driving for some time when we suddenly saw the light of a fire ahead. We were terrified, but decided not to slow down. Suddenly someone stepped out of the darkness and flagged us down with a torch. This was the moment of truth. He was a young man in camouflage clothing who was immediately joined by a number of others. Great was our relief when they told us that they were Frelimo soldiers. All they wanted was food. Relieved and thankful, we shared everything we had, which was not much more than a bag of mangoes. They were friendly and told us to stop in the no man's land and not to go right up to the border. We drove at a steady pace until we reached the area they had indicated. We considered ourselves extremely lucky to have made it.

Prior to our departure to Mozambique on December 18, 1981, the offices of the ruling ZANU (Zimbabwe African National Union) PF party in Zimbabwe were blown up in front of us. We were some of the first people on the scene. This was an attempt to assassinate senior members of the ZANU PF, including the prime minister. Seven civilians in the street and in the shops nearby were killed, and 124 were injured. Again, South African agents were arrested for involvement in this attack. On the day we returned to Europe from Zimbabwe in August 1982, Ruth First, academic and political activist, was killed by a letter bomb in Maputo. We realized how lucky we were to have survived this war zone. Five years later, there were further attacks on the ANC office in Angwa Street and on the same house in Ashdown Park where Joe Gqabi was killed.

I returned to Cape Town in 1993 after twenty-six years in exile. I had not seen most of my family, including two brothers and two sisters, since I had left. My niece Geraldine returned earlier, despite another attempt to assassinate her after her return to Johannesburg. The ANC security in Johannesburg was able to foil the attempt. Geraldine Fraser-Moleketi became the minister of welfare in the Mandela cabinet and is presently the minister of public service and administration in the Mbeki cabinet. She still says that our arrival and presence in Harare on July 31, 1981, saved their lives. The narratives of my mother, my sister, Cynthia, and all the other women remain unwritten. My sons only made the journey "home" when their father suddenly died in Johannesburg in March 1994. He had returned to South Africa in January to work for the Institute for African Alternatives. They were organizing seminars and workshops to inform people about their voting rights in the upcoming first democratic elections. He wanted to participate in the new South Africa and was hoping to prepare the way for our possible return as well.

CONCLUSION

South Africa has to confront two challenges simultaneously: working for an equitable society oriented toward development and pursuing this path of equity for all people in the context of democracy. To a large extent, whites still control knowledge production. Sometimes, when black women's political activities are described as not feminist, it is done from an essentialist interpretation of feminism. Desiree Lewis describes this oversight as follows: "In contexts where oppression takes a variety of forms, and where the subjection of individuals derives from different relations of power and exploitation, it becomes extremely difficult to specify any single form of oppression as dominant. It also becomes very easy to conclude that gender struggles, because they are so bound up with other political struggles, are underdeveloped or absent" (1992).

Feminism and racism make uneasy bedfellows. It remains questionable whether feminism and racism can coexist. In the quest for a counterhegemonic discourse, black women may temporarily have to work within a hegemonic framework. For as long as they are still dependent on such "others" as editors, researchers, and publishers for access to the world of publication, they will have to tailor their narratives to accommodate that dependence. In order for some of the narratives written and/or edited to be understood, their ideological subtexts and context should be explained. Black women's discourse has to be foregrounded for a dialogic interaction between the old (colonial/hegemonic) and the new (counterhegemonic). This will reconstitute and reconfigure the physical and the psychological climate of the imagination of this historical period. Furthermore, for a deeper understanding of the gendered subjectivity of black women, their own voices should be heard.

REFERENCES

Baard, Frances, and Barbie Schreiner. 1986. *My spirit is not banned.* Harare: Zimbabwe Publishing House.

Barrett, Jane, Aneene Dawber, Barbara Klugman, Ingrid Obery, Jennifer Shindler, and Joanne Yawitch. 1985. *Vukani makhosikazi: South African women speak.* London: Catholic Institute for International Relations.

Bennett, Tony. 1990. *Outside literature.* London: Routledge.

Bernstein, Hilda. 1985. *For their triumphs and for their tears: Women in apartheid South Africa.* London: International Defence and Aid Fund.

———. 1994. *The rift: The exile experience of South Africans.* London: Jonathan Cape.

Bozzoli, Belinda, and Mmantho Nkotsoe. 1991. *Women of Phokeng: Consciousness, life strategy, and migrancy in South Africa, 1900–1983.* Johannesburg: Ravan Press.

Brah, Avtar. 1996. *Cartographies of diaspora: Contesting identities.* London and New York: Routledge.

Budlender, D. 1999. Women and the economy. Paper presented at the conference on Women and Gender in Southern Africa held at the University of Natal, Durban, January.

Cock, Jacklyn. 1980. *Maids and madams.* Johannesburg: Ravan Press.

Dido, E. K. M. *Die storie van Monica Peters.* Cape Town: Kwela Books, 1996.

Gordon, Suzanne. 1985. *A talent for tomorrow: Life stories of South African servants.* Johannesburg: Ravan Press.

Griesel, Hanlie. 1987. *Sibambene: The voices of women at Mboza.* Johannesburg: Ravan Press.

Guy-Sheftall, Beverly, ed. 1995. *Words of fire: An anthology of African American feminist thought.* New York: New Press, 1995.

Head, Bessie. 1974. *A Question of power.* London: Davis-Poynter.

Jabavu, Noni. 1960. *Drawn in colour: African contrasts.* London: John Murray.

———. 1963. *The ochre people: Scenes from a South African life.* London: John Murray.

Jameson, Fredric. 1983. *The political unconscious: Narrative as a socially symbolic art.* London: Methuen.

Joubert, Elsa. 1978. *Die swerfjare van Poppie Nongema.* Cape Town: Tafelberg Uitgewers Beperk.

Karodia, Farida. 1986. *Daughters of the twilight.* London: Women's Press.

Kuzwayo, Ellen. 1985. *Call me woman.* London: Women's Press.

Lipman, Beata. 1984. *We make freedom: Women in South Africa.* London: Pandora Press.

Luckhardt, Ken, and Brenda Wall. 1980. *Organize or starve.* London: Lawrence and Wishart.

Mabuza, Lindiwe. 1991. *Letter to Letta.* Johannesburg: Skotaville.

Magona, Sindiwe. 1990. *To my children's children.* Claremont, South Africa: David Philip.

———. 1998. *Mother to mother.* Claremont, South Africa: David Philip.

Makeba, Miriam, with James Hall. 1987. *Makeba: My story.* London: Bloomsbury.

Mamdani, Mahmood. 1996. *Citizen and subject*. Princeton, NJ: Princeton University Press.

Mandela, Winnie, ed. 1985. *Part of my soul went*. Middlesex, UK: Penguin Books.

Matlanyane Sexwale, Buni. 1994. Violence against women: Experiences of South African domestic workers. In *The dynamics of "race" and gender: Some feminist interventions*, edited by Haleh Afshar and Mary Maynard, pp. 196–221. London: Taylor & Francis.

Meer, Shamim, comp. and ed. 1998. *Women speak*. Cape Town: Kwela Books.

Mhlophe, Gcina, Maralin Vanrenen, and Thembi Mtshali. 1988. *Have You Seen Zandile?* Portsmouth, NH: Heinemann Educational Books.

Mikell, Gwendolyn. 1997. *African Feminism*. Philadelphia: University of Pennsylvania Press.

Minh-ha, Trinh T. 1989. *Woman, native, other*. Bloomington and Indianapolis: Indiana University Press.

Ngcobo, Lauretta. 1981. *Cross of gold*. London: Longman.

Orange River Colony. 1904. *Census of the Orange River Colony, Sunday, April 17, 1904*. Bloemfontein: n.p.

Orr, Wendy. 2000. *From Biko to Basson*. Johannesburg: Contra Press.

Peterson, Bhekizizwe. 2000. *Monarchs, missionaries, and intellectuals*. Trenton, NJ: Africa World Press.

Petition to Louis Botha, Prime Minister of the Union of South Africa, from native and coloured women of the province of the Orange Free State, March 11, 1912. Pretoria: South Africa State Archives.

Ramphele, Mamphela. 1997. *Across boundaries*. New York: Feminist Press.

Reyher, Rebecca Hourwich. [1948] 1999. *Zulu woman: The life story of Christina Sibiya*. New York: Feminist Press.

Rodgers, B. 1980. *Divide and rule: South Africa's Bantustans*. Rev. and enlarged ed. London: International Defence and Aid Fund.

Rosenthal, E. [1949?]. *Bantu journalism*. Johannesburg: n.p.

Sikakane, Joyce. 1977. *A window on Soweto*. London: International Defence and Aid Fund.

South African Native Affairs Commission. 1903–1905. *Miscellaneous reports before 1910*, Cd. 2399. South Africa: Government Publications.

Thula Baba. 1987. Johannesburg: Ravan Press.

Tsikang, Seageng, and Dinah Lefakane, eds. 1988. *Women in South Africa: From the heart—an anthology.* Johannesburg: Seriti sa Sechaba.

Tutu, Desmond. 1999. *No future without forgiveness.* London: Rider.

Walshe, Peter. 1970. *The rise of African nationalism in South Africa: The African National Congress, 1912–1952.* London: C. Hurst.

Wells, Julia C. 1993. *We now demand: The history of women's resistance to the pass laws in South Africa.* Johannesburg: Witwatersrand University Press.

Wicomb, Zoe. 1987. *You Can't Get Lost in Cape Town.* New York: Pantheon Books.

———. 2001. *David's Story.* New York: Feminist Press.

Wilson, Monica, and Leonard Thompson. 1975. *The Oxford history of South Africa.* Vol. 2. *South Africa, 1870–1966.* Oxford: Oxford University Press.

Yawitch, J. 1980. The role of women in the struggle for liberation in Zimbabwe, Namibia, and South Africa. Paper presented to the World Conference of the United Nations Decade for Women, Copenhagen, July 1.

11. The Cultural Debate over Female Circumcision

The Sudanese Are Arguing This One Out for Themselves

Ellen Gruenbaum

Taking issue with certain analyses that have tended to view female circumcision as a "maladaptive cultural pattern," Gruenbaum proposes an alternative theoretical framework that situates female circumcision within the context of the political economy. In this respect, Gruenbaum's essay differs markedly from the majority of Western feminist scholarship, which has typically identified "tradition" as the sole reason for the evolution and continuation of this practice. This focus on "tradition," according to Gruenbaum, has only served to divide Western feminist academicians from African women and detract attention away from the ongoing economic exploitation (which has enormous impact on health conditions) of poor countries.

Using historical and ethnographic data, Gruenbaum analyzes the situation of female circumcision in central Sudan. She documents the effects of both pharaonic circumcision (infibulation) and Sunna (clitoridectomy) in order to trace the ongoing changes and debates surrounding these practices. Contrary to the widespread belief that female circumcision is harmful to the overall population of a particular group (i.e., a maladaptive cul-

314   women and globalization

tural pattern), Gruenbaum is unable to make any direct correlation between female circumcision and decreased population growth. However, she does note that the high rate of death among children of both sexes stems from inadequate health care services, sanitation, and water storage—all social services that have been drastically cut in the midst of rapid capitalist expansion.

Gruenbaum's analysis of female circumcision is an important interrogation of contemporary feminist theory. She poses a much-needed challenge to those Western feminist academicians who continue to isolate and sensationalize this practice without paying any attention to the debilitating (health) effects of economic globalization on the poor nations of Africa.

W hy have some societies developed cultural practices that lead people to endanger the lives and health of their girls and women with unnecessary genital surgeries? The explanation of what is euphemistically known as "female circumcision" has been a difficult issue for anthropology and the feminist movement.[1] Strong negative reactions—based on humanitarian and feminist values rather than prejudice—are commonly evoked by this practice. Seen as both socially oppressive and physically harmful to women and girls, the discontinuance of the surgeries is logically advocated as a goal of improving the status of women.

Yet these negative reactions are often highly ethnocentric and prejudicial, especially when Western readers and students reject not only the idea of the surgeries but the cultures where they are found as well.[2] Often, upon first hearing of the practices, people react with the assumption that Sudanese people must be "barbaric," "backward," or child abusers. Indeed, when knowledge of Middle Eastern cultures is minimal, these critics may even apply such judg-

Reproduced by permission of the American Anthropological Association from *Medical Anthropology Quarterly* volume 10, 1996. Not for sale or further reproduction.

ments to all "Arabs" and "Muslims" without regard to their cultural variation. The widespread use of phrases like "genital mutilations" (Hosken 1982) and "prisoners of ritual" (Lightfoot-Klein 1989) contributes to the intensity of the rejection of the practitioners along with the practices and implies intentional harm or unthinking obedience to irrational traditions.

It is incumbent upon anthropologists to offer cultural perspectives on this controversy, yet analyses that offer emic interpretations and cultural contextualizations are often criticized as bordering on advocacy. Critics argue that there is no place for cultural relativism here, and we anthropologists are urged to "draw the line" (Gordon 1991) and condemn female circumcision.

Ample voices outside anthropology exercise that option. As examples, numerous journalistic pieces have recently addressed the issue (e.g., Brownlee et al. 1994; Kaplan et al. 1993), and Pat Schroeder introduced legislation in Congress to outlaw these practices in the United States. Frequently, however, critics offer grossly inadequate cultural contextualization, as did the renowned novelist Alice Walker, who portrayed female circumcision in a generalized African culture.[3] Although anthropologists may passionately oppose female circumcision, I believe the most useful role is to provide cultural perspectives on it, offer a sophisticated analysis of why these practices continue, and describe the forces for change in various cultural contexts.

Efforts to change circumcision practices that have neglected to analyze its causes—and resort to "tradition" as the sole explanation—are problematic. When reformers assume that people follow "tradition" for no conscious reason, they overlook the complexity of decision-making processes within a culture and the competing demands on individuals. As a result, reform programs can result that do nothing but preach against "ignorance." Thus international efforts to "eradicate" female circumcision (as if it were a disease), though often couched in seemingly progressive feminist rhetoric, sound condescending to many African women. The response has often been a cultural backlash, characterized by a defense of traditions by African women against what is perceived as Western cultural imperialism.

Elsewhere I have argued that the international chorus of criticism against female circumcision has served as a smoke-screen, focusing attention and resources on "traditions" while drawing attention away from disastrous situations of economic exploitation and neglect in poor countries (Gruenbaum 1982). Anthropological theories that offer a static view of culture are partly to blame for this distortion. Even theories of cultural adaptation, as dynamic as they may be in viewing culture as capable of changing in response to new conditions, have sometimes left female circumcision with an analytical label—"maladaptive"—that sounds equally as disparaging as the static "traditions" explanation. Thus, in order to reduce counterproductive public invective against the practitioners of circumcision and their cultures and thereby move forward efforts for social change, it is important for anthropologists to develop analyses that offer a more thorough understanding of the cultural and historical contexts of social change and of women's priorities for it.

Although a great deal of descriptive and statistical information is already available, anthropologists need to contribute to the current debate over female circumcision in at least three ways: discovering and explaining the meaning of these practices in their various cultural contexts; analyzing issues of causality; and exploring the forces and prospects for change. Each can contribute to change but does not presuppose an outcome. The first has been adequately explored in the literature (see, among others, Assaad 1980; Boddy 1982, 1989; Gruenbaum 1982, 1988; Hayes 1975; Toubia 1988) and will not be discussed here. This article concentrates on analyzing contributing factors to circumcision and on prospects for its change.

In my view, the commendable goal to end these practices is unlikely to be achieved without a sensitive approach that respects the sentiments of those who practice these surgeries. Thus I critique the medical, ecological interpretation of female circumcision as a "maladaptive cultural pattern" and offer a political-economic analysis of female circumcision in central Sudan. Acknowledging the key element of the views of the practitioners, I then explore the process of change currently under way in rural central Sudan and illustrate the dynamic debates within Sudanese society, drawing on my field research there in the seventies, in 1989, and in 1992. Finally, I discuss the internationalization of this issue and suggest directions for further developing theory that incorporates political-economic analysis into a dynamic view of social ecology, one in which circumcision is understood as just one of many obstacles to healthy lives for women and girls.

IS FEMALE CIRCUMCISION A MALADAPTIVE CULTURAL PATTERN?

In their popular medical anthropology text, Ann McElroy and Patricia K. Townsend use female circumcision as one example of what they term a "maladaptive cultural pattern" (1989, pp. 102–104). The basic idea here is that we should not assume that culturally institutionalized patterns are necessarily going to promote health and well-being: "Humans do not invariably make maximally adaptive responses or wise, healthful choices." While it is certainly true that our species is not as sapient as we might wish, the question of whether female circumcision or any other cultural pattern is "adaptive" or "maladaptive" is more complicated to analyze than it first appears. Does the fact that it is dangerous and potentially harmful to health mean that it is essentially negative and maladaptive? If so, then resistance to health education against female circumcision may be judged as ill advised and irrational.

If adaptation is, as McElroy and Townsend define it, "the processes of adjustment and change that enable a population to maintain itself in a given environment" (1989, p. 72), then maladaptive practices impede those processes and, presumably, make population survival less likely. McElroy and Townsend use the term *maladap-*

tive to emphasize that female circumcision is not a "healthful choice" and therefore maladaptive. Thus something that is performed for "both social and religious reasons" can be labeled "maladaptive for individual physical health and fertility" (1989, pp. 103–104).

But Nile Valley populations have survived very well for centuries, if not millennia, with these practices. Leaving aside for the moment the degree to which the practices influence fertility, I would also question the assumption of a link between individual physical health and adaptation. If a condition is bad for individual health, is it maladaptive in relation to the population's survival? Not necessarily. Unhealthy individuals often reproduce in large numbers, particularly if their conditions are not debilitating until after the reproductive years, and deaths among the young can serve as an adaptive process that selects against certain genetic or other health problems being passed on. In short, one must agree with Hans Kummer's view, cited by McElroy and Townsend, that a trait preserved by a species need not be considered adaptive simply because it has been preserved: "all we can say with certainty is that it must be tolerable since it did not lead to extinction" (cited in McElroy and Townsend 1989, p. 119). The same applies to cultural practices. A trait should not be labeled maladaptive merely because it is risky or harmful to individual health.

But if a practice inhibits the fertility of a population, there is a stronger case for arguing that it is maladaptive, since reproduction is necessary to population survival over time. In the late twentieth century, of course, we are aware that maximizing reproduction should not remain an unquestioned indicator of long-term "survival," since adaptive success clearly requires maintaining a balance between population and resource use. But if female circumcision inhibits fertility in any way, an argument could be made that it is maladaptive to population survival.

In order to persuade people from pronatalist cultural environments to end female circumcision, some critics would like to assert that female circumcision inhibits fertility. Certainly, pharaonic circumcision (infibulation) is associated with lowered fertility for individuals, as a result of scar tissue inhibiting sexual activity; of chronic infections resulting in higher rates of miscarriage, stillbirth, and infertility; or of obstructed labor and consequent damage to reproductive organs.[4] However, I know of no strong evidence that group fertility is seriously impaired, from either a population or even an extended family perspective, and my own ethnographic research supports this. Although more extensive demographic research is needed, I found that achieving high fertility did not, in fact, seem to be a problem in rural Sudan, where pharaonic circumcision is practiced.

In 1989, I collected twenty-nine reproductive histories from married Sudanese women in a village in the southern part of the Rahad Irrigated Scheme, east of the Blue Nile.[5] This work was part of a long-term project with two ethnic groups, the Kenana and the Zabarma, with whom Jay O'Brien, Salah-el-din El-Shazali, and I had done research in the mid-seventies.

The groups have different traditional female circumcision practices. The Kenana perform the most severe pharaonic circumcision, characterized by total excision of clitoris, prepuce, labia minora, and labia majora, and infibulation, which closes the vaginal opening except for a tiny opening for urination and menstrual flow. The Zabarma, however, practice clitoridectomy (or partial clitoridectomy) only, which they call *Sunna* circumcision. The term *Sunna* suggests that the practice is acceptable, or even recommended or required for Muslims, although most Islamic theologians consider it to be either optional or discouraged by Islam. Table 11.1 gives the results of the study.

A comparison of my network samples from the two groups offers insight into the effect of pharaonic circumcision on fertility. If we hypothesize that reduced fertility of circumcised women is due either to failure to become pregnant or to childbirth difficulties leading to stillbirth or perinatal death, the number of live births among pharaonically circumcised women would be lower than

Table 11.1. Comparison of Zabarma and Kenana fertility (live births only)

| | Zabarma (Sunna, n = 10) | | Kenana (pharaonic, n = 19) | |
	Total	Average per woman	Total	Average per woman
Births to all women in sample	68	6.8	136	7.15
Births to women with completed childbearing only	64	8.0	92	9.2
Apparent sterility	0		1	

among Sunna-circumcised women. But as is clear from the table, the birthrate (an average of 6.8 births per woman for the Zabarma sample and 7.15 for the Kenana sample) is approximately the same for both groups, even though the samples include some young women who have not yet completed their reproduction. For women with completed reproduction, the averages are 8.0 for Zabarma women and 9.2 for Kenana women. Thus birth rates are actually somewhat higher for the pharaonically circumcised sample. Only 1 of the 29 women—a pharaonically circumcised Kenana—was apparently infertile: she had already been divorced twice, although she was still in her twenties.

Although my data do not include adequate information on maternal mortality, they suggest nevertheless that female circumcision per se does not seriously imperil fertility.[6] Although a poorly performed surgery or related complications may contribute to infertility for some individuals, particularly where adequate health care is unavailable, certainly for the community as a whole there is no danger of dying out due to the presumed maladaptiveness of the practice. And for rural central Sudan, where divorce is easy and polygyny not uncommon, patrilineal kin groups do not seem to have experienced any difficulty in generating offspring due to female circumcision. The lack of dramatic negative effect on group fertility allows these sociocultural and kin groups to perpetuate their beliefs and practices. Nevertheless, the risk to fertility for the individual may yet be an important argument for reformers to use.

Although female circumcision and its complications are certainly a factor in death rates, high rates of fertility can offset them, thereby making female circumcision a relatively minor factor in net population survival. In the reproductive histories of Sudanese women that we collected, for example, none of the forty-nine deaths of offspring that women reported was due to complications of circumcision. In only one case, the death of a twelve-year-old girl, was circumcision possibly related to death; but the link is unknown because the mother did not report the cause of her death. The vast majority of deaths of children of both sexes were attributed to fever, diarrhea, or malaria. In my estimation, improvements in water supply and storage, sanitation, mosquito control, and nutrition, as well as improved basic heath services, are what are needed to reduce child and infant mortality.

Clearly then, even if female circumcision contributes in some small way to lowered fertility or premature deaths, it is not as significant as malaria and diarrheal diseases. Since so many pharaonically circumcised women are fertile, it is unlikely that people observe it as a problem for fertility or that it functions as a selective factor in adaptation. In these senses, it is thus inappropriate to argue that female circumcision is maladaptive.

Even so, we are left with an interesting problem. Why do societies that practice female circumcision preserve it and, in fact, give it a prominent symbolic role? Does it serve a positive function? Or does it fall into Kummer's "tolerable" category?

Those who have argued that there is a symbolic value for female circumcision in maintaining gender relations and kin group cohesion (e.g., Boddy 1982, 1989)—a position that suggests a positive function for the practice—leave themselves open to occasional accusations of complicity via excess "cultural relativism" (cf. Gordon 1991; Hosken 1982). One might even argue that it is precisely because practices like circumcision are important symbolically that they be preserved despite their drawbacks. There is some merit in this argument, particularly because practices of circumcision are entwined with gender identity (Boddy 1982, 1989) and ethnic identity (Gruenbaum 1988), both of which are very closely guarded and not easily changed.

One can speculate that when people make sense of harmful practices of unknown origins such as infibulation, there were formerly some practical reasons for doing it (e.g., in areas where girls might be exposed to strangers on caravan routes the scar barrier made rape less likely). Today, such practices are preserved in the "tolerable" category.

It is important to remember that, as Soheir Morsy (drawing on the work of historian Christine Delphy) pointed out for zar spirit possession, to know the origin of a social practice cannot explain its present existence (1991b, p. 193). Thus the persistence of a practice that has negative consequences still must be explained in terms of present circumstances that encourage or discourage its continuation. No meaningful effort to change cultural practices can neglect this inquiry.

FORCES FOR CONTINUITY AND CHANGE

More progress in ending the harm of female circumcision might be possible by asking the old political economy question "Who benefits?" rather than by asking the functionalist question "What functions does it serve?" The former inquiry allows us to explore the different, even conflicting, interests among various groups within a society. As Edgerton argues, "in all societies . . . some people are better served than others" (1992, p. 102). Questions of patterns of adaptation and maladaptation then become embedded in the political aspects and power relations of cultural patterns. Some cultural patterns, in this view, are good for some people but bad for others, harmful to the health of some but good for the power or wealth of others. A careful analysis of this sort might lead us to better understandings of whose interests are served by the preservation of—or challenges to—certain cultural patterns, understandings that in turn may suggest where to look for resistance to—or fostering of—change.

Where pharaonic circumcision is widely practiced and accepted—such as the Arab-Sudanese in my Gezira research site in the seventies (see Gruenbaum 1991) and currently in the Kenana ethnic group in the Rahad community—definite differences exist in the social effects of the surgeries on different groups of people, such as women and men, or different ethnic and social class groups.

Critics and practitioners alike think that pharaonic circumcision serves the interests of men. Although tight infibulation can obstruct first intercourse (and requires repeated efforts over time or even a small incision to widen the opening), the opening remains fairly tight and is retightened after each childbirth. Both men and women in my research communities told me that men derive far greater sexual pleasure from intercourse with a woman whose vaginal opening has been surgically narrowed in this way. This view is widely held as a reason for the continuation of the practice, even among middle-class urban women, including those who actively oppose the practice. For instance, one well-known urban midwife I interviewed said parents often tell her they are afraid a future husband will not like sex with their daughter if she is not infibulated. To discourage pharaonic circumcisions on young girls, this midwife counsels parents that daughters can be infibulated later if they and their husbands want it. She reported that some clients have been persuaded by this reasoning.

A second male interest served by infibulation is control of women for the goal of maintaining family honor. By assuring verifiable virginity (the scar-tissue barrier and reduced sensation are believed to make women less likely to engage in premarital sex), family prominence can be more easily achieved through appropriate marriages and the reproduction of large numbers of legitimate offspring. Since close-kin endogamy is preferred, the control of female sexual morality affects the entire kin group by fostering a sense of enclosed, inclusive, extended family units. Even in exogamous marriages, which are often arranged to build strategic interfamily linkages, females still depend on the success and reputation of their fathers and brothers (tied to family honor) because they are likely to need to rely on their natal families for support in times of economic hardship or after divorce or widowhood.

Also related to family well-being is the economic control of women's labor, including women's tasks in biological reproduction, social reproduction (including domestic labor), and other economic work. Women's and children's contributions to farming, herding, food processing, and other economic enterprises all enhance men's wealth. Insofar as female circumcision contributes to the subordination of women, it plays a role in these economic relations between the sexes and among men. While control of women's labor has dramatic consequences for rural farmers, herders, and peasant proletarians, it has significant consequences for urban workers and entrepreneurs as well.

The practice of pharaonic circumcision also serves ethnic group and class superiority because it functions as an ideological marker of superior morality and propriety for the dominant ethnic groups, justifying the socioeconomic subordination of West African and southern Sudanese groups that do not practice pharaonic circumcision. (See Gruenbaum 1988 for a fuller discussion of the role of pharaonic circumcision in ethnic and class stratification.)

One other interest that plays a minor but significant role is that of rural midwives, whose income depends in part on performing circumcisions, marriage-related openings, and reinfibulations. Since health-policy makers have often looked to midwives to play a role in educating their clients about the dangers of circumcision, their interests certainly need to be understood as a possible contributing obstacle to change.

We must also consider who is harmed by the practice of female circumcision. Clearly, the health of women and girls is seriously harmed; there are both immediate and long-term physical consequences and potentially serious psychological effects. In spite of their recognition of such risks, most women and girls react with acceptance—as well as with some fear. Their attitude is that although circumcision is difficult, it is just one aspect of being a woman, a part of life that they must endure to achieve the status and joys of womanhood: getting married, pleasing a husband, and having children.

Women's sexuality is also often harmed. Since the amount of tissue removed during infibulation is variable, it is impossible to generalize about its effects on sexual functioning. My observations and interviews with midwives and other women suggest that many midwives, fearing hemorrhage, leave much of the clitoral (erectile) tissue intact beneath the infibulation when they perform the surgeries. This probably explains how some women have orgasmic response despite the scarring. But in surgeries I have seen and in most of the descriptions of clitoridectomy and infibulation in Sudan that I have read, clitoral tissue is removed. It is therefore not surprising that infibulated women often report that, other than feeling happiness by making their husbands happy, sex is unsatisfying and they do not "finish" (i.e., achieve orgasm) as men do.

It is important, however, not to overgeneralize about sexual response. One evening, during my fieldwork in the Gezira village discussed below, I wanted to ascertain that a group of women with whom I was discussing orgasm were talking about true orgasms and not some vague conceptualization by women who had never personally experienced them. I pressed them for a clearer description. Somewhat exasperated that I didn't seem to understand, one woman grabbed my hand and said, "Look, Ellen, some of us do 'finish.' It feels like electricity, like this . . . ," and she proceeded to flick her finger sharply and rhythmically against my hand. I was convinced that we were talking about the same thing.

Although women are harmed and men are benefited by infibulation, we cannot conclude that the practice is simply a matter of male exploitation of subordinated women. We must first understand how various interest groups conceptualize and justify the practice. Western critics often utilize Western values and feminist consciousness in their analysis of infibulation (a common enough reaction especially for feminists schooled in "consciousness-raising" groups of the sixties). As a consequence, these analyses portray Sudanese cultural values as examples of "false consciousness." Values relating to morality and honor that require pharaonic circumcision are dismissed. They similarly dismiss as "unnatural" or perhaps "maladaptive" the aesthetics of infibulation, that the labia and clitorises are the "ugly," "masculine" parts of girls, and removal results in beauty and cleanliness.

Such responses strike many African women scholars as arrogant, especially because Western culture has its own aesthetically motivated medical disasters, such as silicone breast implants and useless cosmetic surgeries. The ethnocentric views of outsiders fail to recognize the dynamic nature of cultural patterns, imagining "the other" perhaps as frozen in time, bound by "traditional" ways of doing things, and as "prisoners of ritual" who are not rational makers of their own history. But as Edgerton makes clear in his discussion of customs such as sati in India as well as female circumcision in Africa, insiders to such cultures often have widely differing opinions and disagreements about them (1992, p. 139). Culture, in fact, is far from static, as the cultural debates now raging in Sudan over the issue of female circumcision illustrate.

FORCES FOR CHANGE:
CULTURAL DEBATES IN SUDAN

Sudanese practice the severest form of surgery. In a large sample survey of 3,210 women in several provinces of northern Sudan, a research team found that only 1.2 percent of the women were uncircumcised, a few others did not know what type they had, and only 2.5 percent had the Sunna. The rest had either an intermediate (12 percent) or pharaonic (83 percent) circumcision (El Dareer 1982, p. 1). These figures are consonant with my own observations in rural central Sudan.

In field research in the summer of 1989 I observed that changes in female circumcision practices had taken place since my first fieldwork in Sudan from 1974 to 1979. In the seventies many rural and urban women believed that the practice of infibulation was part of being a Muslim. They interpreted their "way of life" as being synonymous with the religion and (especially in the case of uneducated and rural women) were not fully aware of the degree of cultural variation within the Islamic world.

By the seventies numerous individuals and organizations within Sudan had already spoken out against female circumcision. Some supported the modified, Sunna type over the pharaonic; others supported total abandonment of all of its forms. It seemed that efforts for change were poised to take off after the 1979 Khartoum Conference and the renewed commitment of doctors and the Ministry of Health to pursue a policy against all forms of female circumcision. This policy shift was attended by wide discussion among health workers and educators of the need for change and by a survey documenting the extent and variation of female circumcision practices in several provinces, reported in El Dareer (1982) and Rushwan et al. (1983).

My own participant-observation and interviews in two cities and two rural villages indicate that, although much has changed in the past decade, including some reduction of the incidence and a shift toward the less severe forms, pharaonic circumcision has not been displaced as the operation of choice among the majority of families. Still, there is every reason to believe that the cultural debates that have been stirring for the last several decades have accelerated and that a fairly dramatic process of change is under way.

Cultural debates concerning the proper way to be Sudanese, Muslim, or a member of any ethnic group need to be analyzed in light of the differential effects such debates have on different groups. Power struggles in Sudanese communities and in the nation require that discussion of infibulation be contextualized politically. In the following sections I explore some of the positions taken in the Sudanese debates over female circumcision to underscore the political element in the ecology of health. I focus not so much on the articulated arguments of intellectuals or other political elites, but I profile the views and activities of a number of rural and urban people I observed and interviewed in Sudan in 1989 and 1992, people who are making the actual decisions about infibulation for the girls of their communities.[7]

Debates about female circumcision, whether articulated or not, revolve around four major axes: health education/health policy; ethnicity and social class relations; sexuality; and religion. As one might expect, gender, generational, class, and educational differences often play significant roles in peoples' attitudes toward female circumcision. But the pattern is far from simple, as is evident from the following case.

The Politics of Sudanese Change Efforts

Change in circumcision practices should not be seen as an isolated, spontaneous phenomenon. It has been and continues to be connected to the education, health, and development programs of the government and private organizations. Extensive public health education, including media programming, lecture tours by teachers, and magazine articles, has already taken place under the previous military and elected governments. But of course their influence on educated and urban residents is greater than on people in rural areas.

Another significant and growing influence has been the Islamic movement. Ever since the religious pronouncement (*fetwa*) denouncing pharaonic circumcision (but favoring Sunna) was issued by Sudan's religious leaders in the forties, some Muslims (particularly literate and educated people) have been convinced that their religious duties do not require pharaonic circumcision. With increasing international influences in the Islamic movement, and as Muslims are exposed to other Middle Eastern cultures' interpretations of Islam, pharaonic circumcision has become even less justifiable. As the Islamic activist movement gained increasing influence in Sudan (despite the fact that the extremist elements are a minority and the National Islamic Front–influenced government came to power in a coup), questions about the authenticity of cultural practices have increasingly centered around interpretations of Islamic teachings.

Ideological struggle is quite vehement at present and often focuses on women's roles. Islamists are especially concerned about Islamic dress, female employment, and what they view as non-Islamic practices such as zar spirit possession rituals (practiced by women primarily) and pharaonic circumcision. Although circumcision has received less public attention recently, the ideological position that has been espoused by the Islamist movement is important to understand: it frames the arguments on all of these issues in terms of cultural authenticity, arguing that their definition of authentic *Islamic* culture should supplant Sudanese cultural practices they consider pre- or non-Islamic. The Islamists who claim to love Sudan and want it to conform to Islamic rules (by instituting an Islamic constitution and the much-hated *hudud* punishments, such as hand amputation) are reviled by the dissidents for "loving Sudan as if they hate it," since so many Sudanese traditions are being criticized.

Citing extensive foreign assistance from Iran and exposure of many Sudanese to the conservative Islam of other Gulf countries, some oppositional voices view the criticism of Sudanese cultural practices as a new form of cultural imperialism from the central Middle East. Although political resistance has been repressed (by

extrajudicial detentions, arrests, and extensive firings of government employees, which have driven many into exile), some resistance has taken cultural forms. Some have defied recommended
dress codes, either by asserting national pride by wearing traditional *robes* (the long head and body covering worn over clothing,
which traditionally has been acceptable wear for Muslim women,
even while on pilgrimages to Mecca, but which is now criticized as
insufficiently modest) or by defiantly wearing Western clothes and
short, uncovered hair (see Gruenbaum 1992).

Other dissidents argue that the leaders of the Islamist movement
are cynically pursuing Islamism as a cover for their rapacious
exploitation of the Sudanese economy. Even though that may be true
of some, the sincerity of many followers is evident and should not be
underestimated as a force in the current ideological struggles.

The implications of these struggles for female circumcision, as
I read it, are (1) that the serious interest in religious study and practice evident among so many of the younger educated people will
reinforce the public health efforts to modify or abandon the practice
of circumcision and (2) that cultural arguments favoring the practice as part of "Sudanese heritage" will become less acceptable
under a hegemonic interpretation of Islamic heritage. However, it is
unfortunate that the term *Sunna* has been associated with any form
of the surgeries, since the role of religion in the ideological debates
might lead some to feel that they *ought* to do the Sunna type rather
than none at all.

Manifestations and variations of these political and cultural
struggles are illustrated by examples from the two villages where I
did my research.

A Village in the Gezira Irrigated Scheme

The Gezira Irrigated Scheme was opened in 1925, and the villages
in this area benefited from health care and schools for a much
longer period than most other areas of the country. The village

where I worked experienced a great deal of temporary and permanent migration, including permanent in-migration of West African (Hausa) workers, as well as temporary and long-term out-migration of Arab-Sudanese to cities and oil-rich countries of the region. The village has electricity and a growing number of televisions, which offer access to strong ideological influences not found in many other parts of the country. Although in the past girls generally received less schooling than boys, there are a number of educated women in the village who (with the exception of two or three older women who married in from other areas) are in their forties.

Such external influences are apparent in the intergenerational differences about female circumcision evident in families such as that of Sittana and Laila.

Sittana is a woman of about fifty who has held a job as a janitor at the primary school in her village. Zar spirit–possessed, she formerly held twice-weekly clinics for women until a disabling injury made it difficult for her to pursue her normal activities. In these sessions she went into a trance and gave out advice and treatments for a variety of social and emotional ills. She is adamantly opposed to giving up pharaonic circumcision, but her daughter Laila, who is in her twenties, wanted her own daughter to have only the Sunna.

Because the village midwife (discussed below) always performed very severe pharaonic operations and in an effort to avoid a confrontation with her mother over the issue, Laila arranged to have a midwife from a nearby town perform her daughter's circumcision. Laila's midwife did an intermediate form of surgery. At the time, Sittana said she did not realize how little had been taken off. Then, a couple of weeks later, she wanted the operation done over, but Laila, a determined and confident young woman, was quite certain that her mother would not dare go against her. Sittana, however, was given a very young grandniece to raise and intended to circumcise her the pharaonic way.

Part of Laila's confidence that she could resist her mother's desire to have her daughter's circumcision redone stemmed from a widespread change in attitudes about the practice in the Gezira village that was attributable to public discussions that had been stimulated by educated community members. A few months prior to my 1989 visit, the medical assistant in charge of the clinic—a confident, educated man who believed that health workers should also be resources for guidance on a variety of subjects including values and religion—held two public meetings (for men and women separately) on the subject of female circumcision. Numerous people mentioned these meetings to me, so they clearly had a significant impact. Citing the serious health risks of the surgeries and the lack of justification under Islam, he apparently convinced a large number of people that pharaonic circumcision should be abandoned in favor of Sunna, or nothing. Although these talks were at his own initiative, they were linked with the work of the government health system, and he was in touch with doctors and midwives at the nearby medical facilities.

The influence of migration on the local debates is illustrated by the case of Besaina, the village midwife mentioned above. When I interviewed her in 1989, she informed me that she had decided to discontinue pharaonic surgeries and do only Sunna. The medical assistant's influence was apparent, but so too was the influence of religion. Increased religiosity is not uncommon for older women, but the growing Islamic resurgence in the region was probably also a factor in Besaina's increasing religiosity, particularly since one of her sons had gone to work in Saudi Arabia, where he was influenced by religious experiences and accumulated enough wealth to send her on the pilgrimage to Mecca.[8] So by 1989 Besaina had begun to listen to arguments that pharaonic circumcision was not Islamic. In addition, her son, after marrying a pharaonically circumcised woman, criticized her for the damage that was done to women by the practice and "ordered" her, she said, not to do it anymore. When I visited her again in 1992, however, she said she still had not stopped doing pharaonic for those who wanted it, but she claimed it was still her desire to do only Sunna circumcision in the future.

Some people who favored the change from the pharaonic form to the Sunna form have recently become more open about their views. For example, Selwa and her husband (both teachers) had their daughters circumcised in the seventiess. At that time they decided to avoid the midwife's severe pharaonic surgery by arranging for the operation to be done by an urban doctor who did the Sunna. At the time, fearing village disapproval, she had not made it widely known that the girls received Sunna; but by 1992, she was openly advocating Sunnas.

A major factor influencing attitudes was women's concern about men's sexual preference for infibulated women. For example, Su'ad, an educated woman who taught high school in a nearby town, argued about this with her visiting cousin from Port Sudan one evening. An advocate of Sunna circumcision, Su'ad argued it was the only type permitted by Islam. The cousin, however, dismissed that argument, insisting that men's sexual pleasure was far greater with a tight infibulation. She believed that Sudanese women and men would never give up pharaonic circumcision.[9]

Another advocate of the pharaonic form was my friend Fatma, a jovial woman in her fifties. She told me that the tight reinfibulations following birth make intercourse so difficult and frustrating for a time that it makes sex extremely exciting, both for the man and the woman. She imagined uncircumcised women as having gaping openings, hardly capable of giving pleasure. She, too, thought Sudanese women would never give it up.

Fatma's married daughters, however, who had been listening carefully to the views of educated people, particularly regarding the religious implications of pharaonic circumcision, were far more open to modification of the surgeries (although they themselves were infibulated). Fatma's eldest daughter shared the opinion of numerous other women and men in the village that Sunna would eventually be the only type done, even if it took many years.

An issue that was of special concern to the parents of younger women was the dramatic increase in the cost of marriage. The influx of earnings from lucrative jobs in the oil countries had the effect of driving up the going rates for bride wealth and gifts to levels that were unaffordable for young men who stayed home. As a result, a large number of young women, even those with educations and with jobs, find themselves facing the end of their twenties with no marital prospects. In order to encourage more couples to wed, other villages had by agreement of all families (typically in a meeting at the mosque) set an upper limit on marriage offers. Since no such agreement was in place in this village, many parents of unmarried women were deeply concerned. In such an atmosphere, few women were willing to further risk their daughters' prospects for marriage by abandoning circumcision, particularly since it was not unprecedented (though extremely rare) for a groom to divorce an uncircumcised bride shortly after their wedding night. Such a divorce also jeopardizes a woman's future marital prospects, since people assume that she was probably not a virgin.

To complete the case study of this Gezira village, it should be noted that Muslim Hausa women, of West African origin, who lived in a separate quarter of the village, never adopted female circumcision despite the fact that for over half a century their Arab-Sudanese neighbors criticized them as unclean.[10] The Hausa still believe it is best not to be circumcised at all and do not wish to adopt either the Sunna or the pharaonic form.

A Village East of the Blue Nile

Garia Wahid is a multiethnic village that was formed by settlers from several older villages when the new Rahad irrigated development project was opened in 1978. Most people are uneducated. Here, the Arabic-speaking ethnic groups, such as the Kenana, practiced severe pharaonic circumcisions, and they generally believed there would never be change in the practices. In fact, very few of them had heard much about the idea of abandoning circumcision, and those who had saw it as an urban phenomenon: "That hasn't come to us yet." Generally, Kenana women considered female circumcision to be a humorous topic, important to male sexual gratification, but not to be discussed in front of them.

Of the Kenana I interviewed and observed, only one young married woman of about sixteen did not plan to circumcise her future daughters. But even she later retracted this statement and said that her mother-in-law would surely insist on circumcision and that she would not be able to refuse doing it.

Another ethnic group in the village, the Zabarma (who had migrated from West Africa several generations ago), never adopted pharaonic but did practice Sunna, which their neighbors insisted amounted to no circumcision at all. Despite pressure to do so, most said they had no intention of abandoning Sunna. I did, however, learn of three cases of pharaonic circumcision. In one case, a Zabarma husband who married a third wife who came from a different village and was pharaonically circumcised persuaded a more senior wife to have it done also, reportedly because he preferred how it felt during sex. The older wife, who acceded to his wishes, later regretted the decision, saying it made both sex and childbirth *harr* (hot, painful). She advocated maintaining the custom of Suma.

Zabarma daughters, even though they were Sunna-circumcised, were subjected to name-calling by other girls (*Ya, ghalfa!*— roughly, "Hey, unclean!"), names that were applied to uncircumcised girls as well. Some Zabarma mothers reported that their daughters began to complain to them, asking to be circumcised, pressuring mothers with comments like, "What's the matter, don't we have razor blades like the Arabs?"

Some of the Zabarma girls invented names to call back at the pharaonically circumcised hecklers; *Ya, mutmura!* they answered, referring to the underground grain storage pits that are opened and closed, opened and closed, just as is scar tissue (for birth, after which it is reinfibulated). "When you run out of meat [i.e., tissue lost from repeated cutting and sewing], will you buy some in the market?!" These taunts were reported to me with great pride by several mothers, who saw their daughters as sticking up for their group's practices. All the Zabarma women I asked favored continuing Sunna circumcision.

In this village, issues of ethnic superiority and religious piety also entered into the debate. The Kenana, who claim descent from the Prophet Mohammed, are respected for this heritage and consider themselves superior people to the West African–originating Zabarma.[11] Both men and women of the Kenana are very proud of their group's pharaonic circumcision and occasionally say things that indicate their disdain for the physical appearance, hygiene, circumcisions, and ancestry of the Zabarma, in spite of their neighborly behavior toward each other. One of the few explicit insults I heard a Kenana man express about a Zabarma man (but not to his face) referred to the open (i.e., uninfibulated) vagina of his mother.

Zabarma men and women, as members of the Tijaniya sect, are proud of their great religious piety. Although the move to the village in the irrigation scheme where they now live led to some relaxation of the stricter female seclusion practices they had observed in their old village, women's ideas about the importance of deference to husbands and about daily religious observances made them feel superior in religious piety to Kenana women, who seldom seemed to pray. Their religious pride no doubt helped them to resist Kenana pressure to circumcise in their way, despite their claims of social superiority.

The village midwife who regularly served the Kenana and sometimes the Zabarma neighborhoods where I did my research did not advocate Sunna circumcision and continued to do pharaonic. Although she was aware of the discussion among health workers of the Sunna being preferable, she had not gone through the formal government midwifery training. Since the majority of her clientele preferred the pharaonic type, she continued to perform them. If called upon to deliver a baby for a Zabarma mother, however, she followed their custom and left the mother uninfibulated.

The City of Wad Medani

My final examples are drawn from interviews in the capital of Gezira Province, Wad Medani. An old city on the west bank of the Blue Nile, it is the main trading center of the region. The people of both the Gezira scheme and the Rahad area regard it as the nearest large city with well-staffed hospital facilities, although another city, Fau, also serves the Rahad area. Of the women I interviewed in Wad Medani, two in particular shed light on the cultural debate surrounding circumcision.

Sister Battool is a renowned nurse-midwife who supports the public-health education efforts to inform people about the dangers of the pharaonic form and who trains other health workers. Sister Battool reported having considerable success in influencing her clients to opt for minimal tissue removal, success that she attributed to changing social attitudes. When parents feared that a daughter's future husband might reject her if she were uninfibulated, Sister Battool tried to convince them that the couple could decide this issue for themselves later on. For those parents who insisted on infibulation, she tried to preserve the clitoris and erectile tissue inside, so as to minimize bleeding and preserve sexual sensitivity.

In interviews in 1989 and 1992, Sister Battool noted that more than half of her clients (perhaps 70 percent) asked for Sunna circumcision for their daughters and of those who wanted pharaonic, some asked that it be *nuss* (half). In 1992, she estimated that about 10 percent of the community were not circumcising at all. Although it would take further research to confirm her estimates, it is clear from the reputation of this midwife and her surgeries that the discussions she is having with her clients are influencing and influenced by a dramatic process of change, compared with the seventies. She believed that changing community sentiments were due not to the Islamist movement but rather to education, especially public-health education.

In contrast, Dr. Fahima, a female physician, believed that

change efforts should be guided by Islamic principles as well as by health concerns. Although she was involved in the Islamist movement, she was not involved in the political version represented by the more coercive policies of the National Islamic Front holding power in the government. When I interviewed her in 1989, she was finishing a community health research survey in another rural area, in which people were not yet willing to give up circumcision completely. Observing such popular opposition to the Ministry of Health policy of complete abandonment of the practice, a policy she accepted, she considered becoming an advocate for a form of surgery that would remove only the clitoral prepuce. That procedure, she felt, might satisfy people's desire to circumcise, yet would leave the clitoris better exposed to sexual stimulation and actually improve women's sexual response. She considered calling it "proper Sunna" to emphasize that the clitoridectomies commonly called Sunna were actually not approved of by the Prophet Mohammed in the *Hadith*.

Dr. Fahima came to this conclusion from studying religious texts. Her views are radically at odds with the prevalent interpretation (of predominately male religious scholars) that female circumcision was intended to decrease sexual pleasure for women. She concluded that "proper Sunna," like the controversial surgeries for anorgasmic women she read about in American medical journals, enhanced female sexuality. She reasoned that because both men and women believers are enjoined not to have sex outside of marriage, there was no reason to prevent women from enjoying sex with their husbands.

Sister Battool's and Dr. Fahima's creative responses—surgical and ideological—suggest a dynamic situation, where a need for cultural change is felt but where the process and outcome are still in the making. The approaches being considered by contemporary Sudanese health workers such as these are embedded in the political and economic situation of Sudan.

TOWARD A POLITICAL ECOLOGY OF HEALTH

Analyses of health problems would benefit from greater attention to political and economic questions. Cultural adaptation and maladaptation cannot be divorced from the question of differential effects of a practice or social institution on different categories of people in a society.

If the goal of medical anthropology is to make human lives better and to improve health, what might contribute to these ends? Who will define the goals and priorities? How will we move toward desired ends? These questions are at the heart of the issue of adaptation and cultural change, and they are as much political and economic as they are cultural and ecological. Whether a cultural practice is adaptive or maladaptive depends to a large extent on whose viewpoint is taken, where the political forces for and against it lie, and whose interests are served by change.

Unlike the spontaneity of genetic variations (i.e., mutations and chance combinations) that serve as the raw material for adaptation, cultural variations are the product of thinking human beings, who actively search out their best interests and who argue and decide, alone or in groups, whether to preserve one way of doing things or to invent others. Thus biological adaptive constraints—differential death and birth rates—are only a small part of the process of cultural adaptation, and it is necessary, therefore, to ask political and economic questions as well as ones about biological adaptiveness (cf. Singer 1993).

From my summary of the current Sudanese discourse on female circumcision, I suggest that the efforts to change it are not simply "adaptive" improvements on an otherwise "maladaptive" cultural pattern. Rather, both change efforts and resistance to such efforts involve contradictory political-economic implications. Forces for preservation of "Sudanese traditions" may be motivated by nationalist or partisan opposition to political repression and yet at the same time contribute to suppression of the female population (via the harmfulness of female circumcision). The Islamist movement may oppose pharaonic circumcision for religious reasons and yet contribute to more restrictions on women in the workplace, in dress, and in the curtailment of freedoms labeled as Western or un-Islamic—with the result that such cultural practices are suppressed without improving women's lives. The biomedical establishment supports abolition of all forms of these surgeries through education and by recommending against it, positions that are perceived by many rural people as somewhat elitist (i.e., they see it as a view of educated, middle-class, urban people). Many educated Sudanese, especially feminists, support the idea of gradual elimination of female circumcision while maintaining respect for the sentiments of those not espousing their view (Toubia 1993) and at the same time view the circumcision issue as only one of dozens of obstacles to balanced lives for women.

The international dimension of political-economic issues should not be overlooked. When outsiders take strong positions on practices such as pharaonic circumcision they can appear to be ethnocentric or arrogant. Their posturing can seem to deliberately ignore the salient issues of Third World poverty and health (such as centuries of economic exploitation and political interference) and place blame instead on the people themselves or their cultural maladaptation. To echo Boddy's rejoinder to Gordon (1991), "of what practical consequence" is it to draw the line at female circumcision if we have not analyzed how change might occur (1991, p. 16).

Outsiders must recognize that our knowledge about the existence of this practice does not turn the tide: it is the women who practice circumcision who will be the ones to change it (Gruenbaum 1982). Toubia has commented, "Over the last decade the . . . West has acted as though they have suddenly discovered a dangerous epidemic which they then sensationalized in international women's forums creating a backlash of over-sensitivity in the concerned communities. They have portrayed it as irrefutable evidence of the barbarism and vulgarity of underdeveloped countries . . . [and] the primitiveness of Arabs, Muslims, and Africans all in one blow" (1988, p. 101). Thus for outsiders to target female circumcision as the social problem in need of the most urgent attention seems outrageous to many Arab women (among them anthropologist Soheir Morsy [1991a]), since there are so many worse problems that wealthy countries have caused, exacerbated, or at any rate failed to help solve.

In Sudan, for example, at least a quarter of a million people died of starvation due to drought and war in 1988–89. In 1991, millions of people were at risk of death from starvation, due to an unhappy combination of failed rains, protracted civil war and population displacement, repressive government, and international isolation following the Sudanese government's refusal to support the coalition against Saddam Hussein during the Gulf War. Although the United States and other countries offered some assistance, it was too little and too late, relating to the "donor fatigue" phenomenon. Thousands of little Sudanese girls died—whether circumcised or not—along with their brothers and elders.

But my purpose in this article has not been to analyze international injustices and human tragedies, as important as those are for anthropology to address. Instead, I suggest that our theories of cultural adaptation be subjected to multiple viewpoints by examining differences in interests by gender, by ethnicity, by age, and by social class. For the case of Sudan, arguments for the abandonment of controversial cultural practices such as female circumcision can serve a variety of political ends, from hiding international injustices to undercutting authenticity of traditional Sudanese culture under the banner of the Islamist movement, to advocating women's liberation, to advocating stricter Islamic interpretations of limitations on women's roles.

If such widely divergent interests can be served both by a cultural practice and by opposition to it, it is important that analysts increase the sophistication with which questions are approached, including not only health effects but the political economic context in which the cultural practices are pursued. In the end, the data I have presented on the cultural debates underway in Sudan are intended to underscore the advice of Morsy (1991a), Scheper-Hughes (1991), and others to look to Sudanese and Egyptian women to lead their own struggle on female circumcision: it is, in Scheper-Hughes's words, something for Egyptian and Sudanese women "to argue out for themselves" (1991, p. 26).

NOTES

I am grateful to the Development Studies and Research Centre of the University of Khartoum for research affiliation in 1989 and 1992 and the Department of Rural Development at the University of Gezira for affiliation in 1989. Funding was provided by California State University, San Bernardino (travel grant and sabbatical), a grant-in-aid from the American Council of Learned Societies, and a summer fellowship from the National Endowment for the Humanities. I am especially grateful to my Sudanese academic colleagues, three research assistants, and the people of the communities where I did my research for their assistance, insight, hospitality, and friendship. For their very helpful comments on earlier drafts of this article I thank Hans Baer, Merill Singer, and three anonymous reviewers. And for her help in manuscript preparation I thank Cynthia Black-Turner.

1. I continue to use the term, following the usage of my Sudanese colleagues who have written in English about these practices (e.g., Toubia 1988), and because "female genital mutilation" (or FGM) has sounded judgmental. However, the latter term has rapidly gained greater acceptance. Toubia, for example, uses both terms in her 1993 work.

2. To guard against such strong ethnocentric reactions in teaching, Sondra Hale recommends that these practices should not be introduced casually as exotica but should be covered only when the teacher is knowledgeable and prepared to spend the time necessary to allow students to get past the initial strong reactions to achieve a clearer understanding of the multifaceted real-life problems faced by the women involved (1989).

3. I am referring here to her best-selling novel *Possessing the Secret of Joy* (1992)—which does not mention any specific culture or country, but is set in "Africa"—rather than the more recent *Warrior Marks* (1993), Alice Walker's collaboration with Pratibha Parmar, which describes their nonfiction filmmaking project against female genital mutilation.

4. Pharaonic circumcision is the most severe form of the surgeries, still practiced widely in Sudan and Somalia. It consists of removal of the clitoris, prepuce, inner labia, and part of the outer labia, followed by the closure of the tissues over the vaginal opening. The resulting scar tissue occludes the urethral and vaginal openings, with only a single tiny opening preserved for the passage of urine and menses. First intercourse often requires tearing or cutting, and childbirth requires cutting followed by re-infibulation (restitching) of the opening.

5. The interviews were conducted in Arabic using an outline of topics, including personal background, a reproductive history, and questions on labor tasks of the women and children. I was assisted by a Sudanese woman schoolteacher who accompanied me on the majority of interviews, who explained in standard Sudanese Arabic unfamiliar words from the local speech. Her assistance in facilitating the interviews through her friendliness, personal knowledge of families and relationships, and her stature in the community was very valuable. She also used the opportunity to encourage mothers to send their children to school.

6. From my discussions it seemed that maternal mortality was not a major problem in this region at the present time. These families moved to the development project village—which has a clinic staffed by a medical assistant—in 1978. Births are attended, and circumcisions performed, by the village midwife, who has not received full formal training but who sterilizes her instruments, uses local anesthesia for incisions and suture, and participates in Ministry of Health seminars from time to time. It is quite possible that maternal mortality had been more of a problem in the recent past.

7. The urban interviews were conducted in Khartoum and Wad Medani. I have used pseudonyms for all individuals, even those who gave me permission to use their names, due to the current political situation in Sudan and recent government actions that make it illegal to write or broadcast anything, inside or outside Sudan, that the government deems damaging to the reputation of the country.

8. Some of this has been spurred by the extensive labor migration to the oil-rich countries, where Sudanese have been exposed to stricter Islam and have had the opportunity to go on the pilgrimage to Mecca. The midwife's son had worked abroad, and she had done the hajj.

9. She quipped, laughingly, "If your husband ever had the opportunity to have sex with a Sudanese woman, he would divorce you immediately!"

10. These Hausa migrated to this village in 1928 in response to labor opportunities on the irrigated scheme and with the encouragement of the British colonial government. Although most of the present residents were born in Sudan, the Arab-Sudanese generally consider them foreigners.

11. The Zabarma group originated in what is now Niger but migrated to western Sudan in the last century, settling in the Rahad River valley by the 1930s. Although their Songhay language is still spoken in the home, most adult women in the scheme have now learned Arabic very well, as the men had done earlier.

REFERENCES

Assaad, Marie B. 1980. Female circumcision in Egypt: Social implications, current research, and prospects for change. *Studies in Family Planning* 11 (1): 3–16.

Boddy, Janice. 1982. Womb as oasis: The symbolic context of pharaonic circumcision in rural northern Sudan. *American Ethnologist* 9:682–98.

———. 1989. *Wombs and alien spirits: Women, men, and the zar cult in northern Sudan.* Madison: University of Wisconsin Press.

———. 1991. Body politics: Continuing the anticircumcision crusade. *Medical Anthropology Quarterly* 5:15–17.

Brownlee, Shannon, and Jennifer Seter, with Betsy Streisand and Louise Tunbridge. 1994. In the name of ritual. *U.S. News & World Report,* February 7, pp. 56–58.

Edgerton, Robert. 1992. *Sick societies: Challenging the myth of primitive harmony.* New York: Free Press.

El Dareer, Asthma. 1982. *Woman, why do you weep? Circumcision and its consequences.* London: Zed Press.

Gordon, Daniel. 1991. Female circumcision and genital operations in Egypt and the Sudan: A dilemma for medical anthropology. *Medical Anthropology Quarterly*, n.s., 5:3–14.

Gruenbaum, Ellen. 1982. The movement against clitoridectomy and infibulation in Sudan: Public health policy and the women's movement. *Medical Anthropology Newsletter* 13 (2): 4–12.

———. 1988. Reproductive ritual and social reproduction: Female circumcision and the subordination of women in Sudan. In *Economy and class in Sudan*, edited by Norman O'Neill and Jay O'Brien, pp. 308–28. Avebury, UK: Aldershot.

———. 1991. The Islamic movement, development, and health education: Recent changes in the health of rural women in central Sudan. *Social Science & Medicine* 33 (6): 637–45.

———. 1992. The Islamist state and Sudanese women. *Middle East Report* 179 (November–December): 20–23.

Hale, Sondra. 1989. The politics of gender in the Middle East. In *Gender and anthropology: Critical reviews for research and teaching*, edited by Sandra Morgen, pp. 246–67. Washington, DC: American Anthropological Association.

Hayes, Rose Oldfiel. 1975. Female genital mutilation, fertility control, women's roles, and the patrilineage in modern Sudan: A functional analysis. *American Ethnologist* 2:617–33.

Hosken, Fran. 1982. *The Hosken report: Genital and sexual mutilation of females*. Lexington, MA: International Network News.

Kaplan, David, with Shawn Lewis and Joshua Hammer. 1993. Is it torture or tradition? *Newsweek*, December 20, p. 124.

Lightfoot-Klein, Hanny. 1989. *Prisoners of ritual: An odyssey into female genital circumcision in Africa*. Binghamton, NY: Haworth Press.

McElroy, Ann, and Patricia K. Townsend, eds. 1989. *Medical anthropology in ecological perspective*. 2nd ed. Boulder, CO: Westview Press.

Morsy, Soheir. 1991a. Safeguarding women's bodies: The white man's burden medicalized. *Medical Anthropology Quarterly*, n.s., 5:19–23.

———. 1991b. Spirit possession in Egyptian ethnomedicine. In *Women's medicine: The ZarBori cult in Africa and beyond*, edited by I. M. Lewis, Ahmed Al-Safi, and Sayyid Hurreiz, pp. 189–208. Edinburgh: Edinburgh University Press for International African Institute.

Rushwan, Hamid, Cony Slot, Asthma El Dareer, and Nadia Bushra. 1983. *Female circumcision in the Sudan: Prevalence, complications, attitudes, and changes.* Khartoum: Faculty of Medicine, University of Khartoum.

Scheper-Hughes, Nancy. 1991. Virgin territory: The male discovery of the clitoris. *Medical Anthropology Quarterly*, n.s., 5:25–28.

Singer, Merrill. 1993. A rejoinder to Wiley's critique of critical medical anthropology. *Medical Anthropology Quarterly*, n.s., 7:185–91.

Toubia, Nahid. 1988. Women and health in Sudan. In *Women of the Arab world*, edited by Nahid Toubia, pp. 98–109. London: Zed Books.

———. 1993. *Female genital mutilation: A call for global action.* New York: Women, Ink.

Walker, Alice. 1992. *Possessing the secret of joy.* New York: Harcourt Brace Jovanovich.

Walker, Alice, and Pratibha Parmar. 1993. *Warrior marks: Female genital mutilation and the sexual blinding of women.* New York: Harcourt Brace.

12. Gender, Race, Militarization, and Economic Restructuring

in the Former Yugoslavia and at the U.S.-Mexico Border

Anna M. Agathangelou

Arguing that economic globalization is constituted through militarization, Agathangelou examines how gender and race are articulated in the process. To support her analysis, she explores and compares two sites: the militarization of the U.S.-Mexico border and the militarization of Yugoslavia during the "ethnic conflict." How have feminists responded to these conflicts? In a detailed and timely paper, Agathangelou indicts radical and liberal feminist perspectives for their failure to issue a critique against capitalism and U.S. foreign policies developed after the Cold War. To effectively organize against militarization, Agathangelou proposes utilizing a "transborder" feminist movement collectively committed to eradicating all forms of exploitation based on gender, race, and class.

The September 11, 2001, attacks on two major symbols of economic and political power, the World Trade Center and the Pentagon, made apparent that First World countries are sites of conflict and insecurity as well as those of the Third World. Although rendered readily apparent by events following the Sep-

347

tember 11 attacks, the accelerating pace of militarization's global-ization stems from deeper roots. The post–Cold War world of neoliberal, economic globalization provides a fertile seedbed for militarized violence in the global context. With the fall of the former Soviet Union and the Eastern European bloc, the global cap-italist system—with its major proponents, the United States, along with the World Trade Organization (WTO), World Bank (WB), and International Monetary Fund (IMF) further institutionalized vio-lence in the name of stability and prosperity in the world. But sta-bility and prosperity for whom? The IMF policies in the wake of Asia's financial crisis (1997–98) provoked riots, widespread strikes, and ethnic violence. The IMF paved the way for Western corporations to buy out Asian ones at "fire sale" prices (Ling 2002). The promises of globalization that more and more people will have access to the economic benefits of the global economy ("free trade," mass privatization, deregulation, and a quest for short-term profits) did not come to fruition. Armies of people (Third World women, workers, migrant workers, rural sectors, and indigenous peoples) are locked out of the gains (Klein 2002, p. xxi). Yet many of these "fenced-out people" are moving "from countryside to city, from country to country, and do not turn to violence even when they organize to resist the dramatic consequences of this develop-mental model of capitalism and to create alternative practices, models, and alliances (see Seattle; Washington, DC; Toronto; and Mexico). Yet they face violence daily as a consequence of resisting the international order (*Globe and Mail* May 31, 2000; June 7, 2000; May 2, 2001).

This paper is guided by the following questions: is globaliza-tion constituted through militarization? What does the neoliberal world order find productive in the systemic strategy of militariza-tion? How is this process gendered and how is race a factor in it?[1] Here I examine and compare two sites, Yugoslavia's militarization in the "ethnic conflict" of the nineties (Nikolic-Ristanovic 1999, p. 1) and the militarization of the U.S.-Mexico border, to show how globalization of militarization constitutes relations and processes across nation-states, classes, and genders.[2] I contend that militarization has become a vital strategy in the constitution of globalization, and both sites, albeit quite different from each other, exemplify this set of social relations and processes. I then critique "global" feminist discourses on this topic promulgated by liberal and radical U.S. feminists, and I conclude with a discussion of feminist decolonizing practices in these two sites.

GLOBALIZATION AND MILITARIZATION: TWO SIDES OF THE SAME COIN?

For most feminists, militarization is more than war and war preparations (Enloe 2000). Militarization is, they argue, a worldview and a structure based on the objectification of "others" as threats and enemies and operates through specific military institutions and actions (Reardon 1985). It is a strategy that "spreads military values and structures (discipline and conformity, centralization of authority, hierarchization, and so on) into the mainstream of national economic and sociopolitical life" (Zwick 1984, p. 2) and depends "in part upon the [continuation] of structural violence of organized gender inequality" (Peterson and Runyan 1999, p. 124). This strategy depends on redirecting resources to increase military budgets, and leads to military leadership of civilian organizations and institutions, especially at a time when "social needs, so long neglected during the Cold War, are massive" (Peterson and Runyan 1999, p. 125). Since the foreign policy of the most powerful countries in the world is informed by the privileging of military concerns over any other national and international aims and objectives, it is no wonder that the leadership of most countries equates military experience and expertise with successful political leadership (Enloe 2000, p. 2). Militarization is becoming a dominant strategy at many political levels: the civic, the national, the international, and the transnational. Police, army, and paramilitary forces are growing in strength and brutality to control and crush their own citizens, particularly if they act against repression (Huggins 1998; Kirk and Okazawa-Rey 1998). Moreover, foreign policy, constantly informed by the desire to access regional markets more freely and the "male politician's angst" to appear "manly" (Enloe 2000, p. 1), is becoming increasingly militarized, and this has substantive implications on the lives of women and men.[3]

The predictions that globalization would bring security, stability, and abundance to the world similar to that achieved in contexts such as those of the United States, Western Europe, and Japan have not been realized. On the contrary, as the WB and the United Nations Development Program (UNDP) attest, two decades of globalization have resulted in enlarging rather than shrinking the gaps between rich and poor, both within and among countries (Robinson 1998; Amin 1996). Throughout Asia, Africa, and the Caribbean, many people, a great number of whom are women, are squeezed out by U.S. imports and relegated to the informal economy or sweatshop labor for multinationals. The G-8 countries' dominance in decision-making in the IMF and the WB led to the implementation of structural adjustment packages, which provided conditions for loans and debt relief but in the end served to keep many poor countries and their citizens locked in poverty. The benefits of global market liberalization and integration have accrued disproportionately only to wealthy U.S. citizens, Western Europeans, and a small group of middle- and upper-class people in the Third World (Amin 1996). Many regions of the world, faced with economic pressure and increased ethnic and domestic violence have organized against the corporatization of their lives and their lands (Klein 2002).

Large institutional investors and firms such as MacDonald-Douglas and Lockheed Martin, some of whom dominate systems of defense, production, and finance, promised their slice of the economic miracle to poor regions. These same agents are the ones who can move production overseas and back again, using the military to discipline Third World peoples (Klein 2002) whenever necessary, with few constraints from the political "state," whose interest is maximization of profits (Aguilar 1997, p. 316). The constitution of these global power dynamics is based on the strategy of militarization, which in turn is based on gendered, classed, and racialized dimensions. Women are sexually violated if they resist militarization of their lives and lands. The marginalized poor are assaulted in the streets all over the world if they organize against corporate globalization; whole nation-states and continents are written off, such as Argentina and Africa (Klein 2002, p. xxi). Indigenous peoples from Columbia to Canada are crushed if they oppose corporatization of their lands. When national security interests are seen as threatened by the cries of the poor or when the global economy seems to be "unstable," more and more repression is necessary to create "stability" locally for the sustenance and constitution of the neoliberal economy. Thus military investment and aid becomes a priority of the national states and now, of particular nationalist groups. As Wilson argues, "the 'health' of the economy is considered the primary national security interest of [all countries]. Social and economic justice are given mere lip service" (1997, p. 1).

In the eighties, in both industrialized and developing countries, the state, following rules endorsed by financial institutions such as the WB, withdrew from social reproduction through deregulation, the corporatization and privatization of social needs such as public education and welfare, and the lifting of regulations that hinder market forces. The state redirected resources from social subsidies into military expenditures and military-oriented industries. This process, which facilitates private capital accumulation and shifts income and power from labor to capital, forms a transnational class in tandem with a modification of the national states as a mediating element (Robinson 1998). Critical understandings of international relations (IR) argue that this transnational class formation "has involved the accelerated division of the world into a global bourgeoisie and a global proletariat, and has brought changes in the relationship between dominant and subordinate classes" (ibid., p. 8). But the same theorists who argue that class is transformed in the process of the state's transnationalization seem to be assuming that labor and capital are masculine social relations that simultaneously represent and subsume the feminine ones (Agathangelou 2002; Chang and Ling 2000). Feminist scholars have shown that gender, or the "socially learned behavior and expectations that distinguish between masculinity and femininity" (Marchard and Runyan 2000, p. 8, citing Peterson and Runyan 1999), operates in international relations ideologically, socially, and physically as well and is linked to class. Demonstrating that race operates on these same levels (Chowdhry and Nair 2002), postcolonial feminists ask, who are the leaders of this transnational class? Are they women or men, where are they from, and what are their major goals and objectives? What is their vision of the world?

Setting social and market policies, mobilizing resources, creating credits, redistributing taxes, and controlling capital and labor allocations, this transnational class constitutes a transnational apparatus moving toward the creation of a new world order. These policies are designed "supranationally" and executed by nation-states (Robinson 1998). As Robinson argues, the "state as a class relation is becoming transnationalized. The class practices of a new global ruling class are becoming 'condensed' in an emergent TNS [transnational state]" (1998, p. 5). This comprises institutions (IMF, WB, WTO) and practices (e.g., using military and police forces to control workers and protesters [Genoa, Seattle] who challenge capitalism and its agents) "that maintain, defend, and advance the emergent hegemony of a global bourgeoisie [mostly male] and its project of constructing a new global capitalist historical bloc" (ibid.). It is against this global matrix of power that the United States, Mexico, and the Yugoslavian states are struggling to integrate themselves as components of this transnationalized apparatus. Despite their sharply different economic and political histories and trajectories, these states, with the intervention of international institutions such as the WB and agreements such as NAFTA, are participating in transnationalization (that is, making it possible for capital to move anytime it wants anywhere without any constraints). The maintenance of these social relations of capital, which exile millions to poverty and exclusion, depend on militarization. Here is what Naomi Klein had to say about this restructuring:

> [globalization] puts resources out of the hands of so many. It simply isn't possible to lock away this much of [people's] wealth without an accompanying strategy to control popular unrest and mobility. Security firms do the biggest business in the cities where the gap between rich and poor is greatest—Johannesburg, Sao Paulo, New Delhi—selling iron gates, armoured cars, elaborate alarm systems and renting out armies of private guards. . . . It now seems that these gated compounds protecting the haves from the have-nots are microcosms of what is fast becoming a global security—not a global village intent on lowering walls and barriers, as we were promised, but a network of fortresses connected by highly militarized trade corridors. (2002, p. xxiii)

Applied to these two states, a historical materialist feminist analytical lens leads us to identify the following:

- *Militarization.* Militarization is a strategy used by the following three agents: (1) developmental states such as Yugoslavia and Mexico, to dominate the "civil" societies under the rubric of national interest; (2) local men using violence against women and working-class people in order to sustain the health and wealth of the patriarchal family-state-economy (Ling 2000); and (3) neoliberal leader states of the neocapitalist economy such as the United States, who use this strategy to constitute global power by intervening through war, military aid, and paramilitary forces at the U.S.-Mexico border and Yugoslavia to protect wealthy interests within

Mexico, the United States, and Eastern Europe. Along with other states, the national state plays a critical role in "maintaining class division, unequal power based on asymmetrical property relations, and transnational capital accumulation" (San Juan 2000, p. 183).

- *Accountability.* Upper-class political and economic agents in these Third World sites and the leader economies are jointly involved in the global changes in these sites. They "both transfer the cost of the crisis to ordinary folk, who had little to do with the massive borrowings of capital that transpired in the late 1990s in the region but now bear the brunt of its consequences" (Ling 2000).

- *Agency.* This relationship of global interactions between elites in Third World and leader sites is a relational and a parallel one. Local strategies of cultural chauvinism in the global political economy sustain these global processes of imperialist domination. The sooner we recognize this relationality and parallel connection, the sooner we can work with local peoples in "periphractic spaces" (Psimmenos 2000) who are feminized or fenced out of the political process to devise a more democratic world (see "Democratizing the Movement," "Rebellion in Chiapas," "Italy's Social Centres," "Limits of Political Parties").

- *Transformation.* If militarization is a strategy of gender, class, and racial domination, then feminist organizing should aim to expose the neoliberal myth that "capital is objective, purely interest-driven, and culturally neutral" and independent of politics (Ling 2000), and that capital's expansion depends on political violence in both peripheralized and core sites as strategies to continue exploitation and oppression. Historical materialist feminists as well as with people who are focusing on identifying "windows to democracy" need to analyze how militarization has become such an indispensable process in capitalist relations. Highlighting contradictions and transgressive possibilities in neoliberal capitalist relations can serve to challenge sexual, racial, class, and other social inequalities.

This article shows how women in different ethno-national sites take a leading role in resisting the redistribution of income and power. More specifically, I focus on the political mobilization of women in the former Yugoslavia, Mexico, and the United States. Women are interested in gaining autonomy and a larger say in political organizations in the move toward the creation of a more democratic global community. I will examine such major processes as the (re-)colonization of local and national economies and their militarization in the process of creating the new global capitalist-security state.[4] I will focus on Third World women workers' experiences and repression.

THE POLITICAL ECONOMY OF MILITARIZATION IN YUGOSLAVIA

The militarization of Yugoslavia began long before the 1991 war. To understand the use of the military in the class and ethnic struggles of Yugoslavs it is crucial to expose the links between economics and politics and how the military is not used to protect democratic spaces but rather the corporate interests of the local or international capitalist elites. The Yugoslav war of 1941–45 among various ethnic and foreign groups led to a wave of killing and retaliation upon Chetniks, Muslims, Orthodox Serbs, and Romanys (Gypsies). For example, in the Sandzak region, surrounded by Montenegro, Bosnia, and Serbia, Chetnik and Serbian guerrillas killed 9,000 Muslims. The Croatian Ustase massacred some 60,000 Jews, 26,000 Romanys, and 750,000 Orthodox Serbs. Out of this bloody struggle, the Communists under Tito emerged as sole rulers without major Soviet assistance. On March 7, 1945, a single provisional Yugoslav government took office, with Tito as prime minister and war minister, Subasic in charge of foreign affairs, and Tito supporters in charge of almost all cabinet posts. A Communist-dominated Provisional Assembly convened in August. The Yugoslav Communist Party (CPY)

> [came to] regard itself as a revolutionary power that embodied within itself the national aspirations of all the Yugoslav nations, now synthesized in the dialectically higher form of a Yugoslav national consciousness. . . . The leadership held . . . the view that national differences were a reflection of regional differences, of the division of the country into advanced and retarded areas, the retarded having been the victim of exploitation by the advanced. Rapid industrialization, which was to be accomplished through the mechanism of Stalinist central planning, would assuredly bring about an equalization of these differences, which divided the land into a progressive northwest and a backward southeast. (Curtis 1992a)

The newly elected Constituent Assembly dissolved the monarchy and established the Federal People's Republic of Yugoslavia on November 29, 1945. Two months later, it adopted a Soviet-style constitution that provided for a federation of six republics under a strong central government. The Communists quickly implemented the Stalinist model for rapid industrial development, and by 1948 they had nationalized virtually all the country's wealth except privately held land. They redirected the bulk of the trade toward the Soviet Union and Eastern Europe. The first five-year plan (1947–52) was designed to overcome economic and technological "backwardness," strengthen economic and military power, enhance and develop the socialist sector of the country, increase the people's welfare, and narrow the gap in economic development among regions.

This (re-)organization of social relations within Yugoslavia was short-lived. In the first half of the planning period, economic development was relatively successful and approximately on schedule.

However, Yugoslavia's 1948 ouster from the Communist Information Bureau (Cominform) resulted in a boycott that contributed to
an economic slowdown. Many treaties and trade agreements among
the Soviet Union, Eastern Europe, and Yugoslavia were abrogated.
Additionally, loans were cancelled, and nearly all trade with the
Soviet Union and Eastern Europe, which made up approximately
50 percent of Yugoslavia's imports and exports in 1948, was halted.
This figure was reduced to zero by 1950. The economy of Yugoslavia suffered when it did not receive goods, particularly
machinery and capital goods, for which it had already paid. When
these established social relations were severed, the Yugoslavian
leadership moved to counter the threat of economic isolation. They
instituted self-management, and with the slogan "The Factories to
the Workers," policymakers transferred economic management
from the state to the workers.

In the sixties Yugoslavia was forced to create an alternative to
this structural economic "cut-off" by allowing greater market
freedom. Through a series of five-year economic plans, it introduced market socialism, in which workers were able to manage
enterprises, using domestic and foreign market forces as a management guide. Decision-making was decentralized, and the federal
government loosened its control over investment, prices, and
incomes, and capitalist economics was allowed to play a greater
role. The federal government could only intervene with emergency
measures in times of crisis in the local market. It introduced liberal
measurements to reorganize its socialist economy into a market
one, and it implemented economic reforms to satisfy IMF preconditions for loans. Between 1958 and 1965, the Yugoslav leadership
worked to satisfy the conditions of membership in the General
Agreement on Tariffs and Trade (GATT) and reformed the
economy to favor an export orientation to Western hard-currency
markets as well as increased labor productivity with imported
Western technology. Despite such changes, the Western recession
that began in 1975, which intensified into a worldwide depression

in the eighties, forced most of the workers in Germany to go home, which in turn affected the "invisible" remittances (averaging US$2 billion in the late seventies) arriving into the country. About one-third of all guest workers were women, a percentage that corresponded to their share in Yugoslavia's overall domestic workforce.

Simultaneously, the IMF, backed by Washington, stiffened its policies requiring dramatic changes to achieve restructuring (Woodward 1995), a strategy that pushed Yugoslavia to borrow heavily to fuel its economic growth. These loans supported the economy in two ways: first, Yugoslavia imported advanced technology to improve its international competitiveness, and second, these loans gave time to domestic industries to adjust to higher prices of oil and other primary commodities and to a variety of non-tariff barriers against Yugoslavian exports of steel, textiles, tobacco, and beef.

Despite economic hardship between 1979 and 1989, Yugoslavia attempted to liberalize its economy, to decentralize political power, to reach association agreements with the European Community and the European Free Trade Association (EFTA), and to create conditions for relative prosperity and a "landscape of multicultural pluralism" (Woodward 1995, p. 1). But a shift from higher to lower value-added products (i.e., from manufacturing to primary commodities) meant declining revenues and "a relative shift of purchases and earnings to areas producing primary commodities— areas such as Serbia, Kosovo, the poorer interior in Croatia, Bosnia-Herzegovina, and Macedonia" (ibid., p. 48). In the eighties Yugoslavia had depleted foreign reserves, and with falling exports it had great difficulty financing its debt, which had ballooned to $20 billion. Despite his previous resistance to IMF intervention, in 1982 Prime Minister Branko Mikulic turned to the IMF, which created a new facility—a three-year standby loan. The IMF proposed that the country finance its debt through a series of anti-inflationary, macro-economic liberalization policies, trade, and price policies. However, these changes, strongly advocated by economic liberals within Yugoslavia, carried risks.

The economic reform and the implementation of long-term macroeconomic stabilization unleashed a multilayered political struggle in 1982 that "had a drastic effect on most citizens' welfare, and led to major political quarrels between the republics and the federal government over the federal budget, taxation, and jurisdiction over foreign trade and investment. Expectations of greater economic integration were not realised. Instead, the result by the end of the decade was a breakdown in all elements of the domestic order, political disintegration, and rising nationalism" (ibid., p. 50).

Austerity measures taken to refinance the debt led to a decline in security of the solid middle class (public sector managers, urban professionals, artisans, and farmers) that had been growing since the fifties. Sixteen percent of this class was able to sustain or improve its living standards; the remaining 84 percent experienced a decline in their economic fortunes and their sense of personal security (ibid.). Massive delegations of workers from Croatia, Vojvodina, and Serbia took their protests to the federal parliament in Belgrade. The U.S. State Department pressed for refinancing the debt despite public opinion against this course of action, because they believed that legislating economic reforms on the basis of a "long-term program for economic stabilisation" would be the best strategy to transform the Yugoslav economy into a market economy. The parliament only had to approve this proposal in principle (ibid., p. 57). Furthermore, the IMF and domestic liberal economists argued that the country could generate growth and improve efficiency at home by integrating itself into the capitalist model of production and finance, the "global division of labour," and by reorienting itself to the production of exports that would be competitive in Western markets.

This "globalization" process required implementing a transnational, neoliberal formula, as well as ignoring the gaps between rich and poor within Yugoslavia and the structural position of Yugoslavia within the global economy. The financial institutions and the leaders of liberalism with Yugoslavia worked hand in hand to integrate this state-socialist system into the neoliberal economy. To recreate its economic and masculine power within the global structure, the Yugoslav state moved in ways that proved detrimental to the whole of the Yugoslav society by following the policies of the WB and the IMF. The more the leadership moved to create itself in the image of the neoliberal state, the more it gave the power to international financial institutions to "take power away from the communities, give it to a central government, then give it to the corporations through privatization" (Klein 2002, p. 36, citing Vandana Shiva). Alternative institutions and frameworks were lacking within the Yugoslav context to challenge the intervention of the military to resolve these socioeconomic crises locally. This lack of alternatives further enabled the intervention of one of the major proponents of the global capitalist system, the United States, to intervene militarily and to control what came to be called an "ethno-nationalist" war.

MILITARIZATION, GENDER, AND RACE

Contradictions of the international world order, as expressed locally, precipitated the dissolution of the Yugoslav state and the consequent war in Yugoslavia. Although loans and aid from the WB and the IMF arrived to restructure the economy of Yugoslavia, the state was pushed to reduce social spending, privatize more resources, and eliminate support to local industries, all in the midst of an economic crisis deepened by the policies demanded by the international financial institutions. With loans, aid, and centralized resources and power in their hands, the elites continued to borrow in order to redirect a socialist economy into a market economy, and moved to feminize larger parts of the Yugoslav society (e.g., to exploit and oppress women, the working class, and particular regions of the country).

Slovenia, Croatia, and most of Serbia emphasized high technology in building production capacity and attracting foreign investment. By contrast, the less developed southern regions, especially Kosovo, Macedonia, Montenegro, and southern Serbia, were pushed to focus on traditional, labor-intensive, low-paying economic activity such as textile manufacture, agriculture, and handicrafts. This contrast produced sharp differences in employment, investment, income potential, and social services among the eight political units of the federation. For example, in the late eighties, the average income for social sector workers in Macedonia was half that of a similar worker in Slovenia. Especially in Kosovo and Macedonia, poor economic and social conditions exacerbated longstanding ethnic animosities and periodically ignited uprisings. Resources from rich regions like Slovenia and Croatia, invested into the Fund for Underdeveloped Regions, were curtailed in nineties because these rich regions saw the fund being mismanaged by the central government. Croatia threatened similar action if the federal government did not make concessions. By this time, economic autonomy and membership in the EEC had become attractive and plausible alternatives for Slovenia.

The state's approach to women within different regions was also based on a strategy of further exploiting and oppressing the Yugoslav society. Although women became better educated and increasingly employed within these different regions, they did not gain access to the job market or advancement to high social and political positions. In the eighties, the percentage of women in low-level political and management positions was quite representative, but representation declined toward the top of the administrative pyramid. Women constituted 38 percent of Yugoslavia's nonagricultural labor force in 1987, up from 26 percent thirty years earlier. The participation of women in the Yugoslav workforce varied dramatically according to region. In Slovenia, women made up 44 percent of the workforce; in Kosovo, 20 percent. In 1989, Yugoslav women worked primarily in three fields: cultural and social welfare (56 percent of the persons employed in the field), public services and public administration (42 percent), and trade and catering (42 percent).

In response to the economic crisis in Yugoslavia, Slobodan Milosevic and other leaders sought to control and police the structural socioeconomic troubles by drawing on "the ideology of state and ethnic nationalism (based on patriarchal principles)" as a tool that could mystify the restructuring of the economic and political landscape, including racial, ethnic, and gender relations (Papic 1999, p. 154). Since the restructuring of Yugoslavia meant that the central state, along with the international financial institutions, was putting resources and wealth out of the hands of so many, and since many citizens in Yugoslavia discovered that "the true price of 'free trade' is the [loss] of the power to govern themselves" (Klein 2002, p. 43), it simply was not possible for the state not to accompany its neoliberal policies with a strategy to control potential unrest from the people. Thus, militarization, a process that consumed millions of dinars and further led to the redirection of people's resources, became part and parcel of the practices of corporate globalization.

The military institution conscripted many working-class soldiers. In 1990, about one-half of all conscripts came from rural backgrounds. Additionally, the only language used in the armed forces was Serbo-Croatian. Although Article 243 of the 1974 constitution guaranteed the equality of all national languages in the armed forces, it also stated that a single, unspecified language could be used for military training and command. For most of the eighties, for some, the military played an important role in sustaining a sense of unity. But the death of Tito marked a dramatic rise in ethnic tensions in the eighties. By 1990, serious problems had developed in the Yugoslav People's Army (YPA) ranks and in its relationship to society as a whole, even though it had been very popular in Serbia in the eighties. Its predominantly Serbian leadership made high-profile appeals for national unity and public order. However, non-Serbs saw this call as a demand for further centralization of political power in the hands of the Serbs.

Civilians of other nationalities heavily criticized the military institution. Although the organization remained unified, divisive tensions paralleled Yugoslavia's growing social and national problems. The growing number of nationalist movements in several regions of the country complicated the mission of the military. How was this institution going to defend the country against external threats while trying to suppress internal ones? For example, the civilian press, especially in Slovenia, heavily criticized the military by calling it an undemocratic institution that favored Serbs over other nationalities. Furthermore, this press described the use of military labor to build expensive villas for the League of Communists of Yugoslavia (LCY) and YPA leadership as well as military involvement in acting as an intermediary in Swedish arms sales to Libya. These reports led the military to react. In 1988, the former secretary for national defense "asserted that hostile elements were tarnishing the military's reputation and stirring ethnic unrest among military personnel. Alleged uprisings plotted by ethnic Albanians in the YPA were mentioned prominently in his speech. He claimed that attacks on the YPA destabilized the country's constitutional order by undermining one of its most important institutions" (Curtis 1992b).

These social and national struggles affected the functioning of the military, and the ethnic makeup of the military also had a serious impact on the military's effectiveness:

Article 242 of the Constitution requires that the senior YPA command and officer corps reflect proportional representation of all nations and nationalities. However, the proportion of Serbs in the YPA was higher than that in the total population. In 1983 Serbs made up more than 57 percent of the YPA officer corps. . . . Among the other nationalities, Montenegrins had a strong military tradition and close ties to Serbia. They made up over 10 percent of the officer corps but only 3 percent of the total population. Croats and Slovenes were the most seriously underrepresented nationalities in the YPA officer corps. They made up only 15 and percent, respectively, of all officers, and 20 and 8 percent respectively of the civilian population. Croats confronted some discrimination in the YPA because of lingering doubts about their loyalty to the Yugoslav state. Muslims, Albanians, Macedonians, and Hungarians constituted a small fraction of the officer corps. (Curtis 1992b)

The friction associated with this ethno-nationalist composition in the armed forces became a serious problem by 1990. Doubts arose about the dependability of troops from certain nationalities (e.g., Croats, ethnic Albanians, and Slovenes) in defending Yugoslavia against external attack because of political and economic conditions that had emerged in their regions in the eighties. When Croats and Kosovans demanded military autonomy or brought to the fore that the military was excessively brutal against the nationalist uprisings in Kosovo, the YPS doubted their loyalty and purged officers out of the military echelons. Similarly, the hostilities began with the Slovenes. Under the weight of nationalism, the YPA began expressing the global contradictions of the neoliberal economy within the military institution.

The U.S. and European powers explained the ensuing crisis in terms of civil war and ethnic conflicts constituted through historical enmities and aggressions. These explanations lack a structural analysis of the global conditions that made possible acts of violence such as "ethnic cleansing." Why did such agents as the liberal elites and the military of this socialist state utilize militarization as their strategy while trying to restructure gendered divisions of labor and resources?

Women workers had been searching for new strategies for survival after the decline of the former Soviet Union and the internal economic and social upheavals in Yugoslavia. The shift toward a market economy meant that state benefits were no longer forthcoming. The number of unemployed women needing a means of livelihood rose. These women workers were seen as dangerous to the reorganization of capital. Despite the formal legal equality accorded to women in the former Yugoslavia, they still experienced patriarchal rule and were considered men's property. As hostilities erupted, the Croatian and the Serbian military used violence against women as a military strategy through which to reconstitute their power against other ethnic groups. More particularly, the military used rape as a tool to produce boundaries between "us" and the enemy other "through the fluid and mixed lines of religion, culture, and ethnicity, and gender, thus reflecting the contemporary redefinition of racial hostility" (Papic 1999, p. 155, citing Eisenstein 1996; Human Rights Watch 1995, p. 1). Rape redistributed the ethnic-gender power "by defining new ethnic and subethnic borders between men and their respective (often militarized) elite structures" and women workers (Papic 1999, p. 155). The different ethno-nationalisms, via the agents of particular states, sought to essentialize identity. In the process, citizens of such ethno-nationalisms came to imagine themselves in relation to 'others' and their women. Women were mythologized "as the Nation's deepest 'essence'" and instruments of its birth (ibid.). Their bodies became a site upon which the power of each ethno-nationalism was contested. Serbian men raped Bosnian girls and women, impregnated them, and demanded that they keep the babies. For them, violating the enemies' women and impregnating them meant the "[re--]creat[ion of] the future of their own community by extinguishing" the other community (Wobbe 1995, p. 99).

The ethno-nationalist abuse of women sheds light on the constructions of power of "totalitarian ethnic nationhood." When ethno-nationalisms are constructed as "naturalised fraternal order[s]," women become targets of decisions to use one's masculine power to violate (ibid.). Muslim women in the former Yugoslavia were doubly subjugated: as insiders, they were colonized and instrumentalized in their "natural" function as "birth machines," and as outsiders they were reified into targets of destruction. The abuse of women and their bodies in the "pure" nation building process results in two interdependent forms of violence against them: highly restricted access to abortion for the insiders, and, in extreme but consistent cases, rape for the outsiders (ibid.). The discourse of the Serbian man who rapes the Muslim woman is interpreted to mean that only Muslim women are the targets of rape and that Muslim men do not rape. Non-Muslim, non-Bosnian men are constructed as rapists, whereas non-Muslim, non-Bosnian women are constituted as not being raped.

When the first rapes occurred, Zagreb feminists raised the issue internationally, but their presentations did not gain prominence because international institutions such as the United Nations viewed them as lacking a "clear national approach." However, when the warring parties such as the Bosnians and the Serbians recognized the propaganda value of women's suffering and violation, rape stories spread all over the world (North American News Analysts Group 2002). Rape was presented as a crime against ethnonationalism and not as a gendered militarized strategy with a goal to legitimate and sanction the state's masculinity (that is, class and gender power). As Enloe argues, militaries require men to act as "'men,' that is, to be willing to die on behalf of the state to prove their 'manhood'—[and] militaries also need women to behave in accordance with their gender as women. In other words, women must be properly subservient to meet the needs of militaries and of the men who largely constitute them" (Peterson and Runyan 1999, p. 119, citing Enloe 1983). Identities were constituted as dichotomous constructions so that "we" and "our" women emerged as polar opposites to "them" and "their" women in all fundamental respects. These ethno-national identity constructions became the basis upon which each ethno-nationalism worked to build up its case and capture the attention of international organizations. Beverly Allen notes, "The rape of thousands of women had been documented. The Serbs even had camps for the sole purpose of detaining women. Serbs had taken 150 Muslim women away from the town of Brcko in Bosnia and Herzegovina" (1996, p. 66).

Using rape to explain the violence and the commitment of atrocities (see United Nations n.d.; UN Resolution 798 and Condemnation, quoted in North American News Analysts Group 2002; Mazowiecki 1993), each ethno-nationalism hoped to gain its argument for an independent state. However, rape as the bodily violation of women's bodies becomes resituated in these ideological presentations, and sexual violence is constructed as not the "real" issue (Agathangelou 2000). After all, sexual violence against women happens all the time. The real issue was the ethnically motivated killing. "They [the raped women] did not want in any way to let rape overshadow the real problem, which is the extermination and execution of thousands of men and women" (Jacobs, cited in Jones 1994, p. 119). The above text is representative of other texts that claim that nationalism is not a structural, social relation informed by class and race, but it is rather about essentialized identities. It seems from the above text that women participated in their own oppression by setting aside their traumatic experiences while their leaders waged a public-relations war, emphasizing the crimes of other ethnic groups. The women participated in the creation of imagined communities of (trans-)national relations, by foregrounding the "real" problem. Simultaneously, this gendered and racialized strategy, which tends to be presented as an ethno-national war, obscures the conditions that constituted its emergence and sustenance: economic and political power relations working toward constituting corporate globalization locally.

THE MILITARIZATION OF THE U.S.-MEXICO BORDER

In processes parallel to those in Yugoslavia, the U.S.-Mexico border region has been a site of significant military and security measures long before corporate globalization emerged as the new strategy of putting resources and wealth out of the hands of so many. The border itself was constituted by military force: the Texas Revolution of 1836 and the Mexican-American wars of 1846 and 1848. This military conflict led to the U.S. conquest of half of Mexico's national territory in 1848. The Treaty of Guadalupe Hidalgo, signed that year, led to a complex and bitter legacy in the border region: "[By] the third decade of the twentieth century, the U.S.-Mexico border region . . . remained a focal point for special law enforcement and security measures . . . for example, in the deployment of U.S. Border Patrol in the region from 1924 onward and in the mass deportation efforts focused there during the 1930s and 1954" (Dunn 1996, p. 1). Dunn notes that moving economic production from high-wage to low-wage areas diminished the relevance of nation-state boundaries for most economic actors, though far less so in the case of labor. Within the U.S., immigrant workers have provided low-cost flexible labor. Yet they are continually rendered economically exploitable and politically vulnerable by immigration efforts initiated at nation-state boundaries that help criminalize them (ibid., pp. 157–58). According to Jimenez (1998), the primary constants between the United States and Mexico are historical migratory streams, economic disparity, and "the need in the U.S. for workers in certain areas of economic growth. Originally these migration patterns began because U.S. employers went to Mexico for contract labor."

In the eighties, the Reagan administration linked the rhetoric of undocumented immigration with the issue of interventionist policies in Central America. In 1982, the administration's ranking official on refugee affairs in the State Department stated, "Pressures on our borders from the Caribbean and Central America—particularly Mexico—make it certain that in the foreseeable future, as never in the past, the United States is going to have to maintain a foreign policy, including pre-emptive and prophylactic measures, which has as one of its objectives the protection of our frontiers against excessive illegal immigration (cited in Dunn 1996, p. 2). Between 1978 and 1992, an array of "alarmist portrayals" of the U.S.-Mexico border as "a vulnerable zone" led to a series of security measures "to repel an 'invasion' of 'illegal aliens,' to win the War on Drugs, and even to counter the threat of terrorism" (ibid., p. 3). Today, "border control" is a prominent topic in U.S. politics. A *Time* article titled "Border Clash" noted, "Private citizens are deputizing themselves as border patrollers to capture illegal aliens pouring across from Mexico in record numbers" (June 26, 2000). The article features a photo of a rancher pointing his gun over a fence towards Mexico. A sign hanging on the fence reads, "Tons of Drugs, Thousands of Illegals Pass this Sign." Such depictions by U.S. corporate media are common and reinforce perceptions of immigration from Mexico to the United States as "national crises with national security implications" (Dunn 1996, p. 1). Washington officials reduce this complex international issue to one-sided domestic border-control problem and identify immigrants as potential threats to national security requiring strong law enforcement and military measures.

Another salient factor is U.S. military assistance to Mexico. This increased dramatically in the eighties, when Mexico implemented IMF and WB structural adjustment policies mandated by the United States as a condition for debt relief. Between 1982 and 1990, Mexico purchased more military goods and services from the United States than in all previous years combined under all categories of assistance, including foreign military sales, commercial sales, excess defense sales, and the International Military Education and Training program (IMET). From 1950 to 1978, total sales had amounted to $29.5 million, whereas from 1982 to 1990 they were $500 million (Barry 1992, cited in Wilson 1997, p. 2). Militarizing the border and increasing Mexico's military capacity is a joint strategy of Mexican political and economic elites and U.S. administrations to control what is considered an "ethnic-nationalist problem." This framing "has served to dispossess and subordinate Mexican-origin people, who have a common history and culture as well as a long-standing claim to large portions of territory—all of which have threatened the state's and the Anglo population's control of the border region" (Barrera, cited in Dunn 1996, p. 6).

As Mexico moves closer to the neoliberal economic model mandated by the Western corporate vision, the security linkage between Mexico and the United States is becoming ever tighter (Wilson 1997, p. 2). Timothy Dunn notes that "the enforcement of national political boundaries, which formally reinforces the separation of First and Third World nations, is crucial to the designation of profitable investment sites in the global 'periphery.' . . . During the 1980s and into the early 1990s there was a positive correlation between an expansion in U.S. investments in and wealth extracted from Mexico, and the increasing militarization of the U.S. Mexico border by U.S. law enforcement and military agencies" (1996, pp. 157–58). Wilson argues that, as a member of the North American Free Trade Agreement, Mexico experiences "new demands for democratisation and justice from its indigenous and poor which threaten the tranquillity of the investment community. . . . The security ties between the U.S. and Mexico have become very tight indeed. On October 23, 1995, then U.S. Secretary of Defense William Perry visited Mexico's military high command. . . . Perry touted the emergence of a new security agreement that complemented the already political and commercial cooperation . . . [and said], 'When it comes to stability and security our destinies are inextricably linked'" (1997, p. 2, citing *La Jornada*, October 24, 1995).

At first sight, the militarization of the U.S.-Mexico border would appear to contradict moves by Mexico, the United States, and Canada to create close economic and political ties (e.g., NAFTA). But border militarization and the implementation of economic integration are not mutually exclusive. Mendel and Munger argue that "the legitimate use of military forces as an element of national power need not be confined to conventional military-on-military conflict. Rather, the use of military force should be considered whenever the nation is severely threatened by any circumstance to which no adequate response is possible solely with civilian forces or resources" (1997, p. 1).

The few brief immigration provisions of NAFTA mainly allow

mobility for business professionals, mostly men (Dunn 1996, p. 165), which in turn create a new, transnationalized professional class among the United States, Mexico, and Canada. Women working in the border area in maquiladoras suffer the health effects of poor working conditions as well as sexual harassment. According to a Human Rights Watch report based on interviews with women from more than forty maquiladoras in the states of Baja California, Chihuahua, and Tamaulipas, women were tested for pregnancy. If pregnant, they were forced to work overtime and do more physically difficult work that resulted in their decision to resign (Human Rights Watch 1996). Another aspect of border militarization concerns incidents of the rape and killing of women; Wilmot (1999) notes that over the last five years 188 women have been brutally raped and murdered in Ciudad Juarez.

Maria Jiménez comments on the seemingly "ironic" juxtaposition of free trade and border militarization:

> I don't think it's an irony. I think it's a function of the global system in which decisions are being made by transnational corporations and by entities that are not democratic. . . . Two billion [people] are in the labor market, and of those something like 1.25 million are actually people who live outside of their countries of origin. . . . When you look at the scheme of globalization and restructuring one sees that the economic and political elites of the world have no problems in getting across borders. . . . The militarized borders, the walls, the agents are really to impede the mobility of the international working poor who attempt to cross borders. In that sense border politics for me is a strategic aspect of economic development policy apparent in our global system. It's a system that seeks to create a world of low wages and high profits. (1998)

Similarly, Wilmot claims, "If the people who cross were not people of color, if they were white, or if they were not exploited as low-waged workers, they would not be disciplined or killed by military or paramilitary forces" (1999, p. 1).

The militarization of the border sustains class exploitation as well as inequalities based on gender and race. The task of the Border Patrol, in effect, is to keep Mexican workers available for work in Mexico. Jiménez continues,

> [Workers are] highly exploited if they do cross. We saw this example with the incident of the deaf people who were brought from Mexico to New York and who literally lived in slave conditions. . . . [People cross the border because of the] conditions in the countries of origin, economic deprivation and the closing of democratic practices and spaces. Most of Latin America has fallen under structural adjustment programs of international banking institutions, which demand a reduction in government services, privatization, and readjustment of land policies. Because these are very harsh measures, the apparatus of political repression grows. (1998)

Despite arguments that NAFTA will reduce the numbers of undocumented workers and increase opportunities for Mexican workers by developing the Mexican economy, feminist labor activists have witnessed the opposite. With increasing militarization of the border, enforcement of immigration policies discipline labor by discouraging Mexican workers from attempting undocumented immigration or by pushing illegal immigrants into staying "underground" (Dunn 1996, p. 167). This "low intensity warfare against immigrants" or "the war without guns" prevents the development of cross-national solidarity networks (Dunn 1996).

FEMINIST PERSPECTIVES ON MILITARIZATION IN THE FORMER YUGOSLAVIA AND AT THE U.S.-MEXICO BORDER

To understand the militarization of the former Yugoslavia and at the U.S.-Mexico border, one needs a theoretical perspective that (1) includes an analysis of hegemony, since it is the "chief target of revolutionary change in Third World formations" (San Juan 2000, p. 183); (2) integrates an analysis of gender, race, class, and nation; (3) illuminates the intersectionalities among these factors; and (4) provides a critical analysis of neoliberalist capitalist structures. Liberal feminist and radical feminist perspectives (MacKinnon 1994; Seifert 1994) that have wide currency among U.S. feminists do not provide critiques of capitalism or the immediate foreign policy goals of the Cold War. However, the global capitalist system, with its major proponent the United States, ensures the reproduction and expansion of its hegemony through the use of military tactics developed during the Cold War. States like the United States who purport to be liberal democracies do not openly exercise their power "through naked and unmediated violence. Rather, they attempt to create the illusion that there is a social consensus about what is and is not legitimate, and thus about what should and should not be suppressed. In order to understand how social consensus is manufactured and how certain sectors of the population consent to the repression of other sectors of society, the ways in which the state promotes conformity need to be examined" (Nagengast 1998, p. 4).

Notable U.S. feminists have explained military rape in former Yugoslavia in terms of human rights violations and genocide and have presented this perspective in international fora such as the United Nations. For example, Catharine A. MacKinnon argues, "What is happening here is first a genocide, in which ethnicity is a tool for political hegemony: the war is an instrument of the genocide; the rapes are an instrument of the war" (MacKinnon 1994, p. 187; Human Rights Watch 1995, p. 8). Ruth Seifert states that rapes are generally "part of the 'rules' of war. . . . Rapes in wartime aim at destroying the opponent's culture. . . . The background to rape orgies is a culturally rooted contempt for women that is lived out in times of crisis" (1996, pp. 58, 62, 65). This perspective is steeped in U.S. geopolitical discourse and assumes that those responsible for these atrocities are all equal, "free," historical subjects despite material realities to the contrary. In suggesting that the military strategy of rapes and reproductive controls are about genocide, misogyny, and cultural destruction, MacKinnon (1994), Seifert (1996), Susan Brownmiller (1994), and Alexandra Stiglmayer (1994a) offer a radical understanding of domination, which assumes the autonomy of the individual in issues of the body. For them, the elimination of this domination depends on proving, in law, that these acts of violence are a form of genocide. When sexual and racialized forms of violence are understood and explained as human rights violations or political violence against the nation-state—equated with the masculine position—without linking this violence to material conditions, then sexual and racial violence is relegated to a *cas de jurisprudence*. The economic and political power relations that relegate "some part of humanity to the status of expendable, which is what waging war necessarily does" (Koehler 2002, p. 3c), depend on sexual violence to further make possible the redistribution of power and resources among some men and women. Yet these social relations are made invisible, and militarization as a colonizing strategy used to reconstruct a capitalist patriarchy in a transnationalized context is completely ignored.

Thus, it behooves us to reexamine the idea that such forms of violence are merely genocide. Peripherally economic nation-states appropriate this notion to invoke support from the international community and consolidate their unstable power and legitimate their existence within the new, emerging transnational context always at the expense of working-class women as well as people of color worldwide, despite daily exploitation and violation of these same people. They come to claim that working-class people, of color and white, are the "blood and soil" of the nation-state and yet exploit, control, and manage their bodies and relegate them to the margins of political decision-making processes. For these nation-states, violence against their women becomes collapsed as ethno-national violence against their power and wealth. It is a great irony that both ethno-national and feminist discourses simultaneously deploy and erase the social relations of both global capitalism and militarization. When U.S. feminists maintain that sexual violence is a war crime or that militarization is direct violence rather than a strategy and insecurity generated by structural inequalities (Peterson and Runyan 1999, p. 115), they disregard crucial factors. Questions that should be asked include, who are these women who are subject to military violence and control? To what end (international and domestic) are they raped (in the former Yugoslavia) or controlled in terms of their productive and reproductive capacity (in the maquiladoras)? In what historical contexts and with what present politics are these U.S. feminists able to define military rape and killings at the border as genocide?

FEMINIST RESISTANCE AND REVISIONING

As long as solidarity exists between women's or other groups across the borders, transnationally, it will be a reminder of other possibilities, even if these are obscured, erased, or reinterpreted in nationalist discourses. (Zarkov 1995, p. 116)

When we talk of the ideal of multiculturalism in enabling social change, the question of leadership of hegemony as a directive force uniting individuals as groups or collectivities cannot be shirked. . . . Bourgeois hegemony in civil society (i.e., the ideological subordination of the masses to the bourgeoisie instead of simple coercive domination) enables the propertied class to control the state. . . . Only when we factor in this historic process of the struggle for hegemony (and, by extension, for state power) among groups can we really begin a substantive discussion on the cognitive and pedagogical value of multiculturalism for "Third World" societies where, in most cases, the violence of the neo-

colonial state often supervenes over a polymorphous society.
(San Juan 2000, p. 211)

Presenting social agents as abstract individuals who interact instrumentally in a market context, neoliberalism does not account for exploitative "private" capitalist and patriarchal power. As capital moves to rid itself of all constraints transnationally, historical materialist feminists need to envision a democratic community that allows for cross-border solidarities among marginalized women and men in Third World nation-states and sites. To challenge neoliberal capitalism, feminists interested in cross-border solidarities need to deal with inequalities within peripheral societies as well as within the global context based on race, class, and nation, and to recognize the ways that such inequalities limit political organizing. To constitute cross-national solidarities that challenge the global neoliberal agenda and its strategy of militarization of social life on all levels, high-income, (mostly) white U.S. feminists need to see the struggles of Third World women both outside and inside the United States who are earning far below the U.S. minimum wage as part of their own struggle. U.S. feminists from the National Organization for Women, for example—a liberal feminist organization—did not take a public position on NAFTA (interview with Pam Sparr, Washington DC, December 1997 cited in Mac-Donald 2000, p. 21) because their liberal understanding of gender blocked their recognition of that project as premised on gender exploitation. Others who understood that the costs of imperial and capitalist relations are being transferred to them organized against NAFTA and tried to hold accountable institutions that consume the social resources necessary for the working class's survival.

Indeed, relatively few upper- and middle-class (mostly white) U.S. feminists seem interested in forging cross-border solidarities for a feminist democratization through a critique of the agents who promulgate a neoliberal global agenda. Of course, here I am referring to U.S. liberal and some radical feminists whose sole focus is the protection of "Third World" women from the postcolonial patri-archies. For example, many U.S. feminists, such as MacKinnon, Brownmiller, and Stiglmayer, reported about the rapes as a form of postmodern genocide. Additionally, I refer to the upper- and middle-class Yugoslavs, Mexicans, and U.S. citizens who are calling for fur-ther liberal policies to combat the militarized violence and the breakout of war. Yet, there have been very few upper- and middle-class (mostly white) U.S. feminists who have even included nation-ality as a dialectic category in their political analysis.

What does it mean to transform the neoliberal vision and mis-sion? It requires work toward feminist democracy. Feminist democ-racy here refers to (1) using one's agency to transform collectively and personally the violence embedded within capitalist social rela-tions, which are sexually constitutive of all social relations by con-stantly recognizing the "web of social relations that enable any sub-ject to exercise transformative agency" (San Juan 2000, p. 210); (2) decolonizing or "modif[ying one's self] fundamentally" (Fanon 1963, p. 37); and (3) transforming the neoliberal structure into a socialist structure by creatively applying historical materialism as a guideline for radical transformation and the people's empowerment. Thus, historical materialist feminist democracy refers to building a structure within which all persons and social groups "have access and opportunity to exercise natural and cultural resources, powers, and capacities" (Marxist Collective 1993, p. 3) and a set of social relations shaped personally and collectively by all.

Marginalized peoples in Yugoslavia, Mexico, and the United States need to simultaneously work to expose the liberal myth that capital is objective and culturally neutral and that its strategies are not militarized. Such transformation will depend on constituting cross-border solidarities that expose the complicit workings of the emerging transnational state and use the state to support popular projects and stop the global economic restructuring process at the expense of working-class women and men. The mobilization of the transnational bourgeoisie from above can only be countered from below. According to Cavanagh and Anderson, "the key to genuine democracy . . . will be the struggle by communities and citizens' organizations to control their own destinies, to take control of their own lands and natural resources, to collectively make the decisions that affect their futures" (1993, p. 161). Marxist feminists can play a leading role in this by developing alliances, networks, organizations, and strategies that will contribute to cross-national solidarity relations. The twenty-five environmental and citizen activist groups who denounced NAFTA are an example of this. They saw NAFTA as a means to empower and enrich corporate capital at the expense of workers and citizens and their capacity for democratic self-determination (Cavanagh and Anderson 1993). Similarly, William Greider (1993) argues that to achieve meaningful democracy, people in the United States will have to reorient themselves toward a more internationalist worldview, which directly addresses global socioeconomic and political asymmetries and oppressions:

> For ordinary Americans, traditionally independent and insular, the challenge requires them to think anew their place in the world. The only plausible way that citizens can defend themselves and their nation against the forces of globalization is to link their own interests cooperatively with the interests of other peoples in other nations—that is, with foreigners who are competitors for the jobs and production but who are also victimized by the system. Americans will have to create new democratic alliances across national borders with the less prosperous people caught in the same dilemma. Together, they have to impose new political standards on multinational enterprises and on their own governments. (Greider 1993, p. 196)

Activists in Mexico and the former Yugoslavia have taken up this call for a historical materialist analysis, and this perspective is also being adopted in the United States, primarily by persons of color. For example, Jiménez and Martinez are members of the U.S./Mexico Border Program, an immigration law enforcement–

monitoring project of the American Friends Service Committee working to educate and organize people of color in the United States about the militarization of sociopolitical life through globalization. For them, decolonization as a premise for feminist democracy entails

> a very collective process. We begin with the victim, the community affected, and help them to articulate the problem, as opposed to substituting. Occasionally, we'll have to be spokesperson for the community when we're asked to testify before Congressional committees. We have always approached this not as advocates but as organizers. From the beginning, the momentum we set in defining this particular project was the involvement of the local border residents in defining the politics. That's why we organized these coalitions and work with persons who articulate their own reality. We simply provide the means, the technical support, to be able to affect these policy decisions and outcomes. (Jiménez 1998)

Women in the former Yugoslavia are working to eliminate the objectification and dehumanization perpetrated by militaries. To resist sexism, ethnocentrism, and war, feminists founded antiwar organizations, crisis lines, counseling centers, and shelters for women and children. Using collective action and civil disobedience, they have transformed women's desperation, trauma, and anger into political action. Since 1990, feminists in Belgrade—with support from U.S. and UK feminists—have created services such as the Women's Center against Sexual Violence, the Incest Trauma Center, SOS Telephone, and political organizations such as the Women's Lobby, Women's Parliament, and Women in Black. Working collectively for peace, feminists from Slovenia, Croatia, and Serbia in Women in Black issued the following statement to protest the war as an imperialist practice: "We refuse that our sons become the victims of senseless militarists. . . . That they should give their lives for imperialist purposes is the project of politicians. It is a disgrace to win a fratricidal war" (Mothers of the Soldiers of Belgrade 1993, p. 8).

Another political aim of Women in Black is to forge alliances among women who have been separated by weapons and borders: "active solidarity between women is the force and the tenderness by which we can overcome isolation, loneliness, traumas. . . . We are the ones who come out in the public with our bodies and our visions of the world without war, rape, violence, and militarism" (Women in Black 1993, p. 50). As these women worked together, their philosophy and approach to resisting the militarization of Yugoslavia changed. Their writings became more overtly political and feminist as exemplified by Stasa Zajovic, who wrote, "the militarization of former Yugoslavia has meant the imposition of military values, and militaristic language; a cult of necrophilia (expressed in slogans as 'the frontiers of Serbia are where Serbs are buried'); and acceptance of political and moral totalitarianism" (1993). Feminists in Belgrade see both private and state violence as stemming from the same source: patriarchy and the capitalist ideology of compartmentalization. An alliance of independent women's groups wrote, "Patriarchy considers that men's violence in the family is a 'private matter'—this ideology or privacy permits violence in all other domains of society. When the SOS hotline for women and children calls the police to intervene in violent scenes, a violent husband standing beside his bruised wife claims, 'This is my wife, it is my issue.' Policemen, also with male understanding, confirm that it is a 'family matter.' That is exactly the model for how the first man of the ruling regime leads the war in Kosovo: 'Kosovo is an internal problem of Serbia.'"

The practices of feminists in the former Yugoslavia and those organizing around the militarization of the U.S.-Mexico border illustrate my contention that feminism must be global, but not in the way liberal international political economists understand this term (i.e., a cosmopolitan appropriation of human commodities to satiate one's own desires). Feminism entails a collective commitment to political action and the production of knowledge that challenge the global division of labor in terms of gender, race (in the form of nationalism), class, and the inevitability of globalization as put forward by the world's hegemonic institutions like the IMF, the WB, and the militaries that sustain them. Our vision should be for a cross-border feminism as gendered, classed, and raced theory and praxis that strives for "freedom from necessity" (Ebert 1996, p. 302) and enables access and control of resources by all women and exploited peoples who currently live in a state of subsistence.

NOTES

I would like to thank the following for their valuable critiques: Delia D. Aguilar, Kyle D. Killian, Gwyn Kirk, Anne E. Lacsamana, and Margo Okazawa-Rey.

1. I use the term *militarization* here to mean values, attitudes, and practices that connote a preference for military means. Militarization also refers to the diversion of socioeconomic resources vitally needed by working-class people in both core and peripheral economies to military ends, which extend to internal repression, state management, policing, external intervention, and alleged deterrence (Wolpin 1986, p. 2; Enloe 1993; Peterson and Runyan 1999; Dunn 1996).

2. Note that a transborder materialist feminist study of militarization allows us to do the following four things: (1) to conceptualize the globalization of militarization as sets of unequal capitalist relations among and between people "rather than a set of traits embodied in all non–U.S. citizens" (Alexander and Mohanty 1997, p. xix); (2) to consider a global structure constituted through a set of economic, political, social, and ideological processes and social relations; (3) to think about women in this structure, albeit in different geographical spaces, as sharing the same analytical field; and (4) to highlight how strategies for generating and managing notions of race, nation, gender, and sexual differences in countries such as the United States are related and parallel to what is occurring in Yugoslavia or Mexico at the same time.

3. The debates over Iraq reveal this anxiety. However, even when war has a rational objective, "war mobilization . . . makes a terrifying demand on a nation's people. It asks them to perform ritual soulectomy

on a bloc of humanity, to hope and even pray (as in Mark Twain's famous War Prayer) for their annihilation: 'O Lord our God, help us to tear their soldiers to bloody shreds with our shells. . . .' We turn them into gooks or nips or, in today's climate of political correctness, 'Muslimists,' so that we need feel no jolt of human horror at their deaths" (Koehler 2002).

4. Referring to the terms of a British loan to Argentina in 1824, Eduardo Galeano wrote in his book *Open Veins of Latin America*, "Such usurious operations put bars around free nations."

REFERENCES

Agathangelou, Anna M. 2000. Nationalist narratives and (dis)appearing women: State-sanctioned sexual violence. In Women in conflict zones. Special issue, *Canadian Woman Studies/Les Cahiers de la Femme* 29 (4): 12–21.

————. 2002. "Sexing" globalization in international relations: Migrant sex and domestic workers in Cyprus, Greece, and Turkey. In Chowdhry and Nair 2002, pp. 142–69.

Aguilar, Delia. 1997. Gender, nation, and colonialism: Lessons from the Philippines. In *The women, gender, and development reader*, edited by Nalini Visvanathan, Lynn Duggan, Laurie Nisonoff, and Nan Wiegersma, pp. 309–17. London and Atlantic Highlands, NJ: Zed Books.

Alexander, M. Jacqui, and Chandra Talpade Mohanty, eds. 1997. *Feminist genealogies, colonial legacies, democratic futures*. New York: Routledge.

Allen, Beverly. 1996. *Rape warfare: The hidden genocide in Bosnia-Herzegovina and Croatia*. Minneapolis: University of Minnesota Press.

Amin, Samir. 1996. *Capitalism in the age of globalization: The management of contemporary society*. London and New York: Zed Books.

Brownmiller, Susan. 1994. Making female bodies the battlefield. In Stiglmayer et al. 1994, pp. 180–82.

Cavanagh, John, and S. Anderson. 1993. Europe offers practical insight. *New York Times*, November 14, 1993.

Chang, Kimberley A., and L. H. M. Ling. 2000. Globalization and its intimate other: Filipino domestic workers in Hong Kong. In *Gender and global restructuring: Sightings, sites, and resistances*, edited by M. H. Marchand and A. S. Runyan. London and New York: Routledge.

Chowdhry, G., and S. Nair, eds. 2002. *Power in a postcolonial world: Race, gender, and class in international relations*. London: Routledge.

Curtis, Glenn E., ed. 1992a. Communist takeover and consolidation. Yugoslavia. AllRefer.com country study & guide. http://reference .allrefer.com/country-guide-study/yugoslavia/yugoslavia33.html (accessed March 12, 2004).

———. 1992b. The military and society. Yugoslavia. AllRefer.com country study & guide. http://reference.allrefer.com/country-guide-study/yugoslavia/yugoslavia185.html (accessed March 12, 2004).

Dunn, Timothy J. 1996. *The militarization of the U.S.-Mexico border, 1978–1992: Low-intensity conflict doctrine comes home*. Austin: Center of Mexican American Studies, University of Texas at Austin.

Ebert, Teresa L. 1996. *Ludic feminism and after: Postmodernism, desire, and labor in late capitalism*. Ann Arbor: University of Michigan Press.

Enloe, Cynthia H. 1983. *Does khaki become you? The militarization of women's lives*. Boston: South End Press.

———. 1993. *The morning after: Sexual politics at the end of the Cold War*. Berkeley and Los Angeles: University of California Press.

———. 2000. *Maneuvers: The international politics of militarizing women's lives*. Berkeley and Los Angeles: University of California Press.

Fanon, Frantz. 1963. *The wretched of the earth*. New York: Grove Press.

Greider, W. 1993. The global marketplace: A closet dictator. In *The case against free trade: GATT, NAFTA, and the globalization of corporate power*, edited by Ralph Nader et al., pp. 195–217. San Francisco: Earth Island Press.

Huggins, Martha K. 1998. *Political policing: The United States and Latin America*. Durham, NC: Duke University Press.

Human Rights Watch. 1995. Global report on women's human rights. New York and Washington, DC: Human Rights Watch.

———. 1996. Mexico's maquiladoras: Abuses against women workers.

Human Rights Watch Web page. http://hrw.org/press/1996/08/mexicomaq96.htm (accessed March 12, 2004).

Jiménez, Maria. 1998. The militarization of the U.S.-Mexico border. Interview by Nic Paget-Clarke. *In Motion Magazine*, February 2, http://www.inmotionmagazine.com/mj1.html.

Jones, A. 1994. Gender and ethnic conflict in ex-Yugoslavia. *Ethnic and Racial Studies* 17 (1): 115–34.

Kirk, G., and Margo Okazawa-Rey, eds. 1998. *Women's lives: Multicultural perspectives*. New York: McGraw-Hill.

Klein, Naomi. 2002. *Fences and windows: Dispatches from the frontlines of the globalization debate*. New York: Picador.

Koehler, Robert. 2002. Common wonders connect the dots. *Houston Chronicle*, November 10, 2002.

Ling, L. H. M. 2002. Cultural chauvinism and the liberal international order: "West versus rest" in the Asian financial crisis. In Chowdhry and Nair 2002, pp. 115–41.

Lutz, Helma, Ann Phoenix, and Nira Yuval-Davis, eds. 1995. *Crossfires: Nationalism, racism and gender in Europe*. London and East Haven, CT: Pluto Press.

MacDonald, Laura. 2000. Trade with a female face: Women and the new international trade agenda. Department of Political Science, Carleton University, Ottawa, ON.

MacKinnon, Catharine A. 1994. Turning rape into pornography: Postmodern genocide. In Stiglmayer 1994b, pp. 183–96.

Marxist Collective at Syracuse University. 1992–93. Late capitalist culture and cultural critique. In *The Alternative Orange*, collectively written as part of the Marxist Collective at Syracuse University, in four parts: October 1992, November 1992, January 1993, and March 1993.

Mazowiecki, Tadeusz. 1993. Situation of human rights in the territory of the former Yugoslavia. Report to the UN Commission on Human Rights, February 10, E/CN.4/1993/50. Michael A. Sells personal Web page. http://www.haverford.edu/relg/sells/reports/mazowiecki_10feb93.htm (accessed March 12, 2004).

Mendel, William W., and Murl D. Munger. 1997. The drug threat: Getting priorities straight. *Parameters*, summer issue, http://carlisle-www.army.mil/usawc/Parameters/97summer/munger.htm (accessed February 2, 2004).

Morokvasic, M. 1998. The logics of exclusion: Nationalism, sexism, and the Yugoslav War. In *Gender, ethnicity, and political ideologies*, edited by Charles N. Hintjens and Helen Hintjens, pp. 65–90. New York: Routledge.

Mothers of the Soldiers of Belgrade. 1993. To the public opinion of the federal secretariat of defense, the senior head of state of the Serbian government, and the Yugoslavian presidency, July 20, 1991. In *Women for peace anthology*, p. 8. Belgrade: Women in Black.

Nagengast, C. 1998. Militarizing the border patrol. *NACLA Report on the Americas* 32 (3): 37–43.

Nikolic-Ristanovic, V. 1999. *Women, violence, and war: Wartime victimization of refugees in the Balkans*. Translated by Borislav Radovic. Budapest: Central European University Press.

North American News Analysts Group. 2002. Rapes in Yugoslavia: Separating fact from fiction. Balkan Repository Project. http://www.balkan-archive.org.yu/politics/rape/nanag/index.html (accessed January 30, 2004).

Papic, Z. 1999. Women in Serbia: Post-Communism, war, and nationalist mutations. In *Gender politics in the western Balkans: Women and society in Yugoslavia and the Yugoslav successor states*, edited by Sabrina P. Ramet. University Park: Pennsylvania State University Press.

Peterson, V. Spike, and Anne Sisson Runyan. 1999. *Global gender issues*. Boulder, CO: Westview Press.

Psimmenos, I. 2000. The making of periphractic spaces. In *Gender and migration in southern Europe: Women on the move*, edited by Floya Anthias and Gabriella Lazaridis, pp. 81–102. Oxford and New York: Berg.

Reardon, Betty A. 1985. *Sexism and the war system*. New York and London: Teachers College Press.

Robinson, W. I. 1998. Capitalist globalization and the transnationalization of the state. Paper presented at the transatlantic workshop titled "Historical Materialism and Globalization," University of Warwick, UK, April 15–17.

San Juan, E., Jr. 2000. *After postcolonialism: Remapping Philippines-United States confrontations*. Lanham, MD: Rowman & Littlefield.

Seifert, Ruth. 1996. The second front: The logic of sexual violence in wars. *Women's Studies International Forum* 19 (1–2): 35–43.

Shiva, Vandana. 1997. *Biopiracy: The plunder of nature and knowledge.* Boston: South End Press.

Stiglmayer, Alexandra. 1994a. The rapes in Bosnia-Herzegovina. In Stiglmayer 1994b, pp. 82–169.

———, ed. 1994b. *The war against women in Bosnia-Herzegovina.* Lincoln and London: University of Nebraska Press.

United Nations. N.d. Excerpts from "Human Rights Questions," United Nations document # S/24991. Geopolitics (Yugoslavia, Bosnia and Hercegovina, Croatia). http://www.balkan-archive.org.yu/kosta/Geopolitics/Risto.Mostarski/rapes02.text (accessed March 12, 2004).

Wilmot, Sheila. 1999. On re-building the Left: Integrating race, gender, and class in the struggle against neoliberalism. *New Socialist* 4 (4). http://www.newsocialist.org/magazine/21/article12.html (accessed February 2, 2004).

Willson, S. Brian. 1997. The slippery slope: U.S. military moves into Mexico. Revolt Web site. http://flag.blackened.net/revolt/mexico/usa/slip_slope_feb97.html (accessed March 12, 2004).

Wobbe, T. 1995. The boundaries of community: Gender relations and racial violence. In Lutz, Phoenix, and Yuval-Davis 1995, pp. 88–104.

Wolpin, Miles D. 1986. *Militarization, internal repression, and social welfare in the third world.* New York: St. Martin's Press.

Women in Black. 1993. Women in Black against war, June 10, 1992. In *Women for peace anthology*, p. 50. Belgrade: Women in Black.

Woodward, Susan L. 1995. *Balkan tragedy: Chaos and dissolution after the Cold War.* Washington, DC: Brookings Institution.

Zajovic, Stasa. 1993. Militarism and women in Serbia. In *Women for peace anthology*, p. 26. Belgrade: Women in Black.

Zarkov, D. 1995. Gender, orientalism, and the history of ethnic hatred in the former Yugoslavia. In Lutz, Phoenix, and Davis 1995, pp. 105–21.

Zwick, Jim. 1984. Militarization in the Philippines: From consolidation to crisis. In *Sentenaryo/centennial: The Philippine revolution and the Philippine-American War*, edited by Jim Zwick. http://www.boondocksnet.com/centennial/sctexts/zwick85a.html# (accessed March 15, 2004).

13. Sex Worker or Prostituted Woman?

An Examination of the Sex Work Debates in Western Feminist Theory

Anne E. Lacsamana

Over the past several years there has been an abundance of research in U.S. feminist theory concerning the topic of prostitution. During this period, there has been a noticeable shift between those seeking to end to the international trade in women (sex trafficking) and those seeking to regulate and treat prostitution as any other form of work (sex worker). This shift in perspective can most certainly be traced to the influence of postmodern theory on U.S. feminist thought. Lacsamana's essay forcefully argues against the notion that prostitution is like any other form of labor. Using the example of Philippine prostitution—now exacerbated by the return of U.S. troops to the Philippines as part of the U.S.-led "War on Terror"—she posits that prostitution is the result of unrelenting impoverishment brought about by centuries of colonialism and neo-colonialism, global capitalist expansion, and onerous structural adjustment programs placed upon "Third World" countries by the IMF and World Bank. The advent of postmodern/postcolonial thought in U.S. feminism effectively works to obscure the dire economic realities now facing "Third World" women in this era of globalization—realities that are largely responsible for the recruitment of young women and girls into the international sex trade.

There is room in feminism for whores, virgins, and everything in between. The advent of postmodernism and queer theory presents both more possibilities and more challenges for feminism. In forging more whore feminisms, we might well begin looking at what purposes are served by using *any* sexual categories to describe women.

—Jill Nagle, *Whores and Other Feminists* (1997)

Now, this is what feminists do when they promote prostitution. They pimp other women in a fantasy framework of sex work and female sexual expression by neutralizing the horrific reality of prostitution with so much intellectual masturbation that it takes it further and further into the realm of ideas. There they don't have to think about or discuss or explain why little girls are doing $5 blow jobs on adult men.

—Kelly Holsopple, "Pimps, Tricks, and Feminists" (1999)

For Marxism *is* the theory of emancipation in global patriarchal capitalism, and there is no emancipatory future, no emancipatory politics without Marxism. I am thus writing to reclaim the critique-al knowledges of historical materialism for feminism in postmodernity and to help revive a revolutionary theory and praxis for third-wave feminism.

—Teresa Ebert, *Ludic Feminism and After* (1996)

A s "America's War on Terror" escalates following the September 11 attacks on the World Trade Center and the Pentagon, the Philippines once again finds itself at the mercy of its colonial master. After meeting with U.S. president George W. Bush and other top-ranking officials in November 2001, Philippine president Gloria Macapagal Arroyo pledged her all-out support for the Bush administration's war efforts. Like previous Philippine presidents,

Arroyo's decision to allow 660 U.S. military personnel to arrive in the country effectively sacrifices the national sovereignty and self-determination of the Filipino people. The deployment of U.S. armed forces in Mindanao and the southern island of Basilan, to help "aid" and "train" the Philippine military in eradicating the Abu Sayyaf (an Islamic extremist group with alleged loose ties to Al-Qaeda) is the largest since the United States began its war in Afghanistan.

If history is any indication, the presence of the U.S. military in the Philippines promises to reopen old and long-standing wounds. Perhaps the most pressing concerns are the constitutionality of allowing the troops back in for an extended stay (six months to one year) and the related social and environmental consequences that accompany foreign military incursions. The military relationship between the United States and the Philippines dates back to the turn of the twentieth century with the beginning of the Philippine-American War, in which over one million Filipinos were killed by U.S. forces in one of the most violent colonial conquests in history. After fifty years of colonial rule, the U.S. officially granted "independence" to the Philippines July 4, 1946—an empty and symbolic gesture, considering the U.S. was allowed to maintain two major military installations (Clark Air Force Base and Subic Naval Base) in the country for several more decades. As the terms of the lease on the bases expired in 1991, the Philippine Senate (under intense pressure from local activist groups) overwhelmingly rejected a new military agreement by the U.S. that proposed to extend their stay for an additional ten years. The success of the campaign against the bases was considered a major step in the direction of reclaiming Philippine national sovereignty. By 1998, however, the Philippines would once again be host to the United States military under the so-called Visiting Forces Agreement (VFA) negotiated by U.S. officials and former Philippine president Joseph Estrada. According to the terms of the VFA, the United States is allowed twenty-two ports of entry to conduct "training" exercises (also known as "Balikatan") with the Philippine army. In addition, the U.S. government is given primary jurisdiction over crimes committed by U.S. personnel while in the country. Although the VFA purports to benefit both countries equally, clearly this military arrangement favors U.S. interests and strengthens the neocolonial stranglehold it has held on the Philippines for over fifty years.

The passage of the VFA, along with the most recent deployment of U.S. troops to help fight the "war on terror," has revived old fears and concerns around the issue of Philippine prostitution. During the Vietnam War, prostitution surrounding Subic Naval Base and Clark Air Force Base became especially acute when U.S. military men would flock to Olongapo and Angeles City in search of "rest and recreation" (R&R). Kirk and Okazawa-Rey report that "[a]t the height of U.S. activity in the Philippines, as many as 60,000 women and children were estimated to have worked in bars, nightclubs, and massage parlors servicing U.S. troops" (1998, p. 311). Fearing a similar situation might arise with the passage of the VFA, GABRIELA (an international federation of women's groups) issued a press statement in early 1998 opposing the military agreement on the grounds that it will only exacerbate the exploitation of women and children. They write, "We have seen this from the experience of Angeles City and Olongapo City, whose economies depended heavily on the 'rest and recreation' industry. With the VFA, such a situation will be duplicated twenty-two times all over the archipelago. The Philippines will be transformed into a country of 'rest and recreation' where the selling of women and children will be done on full scale" (1998). Four years later, GABRIELA's statement appears to be true. Monitoring this year's Balikatan, GABRIELA has reported incidents where women have been brought "inside the Balikatan 02-2 camps in Central Luzon as part of the participants' cultural exposure program" (2002). Describing this situation as a "'take home sex delivery service' in the Balikatan camps [GABRIELA has] blamed the Arroyo government for allowing the U.S. military to do as they please" (2002).

Rejecting GABRIELA's pronouncements, Arroyo has repeatedly argued that she has put laws in place that explicitly prohibit prostitution around U.S. military installations. Arroyo has supposedly warned senior military officials to keep their troops (both those involved in fighting the "war on terror" as well as those participating in the VFA training exercises) from engaging in sexual activities during their periods of rest and recreation. As an alternative, Arroyo has suggested U.S. servicemen participate in guided group tours of tourist spots in the country. Recent stories, however, concerning the influx of women and children around the bases, appear to suggest that the U.S. military has completely ignored Arroyo's warning. In "Filipina Women Hired to Provide Sex to U.S. Troops," the *Philippine Daily Inquirer* reported that women and young girls were already being trafficked into Mindanao around U.S. bases to "service" the troops. Sources monitoring the situation around the bases have "documented thirty-six cases of women [who] had been recruited in Davao City to work as maids, waitresses, and entertainers in bars in Zamboanga City. Girls as young as thirteen were promised free plane rides, pocket money, and huge dollar incomes" (2002). At the time of this writing, local Filipino activist groups continue to protest U.S. military intervention on the grounds that it is not only sacrificing the national sovereignty of the country but also intensifying the exploitation of women and children by encouraging prostitution.

As this sexual exploitation increases in countries such as the Philippines, in the industrialized West the issue of prostitution has begun to figure prominently in contemporary feminist debates. While most discussions have centered on prostitutes in the United States and Western Europe, attention has begun to shift to countries in the "Third World," where "sex tourism" has become a major income-generating business for poor, indebted nations. Whether discussing prostitution locally or globally, the basic contours of the debate have been shaped by those who suggest that feminism should recognize prostitution as a viable form of work (hence the terms *sex work* and *sex worker*) and those opposed on the grounds that prostitution is a fundamentally exploitative practice. In "Feminism, Sex Workers, and Human Rights," Priscilla Alexander argues that those opposed to prostitution (groups such as WHISPER: Women Hurt in Systems of Prostitution Engaged in Revolt, and CATW: Coalition against Trafficking in Women) "deny the existence of voluntary prostitution [and] define all prostitutes as passive, helpless, degraded victims" (1997, p. 83). In response to the antiprostitution forces, Alexander identifies a "countervalent discourse [that] is rooted in two parts of the women's movement: sex workers' rights and prosex feminism" (1997, p. 84). Thus, proponents of prostitution and/or "sex work" seek to legitimize voluntary forms of prostitution and remove the stigma attached to prostitutes/sex workers. In an effort to accomplish this, there have been numerous conferences on the subject, rallies held on behalf of prostitutes/sex workers, and a number of anthologies written by those involved in the industry and other "prosex" feminists. With the publication of *Good Girls/Bad Girls: Feminists and Sex Trade Workers Face to Face* in 1987, several other works have followed, including *Sex Work* (1987), *A Vindication of the Rights of Whores* (1989), *Whores and Other Feminists* (1997), and *Global Sex Workers: Rights, Resistance, and Redefinition* (1998). Although this list is a mere sampling of the range of writing on the subject, it is indicative of how pervasive the pro–sex worker/prostitute stance has become in the field of Western feminist theory.

Using the Philippines as an example, I wondered how a pro–sex worker analysis might account for the lucrative trade in women (as mail-order brides, prostitutes, bar girls, massage parlor attendants, etc.) that has come to characterize the country. As one of the poorest nations in Southeast Asia, "sex tourism" has generated a considerable amount of foreign exchange for the country. During the seventies, international tourism and export-oriented production became important cornerstones in the Marcos administration's development strategy. Along with bolstering the national economy, the administration saw other benefits in the promotion of tourism. According to

Daniel Schirmer and Stephen Shalom, "More important from the Marcos's perspective were the political benefits of tourism: luxurious accommodations and political stability generated good will among foreign business people and international bankers whose support the regime needed" (1987, p. 182). In 1973, one year after Marcos declared martial law, the Ministry of Tourism was established. Headed by a close Marcos ally, Jose Aspiras, the Ministry of Tourism oversaw the construction of "fourteen first-class hotels and a luxurious conference center in Manila at a cost of over $450 million" (ibid.). The majority of these facilities were financed by the Marcos regime with loans obtained from the World Bank.

It was not the extravagant accommodations, however, that became the central feature of Philippine tourism. Instead, the state used the "reputed beauty and generosity of Filipino women as 'natural resources' to compete in the international tourist market" to lure people to the country (Enloe 1990, p. 38). Thus, the growth in prostitution throughout Manila and various other tourist areas corresponded directly to the rise in international tourism. By the late seventies, Philippine tourism brought in "$300,000,000, which [was] $262,000,000 more than in 1972" (Eviota 1992, p. 137). By the mid-eighties, the majority of tourists in the Philippines were Japanese, Australian, and American men who had come to the country as part of a sex tour. Included in a typical sex-tour package were brochures of women that men could select from, transportation (usually by bus) to the various "girlie bars" throughout Manila, and accommodations at some of the most luxurious hotels (most notably those owned or financed by government officials).

Similar to the situation around the bases, prostitution flourished throughout this period primarily due to the collusion between top-ranking government officials, tour operators (pimps), and the local law enforcement agencies. Although the state repeatedly denied any connection between the increase in prostitution and the development of tourism as an "industry," evidence to the contrary was overwhelming. Linda Richter explains that the administration's lack of intervention in the sex trade included a *"quid pro quo*: unflinching support of the administration from the tourist industry" (1982, p. 143). This is certainly evident in the 1978 parliamentary election, in which "Minister Aspiras called all major hotel and tour operators together . . . and pressured them to instruct their employees to vote for the administration, because the opposition would destroy the tourist industry" (ibid.). Of course, the Marcos regime won the election, thus enabling Philippine prostitution to continue to thrive.

Since the eighties, because of campaigns waged in the Philippines and outside, the number of sex tours has declined significantly. As a result, the hospitality industry has resurfaced in new forms: women now migrate overseas to a number of countries as "artists" or "entertainers" (euphemisms for prostitution) or as "brides." For many Filipino feminist organizations, the traffic in women cannot be viewed in isolation but "should be understood in relation to Filipinas' migration overseas" (Enloe 1990, p. 39). At present, over eight million Filipinos (10 percent of the population) leave the Philippines to find work abroad as overseas Filipino workers (OFWs). Of this percentage, the overwhelming majority are women who find themselves employed in low-pay, labor intensive, service-oriented work. As part of the contractual agreement, OFWs must remit 10 percent of their earnings back to the Philippines to help service the foreign debt. OFWs, according to Maita Santiago of *Migrante-International*, "are taking the dirty, difficult, and dangerous jobs that nationals of the host country refuse to take. . . . [A]broad they face racism and discrimination. Many 'disappear' or return home either mentally unstable, in overwhelming debt, or in coffins'" (cited in Alcuitas 2002). *Migrante-International* estimates that four hundred OFW died last year.

For many Filipino activists, the feminization of labor migration (as OFWs, "entertainers," and mail-order brides) is the direct consequence of "globalization" and a ballooning foreign debt. Because there is an absolute *lack* of economic choices and productive work available to women in the Philippines, many are forced to migrate overseas or turn to prostitution as an income-generating activity. The rosy picture painted by proponents of globalization is in stark contrast to the dire reality many are facing in "Third World" countries. Hetty Alcuitas explains that in 2002 the "impact of these policies on the marginalized of the world has burst the globalization bubble. Instead of alleviating poverty of the majority of the world's population, globalization has intensified their exploitation and oppression" (2002). Because women tend to bear the burden of both productive and reproductive work, they are always the hardest hit in times of economic crises. For example, the Center for Women's Resources (CWR) recently released a study indicating that the "unemployment rate of women [in the Philippines] increased from 9.9 percent to 10.3 percent in the first 11 months of 2001" (cited in Alcuitas 2002, p. 2). Furthermore, CWR discovered that "52 percent of employed women were in the informal sector, as own account workers or unpaid family labor . . . or prostitutes" (ibid.). The remaining 42 percent of women employed in the formal sector (wage or salary work) were relegated to labor-intensive, service-oriented jobs such as factory or retail work.

With rising unemployment rates and limited options, it is not surprising that many Filipino women and children have entered the sex industry. In 2002, it was estimated that the "Philippines has the highest number of women prostitutes—600,000. An estimated 100,000 of these are children" (Alcuitas 2002, p. 4). To underscore the severity of the situation, the nationalist feminist movement in the Philippines prefers to use the term "prostituted" women (rather than "prostitutes") to describe those involved in the sex trade. The change in part of speech is significant because it effectively highlights the exploitative nature of the relationship and emphasizes the external material conditions that force many women into the business.

The antitrafficking stance that grassroots groups like GABRIELA and the Coalition against the Trafficking in Women–Asia Pacific (CATWAP) take regarding prostitution is strikingly different from some of the more recent writings on the subject. For example, *Global Sex Workers*, edited by Kamala Kempadoo and Jo Doezema (1998), is one of the first anthologies to apply a "pro–sex work" analysis to conditions facing women and children in the "Third World." Rather than use the term "prostituted" women, contributors to this collection prefer "sex worker" because this phrase "suggests we view prostitution not as an identity—a social or psychological characteristic of women, often indicated by 'whore'—but as an income-generating activity or form of labor for women and men. The definition stresses the social location of those engaged in sex industries as working people" (Kempadoo 1998, p. 3). Thus, one of the central themes to emerge from this book is that prostitution or "sex work" is equivalent to any other form of work or labor in which people are engaged. Pro–sex work feminists argue that the term "'sex worker' insists that working women's common interests can be articulated within the context of broader (feminist) struggles against the devaluation of 'women's' work and gender exploitation within capitalism" (ibid., p. 8). Is prostitution just another aspect of "women's" work? Are prostitutes just like other working women? The answer, according to the authors in this book, is a resounding YES. For those who don't accept the notion of "prostitution as labor" and who tend to view the sale of sex as harmful and exploitative, Kempadoo argues that such a perspective confuses "the sale of one's sexual energy . . . with a particular morality about sexual relations," thereby imposing "essentialist cultural interpretations upon the subject" (ibid., p. 5). To avoid this type of thinking, the editors propose we emulate the work of Wendy Chapkis by situating prostitution within the context of "emotional labor." This form of labor encompasses all "activities and jobs for which care and feeling are required, commodified and commercialized, such as airline service work, acting, psychotherapy, massage work, or child-care" (ibid.). Essentially, then, emotional labor enables sex workers to "distinguish intimacy and love from the sex act itself, much in the same that an actor or therapist is able to separate their work from private life, preserving a sense of integrity and distance from emotionally demanding work" (ibid.). Are actors, therapists, and prostitutes all in the same boat? Is the extraction of their labor power the same? Are their working conditions similar?

Another component to the pro–sex worker analysis is the concept of agency. The authors in this collection maintain that even in "cases where women, men, boys, and girls are clearly harmed within the sex industry or are caught in debt-bondage and indentureship situations, it is the respectful recognition of subjectivity and personal agency that creates continuity in this collection" (ibid., p. 8). According to this logic, there isn't much we can do (or should want to do) for the thirteen-year-old girls currently being recruited to sexually service U.S. troops in the Philippines. At best, we can simply respect their personal agency by recognizing the emotional labor they perform by servicing over one hundred men a week. Just like a therapist, right?

One of the most forceful condemnations of the antitrafficking movement can be found in "Debt Bondage and Trafficking: Don't Believe the Hype," by Alison Murray. Tracing the antitrafficking movement from the early ninetiess to the present day, Murray contends that the most extreme views on the subject are represented by the CATW. In their efforts to eradicate prostitution, CATW resorts to "linking all forms of the sex trade together beneath an emphasis on emotive words like 'trafficking,' 'slavery,' and 'child prostitution'" (1998, p. 52). This "abolitionist" stance, which according to Murray relies on the manipulation of people's feelings, is directly at odds with the "postmodern challenge to conventional feminism, which allows for the cacophony of voices and refuses the binary dichotomy in which all women are constituted as 'other'" (ibid.). Since the various women's groups that compose GABRIELA are often prone to using emotive words such as *trafficking* as well, it would be safe to assume that Murray would see them as belonging to the branch of feminism that fails to "overcome binary oppositions [and] ends up supporting the status quo, impoverishing women and aligning with right-wing fundamentalism and a discourse which has its genesis in homophobia" (ibid.). Arguing that the antitrafficking movement relies on "sensational" stories that highlight the dangers involved in the trade in women and children, Murray provides readers with examples of women and children being trapped and killed in factory fires in Thailand and other parts of Asia to illustrate that "exploitative and dangerous conditions can be found across a range of industries internationally" (ibid., p. 55). Further, she contends that the image of the helpless, passive, Asian prostitute that has been "tricked" or "lured" into the industry has been thoroughly manipulated by middle-class feminists as a means to "enforce the moral condemnation of prostitution" (ibid., p. 59). For her, there is no logical "difference between 'debt-bonded' Asian workers and Australian workers choosing to work for Hong Kong triads for more money than they could get in Sydney: it is racism that says that the former are victims and the latter agents" (ibid., p. 60). I beg to differ. What about North-South relations of power? As a sex worker based in Sydney, it would appear that Murray is woefully unaware of the power differentials between a debt-bonded Asian prostitute and one living in a First World country such as Australia going abroad to make additional money. Why is the prostitute from Asia debt-bonded? Why is the prostitute from Australia not? What I find racist (not to mention class-bound) about Murray's argument is the manner in which she flattens differences between groups of people. Sure, she might allow for a "cacophony" of voices, but are there not significant differences between the multiple voices we are hearing? In her attempt to eschew all binary forms of thinking, she has inadvertently (or maybe not) erased all significant difference based on race, class, nation, etc.

This essay, like others in the volume, is quite slippery in its theoretical formulation. On the one hand, Murray is able to recognize that immiserating debt could be a reason why so many "Third World" women, particularly from Southeast Asia, enter the industry. But attempts to eradicate the trade or traffic in women (such as those undertaken by CATWAP or GABRIELA) are seen by many prosex feminists as creating and contributing to "highly complex and oppressive situations for women if they become involved in sex work abroad" (Murray 1998, p. 17). If we follow this pro–sex worker logic to its conclusion, it would seem that in a magical, discursive twist, the real oppressors in the traffic in women turn out to be those most involved in the antitrafficking debate! Rather than devise strategies to change the structural mechanisms that inevitably lead to the traffic in women ("Third World" indebtedness, global capitalist expansion, etc.) the pro–sex worker feminist analysis seeks ways to make life more comfortable *within* the existing social order.

According to pro-sex worker feminists, I imagine I am one of those people who have been "manipulated" by the antitrafficking contingent. I'm just not convinced that prostitution is equal to being an actor, a therapist, or a flight attendant. I don't believe the hype about emotional labor anymore than Alison Murray believes the hype about trafficking. This should lead us to question how and why feminist theory has gotten to be so divided over this topic. I argue that the pro–sex worker analysis has its roots in postmodernism and postcolonialism. Near the end of the twentieth century, feminist theory became obsessed with the postmodern turn in the academy. Since much has already been written on the subject, suffice it to say that since the eighties, there has been a steady, progressive retreat from radical, transformative politics in Western feminist thought. Adhering to the dictates of postmodern theory, which demands the abandonment of "master narratives" or "totalizing theories" to explain social conditions, feminism has been immobilized by discursive practices that celebrate jouissance, multiplicity, heterogeneity, and most of all, female agency. Carol Stabile designates postmodernism as "critical theories that rely upon an uncritical and idealistic focus on the discursive constitution of the 'real,' a positivistic approach to the notion of 'difference' (one that does not consider the divisiveness of such differences), and a marked lack of critical attention to the context of capitalism and academics' locations within capitalist processes of production and reproduction" (1997, p. 396). The dismissal of capitalist processes in postmodernism can be attributed to the staunch antiessentialist stance that is another feature of the theory. Unfortunately, this has led to the most important casualty of postmodernism: the concept of "class" as a category for analyzing the social and material conditions that constitute our everyday existence. The anti-Marxist perspective that pervades all aspects of the "post" theories (poststructuralism, postmodernism, postcolonialism, post-Marxism, etc.) stems from the refusal to acknowledge capitalism as a world system (which would require a totalizing analysis) that governs our social relations. What we are left with is a theoretical apparatus that gives primacy to discourse, free-floating signifiers, and linguistic play.

Global Sex Workers is a significant contribution to feminist theory insofar as it places "Third World" women and children at the center of its analyses. It fails, however, to provide readers with a tangible strategy for collectively organizing against the structural mechanisms that have led to the increase in the global sex trade. Instead, we are encouraged to negotiate prostitution/sex work within the existing social order by lobbying for unionization of prostitutes, recognition of prostitution as any other form of women's work, better "working" conditions, and the overall *end* to laws that *prohibit* the traffic in women. In other words, there is no alternative (TINA). Has Margaret Thatcher been right all along?

In "Pimps, Tricks, and Feminists," Kelly Holsopple offers a refreshingly different perspective from that of the pro–sex worker analysis. After being involved in the sex industry for thirteen years as a prostitute and stripper, Holsopple is now a co-founder of the Metropolitan Coalition against Prostitution in Minneapolis, Minnesota. Responding to those that propose viewing prostitution like any other form of work, she writes, "Your job description consists of a combination of harassment, exploitation, and abuse at the hands of men or women who pay to penetrate you orally, anally, and vaginally with penises, fists, animals, bottles, guns, and garden hoses. . . . Your job-related activities will be conducted in hotels, massage parlors, vans, doorways, public bathrooms, crack houses, truck stops, executive suites, military bases, bars, stages, and glass booths. . . . Your wages will be negotiated at every transaction and payment will be delivered only when and if your customer cums" (1999, p. 3). Given this description of prostitution, it seems hard to compare it to being an actor, therapist, or flight attendant. The "labor" involved here seems more complicated than just divorcing one's public work from one's private life.

In *Doing the Dirty Work? The Global Politics of Domestic Labour*, Bridget Anderson offers a cogent analysis of domestic work that can also be useful in understanding the situation surrounding prostitution. She explains "with the particular reference to the caring function of domestic labour, that it is the worker's 'personhood,' rather than her labour power, which the employer is trying to buy, and that the worker is thereby cast as unequal in the exchange" (2000, p. 2). Exploring the tension between "body as personhood and body as property" Anderson writes that the "domestic worker is selling, not her labour power (the property in person), but her personhood" (ibid., p. 3). By making this distinction, Anderson is able to draw parallels between contemporary domestic work and slavery in the U.S. South. The "selling of one's personhood" can also be applied to prostitutes. The description of the working conditions Holsopple outlines above vividly illustrate that it is not simply labor power being sold, but the entire person. Prostitution, therefore, is much more than "being able to distinguish intimacy and love from the sexual act itself," as Chapkis and others propose (Kempadoo 1998, p. 5). The "emotional labor" framework is not useful in trying to justify why prostitution should be treated like any other type of work. For both the prostitute and domestic worker, there is no real separation between the public and private because "they are defined in a very real sense by their social relations, characterised by personal dependency on the employer" (Anderson 2000, p. 4). Therefore, rather than occupy one realm or the other, they both exist "in the imaginary space between the two worlds, symbolically ordered and imagined in very different ways" (ibid., p. 4).

The perspectives offered by GABRIELA, Holsopple, and Anderson prove that there are still feminist theorists and activists committed to revolutionary praxis and struggle. It also gives hope that we can begin to break away from the apolitical, conservative brand of theorizing that refuses to imagine an alternative social order. As U.S. military exercises continue to wage on in the Philippines, I cannot help but be reminded of a popular T-shirt worn by U.S. servicemen during the seventies describing Filipino women as "Little Brown Fucking Machines Powered by Rice." I also cannot forget the thousands of Filipino women who leave their homeland to marry Western strangers as mail-order brides—bought and sold in cyberspace. It is not enough to merely figure out ways to "regulate" and "control" the sex industry. What we need, at this historical moment, is a return to a historical materialist critique that enables us to see the totality and root causes of the situation. We need to place women involved in the sex industry squarely within the context of the international division of labor. Only then will we begin to see the manner in which globalization (a now familiar code for U.S. imperialism) is wreaking absolute havoc on "Third World" women's lives.

REFERENCES

Alcuitas, Hetty. 2002. Filipino women under GMA. *IBON* 8 (15). http://www.ibon.org/news/if/02/15.htm (accessed February 2, 2004).

Alexander, Priscilla. 1997. Feminism, sex workers, and human rights. In Nagle 1997, pp. 83–97.

Anderson, Bridget. 2000. *Doing the dirty work? The global politics of domestic labour.* London: Zed Books.

Ebert, Teresa. 1996. *Ludic feminism and after: Postmodernism, desire, and labor in late capitalism.* Ann Arbor: University of Michigan Press.

Enloe, Cynthia. 1990. *Bananas, beaches, and bases: Making feminist sense of international politics*. Berkeley and Los Angeles: University of California Press.

Eviota, Elizabeth. 1992. *The political economy of gender: Women and the sexual division of labor in the Philippines*. London: Zed Books.

Filipina women hired to provide sex to U.S. troops. 2002. *Philippine Daily Inquirer*, March 22, 2002. Kilusan Web site. http://www .kilusan.info/news/stories/20020509_pinayshired.html (accessed February 2, 2004).

GABRIELA. 1998. Women say NO to VFA. GABRIELA home page. http:// www.members.tripod.com/~gabriela_p/ (accessed November 2001).

———. 2002. "Take home sex delivery service" in Balikatan camps condemned.

Kilusan Web site. http://www.kilusan.info/news/stories/20020509 _pinayshired.html (accessed February 2, 2004).

Holsopple, Kelly. 1999. Pimps, tricks, and feminists. CATW International Web site. http://www.catwinternational.org (accessed November 2001).

Kempadoo, Kamala. 1998. Introduction: Globalizing sex workers' rights. In Kempadoo and Doezema, pp. 1–28.

Kempadoo, Kamala, and Jo Doezema, eds. 1998. *Global sex workers: Rights, resistance, and redefinition* New York: Routledge.

Kirk, Gwyn, and Margo Okazawa-Rey. 1998. Making connections: Building an East Asia—U.S. women's network against U.S. militarism. In *The women and war reader*, edited by Lois Ann Lorentzen and Jennifer Turpin, pp. 308–22. New York: New York University Press.

Murray, Alison. 1998. Debt bondage and trafficking: Don't believe the hype. In Kempadoo and Doezema 1998, pp. 51–64.

Nagle, Jill, ed. 1997. *Whores and other feminists*. New York: Routledge.

Richter, Linda. 1982. *Land reform and tourism development: Policy-making in the Philippines*. Cambridge, MA: Schenkman, 1982.

Schirmer, Daniel, and Stephen Shalom, eds. 1987. *The Philippines reader: A history of colonialism, neocolonialism, dictatorship, and resistance*. Boston: South End Press.

Stabile, Carol. 1997. Feminism and the ends of postmodernism. In *Materialist feminism: A reader in class, difference, and women's lives*, edited by Rosemary Hennessey and Chrys Ingraham, pp. 395–408. New York: Routledge.

14. Questionable Claims

Colonialism Redux, Feminist Style

Delia Aguilar

In spite of their claim to be politically progressive and emancipatory theoretical frameworks, Aguilar argues that current fashionable academic trends such as postmodernism and postcoloniality are fundamentally conservative ideological paradigms that conceal the effects of global predatory capitalism and mask the inherently unequal relationship between those countries located in the North and those in the South. She illustrates this by focusing her analysis on contemporary Western feminist theory, which has been heavily influenced by the "postmodern" turn in academia.

Embracing the central tenet of postmodernism, which declares the end of "grand narratives" or "totalizing" theories to explain various forms of oppression, many feminist theoreticians have retooled their scholarship to reveal the complexity, multiplicity, and agency in women's everyday lives and experiences. Drawing on a variety of examples, Aguilar clearly exposes how these microlevel types of examinations, end up dislodging a class analysis. The displacement of class from current feminist writings comes at a curious time, considering that divisions between the "First World" and "Third

World" are occurring at an unprecedented rate as a result of the unfettered movement of globalized capital. This shift in thinking is even more disturbing when one considers that it is women who consistently bear the brunt of capitalist exploitation. Thus, in an effort to recuperate female agency and illustrate the various ways women can "resist" their oppression, contemporary feminist theory has once again managed to marginalize women of color, working-class women, and "Third World" women from its analyses.

Aguilar's critique of feminist theory comes at an important time. If we are to fully account for the worldwide economic changes being brought about by global economic restructuring, the category of class must assume a central position within our writings. It is only by doing this that we can hope to have a truly radical and transformative project.

N ot too long ago I had occasion to chair a panel on "sex work" in an international conference, the overall theme of which was global economic restructuring. Rejecting the projection of "woman as passive victim" that they read into Marxist and radical feminist theories—capitalism and patriarchy, respectively, symbolizing the oppressive forces—the panelists laid new ground for reconfiguring the entire phenomenon. Their approach, one that has tremendous appeal among feminists today, was to highlight the notion of women's consciousness and agency. With women's proclaimed agency arose a wholly different set of motifs: jouissance, desire, pleasure, negotiation. Appropriately enough, one paper was rendered like a performance on stage, mimicking the role of empowered actor it had cast "sex workers" into, transforming a willing audience into voyeurs who watched in rapt attention.

This essay was originally published in Race & Class 41, no. 3 (2000): 1–12. Reprinted courtesy of the Institute of Race Relations.

WOMAN AS EMPOWERED AGENT

The presenters identified their research subjects as practitioners in New York, San Francisco, and Western Europe. Yet the moment they shifted from concrete description to a theoretical mode, that specificity immediately dissolved, with Euro-American women occupying the space of paradigmatic "sex workers." Ironically, the conference theme was global economic restructuring. I asked how their theory might be altered if "Third World" women were part of the picture. Two of the three speakers quickly responded, to my pleasant surprise, by elaborating on the negative impact on "Third World" women of World Bank/International Monetary Fund (WB/IMF) conditionalities such as structural adjustment programs, which require the withdrawal of government subsidies from social services, public utilities, education, etc.

It was a relief to learn that the panelists understood how the resulting immiseration of women make them especially vulnerable to the sex industry, particularly in the context of development schemes in which tourism figures heavily. To forge closer connections between globalization and the sex industry, the presenters could well have proceeded to describe the literal "border crossings" maneuvered by traffickers for hundreds of thousands of girls and women transported from Asia or Eastern Europe to Western Europe (Jeffreys 1996). Unfortunately, all such details counted for little because these proved irrelevant to their narrative. Their thesis, not to be sullied by these other pieces of information, was that "sex work" is a form of emotional labor that is not necessarily exploitative, alienating, or estranging, because of the ability of "sex workers" to exert control over and manage their emotions. In a response that I found instructive, the third speaker, more frank, expressed her exasperation with the Marxist notion of class, explaining that she had deliberately left it out.

I use the above example to broach the key argument of this essay: that contemporary feminist theory has continued to relegate and consign "Third World" women, women of color in general, and working-class women to the periphery of its concerns. In the instance cited, it is what might be labelled "resistance and empowerment theory" that, paradoxically enough, accounts for this marginalization. I am taking the position that for the most part white/Western feminist claims to emancipate women (where such claims still exist) are questionable, in view of prevailing postmodern currents that enunciate a clear retreat from class analysis, political economy, and a distrust of nationalist sentiments and notions of the nation-state. I believe that such a retreat can only aggravate problems of exclusion that feminist theory since the late seventies has tried to redress. Finally, I will point to efforts calling for the reinstitution of the basic concepts of class and social relations of production to suggest directions feminist theory might take in order to address a broader audience and target a wider range of interests than it does at present.

FROM ACADEME TO THE "NEW WORLD ORDER"

If feminist academicians are inclined to depict women as empowered agents posing resistance in multiple sites within the global order, social reality may warrant an altogether different analytical frame. In the face of Asia's current economic maelstrom, to take an example, it is women and girls who carry the heaviest burden of all, winding up eating less and getting battered more, among other routine misfortunes. According to Linda Tsao Yang, the American envoy to the Asian Development Bank in the Philippines, the financial troubles of Asia have resulted in women losing their jobs and pulling daughters out of school and even selling them to brothels (Kristof 1998a, pp. A1, A12). In Indonesia, one study found that the number of street children aged thirteen to fifteen in the major city of Semarang increased by 43 percent since the crisis; 30 percent of girls who took to the streets became prostitutes.

The practice of turning to prostitution for survival is reported to have become more frequent, and because the sex industry is supply-driven, the increase in young "sex workers" has simply served to lower the usual rates for customers. In northeast Thailand a woman sold her fifteen-year-old granddaughter to a brothel. Lamphan, the young girl, eventually escaped the Bangkok brothel owner, who locked her up, starved her, and threatened to force her to eat her excrement. Back in her village, she fancies working in a sweatshop, a dream she apparently shares with innumerable jobless others for whom Asia's woes have made "miserable factories . . . coveted places to work" (Kristof 1998b, pp. A1, A6).

It might seem bizarre, if not risible, for anyone to contemplate these news items on the Asian crisis and its dire consequences for women (not to mention men) and, among the data therein, to seize upon Lamphan's courageous escape as the focal issue, extolling it as a rebellious individual act. Pursuing this line of thinking, one might not be totally off the mark to uncover a certain resourcefulness, though unpraiseworthy, in the grandmother's act of selling Lamphan; after all, hers was a decision purposively contrived to stave off family hunger. While this may smack of parody, it is, in fact, exactly the perspective one commonly finds in feminist writing today.

In a recent book, *Maid to Order in Hong Kong: Stories of Filipina Workers* (1997), Nicole Constable brings much-needed attention to the plight of Filipino women domestic workers who comprise 150,000 "guest workers" in this newly reunified Chinese territory. Her account is rich and dense with the minutiae of maids' day-to-day struggles at the hands of Chinese employers who are often prone to mete out harsh, racialized treatment. Drawing on Michel Foucault's disciplinary regimes, she outlines the ways in which various institutions (employment agencies, state policy, employers) manage, regulate, and control the behavior of these women through the deployment of a variety of disciplinary forms, physical and psychological. To the extent that she exposes the institutions profiting from the extraction of Filipino women domestics' surplus labor, she does a commendable job. However, this is not the task she set out to undertake; proof of this is that she allots but a few pages to the history of labor migration in the Philippines, omitting any meaningful reference to the country's colonial history or to its neocolonial status, the backdrop for today's massive labor exodus; 8 million Filipinos out of a population of 80 million work overseas.

Although Constable states that "Filipino migrant workers are the Philippines' largest source of foreign exchange" (1997, p. 34), this is not quite the same as acknowledging that their remittances have fueled consumerism and kept the economy above water, public knowledge in the country. Nor does the author evince deep interest in probing the reasons for such a situation. Furthermore, even though she describes the operations and instruments of repressive institutions, she ultimately downplays their role. Finally (and from here springs the energy that unmistakably drives her work), she trains the spotlight on the quotidian—everyday practices of "resistance" that she perceives domestic helpers to engage in. As Constable herself declares (unlike the conference panelists, she rejects the passive victim-agent dichotomy), "To regard these women simply as oppressed by those 'with power' is to ignore the subtler and more complex forms of power, discipline, and resistance in their everyday lives" (ibid., p. 202).

With this in mind, Constable devotes the entire book to unravelling the precise mechanisms employed by domestic helpers in myriad acts of defiance and rebellion. The result is a book that explains how those normally purported to be without power are shown to be actually in possession of it. Demonstrations of this "power" range from the use of subtle insider jokes, intelligible only to Filipino cohorts, to cajolery and chicanery, and to confrontation and quitting work. Constable interprets as acts of protest ("in a Ghandian sense") the Sunday gatherings of domestic workers in public spaces, acknowledging that the women themselves may view it as no more than their simple right to be there. On Sundays at fast-food restaurants, Filipino women relish the reversed role of being served instead of serving, even as McDonald's and other establishments "do a roaring business" off of them. Constable cites one woman who protested poor service at McDonald's by writing a letter to the newspaper, another by requesting extra ketchup and napkins. Admittedly, unlike factory workers, who loudly raise voices to protest, domestic workers "whisper admonitions to compatriots . . . imploring them to work harder, to complain less, and to behave better. Their everyday forms of resistance are geared toward surviving their situation with their sense of humanity intact" (ibid., p. 206).

The author acknowledges the discursive character of most of these acts of resistance, herself doubting their efficacy in making changes either in the conditions of work or in mitigating power relations. But she is determined to disprove the idea that women are passive victims, a notion ostensibly stemming from systemic explanations of gender subordination, although this is not made explicit. She accepts the possibility that deferential behavior may indeed signify nothing more than accommodation—that despite all this resistance, relations between predominantly Chinese employers and Filipino women domestics have remained the same and that domestic work persists as a degrading and dehumanizing occupation. Nevertheless, in the final chapter, titled "Pleasure and Power," she concludes, "we can begin to see how Filipina domestic workers derive pleasure, or at least some satisfaction, from attempts to organize their work better and maximize their productivity, to get along better with employers, and to 'professionalize' their image, even at the cost of becoming ever more obedient and hardworking. Their work, after all, is what allows them to remain in Hong Kong, a wealthy and cosmopolitan place that excites their imaginations while extracting their labor" (ibid., p. 210).

In this passage, Constable indubitably wants the reader to view Filipino women domestics as endowed with human agency—individual agency, more specifically. Because she has allowed existing social relations to define the parameters of her conceptual framework, she seems unperturbed by the irony in seeing these women as deriving pleasure from maximizing their productivity and performing in a more organized and "professional" manner the precise activity that solidifies their exploitation. Blind to a social division of labor that is inherently unequal, she can speak of a seemingly neutral, depersonalized entity (a "wealthy and cosmopolitan" Hong Kong) "that excites their imaginations while extracting their labor," in the same breath—as though the two motions were equally benign. Given this stance, it is no surprise that one approving reviewer of Constable's book (Smart 1998, p. 201) prescribed it as useful reading for Chinese employers of Filipino women domestic helpers.

MAKING SENSE OF "RESISTANCE" FEMINISM

How does one fathom such a feminist scenario? In the case of the conference panelists, their "empowerment" thesis functioned to exclude involuntary practitioners in the sex trade like Lamphan, the young Thai. Even their use of the term "sex work," intended to denote occupational dignity and choice, suggests a libidinal economy, contrasting sharply with Filipino women's insistence on the label "prostituted" women (Miralao, Carlos, and Santos 1990; Sturdevant and Stoltzfus 1992), which invokes political economy. But how could the panelists recite a litany of adversities besetting the "other" and, the next instant, casually brush these aside? Perhaps blame can be laid on the persisting tendency of those in dominant positions to universalize from the limits of their own experience. Women of color in the United States repeatedly called attention to just this predilection in white, middle-class women in the seventies, a challenge that many have accepted and responded to. Elizabeth Spelman, noting this solipsism, remarks, "For a feminist theory to end up focusing on one group of women without saying that that is what it is going to do is no mean feat" (1988, p. 169).

That the panelists were aware of structural adjustment at all is in itself already laudable, since few, indeed, have this knowledge. But continuing with Spelman and her critique of the "ampersand problem," the additive response resorted to amounted to an empty rhetorical gesture, since it had no effect whatsoever on the theory ultimately arrived at. Still, these were theorists immersed in postmodern feminism, the politics of difference, and its adjunct, the fierce drive against essentialism. So how did this bugbear, essentialism, slip in without notice? In a conference on global corporativism at a historical juncture when progressive thinking on the whole is in retreat, it is not difficult to detect in this political climate a weather warning, an advisory against colonialism redux, feminist style. This is a thought that I propose we ponder.

Constable's work, to be sure, is not exclusionary on the same grounds, but in the end it makes a mockery of Filipino women domestics' predicament by fetishizing their pragmatic "make-do" coping skills and trivializing their mobilizing activities. For instance, she maintains that their self-discipline (a form of power) tempers and limits their collective resistance, as in their demand that forced remittance be reduced but not revoked (1997, p. 207). Constable's interest in the quotidian, because it is deprived of an explanatory framework that could raise essential questions about a hierarchically organized exploitative system, comes out petty and patronizing under scrutiny. Unlike the conference presenters, because of the nature of her subjects, Constable is denied the position of ignoring class issues outright. Even so, she attempts to discount poverty as a causal factor by asserting that many of these Filipino women domestics do not hail from the poorest or least educated sector in Philippine society. On the whole, I believe it is fair to say that in spite of her close, extended encounter with class-inscribed actors, Constable manages to elude the implications of a class-informed perspective that might have enabled her to imagine alternate forms of power and resistance, ones that do not promote and preserve subservience and servitude.

ESCAPE FROM CLASS
AND POLITICAL ECONOMY

I have chosen to discuss "sex work" and domestic work because their handling in both cases epitomizes a widely practiced way of dealing with matters of class: confronting class-bound issues but, in effect, shunning them. Put another way, the theoretical frames utilized (most of which can be safely classified as belonging to the postmodern constellation) are those that carefully steer clear of the vaguest notions of surplus labor, so that no matter how eloquently empirical data may speak of exploitation, the transcription winds up telling another story. Underpinning both examples is the notion that "class" has come to be perceived as merely another form of identity or "difference."

David Harvey delineates the pitfalls of discussing difference or identity politics and "otherness," both current fixations of postmodern feminism, in abstraction—that is, apart from the social division of labor or material circumstances (1996). He illustrates this by bringing up two events that transpired at about the same time in 1991. The first was the Anita Hill-Clarence Thomas hearings and the sexual harassment issue that rapidly caught feminists' attention; the second, a fire that took place in the Imperial Foods chicken processing plant in Hamlet, North Carolina, which killed twenty-five workers, eighteen of whom were women and twelve African American. The latter merited no equivalent response from feminists. Two things can be observed here: the privileging of cultural forms of oppression and a corollary, their detachment from the social relations of production, which are deemed less significant.

Feminist emphasis on empowerment and resistance, then, might be construed as a deceptive device that gives the illusion of an emancipatory agenda where there is none. For apathy to those of color and less privilege, as shown by Harvey's example, is echoed in the lack of response to what has been described as the worst industrial fire in the history of capitalism (Greider 1997). This was a fire that razed to the ground the Kader toy factory on the outskirts of Bangkok, Thailand, on May 10, 1993, leaving 188 dead and 469 injured. Except for 13, all of the dead were young women, some only thirteen years old. Three thousand workers were employed by the factory to produce stuffed toys and plastic dolls for children in the United States. Why the silence about the exploitation of girls?

Alertness to the tragedy that befell women and girl workers in the Thai toy factory—or to prostituted "Third World" women, or to workers harboring dreams of employment in nineteenth-century-style sweatshops—calls for not only a class analysis but also a comprehension of glaring inequalities characterizing international relations. The two, of course, are hardly separate issues. (Policies enacted in the North have caused the maldevelopment—that is, the lopsided or distorted economic development—of nations of the South.) Unfortunately, few feminist theorists concern themselves with these issues. To begin to know how transnationals operate in conjunction with governments and international lending agencies demands an overarching perspective, a grand narrative that is anathema to postmodernists. As a consequence of this rejection, academic discussions on transnationalism and transculture—trendy topics that elide the economic globalization processes from which they arise—tend to omit, in my experience, any reference to the operation of predatory capitalism embodied by transnational corporations. Academics can indulge this omission because they consciously choose to talk about "transculture" in purely aesthetic terms safely removed from the international political economy.

Conversations about transculture and transnational space in which I have participated are prone to conjure idealized projections: for instance, the prospect of instantaneous cultural and intellectual flows and exchanges, a possibility created by the high-tech knowledge industry. Excitement elicited by the image of people (exactly which people is never fully articulated) all over the world creating a novel, supposedly levelling or equalizing "transculture" via laptops is comprehensible, if somewhat naive. (A team-taught course on transculture in which I was involved took exactly this tack.) Almost inevitably, messier topics such as overseas contract workers, whose bodies are catapulted into transnational space by dint of transnational corporate geopolitics, are either overlooked or administered the "resistance and empowerment" maneuver.

Given the inclination to avoid issues implicating the political economy of the everyday lives of subordinated peoples, the discourse of globalization has become a virtual stand-in for imperialism, the material consequences of which it effectively obscures and negates. At other times it is the rhetoric of postcolonialism that serves this function. In any case, when imperialism is summoned, it appears in discursive form. Mridula Udayagiri (1995) cites Chandra Mohanty's critique of Western colonialism which, though sharp, is centered solely on textual analysis, on how writings by Western feminists silence and homogenize "Third World" women.

Doing her bit in the postmodern war against essentialism, Mohanty (1991) upbraids Western feminists for casting "Third World" women as a unitary category (to wit, poor) without agency (victims of political economy). What underpins her argument is identity or "difference" politics, which seeks to uncover the multifarious self-definitions (ones supposedly not generated by relations of production, thereby conveniently discarding the idea of a historical agent) available to women. Western imperialism needs to be critiqued, but Mohanty's wish to rescue "Third World" women from the status of victims of socioeconomic systems, along with her attempt to delete poverty as a unifying element for struggle, merely gloss over and conceal the imperialism she intends to put down. At best, imperialism becomes reduced to a form of discursive domination. Here I raised the issue of homogenization to Elizabeth Eviota, a Filipino feminist theorist, in a recent visit to Manila. "And what's wrong with that?" she asked, then added unequivocably, "'Third World' people are poor!"

AN ALTERNATIVE
TO "ESSENTIALISM"

Class, suffice it to say, has become a distrusted essentializing category that prevents the development of a genuinely "radical democratic politics" (Laclau and Mouffe 1990). If class concepts are suspect (reductive), so are grand narratives that permit a comprehension of the global economic order (totalizing). Another pernicious view is that the nation-state is in decline and irrelevant, and all forms of nationalism retrograde. Yet these are the very analytical tools needed to allow us to comprehend our place in the world and to envision collective strategies for change. To delegitimize the nationalism of oppressed peoples—and worse, to deny the existence of nation-states at a time when the struggle for national sovereignty (as in the Philippine instance) has become most critical— is hardly conducive to forging solidarity.

True, transnational corporations move about more freely than ever before and penetrate every corner of the globe in the pursuit of maximum profit, now handily supplied by "Third World" women's cheap, subcontracted labor. But as Ellen Meiksins Wood (1997) explains, the permeability of nation-states (erroneously translated into a manifestation of their decline) is premised on the existence of national boundaries and state jurisdictions.

It is the state that is principally responsible for establishing the conditions favorable for investment—political stability and cheap compliant labor, among others. The tautology that peripheral nation-states are subservient to core nations (thus the porousness or permeability referred to) must be seen as accentuating tremendous power disparities rather than proving the nation-state's weakness or demise. For this reason, Meiksins Wood labels as "perverse" the current emphasis on identity politics when state apparatuses retain preeminence as key sites of contestation.

TOWARD A REINSTATEMENT OF CLASS

To recapitulate, in light of feminist theoretical trends, a decolonizing project appears ever more taxing and can prove more arduous and frustrating than in previous decades. Fortunately, there is a growing intellectual countertrend that is impelled by the need to grapple with increasing economic inequalities worldwide. In search of conceptual tools best suited to elucidate contemporary conditions, it is distinguished by its avowed aim to restore a transformative project.

Part of this countertrend are efforts to reinstate basic Marxist concepts that have been discredited by avant-garde theoreticians, particularly after the collapse of socialist regimes and the accompanying loss of an alternative vision. Teresa Ebert unflinchingly presents what to her is the necessary element for social change—an understanding of "the basic structural reality of capitalism: the expropriation and exploitation of living labor (surplus value) in the production for profit" (1996, p. 28). For Barbara Epstein (1995), it is the concept of alienation that must be recuperated. She deploys the existence of basic human needs (against the postmodernist notion that everything is socially constructed) to call to task a social order that fails to meet them.

In an instructive and revealing debate over the culture-economy divide, Judith Butler (1997) and Nancy Fraser (1997) tussle over whether what counts as "material" is always also "economic." Butler maintains that capitalist discrimination against homosexuality is not "merely cultural" but economic, because material, in its consequences. Fraser, deploying Weber as an antidote to economic reductionist versions of Marxism, distinguishes between injustices of recognition (under which homophobia falls) and those of distribution, which have to do with "economics" or relations of production. In this way, she acknowledges the materiality of discrimination but preserves the realm of production as a distinctive domain.

In view of the blindspots connected with labor extraction discussed earlier, I think that it is reformulations of a more inclusive version of class that can prove most fruitful in redirecting feminist energies toward social transformation. I will conclude with two attempts, one by Alan Sears and Colin Mooers (1995), and the other by Sonya O. Rose (1997). I have selected these two because I think that they encapsulate two distinct, competing approaches to the same problem.

A historian, Rose argues against the exclusivity inscribed in the nineteenth-century model of the "quintessential worker" around which she believes present-day versions continue to revolve. She unmasks this universal worker to be a white man doing artisanal or skilled work in what is designated as the public (and male) domain. Finding this specific vision of the proletariat limiting to scholars' views of what is interesting and important, she proposes Sartre's metaphor of seriality, in which class is "conceptualized as 'effects,' as consequences of the structuring of inequality by racialized and gendered capitalisms" (1997, p. 150). In this formulation, class breaks out of the physical boundaries of the workplace into "social space" and moreover is also "formed discursively by cultural and symbolic processes that define a common project" (ibid., p. 151).

Sears and Mooers, in contrast, begin their reconceptualization with the assumption that the part played by human productive relations in shaping social and political life must not be abandoned. "Economy" thus is defined to include "the multiplicity of processes through which people organize socially to transform nature to meet human needs" (1995, p. 218). Formulated within a nonreductionist Marxist paradigm, it becomes possible now for "class" to embrace the whole gamut of human activities conducted to sustain life: productive/nonproductive, employed/unemployed, full-time/part-time, etc. By this reckoning, nothing is untouched by class. Indeed, the everyday practices of resistance (now a familiar motif) that Rose hopes to illuminate through seriality will have a place carved out. Sears and Mooers' inclusive construction of class begins with a grand narrative that can apprehend capitalist social relations where class struggles are not severed from nonclass.

How the two differ is a matter of great significance, because from these divergences can be predicted contrasting outcomes. Whereas Sears and Mooers insist on the use of a totalizing frame and on center-staging an expanded rendition of production relations, Rose repudiates both in favor of an empiricism that valorizes struggles in multiple sites. For Sears and Mooers, the linking of race, gender, class, and other forms of oppression is only possible when these experiences are seen as grounded in a single totality grasped as the complex network of capitalist social relations (p. 229). With the loss of a totalizing frame, the notion of where inequality springs from becomes vague, and indeterminacy results.

Although Sears and Mooers wrote their piece before Rose, their work stands as a prefiguration of the pitfalls that accompany the rejection of a totalizing frame in the formulation of Rose. Without the conception of a totality, Rose can only speak ambiguously of resistance but is unable to specify to what. If the subject positions of contending parties are left unclear, so also is the basis for any kind of solidarity. Within this framework, indeterminacy (where relations cannot be presumed but need always to be discovered) and the fragmentation of experience may well be perceived as virtues.

Yet the real world of "sex workers" and domestics, among others, warrants much more potent analytical instruments. Nuanced and multifaceted narrations of everyday oppositional acts by individual agents can prove enlightening and useful if analyzed within a totality in which the potential for collective action can be sketched. Such potential can be delineated only when the current retreat from class perspectives is reversed and a commitment to social transformation renewed.

REFERENCES

Butler, Judith. 1997. Merely cultural. *Social Text* 52–53 (fall–winter): 265–77.

Constable, Nicole. 1997. *Maid to order in Hong Kong: Stories of Filipina workers*. Ithaca, NY: Cornell University Press.

Ebert, Teresa. 1996. Toward a red feminism. *Against the Current* 9 (5) (November–December): 27–31.

Epstein, Barbara. 1995. Why post-structuralism is a dead end in progressive thought. *Socialist Review* 25 (2): 83–119.

Fraser, Nancy. 1997. Heterosexism, misrecognition, and capitalism: A reply to Judith Butler. *Social Text* 52–53 (fall–winter): 279–89.

Greider, William. 1997. One world ready or not. *Rolling Stone*, February 1997, pp. 37–41.

Harvey, David. 1996. Class relations, social justice, and the politics of difference. In *Justice, Nature and the Geography of Difference*, pp. 334–65. Cambridge, MA: Blackwell.

Jeffreys, Sheila. 1996. Feminism, human rights, and the traffic in women. *Sojourner* 22 (2) (October): 12–13.

Kristof, Nicholas. 1998a. As Asian economies shrink, women are squeezed out. *New York Times*, June 11, 1998, pp. A1, A12.

———. 1998b. Asia's crisis upsetting effort to reduce sweatshop blight. *New York Times*, June 15, 1998, pp. A1, A6.

Laclau, Ernest, and Chantal Mouffe. 1990. *Hegemony and socialist strategy*. London and New York: Verso.

Miralao, Virginia, Celia Carlos, and Aida Santos. 1990. *Women entertainers in Angeles and Olongapo*. Quezon City, Philippines: WEDPRO and Kalayaan.

Mohanty, Chandra. 1991. Under Western eyes: Feminist scholarship and colonial discourses. In *Third world women and the politics of feminism*, edited by Chandra Mohanty, Ann Russo, and Lourdes Torres, pp. 51–80. Bloomington: Indiana University Press.

Rose, Sonya O. 1997. Class formation and the quintessential worker. In *Reworking class*, edited by John Hall, pp. 133–66. Ithaca, NY: Cornell University Press.

Sears, Alan, and Colin Mooers. 1995. The politics of hegemony: Democracy, class, and social movements. In *Post-ality: Marxism and postmodernism*, edited by Zavarzadeh Mas'ud et al. Washington, DC: Maisonneuve Press.

Smart, Alan. 1998. Maid to order in Hong Kong. *American Anthropologist* 100 (1) (March): 200-201.

Spelman, Elizabeth. 1988. *Inessential woman*. Boston: Beacon.

Sturdevant, Saundra, and Brenda Stoltzfus. 1992. *Let the good times roll.* New York: New Press.

Udayagiri. Mridula. 1995. Challenging modernization: Gender and development, postmodern feminism, and activism. In *Feminism, postmodernism, development*, edited by Marianne Marchand and Jane Parpart, pp. 159–77. New York and London: Routledge.

Vickers, Jeanne. 1993. *Women and the world economic crisis.* London: Zed Press.

Wood, Ellen Meiksins. 1997. Globalization and epochal shifts: An exchange. *Monthly Review* 48 (9) (February): 21–32.

Contributors

ANNA M. AGATHANGELOU is founder and director of the Global Change Institute in Cyprus. She has published in the areas of postcolonial feminist theory, nationalism and feminism, sex work, and feminist pedagogies. Her major research interests are political economy of gender and race, feminist methodologies, militarization of societies, and women's health. She is currently writing a book examining sex and domestic workers in Cyprus, Greece, and Turkey. She has also published poetry in English and Greek.

COMITE FRONTERIZO DE OBRERAS (CFO; Border Committee of Women Workers) works along the Mexico-Texas border to represent the needs and interests of maquiladora (assembly) workers in foreign-owned plants. It is the only maquiladora organization whose membership is composed of maquiladora workers themselves. The CFO was formed twenty years ago with support from the American Friends Service Committee (AFSC). Today it continues to work in partnership with the AFSC as an autonomous grassroots organization.

DELIA D. AGUILAR was associate professor in Women's Studies and Comparative American Cultures at Washington State

University and at Bowling Green State University. She is the author of *Filipino Housewives Speak*, *The Feminist Challenge*, and *Toward a Nationalist Feminism*, all of which were published in the Philippines. She has written numerous articles on Filipino women, feminist theory, and women and development that have appeared in *Feminist Review*, *Women's Studies International Forum*, *International Journal of Intercultural Relations*, and *Monthly Review*, among others. She now teaches courses in women's studies at the University of Connecticut.

BRIDGET ANDERSON did her first degree in philosophy and modern languages at the University of Oxford. She applied her learning to theoretical and empirical questions in her doctoral research on migrant domestic workers in private households in the European Union, in which she explored liberal notions of contract, labor power, and the public/private distinction as played out in the lives of undocumented migrants. *Doing the Dirty Work? The Global Politics of Domestic Labour* was awarded the Philip Abrams Memorial Prize. She has spent many years involved in the voluntary sector and is currently chair of Kalayaan, an advocacy group for migrant domestic workers. She is currently researching the "pathways to legitimacy" of recently regularized workers who find significant obstacles in their attempts to move into legal employment.

ROHANA ARIFFIN is a lecturer in the Department of Sociology at the Science University of Malaysia, where she has been teaching courses in industrial sociology, women's studies, and poverty and inequality since 1982. She holds a postgraduate diploma in community development from the University of London and a PhD from the University of Malaysia. She has worked as a community development officer, where she planned programs for settlers' wives and daughters.

GRACE CHANG is a writer and activist in struggles for immigrant and welfare rights. Her essays on immigrant women and welfare and work have appeared in *Radical America*, *Socialist Review*, and the anthology *Dragon Ladies: Asian American Feminists Breathe Fire*. She was a co-editor of *Mothering: Ideology, Experience and Agency* and is the author of *Disposable Domestics: Immigrant Women Workers in the Global Economy*. Currently, she teaches ethnic studies, women's studies, and globalization at Evergreen State College and is working on a book about the violence of the family law against women of color and their children. She is a single mother of two sons.

NANCY CHURCHILL is an urban anthropologist who works as a researcher and graduate program instructor in the Sociology Program at the Institute of Social Sciences and Humanities of the Autonomous University of Puebla, Mexico. She received her PhD from the University of Connecticut, writing her dissertation on welfare reform in Hartford, Connecticut. She has worked for over fourteen years in a variety of social service programs and community-based organizations in the United States. Her current research addresses the connected themes of urban renewal, planning and policy, and popular culture in Puebla, Mexico.

ELIZABETH UY EVIOTA lectures in the Department of Sociology and Anthropology at the Ateneo de Manila University, Philippines. She received her MA from the New School of Social Research and her PhD from Rutgers University. She is the author of *Political Economy of Gender: Women and the Sexual Division of Labour in the Philippines*. She has published a number of articles on gender and economic restructuring, sexuality, migration, poverty, and development. She has also worked on women and development projects for the Philippine government and a number of international development agencies, including the World Bank, Asian Development Bank, UNICEF, and the Canadian International Development Agency.

ELLEN GRUENBAUM is a professor of anthropology and dean of the College of Social Sciences at California State University, Fresno. Her research in Sudan began during the seventies, when she spent several years at the University of Khartoum carrying out research in three rural areas. In 2000 she published *The Female Controversy: An Anthropological Perspective*. She serves on the Committee for Human Rights of the American Anthropological Association.

HSIAO-CHUAN HSIA is assistant professor at the Graduate Institute for Social Transformation Studies, Shih Hsin University. She has been working on the "foreign brides" issue in Taiwan since 1994. In addition to research, she has organized workshops for these new female immigrants from Southeast Asia, which helps empower foreign brides and the communities that receive them.

RACHAEL KAMEL is education coordinator in the Community Relations Unit of the American Friends Service Committee. She is the co-editor of two recent AFSC books: *The Maquiladora Reader: Cross Border Organizing since NAFTA* and *Resistance in Paradise: Rethinking 100 Years of U.S. Involvement in the Caribbean and the Pacific*. She is also the author of AFSC's landmark publication, *The Global Factory: Analysis and Action for a New Economic Era*. She is currently working on a video documentary and study guide about immigrant communities in the United States.

APRIL ANE KNUTSON is an adjunct lecturer in both French and women's studies at the University of Minnesota. Her research focuses on novels by women in former French colonies, particularly in the Caribbean. In the summer of 1999, she led a group of students to Haiti to conduct independent research in linguistics, sociology, medical anthropology, and agroforestry.

ANNE E. LACSAMANA holds a PhD in American culture studies from Bowling Green State University, where she completed her dissertation titled, "Colonialism, Globalization, and the Filipino Mail-Order Bride." She is currently an assistant professor in the Department of Women's Studies at Minnesota State University, Mankato. She has published in *Amerasia Journal, Socialist Review, Nature Society & Thought, Against the Current, Critical Asian Studies*, and *Synthesis*.

THELMA RAVELL-PINTO is currently teaching in the Africana Studies Program at Hobart and William Smith Colleges in Geneva, New York. A South African who spent twenty-six years in exile mostly in the Netherlands, she has taught and worked in South Africa, the Netherlands, Zimbabwe, the United States, and Tunisia. She set up and was the first director of the Melfort Women's Educational Centre for ex-combatants, just outside Harare, Zimbabwe, in 1981–82. She worked as a consultant for foreign women in East Brabant, the Netherlands. She taught at Spelman College (Atlanta) and Temple University (Philadelphia) from 1984 to 1991. She taught at Olympus College and Nieuw-Zuid in the Netherlands from 1991 to 2001, while at the same time working as a freelance translator from Afrikaans into Dutch for National Dutch Television. She has published two books, numerous papers in English, Dutch, and German, and has edited several books and scholarly journals.

NANCY WIEGERSMA is professor of economics at Fitchburg State College in Massachusetts. She worked from 1969 to 1973 for the U.S. Department of Agriculture, Economic Research Service, on the Southeast Asia Desk, and she was UN representative on a World Food Programme mission to Vietnam in 1987. She has authored numerous journal articles about land tenure, gender, and development as well as two books: *Vietnam: Peasant Land, Peasant Revolution* and (with Joseph Medley) *U.S. Economic Development Interventions in the Pacific Rim*.